# ENTHRONED ON OUR PRAISE

OTHER BOOKS IN THIS SERIES:

NAC STUDIES IN BIBLE & THEOLOGY

# ENTHRONED ON OUR PRAISE

## AN OLD TESTAMENT THEOLOGY OF WORSHIP

## TIMOTHY M. PIERCE

### SERIES EDITOR: E. RAY CLENDENEN

ACADEMIC

NASHVILLE, TENNESSEE

ISBN: 978-0-8054-4384-4

Published by B & H Publishing Group
Nashville, Tennessee

Dewey Decimal Classification: 248.3
Subject Heading: WORSHIP/GOD—APPEARANCES

Printed in the United States of America
1 2 3 4 5 6 7 8 9 10 11 12 • 15 14 13 12 11 10 09 08
LB

*To My Parents*

*Dean and NaDean Pierce*

# TABLE OF CONTENTS

# LIST OF ABBREVIATIONS

| | |
|---|---|
| AB | Anchor Bible |
| ABD | *Anchor Bible Dictionary*. Edited by D. N. Freedman. 6 vols. New York, 1999. |
| ANET | *Ancient Near Eastern Texts*, ed. J. B. Pritchard |
| AOTC | Abingdon Old Testament Commentaries |
| AUSS | *Andrews University Seminary Studies* |
| BA | *Biblical Archaeologist* |
| BB | Blackwell Bible Commentary |
| BASOR | *Bulletin of the American Schools of Oriental Research* |
| BibInt | *Biblical Interpretation* |
| BJRL | *Bulletin of the John Rylands University Library of Manchester* |
| BSac | *Bibliotheca Sacra* |
| BTB | *Biblical Theology Bulletin* |
| BZ | *Biblische Zeitschrift* |
| CBC | Cambridge Bible Commentary |
| CBQ | *Catholic Biblical Quarterly* |
| CBR | *Currents in Biblical Research* |
| ConBOT | Coniectanea biblica: Old Testament Series |
| CTQ | *Concordia Theological Quarterly* |
| CTR | *Criswell Theological Review* |
| CurBS | *Currents in Research: Biblical Studies* |
| EBC | Expositor's Bible Commentary |
| ECC | Eerdmans Critical Commentary |
| EncJud | *Encyclopaedia Judaica*. 16 vols. Jerusalem, 1972 |
| EvQ | *Evangelical Quarterly* |
| EvT | *Evangelische Theologie* |
| ExpTim | *Expository Times* |
| FaiPhil | *Faith and Philosophy* |
| GJ | *Grace Journal* |
| GTJ | *Grace Theological Journal* |
| HAT | Handbuch zum Alten Testament |
| Her | Hermeneia |

| HTR | *Harvard Theological Review* |
|---|---|
| HUCA | *Hebrew Union College Annual* |
| IBHS | B. K. Waltke and M. O'Connor, *Introduction to Biblical Hebrew Syntax* |
| IDB | *The Interpreter's Dictionary of the Bible*. Edited by G. A. Buttrick. 4 vols. Nashville, 1962 |
| Int | *Interpretation* |
| INT | Interpretation: A Bible Commentary for Teaching and Preaching |
| IRM | *International Review of Mission* |
| JBL | *Journal of Biblical Literature* |
| JBR | *Journal of Bible and Religion* |
| JETS | *Journal of the Evangelical Theological Society* |
| JP | *Journal for Preachers* |
| JPSTC | Jewish Publication Society Torah Commentary |
| JQR | *Jewish Quarterly Review* |
| JSNT | *Journal for the Study of the New Testament* |
| JSOT | *Journal for the Study of the Old Testament* |
| JSOTSup | Journal for the Study of the Old Testament: Supplement Series |
| JSS | *Journal of Semitic Studies* |
| JTS | *Journal of Theological Studies* |
| Judaism | Judaism |
| KB³ | L. Koehler, L., and W. Baumgartner, *The Hebrew and Aramaic Lexicon of the Old Testament*, trans. M E. J. Richardson. Leiden, 2000 |
| NAC | New American Commentary |
| NACSBT | New American Commentary Studies in Bible and Theology |
| NCB | New Century Bible |
| NIGTC | New International Greek Testament Commentary |
| NICNT | New International Commentary on the New Testament |
| NICOT | New International Commentary on the Old Testament |
| NIVAC | NIV Application Commentary |
| NovT | *Novum Testamentum* |
| OTL | Old Testament Library |
| Proof | *Prooftexts: A Journal of Jewish Literary History* |

| | |
|---|---|
| *RB* | *Revue biblique* |
| *RevExp* | *Review and Expositor* |
| SBLAB | Society of Biblical Literature Academia Biblica |
| SBLDS | Society of Biblical Literature Dissertation Series |
| SBT | Studies in Biblical Theology |
| SemeiaSt | Semeia Studies |
| SJLA | Studies in Judaism in Late Antiquity |
| *SwJT* | *Southwestern Journal of Theology* |
| *THAT* | *Theologisches Handwörterbuch zum Alten Testament.* Edited by E. Jenni, with assistance from C. Westermann. 2 vols., Stuttgart, 1971–1976 |
| *TDOT* | *Theological Dictionary of the Old Testament.* Edited by G. J. Botterweck and H. Ringgren. Translated by J. T. Willis. G. W. Bromiley, and D. E. Green. Grand Rapids. |
| TLOT | *Theological Lexicon of the Old Testament,* ed. E. Jenni and C. Westermann. Peabody, MA, 1997 |
| *TJ* | *Trinity Journal* |
| TOTC | Tyndale Old Testament Commentaries |
| *TRE* | *Theologische Realenzyklopädie. Edited by G. Krause and G. Müller.* Berlin. |
| *TToday* | *Theology Today* |
| *TynBul* | *Tyndale Bulletin* |
| *TWOT* | *Theological Wordbook of the Old Testament.* Edited by R. L. Harris, G. L. Archer Jr. 2 vols. Chicago, 1980. |
| UF | Ugarit Forschungen |
| *VT* | *Vetus Testamentum* |
| VTSup | Supplements to Vetus Testamentum |
| WBC | Word Biblical Commentary |
| *WTJ* | *Westminster Theological Journal* |
| WMANT | Wissenschaftliche Monographien zum Alten und Neuen Testament |
| WUNT | Wissenschaftliche Untersuchungen zum Neuen Testament |
| *ZAW* | *Zeitschrift für die alttestamententliche Wissenschaft* |

# SERIES PREFACE

We live in an exciting era of evangelical scholarship. Many fine educational institutions committed to the inerrancy of Scripture are training men and women to serve Christ in the church and to advance the gospel in the world. Many church leaders and professors are skillfully and fearlessly applying God's Word to critical issues, asking new questions and developing new tools to answer those questions from Scripture. They are producing valuable new resources to thoroughly equip current and future generations of Christ's servants.

The Bible is an amazing source of truth and an amazing tool when wielded by God's Spirit for God's glory and our good. It is a bottomless well of living water, a treasure house of endless proportions. Like an ancient tell, exciting discoveries can be made on the surface, but even more exciting are those to be found by digging. The books in this series, NAC Studies in Bible and Theology, often take a biblical difficulty as their point of entry, remembering B. F. Westcott's point that "unless all past experience is worthless, the difficulties of the Bible are the most fruitful guides to its divine depths."

This new series is to be a medium through which the work of evangelical scholars can effectively reach the church. It will include detailed exegetical-theological studies of key pericopes such as the Sermon on the Mount and also fresh examinations of topics in biblical theology and systematic theology. It is intended to supplement the New American Commentary, whose exegetical and theological discussions so many have found helpful. These resources are aimed primarily at church leaders and those who are preparing for such leadership. We trust that individual Christians will find them to be an encouragement to greater progress and joy in the faith. More important, our prayer is that they will help the church proclaim Christ more accurately and effectively and that they will bring praise and glory to our great God.

It is a tremendous privilege to be partners in God's grace with the fine scholars writing for this new series as well as with those who will be helped by it. When Christ returns, may He find us "standing firm in one spirit, with one mind, working side by side for the faith of the gospel" (Phil 1:27, HCSB).

E. Ray Clendenen
B&H Publishing Group

# AUTHOR PREFACE

There is always a danger of being placed into one of two categories when writing a text about something as meaningful and central as worship—the legalist or the radical. In the event either assignment occurs, the unfortunate result of being assigned to the category of insignificant will soon follow. It is my sincere desire that as you read this text, you are able to look beyond the limitations of the writer into my heart and understand that all that I desired to accomplish was to bring the biblical text back into the center of the discussion of an issue that is often more categorized either by tradition or by the latest survey results. To that end, I avoided a direct evaluation of the matter of style, except when discussing barriers which the debate itself creates to getting back to what God desires of this life reality most centrally rooted in Him called worship. No doubt I also took a risk by not interacting with many of the more style and form oriented texts presently available on the market. While, I discuss this in more detail in my conclusion, please allow me to say here that my avoidance of those texts was simply an attempt to stay on task. Furthermore, that I do sometimes comment on current situations grows out of a belief that any biblical theology must be normative in some regards if it is going to be of any use to the Church or to those who lead it.

As with any production of a project of this nature, there are many people to thank. To those who helped in its production I want to express my appreciation and to acknowledge that any failures or limitations in the work are my own. Thank you, Dr. McConville and Dr. Johnson for reading through the manuscript and making suggestions along the way. You enriched the project and my life with your demeanors and with your contributions. My appreciation goes out to David Hutchison and Jonathan Blackmon for their assistance with bibliographical research. To the administration of Southwestern Seminary for allowing me a sabbatical leave so that I might complete this project I am very appreciative. Finally, I want to thank Ray Clendenen for his support of the project and for the suggestions he made along the way.

I also need to express my appreciation to those who have influenced me on a personal level. To my parents, to whom this book is dedicated, thank you for instilling in me a love of God. Dad, you will be missed and I look forward to praising the Father with you throughout eternity. I would like to thank my professors along the way for their investment in me and for showing me that spirituality is not only a heart issue, but also involves the mind. Kristy, thank you for your love and support (and for all the proof-reading)—God blessed me greatly when He gave me you. Lauren, Will, and Jonathan—your love and support of me and your ability to keep me grounded in life and outlook mean so much to me as well.

In the end, I do hope this book raises issues that have not been considered in the past. None of the observations in the text itself stand alone, but are designed to be taken holistically in consideration of the balance of freedom and accountability to which the biblical text calls each of us. The biblical text is our guide to life. It is my earnest prayer that I have been faithful to its letter and spirit as I have sought to expound on its content. Indeed, it is my hope that it is His sufficiency that guides all that I do, and not my own (2 Cor 3:5). May God be truly be enthroned on the praises of my life.

Timothy M. Pierce
Southwestern Baptist Theological Seminary
Fort Worth, Texas
2007

# INTRODUCTION

The psalmist said, "But You are holy, enthroned on the praises of Israel" (Ps 22:3 [Hb. 22:4]).[1] He was in the midst of despair and felt abandoned. In spite of this, he moved from suffering to praise, from focusing on feelings to accepting the way things are as he acknowledged God's sovereign position. By his choice of words the psalmist alluded to the nature of worship that goes to the heart of what true worship is—the enthronement of God.

In recent years, the issue of worship has created the opposite effect. As churches and educational institutions argue over the appropriateness of one style of worship versus another, God is removed from His throne and human plans and desires become preeminent. But the news is not all bad.

A fundamental thirst has awakened in people to recognize someone who is bigger than they are, to relate to Him in a personal way and to experience community with like-minded individuals in the process. More books are being produced on worship than perhaps at any other time in history. It is difficult to find a Christian artist who has not recently produced a praise and worship recording, and often the recording includes many old hymns. Conferences focused on worship draw tens of thousands of people each year, most of whom are in the college and university age group or even younger. In addition, the battles themselves reveal that people are interested not only in worship but also in its appropriate expressions.

[1] The difficulties of translating this verse are well known. E.g., see P. C. Craigie, *Psalms 1–50*, WBC (Waco: Word, 1983), 194–96 and alternately, H. Kraus, *Psalms 1–59*, CC (Minneapolis: Fortress, 1993), 290–95. The use of the words "holy" and "praise" as titles, adjectives, and in the case of the former, metonymy, is well represented in scholarly works. This rendition, which seems the most straightforward grammatically, is contextually supported. The contrast the psalmist made as his perspective was transformed between vv. 1–2 and vv. 4–5 and the placement of God in His proper position of authority seem to be of primary interest. The preposition "on" should be viewed in light of the fact that the preceding verb intimates a "dwelling within" as well as an enthronement on the praises of the people. As such, God is the focus of all praise. This position of worth forces the psalmist to deal with the disparity between what he was experiencing and what he knew to be true, which is the crux of this lamentation psalm. In this book verse numbering follows English versification. Where the Hebrew numbering differs, it is provided in brackets and signified with the abbreviation "Hb." Unless otherwise noted, all Scripture references are taken from the Holman Christian Standard Bible.

In the midst of all this seeking, however, one has to be careful about what voices to hear and what advice to heed. Ask a group of people what worship is and you are likely to receive as many different answers as the number of people asked. This fact grows out of the personal nature of the practice and the myriads of comments being made about worship by Christian leaders and speakers. In some respects, worship has become an almost humanistic endeavor as we, in effect, argue for a view of worship directed by our own perspectives and desires. People who follow a more contemporary pattern of music often say that their method best appropriates who they are and is therefore more genuine. People who follow a more traditional pattern will argue that their approach is more appropriate because it instills a more reverent position and perspective.[2]

The main question we should ask ourselves about the so-called worship wars seems to be this: How do we find a balance between being able to express something genuinely (an expression of who we truly are) and being submissive to the recognition that worship is not about us? Stated another way, How do we know where we have confused our desires with God's position?

The answer resides in defining two key presuppositions about where we derive our information. The first foundational concept is that the starting point for all of our decisions must be the biblical text and its proper interpretation. The second indispensable conclusion is that proper communication of any practice and belief begins with accurate definitions.

## To Whom Do We Listen?

Evangelicals believe that the Bible, as the primary document of the Christian faith, is the source that we must seek out in determining what the Christian beliefs are on any particular topic.[3] In a world where feelings and personal autonomy have become the norm, submission to biblical authority must be the basis and stan-

---

[2] Obviously, this is a slight overgeneralization; however, it is not all that uncommon to hear individuals on both sides claim that they simply cannot worship in *that* manner when referring to other styles.

[3] J. Bright, *The Authority of the Old Testament* (Nashville: Abingdon, 1967), 26.

dard by which worship is rescued from the realm of temporal feelings and empty words to that of truth that can transform and renew both the individual and the Church universal.[4] A biblical study of worship suggests that the issue is worth struggling over and that there is indeed an appropriate way to identify the nature of worship. One striking realization is that theology and worship are inextricably tied because the foundation of both is the question, "Who is our God?" The purpose of this book is not to propose a specific style of worship (the topic will barely be broached) but to suggest that the relational God who is presented in the Bible has expressed who He is and how our relationship with Him should manifest itself in worship.[5]

## What Is Meant by "Worship?"

Already the term *worship* has appeared many times in this introduction. A definition, therefore, is required. Many definitions of worship have been offered in the past. The first book I ever encountered on the subject defined worship as "an active response to God whereby we declare his worth."[6] A more recent work defined worship as "an engagement with [God] on the terms that he proposes and in the way he alone makes possible."[7] Both of these are worthy descriptions of what it means to worship, but to be a little more specific, worship as used in this book refers to the relational phenomena between the created and the Creator, which find expression in both specific events and lifestyle commitments.[8]

The concept that both the event and the lifestyle of worship are implicit in biblical conceptions of worship is revealed in at least

[4] Of course, one must be careful to recognize that the authority of the Bible is something that is submitted to, not used. Ibid., 47.

[5] In fact, it will be argued that despite the current practice of identifying worship with music, music is but one rather small component of what worship should include.

[6] R. Allen and G. Borror, *Worship: Rediscovering the Missing Jewel* (Portland: Multnomah, 1982), 16.

[7] D. Peterson, *Engaging with God: A Biblical Theology of Worship* (Downers Grove: InterVarsity, 1992), 20.

[8] This is not to say that the aspect of God as Creator is the only perspective of Him that will be addressed within these pages, but it is the positional starting point for any discussion of what it means to ascribe worth to Him.

three ways. First, it is exposed in the two primary terms referring to worship in the OT. One term is a derivative of the root, *ḥāwâ*, which involves the formal expression of bowing, paying homage and making oneself prostrate.[9] Another term, *'ābad*, generally means to "work" or "serve." These two words are used in worship contexts, often in juxtaposition to each other, which demonstrates the biblical perception of the interplay between lifestyle and liturgy. Second, the fact that so many prose sections include embedded psalms (see Exod 15; Judg 5; 1 Sam 2; 2 Sam 22; Hab 3) is suggestive of the close link between God's actions, our actions, and our praise of Him. Third, the diversity and pervasiveness of worship, either in practice or expression, throughout the entirety of the OT corpus suggests that it cannot be limited to only one section of life. Together, these factors help us understand worship as being a reaction from people in a lower position to God in His exalted position through specific actions and expressions of a general worldview.[10] How these experiences within the lives of God's people in the ancient past find verbal expression in the lives of modern believers is something that must now be addressed.

## Why the Old Testament?

When a friend first heard about the topic of this book, he asked, "But what does the Old Testament have to say about *Christian* worship?" Certainly the question of the OT's relationship to Christian thought and practice is one that has always been a matter of debate within the Church. From the council at Jerusalem (Acts 15) to modern debates surrounding Christian reconstructionism, feelings run deep about this issue.[11] After all, few evangelicals would dispute

[9] This root provides special difficulties for the Hebraist. The problem is identifying the word from which the form is derived. Earlier grammars suggest that the word הִשְׁתַּחֲוָה was a hitpalel of שָׁחָה, "bow down." But more recent work has identified it as a reflexive šafel of the synonymous root חָוָה. In either case, however, the agreed meaning is to "bow down" or "to be prostrate before." See KB[3], "חוה."

[10] Because of the wide semantic range of the word *worship* within modern usage and the lack of any desirable substitutes for the word, the reader will be left primarily with the context to determine the intended use.

[11] Reconstructionism is sometimes called Dominionism or theonomy and is driven by a postmillennial eschatology, a strict Calvinism, and a desire to reorder society according to OT

the idea that the Church is under the new covenant relationship in Christ and the old covenant stipulations of ritual sacrifice, diet, and practice are not a part of our relationship with God. Unfortunately, the result of such conclusions is that, at times, the OT has been relegated almost to a "non-essential status."[12]

But the OT is a part of our canon. As Bright put it, "The Old Testament is a problem because it is in the Bible, and because of what the church declares the Bible to be."[13] Therefore, unless one is willing to become Marcionite in practice and belief and make the OT noncanonical, one cannot simply dismiss its content. Instead, the interpreter must determine to what degree and in what way the OT should be appropriated? In answering these questions, one must be careful to recognize both the continuity and the discontinuity between the OT and the NT. Failure to recognize the continuity leads to a dismissal of a sacred text and abrogation of the very instrument the NT church used in its preaching and instruction.[14] Conversely, failure to recognize the discontinuity results either in the loss of the historical revelation of God in the OT (through allegory) or the rejection of clear directives within the NT about many OT practices.

The question remains: Why write an OT theology of worship? There are two answers. First, it can instill, in some small way, a greater appreciation of the OT in the hearts and minds of today's church leaders. My work in churches and in the classroom has revealed that today's church has created a canon within a canon, or a received canon and a used canon. There are pastors who never visit

and NT law. Though written by a reconstructionist, Gary Demars' work on the subject with reactions from Tommy Ice and David Hunt is a good and popular introduction to the matters of debate surrounding the topic and the basic tenets of the position. See *The Debate over Christian Reconstruction* (Fort Worth: Dominion Press, 1988). For a good critique of the beliefs, see the review by M. Kline, "Comments on an Old-New Error," in *WTJ* 41 (1978): 172–89.

[12] This is nowhere more evident than in the widespread use of NT-only editions of the Bible.

[13] Bright, *Authority*, 17.

[14] Childs cogently argued this point by pointing out that the church "neither incorporated the Old Testament within the framework of the New nor changed its shape significantly." B. Childs, *Old Testament Theology in a Canonical Context* (Philadelphia: Fortress, 1985), 7. Paul's statement in 2 Tim 3:14–17 must at the very least be applied to the OT since that was the Scripture available to his readers at that early date in Christendom.

the OT except to preach from Psalms, Isaiah, or Daniel.[15] Similarly, more than once, as a professor I have encountered students who are hard pressed to identify for me basic theological themes and individuals in the OT corpus. Ultimately, one is left wondering whether or not the OT is really a part of the canon of today's church. To respond to this question is more than simply a convenient excuse for a book; it is my duty as a professor of Bible.

Second, the God of the OT is the same God we serve today. The OT presentation of His story transmits a relational vividness and attitude that fills in the gaps about who He is and what He desires in ways that even the NT writers themselves appreciated and recognized. The differences between the OT and the NT are indeed prevalent, but like Goldingay, I would argue that if we believe the differences reside only in areas where the NT surpasses the OT, we miss a vast number of areas where Christians have something to learn about who we are and who our God is.[16] Simply put, there are elements about mankind's relationship to God that we cannot find anywhere except in the OT. Consequently, such essentials, if we realize and implement them, will positively affect the way we worship the God we serve today.

## Methodology

Another essential issue is that of methodology. When one uses the term "Old Testament theology" today, numerous conceptions come to mind. Scholarship has declared the classical expression of the discipline dead; the canonical expression finds numerous proponents and manifestations that are sometimes at odds with one another; and the discipline in general is looking for a direction. Simply stated, the type of OT theology undertaken in this work is something akin to Goldingay's perception of "a statement of what we might believe about God and us if we simply use the Old Testament or if we let it provide the lenses through which we look at Jesus."[17] By way of ex-

---

[15] At my first pastorate, a man who had been in church for over 50 years informed me that the sermon I preached from Leviticus was the first he had ever heard from that book!

[16] J. Goldingay, *Old Testament Theology*, vol. 1, *Israel's Gospel* (Downer's Grove: InterVarsity, 2003), 21.

[17] Ibid., 20–21. Indeed, for some the title *Old Testament Theology* is a misnomer. But my pre-

pression, this methodology takes shape in both a principle-centered interpretation and a reality-centered interpretation.

A principle-centered interpretation recognizes that specific practices within the OT and the Bible may change, but the underlying principle behind those activities remains constant and something on which present action can be established.[18] One such principle of the OT as it relates to worship is that there is, in fact, an unacceptable way to worship. God's rejections of and judgments on Cain (Gen 4), Saul (1 Sam 13–15), and the Israelite people, the latter through the words of the prophets, make it clear that there were expressions of worship that were unacceptable (see Jer 7:16–22; Amos 4:4–5; 5:21–27). Yet each of these cases involved a style of worship clearly advocated and appreciated elsewhere in Scripture.[19] So it seems that the *principle* behind the issues at hand is where much of the answer is found, rather than in the acts themselves. Of course, the principle is implicitly related to the act, but it also transcends it and remains unchanged, even when the manner in which it might be made manifest in history changes.

The advantages of a principle-centered approach to interpretation for explanation and application cannot be overemphasized. For the Christian repulsed by the foreignness of the OT expressions of worship, this method opens the door to application without sacrificing the historical meaning of the text. The latter part of this statement is important because for a theology to be biblical, the foundation must be the meaning found in the biblical expressions and practices—not in modern allegories or recreations. Indeed, the authority to say what we say as pastors and teachers is found in direct proportion to how closely we stay with the biblical text. Such is the heart of the second element of interpretation taken in this book.

A reality-centered interpretation recognizes the truth of both the biblical audience's experience and our own. It begins with an

supposition is the essential unity of the various biblical books to be perused herein, and to the essential unity of the text based, not on some central theme, but on a central individual—God.

[18] Kaiser makes observations similar to this, though with a slightly different conclusion. W. Kaiser, *Toward Rediscovering the Old Testament* (Grand Rapids: Zondervan, 1987), 155–66.

[19] Compare Cain's offering to the grain offering of Lev 2, Saul's sacrifice to David's in 2 Sam 24:22–25, and the prophets' rejected offerings (Jer 7:16–22; Amos 4:4–5; 5:21–27) to the commands of Lev 1–6.

emphasis on the historical particularity of an event or expression
and seeks to interpret it within the confines of that context, while
realizing that unless the event can address the modern milieu it is
a waste of ink and breath. This theology seeks a middle ground between the descriptive and the normative—to find a place where the
OT faith is appreciated for what it was and to demand a re-expres-
sion of its basic relational teachings. Since the commands and laws
cannot be applied directly, it becomes helpful to recognize that the
central emphasis of these OT passages is that they advocate and presuppose a life lived before God.[20] They express life and practice as
responses to a God who has revealed Himself in various ways, which
shape one's view of reality and demand a response. Again, is this not
the heart of worship? The OT is fundamental to developing proper
worship attitudes and practices because of the various ways it portrays God and life before Him. Indeed, if our God is the same God,
we must alter our reality and worldview to conform to the foundational principles on which the various manners of life found in the
OT are established, even if those specific forms of expression are no
longer a part of how we relate those principles.

The book is specifically designated as an *Old Testament* theology.
The terminology specifically reflects that this work is being undertaken within a Christian worldview and perspective. By choosing
the term "Old Testament" we do not mean to denigrate or diminish other perspectives and approaches; we only communicate what
method and approach this discussion uses.[21] The presupposition of
this work is that the texts being considered are part of the Christian
tradition and are therefore to be interpreted in light of the whole
canon, though as stated above they are initially considered on their
own grounds. The expression "First Testament" has merit by relating the value of the text, but in the end there is very little to be
gained through such an expression. So the term is not used since
that would be a superfluous exercise.

---

[20] J. Goldingay, *Approaches to Old Testament Interpretation,* updated edition (Downers Grove: InterVarsity, 1990), 42–43.

[21] There are places where the term "Hebrew Bible" would be appropriate, but this book as a whole is not one of them.

These observations concerning the title might logically lead the reader to inquire as to the reason the Hebrew canonical order is observed rather than the Christian order. The primary answer is that the Christian canon is ordered more in terms of literary classification, whereas the Hebrew ordering takes both literary classification and order of writing into account. Since this work is built on historical as well as literary matters, the groupings of the Hebrew Canon facilitated observations in a way that the Christian ordering could not. Furthermore, the use of the Hebrew canonical titles serves a didactic purpose because their categories in places relate theological truths about their content and not merely literary genre (for example, "Former Prophets" as opposed to "Historical Books").

## *The Dangers and Rewards of Narratives in an Old Testament Theology*

When developing a theology or even principles of activity from the biblical text, the danger of misrepresenting its intentions is always in play.[22] With the possible exception of the NT Epistles, narratives represent one of the most easily misleading genres for interpretation. This danger manifests itself in two ways. First, while it is true that narratives include examples for behavior, this is more often secondary than primary. Often the point of the narrative is not so much the activity of the human as it is the activity of God. For example, the sinful actions of both sides in the struggle between Joseph and his brothers (Gen 37–46) are peripheral to God's activities of deliverance and preservation. When humanity and its activities become the primary focus of our interpretation, the narrative is robbed of its power to establish relationship with God. As Goldingay has stated, "To concentrate on the human deed, then, is often to miss the point of [the text]. Indeed, it is not merely to misuse it: *it is to bring a message that is its opposite.*"[23]

---

[22] The approach taken to the various genres of Scripture will be addressed as each is introduced. Narratives are treated here because they represent the majority of the biblical text and because this genre occurs first in the opening chapters of the biblical text.

[23] Goldingay, *Approaches,* 39 (emphasis added). For further reading on this topic, see G. Wenham, *Story as Torah: Reading Old Testament Narratives* (Grand Rapids: Baker, 2000).

The second danger is as common as the first and sometimes more problematic. In those places where the narrative is offering an example of human behavior as it relates to God's desires, it is emphatically necessary to distinguish whether or not the example is positive or negative. There is perhaps no greater occurrences of this danger than in the book of Judges. How many sermons have been offered on "laying out fleece" in mimicry of Gideon, when the context makes it clear such activity was an example of faithlessness?[24] Similarly, when one looks at the activity of the other judges, it is clear that these leaders, like the people they led, were themselves undergoing a downward spiral away from God.[25] Indeed, from a theological perspective these stories and others often have more to say about what God can do in spite of His people, rather than what He does through them.

By way of encouragement, narratives represent some of the most fertile ground for theological reflection anywhere in the Bible. If indeed, as has been proposed, they are God's story, then they should be able to tell us much about who it is we serve and how He wants us to demonstrate that service to Him in worship. What's more, narratives have the gift of allowing the reader to participate in the event. The result of this participation is that the stories are no longer merely stories about others, but they are about us as well. This is not meant to allow these stories to devolve into parables or allegories—with little or no interest in whether or not they actually occurred. Indeed, we affirm that the theology has no meaning unless there is an actual event behind the story. What value is there in presenting God as the Deliverer if He has never actually delivered anyone?

The methodology of this work is one of description and correspondence. We examine the expressions of the OT as well as the original audience that received them and draw conclusions about God's revelation of Himself that can find expression also in modern

---

[24] D. Block, *Judges, Ruth*, NAC (Nashville: B&H, 1999), 272–74. Less scornful but still dismissive of the practice is A. Cundall and L. Morris, *Judges and Ruth*, TOTC (Downers Grove: InterVarsity, 1968), 109.

[25] Note the complete misunderstanding of the nature of God in the child sacrifice performed by Jephthah and the apathetic approach to his vow taken by Samson, whose life ends in failure, having not even fulfilled his basic role of deliverer.

worship. This examination attempts to be holistic in its approach, although an exhaustive view of worship in the OT is beyond the scope of this work. We identify each section of the Hebrew canon according to its overarching relationship to worship and deal with each book in relationship to its final form.

This approach may be constraining and problematic in some regards, but this methodology provides the greatest opportunity to facilitate both continuity and clarity. Also, because this is a Christian endeavor, we would be remiss if we did not conclude each discussion with reference to the direction the NT takes. The end result, I hope, is a work that opens new avenues to experiencing worship as relationship while reminding the reader that worship without theology is nothing more than an exercise in self-expression.

# Chapter 1

## *THE PRIMEVAL PROLOGUE:*
## *RELATIONSHIPS IN WORSHIP*

God. No word provokes more feelings. In today's culture, few words have more definitions.[1] Even an individual can struggle internally with the word, as the theoretical definition is quite different from the practical one. No doubt this is because how one defines "God" delineates who we ourselves are and because it is easier to be a certain type of person in theory than it is in practice. Perhaps the real problem is that our definitions are too often theoretical instead of practical—outgrowths of knowledge *about* God, rather than the knowledge *of* God.[2] Is it any wonder that churches struggle with worship? Tozer stated half a century ago, "We tend by a secret law of the soul to move toward our mental image of God. This is true not only of the individual Christian, but of the company of Christians that composes the Church."[3] *Worship* has been defined in the introduction as the ascription of worth and a relational phenomenon between the created and the Creator that finds expression in both specific events and lifestyle commitments. If this is true, then the understanding one has of God will, in turn, be the heart of one's understanding and expressions of worship.

Thus it is not surprising that the biblical record begins with a universal focus on the nature of God and His relationship with all humanity. In the primeval prologue (Gen 1–11), one encounters texts that paint the grandeur of God with colors unimagined and with insights few could expect. These texts introduce humanity to a God who is not only transcendent, but also immanent; a God who is not only powerful, but also personal; and a God who is not only austere, but also relational.[4] The wonder of a God who can overwhelm our

---

[1] Of course this is not to suggest that we can make God in our image—simply that we often try to.

[2] Packer's classic work on this topic deals with the issue in a more comprehensive way than will be put forward here. See J. I. Packer, *Knowing God* (Downers Grove: InterVarsity, 1993).

[3] A. W. Tozer, *The Knowledge of the Holy* (Lincoln, Neb.: Back to the Bible, 1971), 7.

[4] T. Fretheim, *God and World in the Old Testament: A Relational Theology of Creation* (Nashville: Abingdon, 2005), 22–27. Caution should be taken in relation to many of Fretheim's con-

categories and yet be a part of our formulations in a meaningful way truly is the starting point of worship.[5]

## The Creator and the Created: The "Confession" of Genesis 1

The first chapter of the Bible is perhaps the most debated single chapter in all of Scripture. From the nature of the first verse to the general questions that arise in relating this text to modern science, a person could make a career studying this one chapter.[6] Yet for all the pontificating and study of the text that goes on, more often than not interpreters lose the main purpose in their attempts to either defend or dissuade. This is not to say that the various discussions concerning this chapter are unhelpful, only that it is advisable from time to time to simply step back and look at why it is there in the first place—to create a vision of the grandeur of our God.

As previously pointed out, one of the fundamental questions of correctly interpreting a text resides in the proper identification of its genre. By identifying the genre of a text, the reader is able to more readily understand its purposes and forms of expression as the author intended them to be read and understood. Such an approach is not only logical but also extremely helpful in answering questions and correcting errors. But a problem is created when the genre is not readily identifiable, and such is the case with Genesis 1. While the overwhelming majority of interpreters reject its identification as pure narrative, they are less successful in agreeing what the form actually is.[7] These scholars are not motivated by a desire

---

clusions and observations since they are adversely affected by an apparent commitment to open theism.

[5] S. Balentine, *The Torah's Vision of Worship* (Minneapolis: Fortress, 1999), 81–95.

[6] It is overwhelmingly recognized by scholarship that the first text in the Bible is not Gen 1 only, but rather extends into chapter 2. The division either occurs after 2:4a (the majority opinion) or at 2:3. The latter option is preferred here. See G. Wenham, *Genesis 1–15*, WBC (Waco: Word, 1987), 6.

[7] Ibid., 10. Wenham constantly refers to the "creation narrative" (*Genesis 1–15*, 6–7), yet acknowledges it is distinct from narrative prose. He ultimately argues that it is a great hymn of elevated prose, though unlikely sung. O. Loretz ("Wortbericht-Vorlage und Tatbericht-Interpretation im Schöpfungsbericht Gen. 1:1–2:4a," *UF* 7 [1975]: 279–87) argues that the presence of poetic elements is undeniable. W. Brueggemann (*Genesis*, INT [Louisville: John Knox Press, 1982], 22) says it is a "poetic narrative that likely was formed for liturgical purposes." Against

to run away from the issues of conflict with modern science or to turn the text into something less than history.[8] Rather, the author's careful use of certain stylistic features,[9] organization of the days in corresponding relationship of sphere with occupant,[10] and apparent interaction with the contents of other ancient Near Eastern texts drive these observations.

Although it was fashionable in previous generations to talk about the dependence of the Genesis writer on his Babylonian and Egyptian counterparts for his cosmogony, numerous studies have demonstrated that the similarities can hardly be defined as borrowing and are better described as correction by means of polemic.[11] This relationship of texts that manifests itself in both reflection and transformation marks some of the most striking forms of communicating God's greatness anywhere in the Bible. The opening verses portray a God who is not at war with the seas, but who demonstrates control over them merely by His presence.[12] The sun and the moon,

---

these positions, J. Sailhamer states the text is "clearly recognizable as a unit of historical narrative" ("Exegetical Notes: Genesis 1:1–2:4a," *TJ* 5 [1984]: 74).

[8] Indeed, it is a false assumption that the lack of a narrative structure brings with it a lack of "history" in its contents. See K. Mathews, *Genesis 1–11:26*, NAC (Nashville: B&H, 1996), 109.

[9] Note, for instance, how the number seven manifests itself in the number of words used in various sections, in the number of times a particular word is used, and in the grouping of various formulae throughout the chapter. Wenham, *Genesis 1–15*, 6–7.

[10] The correspondence of day one and day four, day two and day five, and day three and day six is generally acknowledged, commented on by most without notation or credit. See Wenham, *Genesis 1–15*, 7; and T. Fretheim, *The Pentateuch* (Nashville: Abingdon, 1996), 74.

[11] Wenham (*Genesis 1–15*, 9) said it best: "It is not merely a demythologization of oriental creation myths, whether Babylonian or Egyptian; rather it is a polemical repudiation of such myths." Against that argument M. Unger argued that the comparisons go back to an original form, given by God to mankind that the other nations transformed but which the biblical writer faithfully transmitted. (*Archaeology and the Old Testament* [Grand Rapids: Zondervan, 1954], 37). Unger's faulty premise, however, seems to be that for something to be of divine origin it could not have borrowed language or expressions. Furthermore, such conceptions would completely exclude the possibility of recognizing Israel's relationship with other nations in terms of what God may have been doing in their midst as well. See Fretheim, *God and World in the Old Testament: A Relational Theology of Creation*. Nashville: Abingdon, 2005), 66–67.

[12] This interpretation differs from those who would argue that Gen 1:2 portrays a chaotic power with which God must deal, such as B. Batto (*Slaying the Dragon: Mythmaking in the Biblical Tradition* [Louisville: Westminster John Knox, 1992]), and from those who suggest that there is no relation to the warfare motif of other ancient Near Eastern texts in v. 2, such as C. Westermann (*Genesis 1–11*, trans. J. J. Scullion [London: SPCK, 1984], 105–6). Instead, Moses expected his original audience to be familiar with the primordial warfare images of other ancient texts and the accompanying image of the sea as a monster to be defeated; thus Moses could

viewed as gods by much of the ancient world, are relegated to mere objects when Moses dares to call them merely "greater light and lesser light" (Gen 1:14) rather than addressing them as *šemeš* and *yārēaḥ*.[13] To read that the biblical writer—within a world ensnared by polytheism and myth—has made the audacious claims of God's singularity and power in such a simple yet profound way is to be introduced again to the transformational nature of a relationship with the Creator of the world.[14]

In the end, where are we left regarding the genre of Genesis 1? The passage clearly tells a story, though not in a form even comparable to the chapters that follow. There is certainly a didactic purpose in its structure, repetitions, and language. The text is also evidently covenantal in force and essence.[15] Such a conclusion lends itself strongly to the supposition that the first chapter of Genesis is a liturgical work of some sort that finds purpose within the worship of Israel. Perhaps identifying it as liturgical poetry that functions as a confession is the best approach to its genre category because it admits its liturgical and didactic purpose yet maintains its historical reflection.[16] In any case, that the biblical record begins with a text designed to incite, inform, and increase worship is telling in and of itself.

surprise his readers with the absence of other gods and reinforce concepts of God's power in His mastery over a sea that offers Him no opposition. Support for such an early introduction of the required extra-biblical texts is found in the presence of such texts in pre-Israelite Canaan as demonstrated by archaeology and in W. G. Lambert's suggestion that a later exilic Israelite audience would have had little concern for the mythology of Mesopotamia. See Lambert, "Babylonien und Israel," *TRE* 5 (1980): 70–71.

[13] G. Hasel, "The Polemical Nature of the Genesis Cosmology," *EvQ* 46 (1974): 81–102.

[14] J. Gabler's description is that "none of the ancient cosmogonies, be they myths or philosophical constructions, can be even vaguely compared with the Mosaic cosmogony. It is the simplest and loftiest conception"; see Gabler's introduction to Eichhorn's *Urgeschichte I*, 30–31, as quoted by H. Frei, *The Eclipse of Biblical Narrative: A Study in Eighteenth and Nineteenth Century Hermeneutics* (New Haven: Yale University Press, 1974), 274.

[15] H. Blocher, *In the Beginning: The Opening Chapter of Genesis* (Downers Grove: InterVarsity, 1984), 50–59.

[16] Of course, the term "confession" is used here in its plainest sense—a set of stated beliefs whereby a person or group distinguishes themselves from the beliefs of others in a positive sense. Mathews said, "Though it shows some hymnic echoes, the presentation . . . is cast in a historical framework, analogous to the human week, and not in the genre of descriptive praise. Genesis no doubt is implicitly calling Israel to praise its creator, . . . tied to the historical deeds of God" (*Genesis 1–11:26*, 122). But Mathews later suggested that the text is not liturgical (ibid., 125).

## The Creator Has Spoken to His Creation

The starting point for discussions regarding God's attributes ought to be the aspects He himself emphasizes. A major conception of the Judeo-Christian worldview is the notion that there is a God and He has revealed Himself to us. This revelation not only begins here in Genesis 1, but is in fact emphasized. It is axiomatic that, when interpreting a text, it is the verbs that emphasize the concepts disclosed by the writer. It might be surprising, however, to discover that in Genesis 1 the primary verbs are not centered in creating or making, but rather in speaking.[17] The text is clearly advocating an understanding and perception of God centered on the idea that He communicates with His creation. Man does not have to wander around in darkness wondering what kind of God he serves or owes allegiance to; Yahweh has communicated, and the traits He communicates are worthy of worship.

## The Creator Is Lord of His Creation

The discussion above has already alluded to the power of God, but that power is central to the observations of chapter 1 and so deserves further elucidation here. The power of God manifests itself in two distinctive ways: His method of creation and His power over the sea. The method of creation has been the source of considerable debate, centered specifically on the verb *bārāʾ*. Among the aspects that scholars generally agree on are that God alone functions as the subject of this verb and that there are never materials mentioned when it is used.[18] But the idea that the word demands *creatio ex nihilo* (creation out of nothing) is somewhat less settled. The classical commentators almost universally suggested that *bārāʾ* demands a position of *creatio ex nihilo*, and one can still find some modern commentators willing to take this position. Unfortunately, an exclusive definition of *bārāʾ* in these terms is untenable.[19] Rather, the word

---

[17] Brueggemann, *Genesis*, 24.

[18] KB³, "בָּרָא."

[19] This is most clearly true when cross referencing the creation of things through the use of already existing materials. Most significant is man, with three uses of בָּרָא applied to his creation in Gen 1:27, and yet his being made out of dust in Gen 2:7.

emphasizes the effortless creativity of a sovereign God to whom creation owes its very existence and all its worship.[20]

Modern readers may miss the significance of God's power over the sea demonstrated in this chapter (Gen 1:2,6–10), but it expresses a conception of eminence unparalleled in the texts of the ancient Near East. In many myths of the ancient world, the gods are said to struggle with the waters. Marduk struggled with Tiamat in order to achieve ascendancy in the *Enuma Elish*.[21] Baal yearly had to battle the sea in order to bring about renewal to the land.[22] The gods of the Gilgamesh Epic are said to have "cowered like dogs" before the waters of their flood and fled to the highest heaven.[23] It seems that for the ancients, the sea represented that unknown and unconquered aspect of life that haunted their dreams and made their imaginations run wild (perhaps similar to modern views of deep space). In the face of such terror, Yahweh revealed Himself as unrivaled and unchallenged, even by the sea itself. Neither the waters themselves (Gen 1:2,6–10, Exod 14:15–31; 15:8; Job 38:8–11; Ps 77:16–20 [Hb. 77:17–21]) nor the great monsters in the sea (Job 41:1–34; Ps 74:12–15, 89:9–10; Isa 51:9) ever challenge or threaten Israel's God. Objects and beings, which threaten other so-called gods, are merely an instrument in Yahweh's hands or an object with which He does as He pleases.

## The Creator Provides for His Creation

A God of such power is certainly an inspiring revelation. But left by itself, such a realization might lead toward a perspective of Him driven more by a stifling fear than a liberating awe. The passage does not stop with this revelation since it moves into a reflection that this God is also a God of abounding provision for His creation. As mentioned above, Genesis 1 reveals a correspondence between days one and four, days two and five, and days three and six, in which the first

---

[20] W. H. Schmidt, *Die Schöpfungsgeschichte der Priesterschrift*, 2d ed., WMANT (Neukirchen: Neukirchener Verlag, 1967), 166–67.

[21] *ANET*, 60–61.

[22] M. S. Smith, *The Ugaritic Ba'al Cycle*, Vol. 1, *Introduction with Text, Translation & Commentary of KTU 1.1–1.2* (Leiden: Brill, 1994).

[23] *ANET*, 93–95.

set lists the creation of a sphere of habitation and the second the inhabitant of that sphere. Though this ordering may be nothing more than a form of Hebrew parallelism, perhaps it is also a reflection about God's provision—namely, that God does not place a requirement on His creation for which He has not already made provision. One might argue that the same relationship can be ascertained for the chapter as a whole in how it relates to v. 1.

The relationship of v. 1 to the rest of the chapter has been the subject of considerable debate. While most evangelical scholars agree that v. 1 is an independent main clause, they argue about how exactly it relates to v. 2, v. 3, and the rest of the chapter.[24] This is not simply a question of semantics since the answer can have far-reaching theological implications. One approach argues that the independent clause of v. 1 serves as a title to the chapter or as a description of what follows.

Those who support this view generally make three positive arguments for it. First, it can be argued that the words "the heavens and the earth" form a merism meaning "everything," and the statement describes a finished work of creation in its final form; therefore, it must be a title describing all that follows.[25] Second, since the passage is to be understood as a genealogy of sorts as noted by the closing phrase in Gen 2:4a, the summary statement at the beginning is to be expected.[26] Finally, if v. 1 describes a creative activity prior to day one, the seven-day structure is lost.[27]

In response to these arguments, the following observations need to be made. Regarding the merism of v. 1, Wenham successfully argues that given the special nature of the passage as the first account and event, it is quite feasible that the construction here denotes only

---

[24] The rendering of v. 1 as a subordinate clause that finds conclusion in v. 2 (that the earth was formless and void when God began creating) or as subordinate clause that finds conclusion in v. 3 (that v. 2 is a parenthetical statement and the sentence reads that God began creating by his words in v. 3) is represented in many modern translations. But the former is unlikely because of the structure of v. 2 as a circumstantial clause (Wenham, *Genesis 1–15*, 12), and the latter is unlikely because it would result in an abnormally long sentence, well out of character with the rest of the chapter (Fretheim, *God and World*, 35).

[25] B. Waltke, *Genesis: A Commentary* (Grand Rapids: Zondervan, 2001), 59.

[26] Fretheim, *God and World*, 35.

[27] Ibid.

totality, rather than organization.[28] Concerning the relationship of the passage to other genealogies, such a relationship can hardly be said to be certain since few scholars would place chapter 1 within such a literary family and since the passage ends in 2:3, not 2:4a.[29] Finally, the creative activity of v. 1 need only break the seven-day pattern if it falls outside of the first day. It is perfectly reasonable to interpret the event in relationship to the first day—thus preserving the clear pattern of the text.

Theologically, the most disturbing problem with a position that makes v. 1 a title is that it begins the chapter with preexistent matter. That is, if v. 2 begins the account, one is left without knowledge of where the formless and void earth originated.[30] It would seem strange, however, for the writer to go to the lengths he takes to argue for the singularity of God and yet be so careless in the opening, thus allowing the possibility of something being coexistent with God "in the beginning." Furthermore, as Wenham points out in alluding to Gunkel, if v. 1 is a title, how can it be considered accurate for the title to say that God created the earth when according to v. 2 it was already in existence?[31]

One more notable issue with the view that Gen 1:1 expresses a creative act developed further in v. 2 and following is the interpretation of Isaiah's statement that God did not create *chaos* (*tōhû*, "emptiness, wasteland," Isa 45:18). Some argue that this verse does not allow for God to create a chaotic or unfinished world, but rather one that was complete and total. The word *tōhû* is the same word as in

---

[28] Wenham, *Genesis 1–15*, 15. Waltke's objection that Wenham's argument "violates accredited philology" (Waltke, *Genesis,* 59 n. 20) ignores long-standing precedence for this interpretation. See J. C. M. van Winden, "The Early Christian Exegesis of 'Heaven and Earth' in Genesis 1.1," in *Romanitas et Christianitas: studia Iano Henrico Waszink,* ed. W. den Boer and others (Amsterdam: North-Holland, 1973), 371–82, esp. 373–74.

[29] See note 6 above. Even Fretheim's list of comparative texts falls apart on inspection in that the *toledoth* ("These are the records of . . .") formula he is alluding to introduces the text in question; it never closes it.

[30] This problem does not seem to disturb proponents. Waltke suggests such is the case without comment on the implications (*Genesis,* 59). Fretheim states that their origins "are of no apparent interest or are simply assumed to have had their origins in prior divine activity" (*God and World,* 36).

[31] Wenham, *Genesis 1–15,* 13. Waltke seems to attempt to address this by saying that v. 2 must chronologically precede v. 1 (*Genesis,* 60), but this answers little since the earth is still left without a statement about its creation.

Gen 1:2 for the status of the earth at the beginning. Again, unless one is willing to posit a blatant contradiction between the two passages or argue that the world arrived at its status in v. 2 outside of God's creative activity or against His will, one has to observe that the Isa 45:18 statement that "God did not create the world *tōhû*" expresses something other than the earth's nature at creation.[32] Rather, Isa 45:18 must refer to its purpose—the earth was not created to be empty but to be inhabited.[33]

If v. 1 does indeed represent the first creative activity of God in relation to His creation, it represents yet another example of His provision of a suitable environment and then placement of inhabitants in that environment. Such a provision, rather than simply being expressed in the relationships spanning the specific days, is characteristic of the entirety of creation. God created "the heavens and the earth" empty and unproductive and then proceeded to fill this realm with life and inhabitants.[34] This supposition removes much of the negative connotations created by earlier interpretations and instead insists on a wholly good creation from beginning to end, a creation founded in the provision and love of a God who expresses grace even before the fall (more on this below).

## The Creator Relates to His Creation

The first chapter of Genesis not only describes certain divine attributes, but it also informs us of the fundamental relationships that will characterize the rest of the biblical story.[35] As mentioned above, Fretheim has successfully illustrated that the God of the OT is indeed a relational God. He relates to Himself, His heavenly attendants,

---

[32] The position popularized by the *Scofield Reference Bible* of a gap between 1:1 and 1:2 in which Satan's fall brought about the earth's desolation has all but been abandoned by scholars. See B. Ramm, *The Christian View of Science and Scripture* (Grand Rapids: Eerdmans, 1954), 195–210.

[33] Note HCSB: "He did not create it to be empty, but formed it to be inhabited."

[34] The "formless and void" is therefore not chaos or evil, simply emptiness. See D. Tsumura, *The Earth and Waters in Genesis 1 and 2: A Linguistic Investigation,* JSOTSup 83 (Sheffield: JSOT Press, 1989), 43. This would represent yet another example of the Genesis writer removing other gods from his cosmogony.

[35] Wenham writes, "[Gen 1] introduces the two main subjects of Holy Scripture, God the Creator and man his creature, and sets the stage for the long tale of their relationship" (*Genesis 1–15,* 5).

and His earthly creation. The manner in which He does the first of these is somewhat debated as far as how much of it is revealed in the OT. This book's introduction expressed a warning regarding the danger of losing the truth that God is a God of history and viewing His revelation outside time and space. Therefore, it seems necessary to examine the plurality of the Hebrew word for God (*ʾĕlōhîm*) and the plural pronoun used in Gen 1:26 in order to gain further insights into what the writer is trying to say about the Creator.

Concerning the Hebrew word for "God" (*ʾĕlōhîm*), Christians tend to see it as a reference to the Trinity. This view grows out of the surety that the Trinity is an eternal reality and the fact that the word *ʾĕlōhîm* is formally plural though it occurs with a singular verb—hence, a three-yet-one reality. Unfortunately, there is little to support this hypothesis beyond the tangential coincidence of verbal agreement, so that there are few scholars who would identify such as a marker of the Trinity.[36] Indeed, there are other words that take a plural form and yet use a singular verb or which are plural merely for grammatical reasons.[37] As such, there is little evidence to recommend that the form is advocating a Trinity to a people for whom such an idea would have been impossible to conceive of at best and for whom it might have been theologically dangerous. To people who struggled with rejecting polytheism in favor of monotheism, the teaching of the plurality of God would likely have resulted in a dogmatic polytheism.[38]

The matter of the plural pronoun "us" in Gen 1:26 is a somewhat more difficult issue to address. The fact that the *rûaḥ ʾĕlōhîm* ("Spirit of God") has already been introduced in v. 2 at least opens the door to the possibility of God's self-deliberation with his Spirit,

---

[36] The article in *TWOT* seems to be an exception when J. B. S. Scott states that "in the very first chapter of Gen, the necessity of a term conveying both the unity of the one God and yet allowing for a plurality of persons is found (Gen 1:2, 26)." *TWOT*, "אֱלֹהִים."

[37] Note for instance, adonanu in 1 Kgs 1:43 where the plural form of "lord" (אֲדֹנֵינוּ) in referring to David takes the singular verb. Also there are other words such as עֲטָרוֹת in Zech 6:11 where a plural for crown is used, though only one entity is in mind. See *IBHS*, § 7.4.

[38] This is a perspective that Christianity is often accused of, especially by Islamic individuals. Until the exile, Israel as a whole was largely polytheistic despite the orthodox biblical teaching on the singularity of God. The Bible goes to great lengths to bring them out of this perspective; see Exod 20:3; Deut 5:7; Ps 97:7; Jer 1:16; 25:6. The implications will be examined in subsequent chapters.

a revelation very close to Trinitarian in essence.[39] The problem with this supposition is that other uses of the first person plural pronoun in God's speeches do not have a connection with His Spirit, so the connection may only be coincidental.[40] Secondly, the possibility of translating *rûaḥ ʾĕlōhîm* as "wind from God" or "breath of God," rather than "Spirit of God," cannot be excluded, which would be thoroughly devastating to this position. Finally, the problem of the people's polytheism pointed out above would also apply to such a revelation as this. In short, while the Trinitarian explanation cannot be absolutely excluded here as it can with the plural *ʾĕlōhîm*, it clearly does carry some problematic baggage with it.

Other suggestions have been made concerning God's use of the plural verb. One proposal, which has gained favor with many, views it as a type of self-deliberation, an expression of self-exhortation.[41] This view has the benefit of not requiring an outside referent and also highlights that each event involved is of substantial significance, but it is problematic in that it may not fit the context of subsequent uses of the plural (especially Gen 3:22). Perhaps the most common viewpoint held among scholars today is that God is conferring with His heavenly court—a "plural of deliberation."[42] The commonly raised objection that the divine court (often identified as angels) does not have creative powers is answered in light of the revelation that God alone creates (Gen 1:27), and nothing more is implied here than an announcement of great importance for all to pay attention.[43] This position is clearly the one that seems most appropriate in light of the original author and audience, but one needs to protect the viewpoint of the divine author as well. Therefore, it is appropriate to point out that the language is sufficiently broad so that it preserves a

---

[39] Mathews, *Genesis 1–11:26*, 161–63.

[40] See Gen 3:22; Gen 11:7; Isa 6:8.

[41] U. Cassuto, *A Commentary on the Book of Genesis I*, trans. Israel Abrahams (Jerusalem: The Magnes Press, 1964), 55–56. The closest parallels of such uses include Ps 2:3, which is an individual's song (note the singular pronoun in 2:7–9,12), yet uses the plural "us"; see 2 Sam 24:14.

[42] Fretheim, *God and World*, 42; Waltke, *Genesis*, 64; and Wenham, *Genesis 1–15*, 28; see P. Miller, *Genesis 1–11: Studies in Structure and Theme*, JSOTSup 8 (Sheffield: JSOT Press, 1978): 9–20.

[43] Wenham, *Genesis 1–15*, 28; cp. Job 38:6–7.

revelation consistent with and suitable to the concept of the Trinity without necessarily teaching it. Furthermore, it must be stated that Jesus and the Spirit were indeed involved in creation (Prov 8:22; Isa 40:13; Col 1:15–20).[44]

Whether one holds to the self-deliberative understanding or the idea that God is addressing His heavenly court in Gen 1:26, the fact that He is a relational God is inescapable. The importance of such a conclusion should not be underestimated. Discovering that God is relational means that He is not solely self-interested, that one is called to have a relationship with Him, and that one who is created in His image realizes he was created for relationship.

To be created in the image of God is an often discussed but also often undervalued feature in both our own self-understanding and in relation to the nature of worship. Genesis 1:27 highlights the fact that it is a significant event: "So God created man in His own image; He created him in the image of God; He created them male and female." Here in this one verse, the distinctively important verb *bārā*ʾ is encountered three of the six times it appears in the chapter. Hebrew writers often use repetition rhetorically to emphasize a point or draw attention to a particular truth.[45] Such a usage coupled with God's consideration of His activity in v. 26 creates the sense of pause and tension. The picture is one of regular progression through the activity of creation continuing until this moment when God says, "Stop! Everyone pay attention. I am about to do something here unlike anything you could have imagined." Indeed, the text definitely highlights the beginning of a relationship with God that will be closer than anything that has previously existed.[46]

---

[44] See W. LaSor, "Prophecy, Inspiration and the *Sensus Plenior*," *TynBul* 29 (1978): 49–60. The allusion to Prov 8:22 is based on a development of thought that builds on the presence of Wisdom at creation that Paul later associates with Christ. The matter of the language itself functioning this broadly may not be necessary to the premise here, but it does seem to be a little more than coincidental that the language can function in this way.

[45] The practice is more often limited to adjectives or substantives (GKC, § 133k; see Isa 6:3), but the same principle applies rhetorically in the sense of repetition through parallelism.

[46] N. Sarna, *Genesis*, JPSTC (Philadelphia: Jewish Publication Society, 1989), 11. A. Schüle wrote: "Though there is nothing between heaven and earth that is not created *by* God, it is only Adam who is in a particular sense *like* God"; see Schüle, "Made in the 'Image of God': The Concepts of Divine Images in Genesis 1–3," *ZAW* 117 (2005): 4.

But what exactly is the nature of this relationship? What does it mean to be created in the image of God? It has become fashionable to draw conclusions about this issue within one of two perceptions. The image either denotes a characteristic (essence) of God demonstrated in humanity, or it is meant to suggest a status or function that man performs or fills in God's plan for creation.[47] Among those opting for the essence interpretation, man as a spiritual and intellectual being who is capable of self-awareness, reason, and spirituality is the most common approach.[48] The status or function interpretation is usually divided among matters that relate almost totally to self,[49] matters that relate solely to God,[50] and matters of being an agent between God and the rest of creation.[51] Such lines of distinction about the image of God seem a little ambitious to say the least.[52] Of course, one could take the extreme minimalist position that the terms do not have any sort of definitive meaning and were simply designed to express that humans are not animals.[53] But a more prudent course would be to look at the context to determine if multiple truths exist in the text.

The link to man's relationships (both male and female and as lord over the rest of creation) in the context and the possible rendering of the *waw* in "*and* let them have dominion" as "*so that* they have dominion"[54] indicate that the use of the term "image of God" is at

[47] Irenaeus proposed a distinction between the "image" of God and the "likeness" of God. He proposed that the former consisted of natural endowments (primarily reason) common to every man. The latter he believed consisted of "superadded gifts" (*donum superadditum*) such as immortality, impassibility, and immutability. He further argued that while the image persisted beyond the fall, the likeness was lost. His view has largely been discredited by the recognition that the two words form a hendiadys, though much of his exposition remains utilized by interpreters regarding what man lost at the fall. See Irenaeus, *Against Heresies*, 5.6.1; 5.8.1; 5.16.2.

[48] See W. Eichrodt, *Theology of the Old Testament II*, trans. J. A. Baker, OTL (Philadelphia: Westminster Press, 1967), 122–31.

[49] E. Farley, *Good and Evil: Interpreting a Human Condition* (Minneapolis: Fortress, 1991), esp. xvi, n. 4.

[50] Westermann, *Genesis 1–11*, 157.

[51] Schmidt, *Die Schöpfungsgeschichte*, 131–40.

[52] G. von Rad insisted on both mankind's appearance (essence) and his place in service (function) as being representative of the image issue; see von Rad, *Genesis, 3d ed.,* trans. J. H. Marks, OTL (London: SCM Press, 1972), 58–60.

[53] J. Barr, "The Image of God in the Book of Genesis: A Study of Terminology," *BJRL* 51 (1968–1969): 13.

[54] W. S. Towner argues that it is best read as a subordinating conjunction rather than the

least functional in terms of how we serve God and His creation. Its use probably originated as a polemic against the concepts of humanity in much of the thought of surrounding nations. That is, whereas other peoples perceived only one individual as the earthly marker of their god (the king), the biblical perspective is that all of humanity gets this image of God.[55] Man is clearly distinguished from God as creature, and yet he is called to reflect Him to each other and to the rest of creation. This conclusion requires that there is an intention regarding man's essence as well.

Perhaps the best place to begin an examination of the aspect of the image descriptions that relate to the essence of humanity is in the words "image" (ṣelem) and "likeness" (děmût). Both of these words are most often used in relation to idols.[56] Clines has argued cogently that "likeness" expands and sharpens "image" so that the force of the sentence is that man is created as God's image or representative, and "likeness" brings in the reality that man is also representational in the sense that he possesses elements of God in how he relates to the world and to each other.[57] That is, man is a likeness kind of image. This conclusion is supported by the archaeological discovery of a statue of King Hadduiti of Guzana (eighth century BC) in northeast Syria. This statue contains an inscription (distinctive only to it and the biblical text) that links the words "image" and "likeness" in one phrase. Furthermore, it clarifies that the intention of such usage is that the image will serve in the king's place to make him present even when he is absent.[58] That these two Hebrew words have a clear

traditional coordinating conjunction. He states that this switch is not necessary to make the case for such a relationship between the clauses, but makes it unmistakable to the modern reader ("Clones of God: Genesis 1:26–28 and the Image of God in the Hebrew Bible," Int 59 [2005]: 348). Notice that the waw is left untranslated in the HCSB.

[55] T. Mettinger illustrated the egalitarian nature of the image terminology years ago. See Mettinger, "Abbild oder Urbild? 'Imago Dei' in traditionsgeschichtlicher Sicht," ZAW 86 (1974): 414.

[56] KB³, "צלם," KB³, "דמות."

[57] D. Clines, "The Image of God in Man," TynBul 19 (1968): 73–91. Contrast Waltke who argued that "likeness" limits the "image" (Genesis, 66, esp. n. 51). For him, "likeness" tells us how we are like God, while "likeness" tells us how we are not.

[58] Schüle, "Image of God," 9–11. The original report and description of the statue can be found in A. Abou-Assaf, P. Bordreuil, and A.R. Millard, La statue de Tell Fekheriye et son inscription bilingue assyro-araméenne, Editions Recherche sur les civilisations (Paris: Etudes Assyriologiques, 1982).

parallel in antiquity makes it highly likely that the biblical writer was suggesting something about our appearance in creation as representations of God, while still maintaining the truth that we are in fact not God.

The relationship of our being created in the image of God to the ancient practice of a king placing his statue throughout his kingdom as his representation is at least a possible, if not probable, intention in the biblical teaching.[59] This perspective carries significant theological implications pertaining to worship. The inescapable correlation that must be drawn between God's act here and His prohibition in the second commandment (Exod 20:4–6) should fill us with both wonder and humility. The prohibition of the second commandment ensures that God would never be wholly defined by anything here on earth, primarily because nothing on earth can begin to portray His nature. The fact that He would take the steps here to grant us that magnificent privilege and sobering responsibility is beyond description (see Ps 8).[60] Consequently, man has a charge to reflect God's nature to each other and to the world in the way we live our lives. The connections throughout the primeval prologue to this concept link it to all aspects of life: sexuality (Gen 1:27–28—"male and female" and "be fruitful, multiply"); familial (Gen 5:3—"fathered a child in His likeness, according to His image"); judicial/societal (Gen 9:6—"Whoever sheds man's blood, his blood will be shed by man, for God made man in His image"); and vocational (Gen 1:28—"fill the earth, and subdue it"). Thus, the challenge of reflecting God is all encompassing; it is not limited to religious situations but to every aspect of life.[61] This passage reveals the first biblical reference to the interdependence of service and worship and elevates every other story throughout the Bible because God has invested Himself in humanity. Ultimately, it calls us to worship because—although there is

---

[59] Brueggemann overstated his case when he said that this interpretation is generally agreed to in scholarship (*Genesis*, 32).

[60] Ibid., 31–32. D. McBride put it well: "Adamic beings are animate icons; they are empowered by the 'image' and its correlative blessing to be a terrestrial counterpart to God's heavenly entourage"; see McBride, "Divine Protocol: Genesis 1:1–2:3 as Prologue to the Pentateuch," in *God Who Creates: Essays in Honor of W. Sibley Towner*, eds. W. Brown and D. McBride (Grand Rapids: Eerdmans, 2000), 16.

[61] Schüle, "Image of God," 7.

a sense in which all creation can praise Him (see Ps 148)—we are specially designed for that very purpose.

Genesis 1 is a precious chapter in the lives of God's people as we recognize our place in this world and the core expressions of our relationship with our Creator. That the creation event itself is the source of worship events is evident throughout Scripture (see Pss 8, 29, 74, 89, 104, 148), but the creation event also has a significant impact on worship as a lifestyle. Indeed, losing a creationist worldview can have far-reaching implications for how life is lived before God and each other.[62] The passage leaves us full of hope and assured of God's ultimate purpose. As Fretheim writes, "The recurrent litany that God has created everything good stands as a beacon regarding the nature of God's creative work and God's intentions for creation."[63]

## Barriers of Alienation and Portals of Grace (Genesis 2–11)

Genesis 2 starts a new adventure in the life of humanity and its relationship with God. This is not to suggest that one is dealing with a totally different story in this text. Rather, Genesis 2 represents the recounting of the creation of man and woman in a more concrete manner than in Genesis 1 as a means of relating differing propositions about man's relationship to God and himself.[64] In contrast to the stark grandeur of mankind's existence and status in Genesis 1, the second chapter introduces us to a vulnerability that at once emphasizes our need for God and each other. Man here is formed from the clay, reminiscent of the pottery that Israel would use every day and that was susceptible to breaking (see Job 4:19, 10:9, 13:12; Isa 45:9; 64:8).[65] In this chapter, the good creation of God is identified

---

[62] M. Hanby, "Reclaiming Creation in a Darwinian World," *TToday* 62 (2006): 476–83.

[63] Fretheim, *Pentateuch*, 72.

[64] This convention of relating two stories in the recounting of man's creation has significant representation in other ancient writings (namely *Enki and Ninmah* and *Atrahasis*) without any perspective of contradiction, or even separate authorship. See I. Kikawada, "The Double Creation of Mankind in *Enki and Ninmah, Atrahasis* I 1–351, *Genesis* 1–2," in *I Studied Inscriptions from Before the Flood*, ed. R. Hess and D. Tsumura (Winona Lake: Eisenbrauns, 1994), 169–74.

[65] V. Hamilton argued that there is no metaphor for frailty present, apparently because of his view that such an image is demeaning; see Hamilton, *Genesis 1–17*, NICOT (Grand Rapids:

as having an aspect that relates its limitedness and dependence on God, even in the pre-fallen state. The fragile status of man implicit in his being from the dust reveals an intimacy in God's relationship with man that is as important a truth as anything illustrated in Genesis 1. Indeed, man's finiteness, juxtaposed with God's provision, serves well as a vehicle for introducing the relational concepts of alienation and gracious redemption that are the focus of the remainder of the primeval prologue.

## The Essential Needs of Man Met By God

At the risk of understatement, no human need is as acute as the need for God. The second chapter of Genesis addresses this matter by painting a picture of Yahweh that is intimate and passionate. Like the image language in chapter 1, Genesis 2 relates the fact that God and man are distinctively connected in a relational bond resulting from God's investment of Himself in mankind. When God breathes life into man in Gen 2:7, the "breath" is not the expected *rûaḥ* but instead the *nĕšāmâ*. This term refers to something only Yahweh and man possess and something only they share.[66] The fact that it brings "life" to the man is not a circumstantial connection Moses made but at once expresses both our special status before God and our utter dependence on Him for all that makes one alive.

Moses continued his emphasis a little later when he wrote, "The LORD God caused to grow out of the ground every tree pleasing in appearance and good for food . . . The LORD God took the man and placed him in the garden of Eden to work it and watch over it" (Gen 2:9,15). The abundance of God's gift is evident. The twofold description of the trees results in little doubt that what God was granting man here was, as the previous chapter states, "very good" (1:31).[67]

---

Eerdmans, 1990), 158. Gen 3:19 seems to link the image in the present context to finiteness, and there is no need to see the picture as somehow demeaning of man's origin.

[66] H. W. Wolff, *Anthropology of the Old Testament*, trans. M. Kohl (Philadelphia: Fortress, 1974), 59–60. The shift to using the personal name of God, Yahweh, is driven by the shift in usage of the name in the Genesis narrative itself. The meaning and function of the name will be looked at further below.

[67] This is especially notable in light of the description of the land prior to God's planting in Gen 2:5; see Wenham, *Genesis 1–15*, 57–58.

God made this garden available to man without any merit on man's part, perhaps indicating the first statement of grace in the Bible.[68] Since grace precedes the fall, this has significant implications for our understanding of both grace and our need for it. Although grace would certainly include the notion of God's provision for mankind in connection with his lostness and his need for salvation, it goes beyond this to relate the fact that mankind has always needed God for his survival and existence. Man does not simply need God to redeem him and restore him; man simply and plainly needs God. This is a lesson that a self-absorbed humanity needs to hear—whether it is the ancient world influenced by Mesopotamia, or the present characterized by a misguided confidence in human potential. As Wenham explains, "Genesis is flatly contradicting the humanistic optimism of Mesopotamia [and today's world]: humanity's situation in its view is hopeless without divine mercy."[69]

Even the matter of life itself prior to the fall rests on God's provision. The notable access to "the tree of life" (Gen 2:9,16) before the fall and the restriction from it afterward suggest that life and its continuance is a gift from God. This observation is not intended to broach the topic of immortality at the level of the philosophical structures surrounding the immortality of the soul.[70] Such categories are beyond the focus of the biblical writers. Since access is not restricted before the fall, the tree of life is more than simply symbolic and seems to have served a function regarding man's happiness and possibly even his wisdom (Prov 3:18). This is not to understate its

---

[68] Grace is properly understood as that feature of God's interaction whereby He bestows on His creature a benefit that the creature could neither accomplish on his own nor warrant by his actions. Brueggemann noted the presence of grace, but he rejected an emphasis on any kind of fall being evident in the text (*Genesis*, 41, 45).

[69] Wenham, *Genesis 1–15*, xlviii. Although referring to the flow of the primeval stories following the fall, Wenham's words can aptly be applied to that which precedes it as well.

[70] I reject conditional immortality, which asserts that man is not immortal but that since immortality is a gift from God, only the righteous will see resurrection and the wicked will either not be resurrected or resurrected and then annihilated. The references for this belief, even in evangelicalism, are numerous. See C. H. Pinnock, "The Destruction of the Finally Impenitent," *CTR* 4 (1990): 243–59; J. Wenham, "The Case for Conditional Immortality," in *Universalism and the Doctrine of Hell,* ed. Nigel M. de S. Cameron (Grand Rapids: Baker, 1992): 161–91; and J. Stott in D. L. Edwards and J. R. W. Stott, *Evangelical Essentials: A Liberal-Evangelical Dialogue* (Downers Grove, IL: InterVarsity, 1988), 314–20.

life-giving properties (Gen 3:22); rather, it is simply saying that in a pre-fall setting, giving life could hardly have been its emphasis.[71] Therefore, the presence of the tree should be understood as God's provision of life and serves the function in the garden of pointing man to the fact that he owes his existence to God.[72] Indeed, both life and abundant life have always been the domain and prerogative of God to grant (see John 10:10). That He gives it so freely here should again expand our recognition and praise of God for life itself since His activity in that regard is not merely reactive to sin, for it has always been present.

As the great provider of mankind's need of both Himself and of life, God establishes principles by which both of those ends might best be achieved. God placed in the center of the garden the symbol of His lordship over humanity and the measure by which man's recognition of the same is found. God's prohibition against eating from "the tree of knowledge of good and evil" ( 2:17) should not be divorced from the other elements of the garden. The fact that the tree of knowledge was placed in the center alongside the tree of life suggests a necessary tension that must exist between God's provision and man's recognition of it. For how can man truly understand the nature of God's provision apart from the truth that God is Lord and man is not? The option of autonomy versus dependence that God places before man serves the purpose of clarifying that the provision of God in the garden was not solely for man's purposes, but so that man might rightfully and worshipfully relate to God.

The idea that the tree of knowledge represents the capacity of man to decide for himself what is beneficial and harmful and therefore represents his selection of autonomy over dependence on God is all but a foregone conclusion in much evangelical scholarship today.[73] These interpretations are largely built on the idea that one

---

[71] This realization also speaks to the rather jaded position that Genesis 2 relates a God who is fearful of man and sought to manipulate him into the fall so that he would lose access to the Tree of Life and God could gleefully expel him from the garden and the access it afforded. R. N. Whybray, "The Immorality of God: Reflections on Some Passages in Genesis, Job, Exodus, and Numbers," JSOT 72 (1996): 89–95.

[72] See Mathews, *Genesis 1–11:26*, 202.

[73] See Wenham, *Genesis 1–15*, 63–64; Hamilton, *Genesis 1–17*, 163–66; Mathews, *Genesis 1–11:26*, 204–6. They also list the other prominent proposals in the history of the discussion.

must draw conclusions about the nature of the knowledge accessed through the tree that would be consistent with the description of the immediate results of eating the fruit of the tree (Gen 3:7) and that the knowledge does, in fact, make them like God (3:22). That the man and woman went from being "naked" yet without "shame" (2:25) to knowing "they were naked" and covering themselves (3:7) need not have sexual connotations. The lack of clothing and shame before the fall could have connotations of openness to vulnerability without a knowledge of failure.[74] The effect of the fall, then, is to open their eyes to the fact that whereas before they were in unity, successfully coexisting and under the protection of God, their decision to claim their own autonomy has left them divided, a failure, and outside of God's provision, now vulnerable to the world around them.[75] This event highlights a possible motivation for the biblical writers in their emphasis on right interaction in one's human relationships before one can truly worship God (see Amos 5:4–15; Matt 5:21–24)—the two relationships are intertwined in expression and limited in each by our capacity to love.

The above conclusion brings to mind yet another need and relationship of man that Genesis 2 makes explicit and that God provides—community. In the middle of the chapter stands a statement that is unexpected and significant: "It is not good." In the midst of this intimate relationship between the man and God, in the midst of this glorious paradise abundantly created by God for man, God recognizes something that is unacceptable. God states that it is not good that man is alone. And while the primary thrust of this passage is clearly an introduction to the biblical perspective on marriage, the implications go beyond this to involve every human on earth as each attempts to relate to God and live in a state of worship—man was not made to be alone.[76] What is most striking about God's statement

---

[74] The Hebrew verb related to the noun for "naked" (עָרַה) refers to uncovering or to exposing something whether it be a person or an object (see Isa 22:6) (KB[3], "עָרַה"), while the word used for "ashamed" (בּוֹשׁ) expresses the idea of shame or sorrow, often because of failure (KB[3], "בּוֹשׁ"; TWOT, §222 "בּוֹשׁ.") Indeed, it would seem strange in light of the biblical view of sexual intimacy in marriage for this couple to be ashamed of their bodies in front of only each other.

[75] B. Och, "The Garden of Eden: From Creation to Covenant; pt 1," *Judaism*, 37 (1988): 154.

[76] Och writes, "Solitariness contradicts the basic meaning of human existence; from the beginning, the human being is one who lives in community with another." Ibid., 149.

is that within us there is a built-in need that God Himself has chosen not to fill. Yet He did not leave us to our own devices in this regard, for He has made provision for our need again with His wonderfully creative ingenuity. The idea sometimes expressed that one can simply worship God in solitude and not take time for the corporate setting is incompatible with this basic relational revelation and with God's clear instructions elsewhere. The detrimental effects of the fall did not alleviate this need, nor did it diminish a community's capacity to encourage us in times of difficulty and to enhance a worship event (Heb 10:25).

## The Essential Struggles of Man Faced By God

The fall introduced the basic struggles of humanity that impact our capacity for worship. The conversation between the woman and the serpent represents a type of theologizing that is detrimental to the fundamental aspects of worship because it damages a key component in that (or any) relationship—the component of trust. Several theologians have illustrated that the conversation recorded in Gen 3:1–7 represents an unhealthy approach to theology because it is a conversation about God that leaves Him out of the discourse. Perhaps Brueggemann has put it best: "The new mode of discourse here warns that theological talk which seeks to analyze and objectify matters of faithfulness is dangerous enterprise."[77] The "hermeneutic of suspicion" that characterizes so much of scholarship and that has infiltrated the church is a dangerous undertaking because it undermines the principle of trust. When we as creatures begin to view God and His revelation through the lens of doubt and suspicion, it becomes easy not only to question the content of the message but the intent as well.[78]

But we should also be wary on the other side of the equation, for the woman's quotation of God's revelation about the tree faithfully reports His instructions but then goes on to add her own barrier, "You must not eat it *or touch it*" (Gen 3:3). This first expression of

[77] Brueggemann, *Genesis*, 47; see D. Bonhoeffer, *Creation and Fall* (London: Collins, 1950), 70.
[78] See Och, "The Garden of Eden," 152.

legalism in the text, where she sets up her own boundaries of behavior, presumably to protect herself, is as dangerous to worship as
any doubts raised in the throes of suspicion.[79] For this type of behavior places us over God's revelation, and it is true that the person
who can add to God's word will be all too ready to reject it as the
source of authority in the end.[80] When man modifies God's revelation for our own purposes, we ultimately hurt our relationship with
Him. This is true because taking away from his revelation limits our
understanding of His ability to meet crucial needs; whereas adding
something displaces Him from the throne and places ourselves upon
it. Anything less in our suppositions limits our understanding of His
ability to meet crucial needs; anything more displaces Him from the
throne and places ourselves on it. The serpent's lie and the human's
desire is an affront to the mysteries of God that are responsible for
so much of the awe that leads to worship. Though it seems a human
characteristic to desire extension beyond who we are and what we
can do, there are boundaries we were never meant to cross.[81]

When the man and woman broached the barriers established by
God, they brought consequences of alienation that had to be addressed by the Creator who Himself is relational and made humanity relational as well. This relational tension set up a paradigm that
could easily go the route of either escapism (life does not matter
because God will fix everything) or fatalism (life does not matter
because we are all doomed). Instead, the story of human history
recorded in Scripture calls us to realism (life matters because pain is
real) and hopefulness (life matters because God is not finished with
us). This tension is aptly referred to by Brueggemann as "the *strange
resistance of the world* and the *deep resolve of the Creator*."[82] This

---

[79] It is impossible to know whether or not this addition originates with the woman or was
an addition given by the man in reporting God's instructions to her. But the point is clear that it
originated in the mind of man, not in the mouth of God.

[80] This statement is not to be understood as advocating the omission of general revelation or
cultural relevancy that is the notion of some. Indeed, it expresses a wariness of the legalism that
often accompanies those who reject such notions.

[81] In this vein, von Rad wrote, "The serpent's insinuation is the possibility of an extension
of human existence beyond the limits set for it by God at creation, an increase of life not only
in the sense of pure intellectual enrichment but also familiarity with and power over mysteries
that lie beyond man" (*Genesis*, 89).

[82] Brueggemann, *Genesis*, 20 (emphasis in original).

conception of God's investment in humanity is not an easy believism or a cheap grace, but a hard fought recognition of the struggle that epitomizes relationships in the post-fall world—especially the relationship between God and man. God will not relinquish either His right to rule or His commitment to humanity, so each act of treason by us will be met with a proper balance of judgment and grace.

The relationship between judgment and grace as a theme of Genesis 1–11 has been a matter of development in thought over the past several decades.[83] Clines has identified the feature that each act of sin in the successive narratives in these chapters increased in scope, to which God responded with equally increasing expressions of grace and judgment.[84] A question arises, however, in regard to the presence of mitigation related to the Babel narrative. While Clines suggests the possibility that the mitigation rests in the table of nations (Gen 10),[85] it seems more probable that the mitigation is in fact absent from the narrative for purposes of forcing the original readers to ask a crucial question: Where is the grace? The answer, of course, is found not in the primeval prologue but in Genesis 12, when God called Abraham to be a blessing to the nations.[86] By implication, Israel would be led to the conclusion that, as children of Abraham, Israel's mandate was to be a response of grace to a world divided—one more step in the resolve of the Creator. Worship as lifestyle and as event is an outgrowth of our response to God's mercy that helps us as faith descendants of Abraham find our place in God's activities of grace in a rebellious world. Indeed, this interplay of the worship of the true God, with His desire for us to serve as portals of grace, is the fount from which the essential element of missions in the Church flows.

---

[83] von Rad's exposition identifying sin, punishment, mitigation (von Rad, *Genesis*, 152–153) was followed by C. Westermann's sin, divine speech, punishment; see Westermann, "Arten der Erzählung in der Genesis," in *Forschung am Alten Testament* (Munich: Kaiser, 1964), 47 as cited by D. J. A. Clines, "Theme in Genesis 1–11," *CBQ* 38 (1976): 487–88. These two views were then amended by the work drawn on here by Clines (ibid., 483–95) to suggest a pattern of sin, divine speech, mitigation/grace, punishment.

[84] Ibid., 490. Clines rightly points out that it is significant that God's statement of grace precedes His actions of judgment. Ibid., 488.

[85] Ibid., 494.

[86] von Rad, *Genesis*, 153.

## The Essential Purpose of Man Given By God

The first extended story of man following the fall is one of worship. Cain and Abel brought offerings from the produce of their work, and so they apparently were designed to express thankfulness to God.[87] The story does not offer any introduction or explanation of where they learned this method of worship, and it seems at least a possibility that this is the point. If the events of Genesis 1–2 have demonstrated anything, it is that worship is not something that is demanded; it is something that grows out of the relationship between God and humans as our essential purpose. Worship cannot be a half-hearted experience.

The reason for God's favor toward Abel's offering and His disfavor toward Cain's is not that Abel's offering involved blood, since Mosaic law would permit such an offering *(minḥâ)* to consist of grain (see Leviticus 2). Rather, the difference seems to reside in the descriptions of the two offerings—Cain gave only some of the land's produce, while Abel gave some of the first born of his flock (Gen 4:3–4).[88] As Waltke has written, "[Cain] looks religious, but in his heart he is not totally dependent on God, childlike, or grateful."[89] Cain's angry response and God's rejoinder, "If you do right, won't you be accepted? (Gen 4:7)," again link the event of worship with the person's life—they are inseparable. Cain was instructed in the paths of righteousness, but he refused to journey down them. This journey down the wrong path is the necessary outcome for those whose worship is half-hearted and not truly sacrificial. Worship was never to be relegated to second place.

These barriers of sin and portals of grace lead one to the conclusion that our essential purpose on earth is a life including both

---

[87] The offering is called a מִנְחָה. This type of offering is discussed further below.

[88] J. Sailhamer's explanation that Abel's and Cain's offerings were essentially the same in quality based on the conjunction "also" in Genesis 4 seems to place more stress on the conjunction than it can bear; but he is certainly correct that the point of the narrative is more on Cain's response to God's evaluation than on the offerings themselves; see Sailhamer, "Genesis," *EBC* (Grand Rapids: Zondervan, 1990), 2:61. The total picture of the story seems to me to be that Cain possessed a less than righteous spirit about the whole process—hence God's retort and the emphasis in Heb 11:4 distinguishing between the two by stating that Abel's was offered "by faith."

[89] Waltke, *Genesis*, 97.

worship and missions. These two activities are described as a singular purpose in order not to draw too stark a distinction between them, but rather to suggest an inseparable link between the two. Indeed, the climactic exchange at Babel between man and God in these narratives of sin and grace seems to highlight God's intentions for bringing missions and worship together as two aspects of one essential reality. The command in this passage was to "fill the earth" as an expression of worship (Gen. 9:1). By way of negative example, the people of Babel saw in their tower an opportunity for self-deification; they expressed worship of self in rejecting God's mandate. Therefore, one can see that we worship God best when we scatter to a world that needs the message of grace in accordance with His divine commands (Matt 28:18–20).[90]

## Relationships in the NT

It is often said that Christianity is not a religion, but a relationship. Though this statement has often become a stale aphorism with little real power behind it, the NT clearly emphasizes the features of relationship in its pages and tenets. From the reflections of Jesus as the image of God in the Gospels to the presence of the tree of life in the last chapter of Revelation, the NT echoes the features of relationships presented in the primeval prologue of Genesis. Relationships both lay the foundation for our self-identity and move us away from a disengaged introspection to an other- (and Other-) centered engagement in worship as event and as lifestyle.

### God's Clearest Communication: Jesus as the Word and Image of God

"In the beginning was the Word" (John 1:1). So opens the fourth Gospel, reflecting the immanent relationship between the creation text of Genesis 1 and the ministry and work of Jesus Christ. As mentioned above, one of the fundamental revelations about the creation account is that God is a God who communicates with His creation. To observe that Jesus is the Word *(logos)* is at once to say something

---

[90] Clines, "Themes," 495; Fretheim, *God and World*, 89.

about how well He communicates who God is and also to observe His position as Lord of creation.

The NT writers were not lax in illustrating either of these truths. Jesus is the perfect revelation of the Father and the final word spoken to Creation (Heb 1:1–3). John stated that everything was created "through Him" and "apart from Him not one thing was created that has been created" (John 1:3), and Paul declared that Christ is the absolute Lord over everything because he Himself is the beginning (Col 1:15–20). Such passages indicate that the theology of creation was used as a fundamental explanation of God's relationship with man through Jesus.[91] This truth is expanded further with the allusions to Christ as the image of God (2 Cor 4:4, Col 1:15). Christ is more than we are as the image of God, yet the connection between us and God—that we are in His image—suggests much about who we should be as Christians.[92]

## God's Mandates for Our Relationships: Christians as the Image of God

This image language is applied to Christians in expansive and important ways. In Eph 4:23–24 Paul states, "You are being renewed in the spirit of your minds; you put on the new man, the one *created according to God's likeness* in righteousness and purity of the truth" (emphasis added). These words reappropriate the image that, though never lost, was damaged by the fall, and they explain that Christ has formed us to function as a community the way humanity did in the garden.[93] Is it any wonder then that the writer of Hebrews concludes his letter with an expressed interplay of fellowship with man and fellowship with God (Heb 13:1–6)? The advocacy of our imaging God to the world becomes most acute when the image is said to be restored and we take onto ourselves the name *Christian*. What does our lifestyle worship say about who God is to the world that we are called to serve?

---

[91] R. N. Longenecker, "Some Distinctive Early Christological Motifs," *NovT* 16 (1974): 233.

[92] "In Jesus Christ, we are offered a new discernment of who God is and of who humankind is called to be" (Brueggemann, *Genesis*, 34).

[93] Ibid., 34–35.

Our relationship to humanity affects not only the way we take part in lifestyle worship, but also worship as event. In his Sermon on the Mount, Jesus called for a heightened level of response to the world for those who would call themselves worshippers of the Father (Matt 5:3–12, commonly called "The Beatitudes"). He reminded us about Cain when He connected a trip to the altar with broken relationships between brothers (5:23–24). Likewise, Jesus linked the forgiveness God offers us to the forgiveness we offer others (5:38–48). Subsequent NT writers also emphasized both of these features (Col 3:3; Jas 2:8–9; Jude 11).

## God's Answers to Our Need: Babel and Pentecost

The Christ event altered human history forever. In it the resolve of the Creator finds its ultimate response to the resistance of the creation. This not only brings hope in atonement (a matter to be examined in the next chapter), but it resolves the alienation in relationships between humans. Paul's powerful statement in Gal 3:28— "There is no Jew or Greek, slave or free, male or female; for you are all one in Christ Jesus"—is often the passage that individuals reference first when dealing with issues of resolved alienation. But it is an event in the opening chapters of Acts that most directly speaks to the significant division man brought on himself in the final story of the primeval prologue.

The recognition of the relationship between the tower of Babel narrative and the events of Pentecost goes back at least to Augustine. He wrote,

> If pride caused diversities of tongues, Christ's humility has united these diversities in one. The Church is now bringing together what that tower had sundered. Of one tongue there were made many; marvel not: this was the doing of pride. Of many tongues there is made one; marvel not: this was the doing of charity.[94]

God's actions at Pentecost overcame the division caused by mankind's rebellion.[95] Notably, the promise to Abraham as the factor mitigating Babel, as suggested above, finds its fulfillment here among

---

[94] Augustine, *Homilies on the Gospel of John* VI:10 (NPNF1 7:42).

[95] F. F. Bruce, *A Commentary on the Book of Acts* (London: Marshall, Morgan, Scott, 1968), 64.

his progeny—in the One who departed and sent the Spirit and in the people gathered together for worship. This reversal, however, is no simple exchange of unity for division. For in the activities of Pentecost the ultimate obedience to God's demand to "fill the earth" and the requisite scattering so often ignored in the Babel story finds its completion. Whereas God scattered them in confusion before, he now scatters them in a newfound unity in Christ—a clear wedding of the matters of worship and mission that characterizes our relationship to God and man. [96]

### God's Eternal Provision: The Tree of Life

It was suggested above that the tree of life indicates the gift of abundant life from God. This draws one to a conclusion about such endowment and sustenance that expands God's provision beyond simply the reactive to a gifting that has always been present. It should not be surprising, then, that when entering the heavenly realm, where sin and sorrow are left behind, that the apostle John returned to the presence and image of the tree (Rev 22:1–5). Indeed, it ought to be a humbling realization that our heavenly state will also reflect God's provision and our need.[97] As in Eden, man is not beyond his need of God, and as in Eden God does not restrict full access to His provision. How much more must we realize dependence on God and thankfulness for such provision in this life experienced between the two trees.

## Conclusion

As with any relationship, there has to be a beginning. Beginnings in relationships often carry awkwardness as each party learns essential facts about the other. The difference with the primary relationship identified in the biblical text between God and man is that one of the parties already knows the other intimately and has a consider-

---

[96] See H. Wagenaar, "Babel, Jerusalem and Kumba: Missiological Reflections on Genesis 11:1–9 and Acts 2:1–13," *IRM*, 92 (2003), 406–21.

[97] Heaven is not an escape from limitedness. D. Wong makes much of the connection and several references to God's provision of life, health, and happiness in the eternal kingdom; see Wong, "The Tree of Life in Revelation 2:7," *BSac* 155 (1998): 211–26, esp. 217–21. See G. Beasley-Murray, *The Book of Revelation*, NCB (Grand Rapids: Eerdmans, 1992), 80.

able advantage in position and power over the other. The awkwardness, then, exists only on our side as we attempt to adjust to a reality that is well beyond ourselves. Fortunately, God did not leave that journey to our devices—indeed, when we attempt such, it only leads to failure—for He expresses Himself with clarity and ingenuity. How wondrous it is that God condescended to creation so He could reveal Himself, and in doing so He opened Himself up to considerable pain—all the more so since He knew what was coming.

The first eleven chapters of Genesis alone provide accounts of numerous types of relationships. The relationship of man to himself is best understood when glimpsed through the lens of how our Creator would have us see ourselves. The relationship of humans with other humans displays both an unmitigated expression of need for each other and an unavoidable capacity to hurt each other. Perhaps the latter is so true because the first exists. Finally, the primary relationship of God to humanity expresses a connectedness that is both patent and unexpected. It is this relationship that defines the direction of history and theology. It is this relationship that moves the tensions of the narratives. And it is this relationship that creates both the impetus and nature of worship. Therefore, it is to this relationship that the discussion turns and finds further definition in the foundations of worship expressed in the remainder of the Pentateuch.

# Chapter 2

## *THE PENTATEUCH: FOUNDATIONS OF WORSHIP*

The grace of God is fundamental to a relationship with Him. Unfortunately, misunderstanding and sometimes purposeful misrepresentation over the years have led many to believe that in the OT the law was the determinative feature of relationship with God and that His grace is not predominant until the NT. Simply looking at the flow of the story of the OT says otherwise. We have already examined the introduction to God in the opening chapter of Genesis. As one moves into the lives of the ancestors of Israel, the unmerited calling of Abraham, Isaac, and Jacob further illustrates a Creator who persists in reaching out to humanity, even while we are at enmity with Him. As one enters the narrative of Exodus, it is God's saving activity with Israel that dominates the attention of the writer—indeed, it is this act that will dominate all the rest of the OT. It is only after God has saved the people and declared them to be his "own special possession" (Exod 19:3–6) that He begins to outline His expectations by providing the law for them.

The interpretation of the laws of the OT has always been an issue of debate for Christians. This book's introduction has already addressed this question, but it is wise to reflect the primary conclusions previously outlined. Since the OT is part of the Word of God, it claims authority over us. Yet because it does not represent our covenant with God, our approach should be centered on an interpretation based on principle and reality. Using such a methodology, we can derive much from this section of the Bible regarding the nature of God and our relationship to Him—even if we do not carry out the rituals and rites described in them. Indeed, the relationships outlined in the primeval prologue find definition and clarification in the passages that immediately follow. As God lays the foundations of understanding His character through the revelation of Himself and His precepts of behavior and activity, He grants us further glimpses into His nature.

## Knowing the One We Worship

The primeval prologue introduces us to the personhood of God. The tension between His immanence and His transcendence is succinctly and powerfully introduced in the distinctive descriptions of Genesis 1 and 2. The grace and justice of God develop significantly through the succeeding chapters, culminating in His call of Abram in Genesis 12. These fundamental aspects only initiate our understanding of Him and His nature. As stated at the end of the previous chapter, the possibility of a relationship with the Creator forces further inquiry into what else God might be willing to tell us about Himself as He interacts with those He has called out. As the Pentateuch continues, new words begin to be used concerning His nature, such as "holy" *(qādôš)*[1] and "jealous" *(qānnāʾ)*. New names begin to be introduced, and explanations of names already revealed are expressed. These new revelations make clear that the concise introduction we have been granted cannot begin to express His essence and that there are many things about Him that He wants us to know. Therefore, as one begins to discuss the priorities of worship made evident in the Bible, one is drawn to the inescapable conclusion that the foremost priority is getting to know God and His desires better.

### God's Nature as Revealed in His Holiness

There are many attributes of God's personhood that one could focus on. None of them, however, rises to the same level of significance as His holiness, and it is in the Pentateuch that this foundational concept first appears.[2] Holiness has been called the "very Nature of Deity."[3] Some scholars have pointed out that simply by virtue of its number of occurrences and its emphatic placement in Scripture, the concept of holiness demands a unique position in one's assess-

---

[1] Although the first use of this word or one of its derivatives is Gen 2:3, the word is not applied to God Himself until well into the Pentateuch.

[2] The covenant expressions and instructions surrounding the cult in Exodus and Leviticus represent the most thorough expositions of holiness. Indeed, Leviticus 17–26 has conventionally been labeled "the holiness code."

[3] N. Snaith, *Distinctive Ideas of the Old Testament* (Philadelphia: Westminster Press, 1946), 21.

ment of God.[4] In short, more than just an attribute, holiness is what makes God who He is and is also the result of His being God. It is the essence of His being and the element through which we must interpret all other attributes. We often understand other qualities of God based on our own human reference points, but the idea of holiness requires a discussion about what is not human and what is not ordinary (see Lev 10:10). Indeed, "holiness" is best defined simply by the words "other than."[5] To call holiness an attribute, then, may not be altogether correct. It does not necessarily involve righteousness or entail being elevated to a higher status. It is not a component as much as it is a difference or separation—though one should not make the mistake of equating it with remoteness.[6]

Some contrast holiness with mercy, as if it were limited solely to His attributes of justice and righteousness. But it is God's holiness that allows Him to be merciful. Ezekiel 39:25–27 associates God's mercy with the preservation of His holy name and His holy people. The phrase "Holy One of Israel" in the book of Isaiah is directly linked to God's status as Redeemer of His people.[7] Eschatologically, holiness is His desired goal for all the earth. Zechariah 14:20 makes it clear that God's holiness is designed to transform and will ultimately reach its goal of making even the most common of realities distinctly God's. Such a realization is not driven by wrath but by mercy. Only a God who is truly secure in His position and separate from the fallen nature of humanity could demonstrate the mercy it takes to renovate a heart that is radically opposed to Him into one that beats with a passion for the things that He is passionate about.[8] Finally, we come to understand that "Holiness is a state of grace to which men are called by God."[9]

---

[4] W. Eichrodt, *Theology of the Old Testament*, OTL (Philadelphia: Westminster Press, 1961), 1:270.

[5] See *TWOT*, "קָדַשׁ, קֹדֶשׁ." KB[3], "קָדוֹשׁ."

[6] See R. Otto, *The Idea of Holy* (Oxford: Oxford Univ. Press, 1924).

[7] See especially Isa 47:4; 60:9–10.

[8] This is revealed in the close relationship of God's holiness to his jealousy. P. Miller wrote, "The *absolute* attribute of the *holiness* of God as one who is apart from all others, transcendent and distinguished from all other reality, has its correlate in the *relative* attribute of *jealousy*"; see Miller, *Deuteronomy*, INT (Louisville: Westminster John Knox, 1990), 76 (emphasis in original).

[9] G. Wenham, *Leviticus*, NICOT (Grand Rapids: Eerdmans, 1979), 23.

The conclusion that God's holiness works also as an impetus for understanding our position and place begs the question: What relationship does this truth have to worship? First, it should be obvious that since holiness is the very definition of what it means to be God, holiness is also at the very heart of what it means to worship. To have a God who is totally other than, who is different and mysterious, is to have a God worth worshipping. Our knowledge of Him then moves out of the realm of definition into the realm of experience—not experience that one is comfortable with, but one in which we understand there are elements of God that are never to be invaded or understood.[10] Second, since God is holy and therefore in some sense hidden, we understand that our capacity to relate to Him is driven by His revelation to us.[11] This realization causes us to be once again driven back to the components of worship that facilitate such revelation—namely, His word and our reflection on it. Third, the close relationship of God's holiness and His jealousy accentuates the solitary positions both He and His followers possess in the relationship they share. Miller has observed, "The jealousy of God, therefore, is that dimension within the divine encounter with the Lord's people that brooks no other final loyalty and ensures no other recipient of such unbounding love and grace."[12]

Holiness and jealousy are at the heart of our covenant love and the basis by which we function in both the lifestyle and event called worship. God's holiness ought to beckon us to a higher sense of the elevated calling that we are invited to as we seek to live our lives in a status that, like God, is *other than,* yet without being *remote from.* The idea demands a believer's reaction to the world that does not allow us to slip into the profaneness and indignity that characterizes much of humanity, while also preventing us from withdrawing to a position of safety. The holiness to which Israel was called sculpted their lives in such a way that even their meals reminded them of

---

[10] Th. C. Vriezen, *An Outline of Old Testament Theology* (Oxford: Basil Blackwell, 1962), 155.

[11] B. W. Anderson rightly points out that the presupposition of revelation is God's hiddenness (*IDB*, "The Old Testament View of God," 419).

[12] Miller, *Deuteronomy*, 76.

their position before God,[13] while also calling on them to love their neighbor as themselves (Lev 19:18).[14]

## God's Nature as Revealed in His Singularity

As pointed out in the discussion of Genesis 1, the writer goes to some lengths to present the God of Israel as the only God in the universe. In God's revelation to Moses on Mount Sinai in the Ten Commandments—called "the ten words" in Exod 34:28; Deut 4:13 (*ʿăśeret haddĕbārîm*; HCSB, "the Ten Commandments")—the topic is revisited in a more overt yet somewhat more complicated manner.[15] Most evangelicals identify the first Commandment as Exod 20:3, or sometimes Exod 20:2–3: "I am the LORD your God, who brought you out of the land of Egypt, out of the place of slavery. Do not have other gods besides me." However, the view that the first Commandment stops at v. 3 is by no means universally accepted.[16] Most notably, evangelical scholar John Sailhamer has questioned this view, and his argument is that Exod 20:2–6 is one command while Exod 20:17 is two.[17] Since the division one identifies as correct is theologically significant in terms of concluding what it is that God demanded of His people, it is wise to visit the issue before proceeding with this discussion.

Sailhamer essentially built his arguments around cross referencing. His first comparisons are to the golden calf incident of Exodus 32. He argued that the writer of the narrative presents the event as a direct violation of the *first* Commandment. After examining the words of the

---

[13] M. Douglas, *Purity in Danger: An Analysis of the Concepts of Pollution and Taboo* (New York: Frederick A. Praeger, 1966), 51–52.

[14] It is not accidental that this commandment (one of the two greatest), falls squarely in the middle of the holiness code of Leviticus and is itself tied to God's holiness.

[15] The importance of the ten words cannot be overstated. While one needs to be careful not to forget the other commands of God, these commands are significantly established as distinctive in their repetition (Exodus 20 and Deuteronomy 5), their statement apart from the rest of the covenant stipulations within their own narratives, and their reduplication in both Jewish and Church history.

[16] Jewish custom (which is by no means unanimous) generally identifies Exod 20:2 as the first word, and combines vv. 3–6 into the second word. Roman Catholic custom suggests that vv. 3–6 are the first Commandment and that v. 17 should be divided into two separate commandments: i.e., commandment nine is "do not covet your neighbor's house," and commandment ten is "do not covet your neighbor's wife . . ."

[17] J. Sailhamer, *The Pentateuch as Narrative: A Biblical-Theological Commentary* (Grand Rapids: Zondervan, 1992), 283–86.

people in vv. 4,8. Sailhamer opted for the translation, "This is your God who brought you out of Egypt"—as opposed to "These are your gods, who brought you out of Egypt."[18] This approach is based on the idea that *ʾĕlōhîm* can be translated "God" or "gods." The identity of the calf is not as a god but simply as an idol cast in the shape of a calf (Exod 32:4,8). Also, Aaron associated the idol with Yahweh, rather than as a different god (Ex 32:5). Sailhamer attempted to further this argument by pointing out that in Nehemiah's prayer the governor referred to the sin of the golden calf incident using the singular, "this is your God" (Neh 9:18). Therefore, Sailhamer concluded that the sin is one of idolatry, not of following false gods.

Sailhamer's second comparison is to the other account of the Decalogue in Deuteronomy 5. His view is that the commandment regarding coveting is clearly divided into two separate commands, which would then require the commands normally identified as the first two to be only one. His support for this view is the repetition of the verb for covet, the different direct objects, and the use of the *waw* ("and") between them. The latter point grows out of the apparent use of *waw* by the writer to denote each of the last five commandments.

The weaknesses of Sailhamer's arguments are numerous. First, there is nothing in the narrative regarding the golden calf that suggests it is the *first* Commandment that is being broken. Therefore, even if one were to determine that the sin of the golden calf incident is primarily idolatry, the story and the commentary in Nehemiah 9 cannot answer the question of whether the verses in Exod 20:3–6 ought to be taken together or not. Further, based on the grammar of the Hebrew text, the people's statement cannot properly be translated, "this is your God who brought you out of Egypt." If the decision were solely based on the presence of *ʾĕlōhîm* as Sailhamer seems to argue, he might have a case. But both the demonstrative pronoun ("these," not "this") and the number of the succeeding verb (*they* brought you out of Egypt) are plural and thus demand that *ʾĕlōhîm* in this case be translated as a plural, not a singular.[19]

---

[18] The former translation is represented in the HCSB and the NASB. The latter is found in the KJV, ESV, ASV, NRSV, NLT, and NIV and most significantly, the LXX.

[19] Although Nehemiah uses the singular demonstrative and verb, his prayer can hardly be interpreted as a commentary on Exodus 32 beyond the recognition that apostasy took place in

Sailhamer's final comparison with the book of Deuteronomy would seem to be his strongest point, but even here there are difficulties. First, the change in order of the list of objects that must not be coveted between the Decalogue in Exodus and the Decalogue in Deuteronomy seems more comprehensible if the two commands are understood as one command rather than two. The lists reverse the order of house and wife at precisely the point where the division into two commands would take place. This would leave Sailhamer's goal of conformity in a precarious situation since the lists no longer match in what is the ninth commandment and what is the tenth commandment.[20] Furthermore, other than some inconsequential and atypical manuscript evidence, there is no known ancient Jewish tradition that separates Exod 20:17 or Deut 5:21 into two separate commands.[21] Even then it would appear that Sailhamer's attempt to divide the traditional tenth Commandment into two and combine the first two Commandments into one does not have enough evidence to warrant that conclusion.

There is one final and significant observation concerning Sailhamer's proposal. He concluded that combining vv. 3–6 turns the prohibition into one primarily concerned with idolatry, not with false gods. His motivation seems to be to protect the biblical text from recognizing other gods in that he writes, "the expression 'other gods' refers to wooden and stone idols. . . . It does not refer to actual divine beings."[22] At this point he made a distinction in antiquity that simply cannot be maintained. While this will be discussed more below, it is essential to note that biblical writers took the rampant polytheism that characterized the ancient Near East very seriously. The term "other gods" cannot be relegated to the matter of idolatry alone, but instead must include the recognition that such words were calling Israel away from the other gods that the nation struggled not to

the golden calf incident. The difference in the quotation probably arises out of the strict monotheism of the time and should be understood more as a synopsis than as a direct quotation.

[20] Sailhamer's explanation of the difference is that Deuteronomy is more specific than Exodus (*Pentateuch*, 437–38), but this hardly repairs the damage done since his essential argument is conformity.

[21] E. Merrill, *Deuteronomy*, NAC (Nashville: B&H, 1994), 156, n. 59.

[22] Sailhamer, *Pentateuch*, 285.

worship.[23] Furthermore, as both tradition and grammar demonstrate, combining the passage into one command does not bring about an emphasis on idolatry or images, but polytheism.[24] Sailhamer's distinctions seem to be unsupported by either his logic or the text. It remains, therefore, to make a case for the division of Exod 20:3–6 and Deut 5:7–10 into two separate commands.

The argument for dividing the text into two separate commands can be made on the basis of logic, ancient testimony, and textual comparisons. First, logically it is possible to have many gods without making images of them, just as it is possible to have only one God and attempt to represent Him through images.[25] That both would legitimately be the concern of the Decalogue is evident in the importance of both ideas and the fact that the two commands are presented individually in other places in Scripture.[26] Second, while it is clear that there were Jews in the rabbinic period who linked the verses into one instruction, both Philo and Josephus reveal that in the first century AD there were Jews who viewed them as separate commands.[27] Such early testimonies cannot be viewed as inconsequential. Finally, comparisons with other ancient Near Eastern evidence suggests that the prologue in v. 2—"I am the LORD your God, who brought you out of the land of Egypt, out of the place of slavery"—is in fact a preamble to the covenant stipulations that follow. The conclusion suggests that it cannot be considered one of the stipulations or commandments.[28] Therefore, we have the choice of either dividing the first statements of the Decalogue or the last into separate commands. The evidence already presented suggests that there is more to be said for dividing the first.[29]

---

[23] P. Miller, "Preaching the First Commandment in a Pluralistic World," *JP* 27 (2004): 5.

[24] Ibid., 4. The Catholic Catechism's arguments for preserving images in Catholic history grow out of this recognition. *Catechism of the Catholic Church* (New York: Doubleday, 1994), § 2129–2132.

[25] Miller, "Preaching," 4.

[26] The commands against having other gods in the polytheistic sense are found in Exod 22:20 (Hb. 22:19; see 23:13, 34:14), and Deut 13:2–4. Most strikingly, Ps 81:9–10 pairs the two statements of Exod 20:2–3 in reverse order without the reference to idols. The command against images is also found elsewhere (Exod 20:23, 34:17; Lev 19:4, 26:1; Deut 27:15).

[27] Josephus, *Ant.* III:5.5; Philo, *Decalogue*, 65.

[28] B. S. Childs, *Exodus: A Commentary*, OTL (London: SCM Press, 1974), 394, 401–2.

[29] The one item not addressed is the plural "them" in v. 5, whose only antecedent can be the

Having established that Exod 20:3 ought to be understood as a command in its own right, it is now possible to examine the implications such a command has for us in our understanding of God and in relation to worship. In particular, the issue of the passage's relationship to polytheism must be discussed. As already illustrated, some will go to great lengths to try to protect the text from any notion of polytheism.[30] Indeed, one must be careful to avoid suggesting that the Bible recognizes the existence of multiple gods. However, it seems rather unnecessary to suggest the Bible cannot acknowledge that people believed in other gods and that the Israelites would be tempted to follow other gods. It is hard to make much sense of passages that recognize God's superiority in relationship to other gods (see Deut 13:2–6; Pss 82:1; 86:8; 95:3; 97:7–9; 135:5; and 136:2) if one does not allow for this recognition.[31] Additionally, regarding the first Commandment, Childs is correct when he observes the contrast between the statement made here and that of Isa 45:6,14,21: "There is no other."[32] It seems, therefore, that this commandment does not address the ontological nature of God or suggest that it is foolish to worship other gods that do not exist. This point is made elsewhere, but not in this commandment.

Before leaving the subject of God's singularity, we should examine another significant and related command. The *Shema* in Deut 6:4–9 attained its name from the first Hebrew word of the passage *(šemaʿ)*, which is the command, "Listen!" or "Hear!" In many ways, this command became the defining command of Judaism and the central tenet of many of its practices. More important to the discussion here is the clause translated "The LORD our God, the LORD is

gods of v.3. This reference clearly links the ideas but does not demand that they be understood as one command. This is true because "the images we make may become other gods, even if they are images of the God we have" (Miller, "Preaching," 7). Moses used the previous law for purposes of furthering his exposition against idols, without necessarily suggesting that all idols are foreign gods. Further discussion will follow.

[30] E.g., Sailhamer, *Pentateuch*, 285.

[31] See C. J. H. Wright, *The Mission of God* (Downers Grove: InterVarsity, 2006), 149–61. Though his list is much more limited for purposes of discussion and some of his conclusions are troubling, J. Levenson's appraisal is helpful ("Creation and Covenant," in *The Flowering of Old Testament Theology*, ed. B. C. Ollenburger and others [Winona Lake: Eisenbrauns, 1992], 431–35).

[32] Childs, *Exodus*, 403. He did admit that the grammar functions in "categorically eliminating other gods as far as Israel is concerned."

One," (HCSB, NKJV, NIV, ESV). It has also been translated, "The
LORD our God is one LORD" (KJV, ASV, RSV), and "The LORD is our
God, the LORD alone" (NRSV, JPS, NLT, TEV, NAB). The KJV rendering stresses the uniqueness or wholeness of God, while the NRSV
rendering emphasizes His sole claim to the position of the God of
Israel. One's decision will no doubt be influenced by what one understands Israel's thoughts and conceptions to be about Yahweh. On
the other hand, this text more so than the first Commandment does
seem to emphasize the singularity of God in more of an ontological
sense through the use of *'ehad* ("One" or "one"); though it must be
admitted that v. 5 does take the command in the direction of the
people's need to worship Him alone. This text then, like the first
Commandment, highlights the close relationship between Yahweh's
singular nature and His unique position.

It is important not to jump in too quickly to protect the idea of
monotheism in relation to these commands, because doing so robs
them of their true power—the power to call one to absolute loyalty
and subjection to Yahweh. Much like the culture of ancient Israel, our
culture is one permeated with multiple temptations and requests for
our attention and allegiance. The prologue in Exod 20:2 calls Israel to
respond to God because of the history He has with them. In the same
way, the salvation history of Scripture culminating at the cross and
finding manifestations within our own personal and corporate histories also invites God to demand sole allegiance in our lives. Miller has
said it well: "Preaching the commandment will seek out, in the life of
the congregation, those powers that are both threatening and entic-
ing, those attractions that lure the Christian's turn from the Lord your
God to commitments of other sorts."[33]

## God's Nature as Revealed in His Vastness

The second Commandment obviously centers on the topic of making images,[34] so the question is whether the images are of Yahweh

[33] Miller, "Preaching," 9.

[34] A related topic (but not one that will be pursued here) is how early idolatry exited from
the official cult in Israel. T. Mettinger represents much of the scholarship in his argument that
it was not until the sixth century BC that idols were removed from worship; see Mettinger, *No
Graven Image? Israelite Aniconism in Its Ancient Near Eastern Context*, ConBOT (Stockholm :

or false gods. A good case can be made for the latter based solely on the use of "them" in referring to the false gods of Exod 20:3.[35] But the flow of the argument found within the commandment itself leads one to the conclusion that other gods are not solely the focus, and indeed they may not even be primary. The comparison the text seems to make is between the true revelation of Yahweh through His actions and His word and the false one, implied by an image that might be made of Him.[36] That is, God's revelation in history and word correctly reveals who He is and allows for relationship, while not limiting Him to one essence or place. It is a truism of human nature, both ancient and modern, that it is not too difficult for humans to mistake the image for the one it represents. The golden calf incident portrays this fact all too well.

It is true that Aaron sees in the calf a form of Yahwism and an opportunity for worship of Yahweh (Exod 32:5).[37] The phrase "these are your gods" probably represents the confusion of the era and the event. Idols were often understood, especially by the official cult, to function as pedestals for the god.[38] The tension of the moment coupled with such perceptions finds expression in the words of the people as they employ a plural reference (Exod 32:4), probably referring to both the calf and the thought that Yahweh sat on it. Aaron uses the singular (Exod 32:5), viewing it merely as Yahweh's seat or possibly His material representative, thus making the event an act of both polytheism and idolatry.

Such is the danger of images, whether they are physical or mental. For while the original motivation may simply be to enhance an activity or event, if one is not careful the image may begin to replace

---

Almqvist & Wiksell International, 1995). But W. Schmidt has made a convincing case that they were absent from the very earliest periods in Israel's worship; see Schmidt, *Altestamentlicher Glaube in seiner Geschichte* (Neukirchen: Neukirchener Verlag, 1982).

[35] See earlier discussion of vv. 4–6 subjugation to v. 3. The plural pronoun requires a plural antecedent, which can only be "gods."

[36] Childs, *Exodus*, 409. Fretheim concurs, suggesting that the "Law is not to protect God's otherness, but his relatedness with Israel. . . . Images imply that not only does God not think or feel or act in relationship to the world but that this is the very character of God." See T. Fretheim, *Exodus*, INT (Louisville: Westminster John Knox, 1991), 226–27.

[37] Childs, *Exodus*, 567. The same can probably be said for Jeroboam I's actions in 1 Kings 12 (discussed in the next chapter).

[38] K. Galling, *Biblisches Realliexicon*, HAT (Tübingen: J.C.B. Mohr, 1937), columns 202–205.

God Himself.[39] This is not to suggest that artistry has no place in worship; it is also true that symbolism is something that is sorely missing in much evangelical worship and life.[40] Rather, the caution is a simple one about how those who do not carefully consider what they are doing and how it is being received might use and interpret such symbolism.

The rationale of the prohibition of the second command is not merely limited to our understanding of God's essence or nature. It also finds expression in the freedom of God to be sovereign. The ancients perceived their relationship to idols in terms of manipulation toward accomplishing their own ends.[41] It followed that since the god was directly linked to the image, the one who controlled the image also controlled the god. Therefore, the prohibition against images was a direct declaration of Yahweh that He was beyond being controlled, that He was sovereign, and that He would not endure the presence of other gods—whether the gods were some mythical creation or the people themselves who were responsible for those creations.

To the modern reader the challenge is not so much an idol that might be made, but the pride that drives us to create a god that is more manageable in conception and in what He requires of us. Yahweh is vast in essence and power. The second Commandment sets forth principles by which that realization should never be forgotten.

## God's Nature as Revealed in His People

The meaning of the third Commandment has a long history, and much of the discussion concerns the nature of the prohibition in it. Of course, every child who has even a passing knowledge of this Commandment knows that it applies to using God's name as a swear word. But the Commandment means something more than this, es-

---

[39] "To the prohibition of an image is attached a further specification which broadens the prohibition to include every representation" (Childs, *Exodus*, 405).

[40] For an excellent discussion of the place of aesthetics in relation to this command, see W. Dyrness, "The *Imago Dei* and Christian Aesthetics," *JETS* 15 (1972): 161–72.

[41] E. M. Curtis, "The Theological Basis for the Prohibition of Images in the Old Testament," *JETS* 28 (1985): 286–87.

pecially if one examines the literary history of how it has been interpreted. From the Peshitta (the Syriac translation of the Bible) one finds an ancient interpretation that "you shall not swear falsely by the name of the Lord" (see Lev 19:12). Some have suggested translating the sentence as "you shall not give my name to an idol,"[42] and "Thou shalt not cry aloud the name of Yahweh thy God when thou hast brought no sacrifice."[43] The ancient Peshitta interpretation seems unlikely since the condition of false testimony would be adequately addressed by the ninth Commandment (Exod 20:16). The other options have held little sway, and it must be admitted that the rendering of the passage along the lines of "Do not misuse the name of the LORD your God" has yet to be improved on.

The difficulty centers on the interpretation of the verb *nāśā'*, usually rendered "take, lift up, carry, or use," and the translation of the noun *šāw'*, usually rendered "worthlessness, emptiness, or falseness." Viewing the passage relationally, one might see in its prohibition an assessment for how a person of God might present God to the world. Indeed, the commands in Lev 22:2,31–32 draw a very close association between how one behaves and profaning God's name. Therefore, it seems possible, if not probable, that the third Commandment demands that the people of God must not take or carry His name in a way that would render the name worthless in what it says about God.

Such a position has several arguments in its favor. First, since the name of God holds a significant position in one's understanding of God (see Ps 48:10; 86:9), it seems necessary to set forth how one is to characterize that name, not only in speech but also in action. Second, since the first two Commandments deal directly with how God's nature and position are portrayed in the cultus itself, it seems natural that the third Commandment would expand this understanding in how it is applied both to the worship event and worship as a lifestyle. Third, the law understood this way would be the clearest advocacy of the overarching theme of the holiness of God's people found in the ten words. It would thus function as a foundation for the holiness code of

[42] W. E. Staples, "The Third Commandment," *JBL* 58 (1939): 325–29.
[43] L. B. Paton, "The Meaning of Exodus xx. 7," *JBL* 22 (1903): 201–10.

the book of Leviticus and link the various sections of the Pentateuchal presentation in a more cohesive manner. Finally, this interpretation provides one way in which the expansion of God's name throughout the world might find concrete expression in the lives of those who are His own.[44] Of course, this view might be objectionable because it does not give a clear law to break and becomes, therefore, more nebulous and unenforceable. However, this already exists within the third Commandment in its traditional form (hence, the ancients' application of it to vows) and there are other commandments in the ten that also seem to be almost holistically in the realm of attitude and lifestyle rather than in specific action (namely, the first Commandment, and especially the tenth Commandment).[45]

What picture of God do His people portray? It is in the worship wars that this question might find its most damaging and troubling answer. In a realm specifically designated for honoring and valuing God, His people have managed to turn the focus on themselves. Though worship is not a matter of public proclamation in the same way missions and evangelism are, the struggles that characterize many congregations' attempts at addressing the matter have had the horrible effect of presenting a God who is petty and selfish to a world who does not understand the differences of which we speak. When such faulty views of God's character combine with behavior on the part of God's people—behavior that has always had trouble finding a connection between what happens on Sunday and what happens the rest of the week—it is clear that we need to understand the third Commandment with a new sensitivity if we want God's name to be heard by those who so desperately need to hear it.

## God's Nature as Revealed in His Names

Around 1990 the topic of God's names took on a life of its own, and since then it has found numerous expressions in books and studies. Though some of the books have been helpful, some have led

---

[44] Fretheim's argument is similar to this since he argues that taking the name to no effect robs it of its purpose of reaching the world as it is the name that goes out (*Exodus*, 228–29).

[45] Indeed, one might argue that this commandment is fleshed out through the commandments that follow in the rest of the Decalogue.

individuals in directions which are either erroneous or that propose ideas antithetical to the biblical understanding of the use of God's names.[46] The problem, of course, is not a new one. Out of fear of breaking the third Commandment, among other things, the rabbis taught it was wrong to utter the name Yahweh.[47] They did so despite the fact that the biblical text repeatedly calls on individuals to call on, or praise, God using the name Yahweh (see 1 Chr 16:8; Pss 96, 100, 105, 113, 135, 148).

Several observations concerning God's names ought to serve as a warning for their use in our lives, either in worship or otherwise. First, the common view for many years that the giving of a name indicates an expression of dominion of the giver over the recipient[48] becomes untenable when applied to events such as Hagar naming God (Gen 16:13). Instead, naming something seems to arise more from the circumstance than from the individual doing the name change. In fact, one might argue that the only thing the naming of an individual says about the one doing the naming is that it portrays the giver's level of discernment.[49] This linkage between name and circumstance/event is significant. It helps us understand more fully that the importance of God's names is not found in some abstract

---

[46] Such books range from the peripheral (Y. Berg, *The 72 Names of God: Technology for the Soul* [New York: The Kabbalah Center International, 2003]) to the mainline (K. Hemphill, *The Names of God* [Nashville: B&H, 2001]). The misuse of the contents of certain books in this genre, especially those in the mainline tradition, seems more the result of misreading their content than what they actually argue.

[47] For a thorough treatment of the ancient rabbinical aversion to using the name, see S. Cohon, "The Name of God, A Study in Rabbinic Theology," *HUCA* 23 (1951): 579–604.

[48] R. de Vaux, *Ancient Israel: Its Life and Institutions*, trans. John McHugh (London: Darton, Longman, and Todd, 1961; reprint Grand Rapids: Eerdmans, 1997), 43. Note Adam's naming the animals (Gen 2:20), his naming his wife on two occasions (Gen 2:23; 3:20), and certain kings who renamed people under their rule (Gen 41:45; 2 Kgs 23:34; Dan 1:6).

[49] G. Ramsey, "Is Name Giving an Act of Domination in Genesis 2:23 and Elsewhere?" *CBQ* 50 (1988): 34. One may retort that examples such as Gen 41:45 and Dan 1:7 demand an understanding of lordship in the naming. However, even in these texts the writer seems to be intimating a strong disposition concerning the one giving the names having (or lacking ) perception. Joseph's renaming happens after an event and seems to describe the Pharaoh's perception of his abilities. The renaming of Daniel and his friends indeed comes as an act of subjugation, but Daniel the author seems to be using it to show the Babylonian's lack of perception as to who is really in control. In other words, while naming may have been an act of domination in the ancient Near East, it seems that the biblical writers used it primarily (if not exclusively) in terms of reporting a person's wisdom or perception.

meaning that simply describes His character, but in the realization that He is a God invested in history and who can best be known by His actions in history.

Second, since the names of God are linked to a historical circumstance and are *reflective* of that event, one needs to be careful not to turn the separate names or titles for Him into *prescriptive* realities in prayer. Many works on the subject come very close to advocating a position in which the various names are said to unlock doors to God's grace or other benefits. Such a position not only ignores how the names are presented in Scripture, it is the essence of breaking all three of the first Commandments. To use God's names to access that part of Him that might meet a present need is a form of idolatry via attempted manipulation. Such manipulation through the various forms of worship destroys the servant status of worship and places man once again at the center of the activity rather than God.[50]

Finally, all the attention that the names of God have received over the last several years has led to an imbalance of sorts. In the rush to identify the various names and their meanings, we sometimes seem to forget that they all apply to the same person. We almost turn *God* into *gods*, each assigned to his own dominion of activity in life and history. In all the discussion, we should not dissect God to the extent that we lose our capacity to see Him as a person.[51]

Possibly the best place to start in relating the correspondence between the name of God and event is with "the name that is not a name"—God of My Fathers. Albrecht Alt wrote the seminal work on this concept of God. The reference is more to a group of titles used of God, rather than one particular phrase.[52] The titles include "The Fear of Isaac" (Gen 31:42), "The Bull/Mighty One of Jacob" (Gen 49:24), and most importantly, variations of the phrase, "the God of Abraham, Isaac, and Jacob" (Gen 26:24; 29:13; Exod 3:6, 15:4:5; 1 Kgs 18:36;

---

[50] H.-J. Kraus, *Worship in Israel*, trans. G. Buswell (Oxford: Oxford University Press, 1966), 124.

[51] The same could be said of scholars who utilize the various names to propose a polytheistic understanding of the names as presented in Scripture.

[52] E. MacLaurin was certainly correct when he identified these titles more as epithets than proper names ("YHWH, the Origin of the Tetragrammaton," *VT* 12 [1962], 442); hence, the use of the phrase, "the name that is not a name."

1 Chr 29:18). In his article, Alt argued for the idea that each of the gods represented in these phrases were tribal or clan-related gods. He proposed that the later monotheistic priestly writers brought about a convergence of these separate gods with the God of Israel.[53]

Even if one does not follow this trajectory of thought concerning a polytheistic origin for the various titles, there are important lessons in it. While the epithets do not require that this God be understood as anonymous, as Alt has suggested, their presence certainly permitted the individuals involved to have a concept of God that was amenable to subsequent revelations.[54] The titles of God represent a didactic function leading the patriarchs toward an understanding of the one who would eventually reveal Himself as Yahweh. The emphasis is on the fact that He was (and is) a historical God. He had (and has) a history with the people. The patriarchs' concept of God did not exist in a vacuum or even in dictates about His nature. Instead, they resided in His role as the sustainer of their families and in a personal knowledge and remembrance of one who had been with them for centuries.

The name El has a much more difficult route to follow in gaining an understanding of its purpose and function. Multiple references to such a name in other ancient Near Eastern literature forces this question: To what degree should cross referencing be carried out? Furthermore, because the name often appears in connection with another substantive, the issue of translation itself must be raised. For instance, using the name El Olam (*'ēl 'ōlām*), one can render *'ēl* as a name and *'ōlām* as an attributive adjective or substantive—El, the eternal one. One could also render *'ēl* as a substantive and *'ōlām* as a proper name—the god (God) Olam. Finally, one could render both words as a substantive, either in apposition or construct/genitive relationship—god (God), the eternal one or god (God) of eternity.[55] All of these options are both grammatically and contextually

---

[53] A. Alt, "The God of the Fathers," chap. in *Essays on Old Testament History and Religion*, trans. R. A. Wilson (Oxford: Basil Blackwell, 1966), 3–66.

[54] F. M. Cross, *Canaanite Myth and Hebrew Epic: Essays in the History of the Religion of Israel* (Cambridge, MA: Harvard University Press, 1973; reprint, 1997), 12. All citations are from the reprint edition.

[55] Ibid., 47.

feasible.[56] In fact, there is no reason the original audience could not have held these interpretations together in a tension (especially the first and third ones). The result is that El would be understood both as name and a descriptor, similar to modern understandings of the word "God."

What is interesting about El is that when it is used with other appellatives, it is, with the exception of one such name, linked to a specific place. The epithet *ʾēl ʿōlām* (El Olam=God of Eternity) is related to Beersheba (Gen 21:33). The name *ʾēl ʿelyôn* (El Elyon=God Most High) is associated with Jerusalem (Gen 14:18). The title *ʾēl ʾēlōhê yiśrāʾēl* (El Elohe-Israel=God, the God of Israel [the Patriarch]) is connected to Shechem (Gen 33:20). The idiom *ʾēl rōʾî* (El Roi=God who Sees) is attached to Beer-lahai-roi (Gen 16:13). Finally, *ʾēl bêʾēl* (El Bethel=God of the House of God) is noticeably linked with Bethel.[57] Again, the revelation and understanding of the name El commonly occurs with both a place and an event.

The only designation of El that is not immediately recognizable as linked with a place is *ʾēl šadday* (El Shaddai=God Almighty). This term, which apparently transcends locality, found expression in numerous circumstances (Gen 17:1; 28:3; 35:11; 43:14; 48:3). A closer look at *šadday*, however, suggests that it likely originated in the Akkadian word for "mountain" or a range of mountains.[58] Such a conclusion would carry with it the metaphorical implication of strength and immovability, which finds expression in "Almighty." If this etymology is correct, the name would represent an important transitional expression relating God to a place and yet allowing for freedom of expression in numerous ancient settings and situations. Perhaps this is why God makes such an explicit comparison between this particular title and the name *Yahweh* (Exod 6:3).

---

[56] The second option is less preferable on both grammatical and contextual grounds. Cross argues that it is likely in a few cases given that some of the appellations stand alone and that the identity cannot be determined by the biblical material alone (ibid., 47–50). However, unless one acknowledges that it functions in ways similar to other names for God, this view cannot be supported at least in the final form used, and it seems unlikely even in the earlier eras given the polytheistic implications it engenders.

[57] Ibid., 50–57.

[58] KB³, "שַׁדִּי."

Yahweh is generally acknowledged as the term most clearly identifiable as a personal name of God. The name itself (yhwh) is almost
universally accepted as a derivative from the Hebrew verb "to be"
*(hāyâ)*. God Himself made the link in Exod 3:13–16 in the well-
known "I AM WHO I AM" discourse. Significantly, the response
Yahweh gave to Moses in those passages can be translated and interpreted many ways.[59] Most interpret the phrase along the lines of
God's actions, rendering God's response as either "I will be who I
will be" or "I am who I will be." In this way, God was telling Moses
that understanding who He is will only be possible through recognition of how He acts.[60] Thus, the statement amounts to a promise of
God's continued presence with Moses and Israel.[61] Others attempt to
understand the meaning along the lines of the traditional rendering,
"I am that I am." In this perspective the meaning is usually related
to God's self-determination and complete freedom.[62] Finally, following W. F. Albright's lead, some attempt to translate the phrase in the
causative sense, "I will cause to be what I will cause to be."[63] This
denotes freedom and providential care.

What is clear is that the phrase is not ontological in nature—that
is, "I am He who exists," as if God were disclosing His eternality.[64]

[59] Though somewhat dated, G. Barton's discussion of the possible origins of the name
Yahweh is still helpful (*Yahweh Before Moses* [New York: MacMillan, 1912]). For a thorough
discussion of the different approaches to interpreting the name, see C. Gianotti, "The Meaning
of the Divine Name YHWH," *BSac* 142 (1985): 38–51.

[60] R. A. Cole, *Exodus: An Introduction and Commentary*, TOTC (Downers Grove: InterVarsity,
1973), 69; R. Clements, *Exodus*, CBC (Cambridge: Univ. Press, 1972), 23; J. Murphy, *A Critical
and Exegetical Commentary on the Book of Exodus* (Boston: Estes and Lauriat, 1874), 41; and
Fretheim, *Exodus*, 63.

[61] M. Buber, *Moses: The Revelation and the Covenant* (New York: Harper & Row, 1958), 52;
U. Cassuto, *A Commentary on the Book of Exodus*, trans. I. Abrahams (Jerusalem: Magnes Press,
1967), 38.

[62] J. Durham, *Exodus*, WBC (Waco: Word, 1987), 38; C. F. Keil and F. Delitzsch, *Commentary
on the Old Testament*, vol. 1, *The Pentateuch*, trans. J. Martin (Grand Rapids: Eerdmans, 1949),
75 and 442.

[63] W. F. Albright, "Contributions to Biblical Archaeology and Philology," *JBL* 43 (1924):
370–78; D. Daiches, *Moses: The Man and His Vision* (New York: Praeger, 1975), 49; D. N. Freedman, "The Name of the God of Moses," *JBL* 79 (1960): 155. Similarly, based on comparisons
made with Qumran's *Manual of Discipline*, W. H. Brownlee argued for "the one who makes things
happen" ("The Ineffable Name of God," *BASOR* 226 [1977]: 39–45).

[64] He is eternal, but that is not suggested in this statement as it is used in the Old Testament. As MacLaurin noted, such a concept places Greek thought in the lap of a Hebrew writer
("YHWH," 441).

The closest one might come to this interpretation is in the translation of the phrase as "I am who I was." But even here, the emphasis is on the relational aspects of His dealings with the ancestors and reflects the permanency of the covenant, not a statement about His eternality. [65] God protected His freedom through the manner in which He shared his name, thus maintaining the hiddenness illustrated above as essential to His holy status.[66] But in sharing His name He also reveals His empathy and presence with His people—and by extension with us as well.[67] Therefore, whatever else may be said, the most relevant and important reason for the manner of the revelation is to allow for intimacy between God and His people and to permit true worship to occur.[68] The link between the "I am" statements and the name Yahweh make it clear that to best know God's nature, one must go beyond mere knowledge of its meaning and instead live a life in contact with His presence.

One other issue relating to worship and the use of the divine name is the use of the word Jehovah. It is not succumbing to legalism to propose that its usage may be problematic for the modern believer. The word grows out of an error in reading a Hebrew word that the copyists never intended to be read. As stated earlier, Judaism as a whole developed a fear of uttering the divine name, probably sometime not too long after Israel's return from exile in 539 BC. When coming upon the name in the biblical record, they would simply insert either ʾădōnāy (Adonai/"Lord") or haššēm ("the name").[69] Nearly fifteen centuries later, to avoid losing the oral tradition (how the consonantal text was to be pronounced), it became necessary for scribes known as Masoretes to codify the correct reading of the Hebrew text by adding vowels to the consonants. The Masoretes

[65] D. Zeligs, Moses: A Psychodynamic Study (New York: Human Sciences Press, 1986), 65.

[66] L. Köhler, Old Testament Theology, trans. A. S. Todd (Philadelphia: Westminster, 1957), 242.

[67] Fretheim, Exodus, 63.

[68] E. Jacob, Theology of the Old Testament, trans. A. Heathcote and P. Allcock (New York: Harper & Brothers, 1958), 53; S. Terrien, The Elusive Presence: Toward a New Biblical Theology (San Francisco: Harper & Row, 1978), 118; R. Abba, "The Divine Name YAHWEH," JBL 80 (1961): 325–26.

[69] Interestingly, Cohon points out that the rabbinic strictures on usage of the divine name grew to such a level that even Adonai could only be used for liturgical purposes. Cohon, "The Name of God," 590–91.

added vowels to the divine name by adding the vowels of *ădōnāy* to the consonants of yhwh (or when yhwh was used in connection with *ădōnāy,* such as in Hab 3:19, the vowels of *ĕlōhîm* were used). The resulting word is an impossible construction in Hebrew, so that readers would always be reminded to substitute the word Adonai when they came to it. Uninformed scholars of either the fifteenth or sixteenth century simply transliterated the word into their language as *yĕhōwāh,* and the result (with German *J* for Hb. *Y*) was the name Jehovah.[70]

The error has been known for more than a century, yet the use of Jehovah persists even among those who are aware of the error. For some, it would seem the continued use reflects a desire to be understood in a culture that has become accustomed to the use of Jehovah in songs and other places. Such a motivation seems laudable in many ways, yet the use of Yahweh has become widespread enough at this point that it would seem unnecessary to continue to use the erroneous form. For others, the rationale for such usage is that few names are successfully transliterated into English usage from their original, so it is unnecessary to alter this example either.[71] For instance, the name *yĕša'yāhû* bears little resemblance to how it has come into English as *Isaiah.* Indeed, even in languages close to each other in origin and nature, the transfer of a name from one language to another can be somewhat jolting.[72] But the problem here is that the English rendering of Jehovah is not simply a case of a language transferring the symbols of one language into its own as is *yĕša'yāhû* into Isaiah. Rather, the "word" in the original text was not meant to be pronounced as written and is not even linguistically possible. Jehovah, the resulting term in English, is a far more serious mistake than simply an odd way of rendering the name.

It seems a safe assumption that God would not be angry at the use of *Jehovah* from one who is intent on communicating with Him and who holds the name special. Additionally, old hymns or translations that were written in a context prior to widespread understanding of

---

[70] *EncJud,* "God, Names of"; *TWOT,* "יהוה."

[71] F. Denio, "On the Use of the Word Jehovah in Translating the Old Testament," *JBL* 46 (1927): 146–49.

[72] For instance, the Spanish name Ibanez becomes Johnson in English.

the error hardly require revisiting and correction. Yet it would also seem appropriate, for those who know the error and desire to use the name that is revealed instead of the name that is in many senses gibberish, to lay aside the use of Jehovah where possible and use Yahweh instead.

Knowing the meanings of the names of God can expand one's understanding of God and greatly enhance worship. But realizing that the names grew out of specific historical circumstances should caution one against seeing in them some password that allows access to God's special favor in a circumstance of need.[73] Further, there is an implicit lesson to be learned in the relationship of names to events that calls one to adopt the aspects of remembrance and testimony in worship, and the names themselves reinforce a theology of immanence that is necessary if one is going to be successful in carrying out worship as a lifestyle.

## Sacred Space

The discussion above has already alluded to the concept of sacred space in the expressions of God's names when an individual met and experienced Him. Along with these events God often advocates certain locations to be set aside specifically for the purpose of worship. The command to find a central location for worship in Deut 12:4–7 is one of the clearest expressions of the sacredness of one particular place anywhere in Scripture. The most important disclosure in these verses related to sacred space is God's demand that the place of the sanctuary be "the place the LORD your God chooses" (Deut 12:5). God established here as well as in the Tabernacle instructions (e.g., Exod 40:24–38; see below) that there were times when He could only be met in some particular place. Such perspectives became the impetus for the unity prescribed by Josiah's centralization reforms (2 Kgs 23:1–25) and the postexilic drive for the same advocated in the ministries of the Chronicler, Ezra, and Nehemiah.

---

[73] Although the appellatives applied to Yahweh (such as Yahweh Yireh, Yahweh Rophe, and Yahweh Nissi) were not examined, much of the same evidence described for the *El* appellatives applies to them.

The implications of this specific sacred location are significant. While God is indeed everywhere and capable of being worshipped in a number of ways and at innumerable locations, there is an importance to specific locations that transcends this universality for numerous reasons. First, the permanence of a place helps establish the principle of remembrance that has already been demonstrated as central to the biblical concept of how one relates to God. Second, the psychological impact of having a place specifically designated for worship can hardly be overstated. It is axiomatic that it is easier to move into an event of worship in a location where structures and setting advocate such a posture rather than a setting that draws one's attention in other directions. Finally, a specific location for a worship event enhances the notion that worship involves meeting a person—namely, God—and is not simply perfunctory or meaningless activity, for persons are always associated with places.[74]

## The Altar

The most basic form of sacred space is the altar. Altars were not erected at human discretion, but were instead erected because a significant act of God had taken place on that spot,[75] highlighting the God-centered nature of these special structures. The topic of revelation as a precursor to worship was and is a necessary acknowledgement if one is to hold a proper understanding of worship. God reveals Himself and invites the recipient of such a revelation to relate to Him in a special and distinct manner. This interaction is beyond that which is possible from a strictly general revelation evident to all of creation.

An altar could be constructed from many different types of materials. The biblical record records altars of earth—possibly clay brick (Exod 20:24–25), stone (Exod 20:25; Josh 8:31), and wood covered in metal (Exod 27:1–8). The sizes of the altars varied, though they were considerable enough to have ramps built up beside them so that they could be mounted. The altar of the tabernacle was approximately seven and a half feet in length and width and four and a

---

[74] Fretheim, *Exodus*, 273.
[75] De Vaux, *Ancient Israel*, 276–81.

half feet in height (Exod 27:1).[76] The sacredness of the site was preserved in numerous ways, including the regulation that steps were not allowed up to the altar—probably a ramp had to be used—lest the priest on ascending expose himself in some way to the altar (Exod 20:26). Indeed, since the altar primarily served the purpose of carrying out the offerings, the holiness of the location had to be maintained.

Many altars included in their construction the placement of "horns" on top of each corner of the altar.[77] The purposes of these horns remain somewhat of a mystery, though some fair conclusions can be drawn from both the biblical material and ancient Near Eastern comparisons. First, the horns apparently served a role in keeping the sacrifice in place on the altar (Ps 118:27). How exactly this would have been accomplished and why parts of an animal would need to be bound is difficult to say. Indeed, the passage in question is a difficult one to translate, but the implication seems to be a correspondence between the horns of the altar and the reception of the sacrifice by God. Second, the well-known practice of fleeing to the altar in order to grab on to the horns and plead for mercy is recorded in at least three locations. Exodus 21:14 alludes to the practice when it states that if the sin was willful, the person may be removed from the altar for execution. This seems to be what happened in 1 Kgs 2:28–34 in the account of Solomon's judgment against Joab for his backing of Adonijah. Interestingly, Adonijah himself did receive mercy after taking hold of the horns in the preceding chapter (1:50–51).

The rationale behind these activities as they relate to the altar is revealing. Scholars have long recognized the symbolic relationship of the horns of the altar to the very presence of God. This relationship has been expressed in two ways. First, some have suggested

---

[76] The altar before the temple was approximately thirty feet in length and width and fifteen feet in height (2 Chr 4:1).

[77] Though it is generally supposed that such an addition would require working the stone with a tool of some sort (H. M. Wiener, *The Altars of the Old Testament* [Leipzig: Hinrich 1927], 2–3), it is possible to conceive of them as being created using carefully selected stones that simply protruded on top.

that the horns represent God as the epitome of strength.[78] Second, and more likely, is the idea that the altar is a symbolic representation of God's throne.[79] For Israel this meant that an altar represented an opportunity to make supplication before God, to present one's gifts and offerings. One pleaded for His mercy through sacrifice and did the same symbolically by taking hold of the horns. Earthly courts would then be required to hear the request out because any earthly court was required to submit to the presence of the heavenly court. This would also relate to the placement of blood on the horns for purification since an altar served as God's throne and of all places had to be maintained as holy (Exod 30:10; Lev 4, 16:18).[80]

## The Tabernacle

The tabernacle is the subject of much unwarranted allegorical interpretation. From Philo's exposition of the tabernacle as a picture of the universe with the tent representing the spiritual world and the outer court picturing the physical[81] to the countless present studies that unjustifiably see in every element a picture of Jesus,[82] the tabernacle bears a weight it was never intended to bear. Perhaps this is because the biblical record gives so little explanation of the various elements, though it spends chapters outlining the specific details of each of the elements of this sacred building (Exod 25–27). Allegorical interpretations may be simply the outgrowth of the natural human tendency to seek to be the possessor of some special

[78] Eichrodt, *Theology I*, 163; H. T. Obbink, "The Horns of the Altar in the Semitic World, Especially in Jahwism," *JBL* 56 (1937): 43–49.

[79] G. Dalman, *Petra und seine Felsheiligtümer* (Leipzig: Hinrichs, 1908), 79.

[80] This need not be understood as contradictory to the fact that the ark within the holy of holies also is understood as the throne of God (see discussion below). Indeed, repetition of event and symbol seems to be prevalent in any number of articles about the tabernacle and the temple.

[81] Philo, *Vita Mos.* II.71–108.

[82] The number of these studies makes them impossible to list, though one would be hard pressed to find a study on the tabernacle today that does not take it in this direction. Importantly, even in the midst of some of the most typologically laden books (such as Hebrews), the NT writers never explained the tabernacle as a type for Christ (the closest case being John 1:14). Instead they described it as a type for heaven and the new way (Heb 8–9) or in the sense of God's dwelling in the midst of His people (Eph 2:22; Rev 21:3). Childs was certainly well justified in his warning that typology of the tabernacle quickly descends into allegory if one is not careful (*Exodus*, 548–49).

insight into God that few before have recognized. It is difficult to pin down exactly why so much wild speculation centers on this element of Israel's worship, but one would be well served to remember that if the NT writers did not see a need for such comparisons, the NT church should also show reserve. There are lessons to be learned from the tabernacle, but these reside in the original context of the OT and its ancient Near Eastern setting.

In its placement, form, and structure, the tabernacle proclaimed several truths to the children of Israel. The placement of the tent in the center of the camp (Num 2:17) had important significance. First, such a placement was comparable to the tent of the king in a military camp of New Kingdom Egypt (c. 1600–1100 BC). In this tent the king would meet foreign dignitaries and direct the plans and goals of his army.[83] Yahweh had just destroyed the gods of Egypt through the plagues and the crossing of the sea, and He was about to lead the children of Israel into warfare in Canaan, so such a placement speaks volumes. Like the law, the tabernacle had been given to Israel in the wilderness as a message that God would bring order out of chaos and would give shape to a people who had previously known only defeat. Second, the descent of the cloud onto the tent in Exod 40:24–38 also intimates that the one who Moses had met on the mountain and who had asked the people to come to Him would now be going with them. Such visual representations are essential expressions of the relationship between a creative God and his elect people.[84] Finally, since only the priest and Moses could enter the tent, Yahweh maintained that even while completely present, He was not at the beck and call of men but would maintain His status as leader and God.[85]

---

[83] See M. Homan, *To Your Tents, O Israel! The Terminology, Function, Form, and Symbolism of Tents in the Hebrew Bible and the Ancient Near East* (Leiden: Brill, 2002), 113–14.

[84] In the Old Covenant, everything associated with worship had to partake of proper symbolism, so that the presence of God, the purity of God, the superiority of God, and the nature of his salvation could be communicated visually and, at least sometimes, even tactilely, to his people. See D. K. Stuart, *Exodus*, NAC (Nashville: B&H, 2006), 562.

[85] Eichrodt, *Theology*, 1:110; B. Sommer draws this idea from the apparently conflicting reports of where the tent would be established ("Conflicting Constructions Of Divine Presence In The Priestly Tabernacle," *BibInt* 9 [2001]: 41:63).

Somewhat surprisingly, the construction and design of the tabernacle fell into the hands of a man named Bezalel.[86] This man from the tribe of Judah was not a priest or a leader of Israel and yet he holds the honor of being the first person that Scripture says was filled with the Spirit of God (Exod 31:3). The reader should not miss the importance of this information in the text. When it comes to fulfilling the service of God and to carrying out His tasks, His call and gifting fall on any who are receptive. Bezalel was a craftsman who committed his work to God; thus, he fell into place alongside other men and women of the OT that God gave the distinct privilege of receiving the Spirit.[87]

Within the tabernacle were placed several elements that proclaim features suggestive of the nature of worship. The first and probably most important of these elements was the ark of the covenant (Exod 25:10–22). The ark represented the center of worship since it served both as the container of the law tablets and the throne of God.[88] Revelation is always the starting place of worship, so its corollary of proclamation deserves the central position in worship as event. The table of Presence (Exod 25:23–30) held the bread that could only be consumed by the priest and was to be maintained with food and drink on it at all times. Like the ark, the table was covered with gold and clearly proclaimed the presence of God. However, it also advocated that God's presence brought with it the sustenance of His people.[89] The golden lampstand (Exod 25:31–39) has been compared with the light that God brought into the world and therefore served as yet another picture of His presence.[90] However, a closer look at the iconography of the ancient Near East and the descriptions of the lampstand in Scripture has led to the stronger argument

---

[86] The long-held Wellhausen perception that the tabernacle was a late literary construct based on the temple has been answered successfully elsewhere. See R. E. Friedman, "The Tabernacle in the Temple," *BA* 43 (1980), 241–48; and C. Meyers, *Tabernacle Menorah: A Synthetic Study of a Symbol from the Biblical Cult* (Winona Lake: Eisenbrauns, 1972), 182.

[87] Exactly what is meant by "the Spirit" is beyond the scope of this work. For a good discussion of the matter, see J. M. Hamilton Jr., *God's Indwelling Presence: The Holy Spirit in Old and NTs*, NACSBT (Nashville: B&H, 2006).

[88] Durham, *Exodus*, 360; M. Haran, *Temples and Temple—Service in Ancient Israel* (Oxford: Clarendon, 1978), 246–59.

[89] Durham, *Exodus*, 362.

[90] Ibid., 362–63.

that it was a symbol of the tree of life.[91] Such an imposing image in the heart of the sanctuary undoubtedly filled the priest with a sense of God's grandeur and provision and at the same time reminded him of his complete dependence on God. No doubt, it also functioned as a poignant reminder of what was lost at the fall and the reasons behind the need for a building such as the tabernacle and all that took place there. Finally, the altar of incense (Exod 30:1–5) functioned in much the same way as any altar. What is distinct about it is that nothing but incense could be burned on it (Exod 30:9). Therefore, the incense placed on it can only be understood as the prayers of the people (Ps 141:2; Rev 8:3–5). This clearly intimates that it was prayer that most thoroughly brought the ancients into the presence of God and that sought His favor and His glorification.

Many modernists have difficulty with the idea of a distinctly sacred space set aside for the worship event. Whereas previous generations erected buildings designed for worship that to their smallest details pointed to God's presence and an appropriate disposition towards His worship, modern architecture increasingly focuses on utility at the cost of aesthetic values. This is not to say that worship cannot take place in someone's living room or other places as need dictates—indeed, some of the most thoroughly worshipful events in this writer's experience have taken place at services held in squalor on the mission field or in homes of fellow believers. Rather, the observation is simply that previous architectural structures invited and prodded one to look to the sky, to kneel, and to recognize the centrality of the reading of God's word. Today, on the other hand, because many buildings utilized for worship do not offer such assistance, there is the added pressure of making a concerted effort to maintain the sacredness of space devoted to a worship event.

## Sacred Time

For the Israelite, the only element of a life of worship that superseded sacred space was sacred time.[92] From the beginning God set aside or sanctified a certain time for the purpose of experiencing Him

---

[91] Meyers, *Tabernacle*, 96, 118–19, 133.
[92] W. Harrelson, *From Fertility Cult to Worship* (New York: Doubleday, 1969), 16.

more and allowing His people a chance to recover from the trials of life (Gen 2:3). The established times of worship took many shapes, from withdrawal and contemplation to complete relocation of the community for the purpose of joint celebrations. As Israel moved through its seasons, each category of week, month, and year had its distinctive times that served to draw each person's thoughts away from himself toward the God who directed those same seasons.

## The Sabbath

The most basic of sacred times was that of the Sabbath (Exod 20:8–11; 31:12–17, 23:2–4; Num 15:32–36; Deut 5:12–15). Though usually related to the last day of the week, it also found manifestations within the larger categories of months and years (Lev 23:15–31, 25:1–17). The Sabbath rest provided humanity and all creation with an established order that "organizes time into the everyday and the holy."[93] The establishment of certain days as sacred also aids the believer in understanding the distinctions of holiness to which he is called in that its goal is always a deeper devotion and appreciation of the holiness of God.[94] What is so intriguing about sacred times is that not only is God's activity sanctified and descriptive of a relationship, but so is His rest. There is nothing about Him that does not call humanity to a recognition of His presence and, therefore, to their need to worship Him.[95]

In a very real sense, the idea of the Sabbath pulls humanity out of its self-interest and striving. It presses people to find contentment in the idea that God is ultimately in control and does in fact provide for the needs that too often they find themselves attempting to fulfill on their own during the work week.[96] Finally, the fact that the fourth Commandment is based on the actions of God also

---

[93] C. Westermann, *Genesis: A Practical Commentary,* trans. D. E. Green (Grand Rapids: Eerdmans, 1987), 12.

[94] Harrelson, *From Fertility Cult to Worship,* 26

[95] Terrien, *Elusive Presence,* 394; A. Edersheim, *The Life and Times of Jesus the Messiah,* vol. 2 (Grand Rapids: Eerdmans, 1956), 56–57.

[96] W. Brueggemann, *An Introduction to the Old Testament: The Canon and Christian Imagination* (Louisville: Westminster John Knox, 2003), 35–36; G. Cohen, "The Doctrine of the Sabbath in the Old and NTs," *GJ* 6 (1965), 7–15; Fretheim, *Exodus,* 230.

clearly articulates a principle that finds expression throughout the Pentateuch: we must be like God. This impressive invitation is rooted in the *imago Dei* that dwells within us and is at the heart of the two greatest Commandments: "Love the LORD your God" (Deut 6:5) and "Love your neighbor" (Lev 19:18).

## The Sacred Festivals

The sacred calendar of Israel focused on three primary festivals of celebration: Passover, Harvest/Weeks, and Ingathering/Booths (Exod 23:10–19; Lev 23:4–44; Num 28–29; Deut 16:1–17). Scholarship has often taken a position that Israel simply adopted these festivals from the Canaanites and attached them to significant events in the history of Israel.[97] There is no difficulty in accepting such a position as long as we also acknowledge the historicity of these Israelite events. In this view, the adoption of the festivals would serve in a polemical sense as correctives of the false practices of the Canaanites with the recognition that the true deliverer and provider is Yahweh.

Passover is linked with the feast of unleavened bread (Exod 12:1–13,42–50; Num 9:1–14, 28:16–25; Lev 23:6–14), which lasted for seven days immediately following Passover during the month of Abib/Nisan (late March, early April). Along with the consumption of the lamb, bitter herbs, and unleavened bread, the people were also commanded to offer the first fruits of what they had.[98] A similarity in the events prescribed and in the consecration of priests has led Alexander to suggest that the meal represented a consecration of the people—a setting apart for service to the world.[99] Indeed, the two festivals together served as thanks to God for deliverance and advocacy of the resulting call to holiness that such deliverance requires.[100]

---

[97] G. von Rad, *Old Testament Theology,* vol. 1, *The Theology of Israel's Traditions,* trans. D. M. G. Stalker, OTL (New York: Harper & Row, 1965), 27.

[98] Though some would reject the early link of these two festivals, there is good reason to believe that both functioned together from the earliest periods. See T. D. Alexander, "The Passover Sacrifice," in *Sacrifice in the Bible,* ed. R. Beckwith and M. Selman (Grand Rapids: Baker, 1995), 1–6; J. G. McConville, "Deuteronomy's Unification of Passover and Massot: A Response to Bernard M. Levinson," *JBL* 119 (2000): 47–58.

[99] Alexander, "Passover," 8.

[100] A. Ross, *Holiness to the Lord: A Guide to the Exposition of the Book of Leviticus* (Grand Rapids: Baker Academic, 2002), 413.

The Feast of Harvest or Weeks required the offering of two loaves of bread and a whole burnt offering (Lev 23:17–21). Observed fifty days after Passover Sabbath, its historical basis was in the giving of the law following the Lord's deliverance of the Israelites from Egypt. The festival included the requirement that the corner of the fields remain uncut so that the poor could enter and acquire the food necessary for their survival (Lev 23:22). In the face of the bounty that God had brought Israel—not only in its produce but also in its deliverance from bondage—it was appropriate and necessary for Israel to stop and say "thank you," but not just to offer appreciation in word and deed. The people should also offer thanks in the dedication of themselves to the well being of all God's people with the promise that they would not abuse those who had fallen on difficult times.

The Feast of Ingathering or Booths took place at the end of the agricultural year (Exod 23:16; 34:22)[101] and celebrated a year's worth of provision and bounty from God in both the fields and the vineyards (Deut 16:13–15). Even with the preceding two festivals to acknowledge God's gifts (not to mention offerings that did the same), the end of the agricultural year provided yet another opportunity for reflection and gratitude. As Israel looked forward to the new planting season, it acknowledged that its success would be solely God's doing—not in some ritualistic or magical sense but simply in humble recognition that all produce comes from God the Creator. The Feast of Ingathering advocates an understanding of our relationship to God that acknowledges the inexhaustibility of His grace, so our gratitude must not cease.

Contrary to a modern world determined not to recognize its dependence on anything, the festivals of Israel demanded God's people to acknowledge that all they were was the result of the gift of God. At the heart of all these events was an attitude of thankfulness, not just the cursory or passing thankfulness that comes too easy and is forgotten as soon as it is expressed, but the thankfulness that demands giving to others just as one has received. For true gratitude can only be present when one is willing to give to others.[102] Debates

---

[101] See Stuart, *Exodus*, 536.
[102] Ibid., 437.

swirl about the nature of giving to the Lord's work, asking whether the tithe is a Christian practice and if so from what does one give his tithe. The biblical picture of giving has never been of how little one can get away with, but rather how willing God's people should be to give bountifully when they realize how much He has given them.

Another important implication for worship demonstrated in the sacred calendar needs to be heard primarily among those of the free church tradition. The freedom of worship and the commitment to allow the Holy Spirit to move are essential elements that no church should forsake. Openness to moving in new directions and expressions of worship has much in its favor as long as it is limited by biblical propositions and concepts. But there is an unfortunate loss that comes with such a perspective so that it might be helpful for many churches to revisit an issue that for many is closed—the liturgical church year calendar. It draws one's attention to the movement of God throughout the year and allows for reflection and consecration in a way that less regimented approaches cannot fulfill. Following the liturgical year does not mean that we should abandon the free church tradition, but rather that we can learn something from Israel. Regularly scheduled yearly services can draw one's attention to the wholeness of the drama that is God's relationship with the church.[103]

## Atonement

Robert Culpepper wrote the following eloquent words about the atonement:

> The doctrine of atonement is the Holy of Holies of Christian theology. It is a doctrine of unfathomable depth and inexhaustible mystery. Christian theology reaches its climax in it, and in a large measure it is determinative of all other doctrines. Theology is Christian only insofar as all of its doctrines are illuminated by the doctrine of atonement.[104]

Statements such as this reveal the centrality of the word "atonement" to Christian thought and theology. As this work is a biblical

---

[103] These elements could include sacred events in the life of an individual church as well.

[104] R. Culpepper, *Interpreting the Atonement* (Grand Rapids: Eerdmans, 1966; reprint, Wake Forest: Stevens Book Press, 1988), 11. All notes are from reprint edition.

theology of worship from a Christian perspective, a definition of atonement is significant to the discussion.

The beginning of the study of atonement in the OT is in the Hebrew word *kippūr* (root *kāpar*).[105] Although atonement is an expression of *kippūr*, it is not the only way in which the word has been translated and understood. Much debate has gone into the meaning of the root *kāpar* and how this affects its various derivatives. The basic form of the word is used 101 times as a verb and 13 times as a noun.[106] Despite such various uses, or perhaps because of it, arriving at a definition for the word *kāpar* is a rather complicated task. At the core of the issue is the often vexing question of the relationship between its etymology and its usage. Some suggest that the meaning of the word is achieved primarily through a discussion of its origin.[107] In contrast, others argue that the word can only be properly understood in terms of how it is used in each individual passage.[108] As both methods have their benefit, both will be undertaken.

The origin or etymology of the word *kāpar* is found in the sister languages of Hebrew. In general, scholars have approached the word as it relates to either an Arabic or an Akkadian root.[109] For the most part, scholars do not equate the later understanding of the word with its original meaning, but it seems axiomatic that the final translation cannot stray too far from its original cognate.

---

[105] The English word "atonement" originated in the sixteenth century. It was not borrowed from another language, but was created in order to express an idea for which no word existed. The combination of the words "at-one-ment" expressed the idea of reconciliation whereby not just agreement was achieved, but essential unity was acquired. William Tyndale accepted the word as an authentic description of the Hebrew word כפר, and used it in his translation of the Old Testament. Subsequently, the translators of the King James Version, using much of Tyndale's work, also rendered כפר the same way. See O. Baab, "The God of Redeeming Grace: Atonement in the Old Testament," *Int* 10 (1956): 136.

[106] A. E.-Shoshan, ed. "כפר," in *A New Concordance of the Bible* (Jerusalem: Sivan Press, 1990), 560.

[107] B. Levine, *In the Presence of the Lord: A Study of Cult and Some Cultic Terms in Ancient Israel*, SJLA (Leiden: Brill, 1974), 56.

[108] B. Janowski, *Sühne als Heilsgeschehen*, WMANT (Neukirchen-Vluyn: Neukirchener Verlag, 1982), 105–6.

[109] The similarities between the Hebrew כפר and the Babylonian *kaparu*, which means "to cut," seem striking at first, but from comparative studies it becomes clear that these words are merely homonyms. Levine, *Presence*, 57.

The traditional approach to identifying the meaning of *kāpar* has been to associate it with the Arabic root that means "to cover." Gustav Oehler has given the clearest expression of this view. For him the word always represented a veiling of sorts. Whether the act covered a sin from the presence of the deity or was used as a bribe that veiled the truth from the human judge's eyes, the word's use always carried this connotation.[110] Additionally, Ralph Elliott observed that the covering should be understood as a protection or nullification of a normal consequence.[111] Indeed, many commentaries begin discussions of the word with this assumption already made.

The arguments for understanding the word as meaning "to cover" center on three primary pieces of evidence. First, the use of *kāpar* with the preposition *'al*, "on, over, above," suggests that the word is to be understood as being on or over something else. Second, Neh 4:5 paraphrases Jer 18:23 by replacing the word *kāpar* with *kāsâ*—a term that definitely means "to cover." Third, the derivative word *kappōret* is understood as the covering for the ark of the covenant, and therefore the root from which it is derived most likely meant "to cover."[112]

A second understanding of the origin of *kāpar* is to associate it with the Akkadian *kapāru*, which means "to wipe off." Though this suggestion was made as early as 1881,[113] it was not until much later in the twentieth century that this view began to gain wide acceptance in OT theologies. The evidence for an association of the Hebrew *kāpar* and the Akkadian *kapāru* is offered along similar lines as that of its association with the Arabic *kafara*, "to cover." The previously mentioned Jeremiah passage places *kāpar* in parallel usage with the word *māḥʾâ*, which means, "to blot out."[114] The uses in biblical and Akkadian sources mirror each other in both cultic and non-cultic contexts. This is true even in the implicit cultic references to puri-

---

[110] G. Oehler, *Theology of the Old Testament*, trans. G. Day (New York: Funk & Wagnalls, 1883), 276–80; see Eichrodt, *Theology of the Old Testament*, 1:162.

[111] R. Elliott, "Atonement in the Old Testament," *RevExp* 59 (1962): 18–19.

[112] E. König, "The Hebrew Word for 'Atone'," *ExpTim* 22 (1910–1911): 232–33.

[113] G. Gray credits W. R. Smith with this identification. G. B. Gray, *Sacrifice in the Old Testament: Its Theory and Practice* (Oxford: Clarendon Press, 1925), 69.

[114] Gray, *Sacrifice*, 73; Levine, *Presence*, 58; and D. McCarthy, "The Symbolism of Blood and Sacrifice," *JBL* 88 (1966): 169.

fication through magical manipulation.[115] Furthermore, within the OT itself there are numerous places where *kāpar* is placed in synonymous relationships with words that mean to "erase," "remove," or "to set aside."[116]

Those who connect *kāpar* with "to wipe off" argue against the suggestion that the term means "to cover." First, they argue that the appearance of *kāpar* with *'al*, "upon," is inconclusive because the word also appears with the prepositions *bĕ*, "in, on," and *lĕ*, "to, for," which do not indicate a covering. Second, the relationship of the Nehemiah and Jeremiah passages should be discounted because the comparison is in the general intent of both verses with regard to the denial of forgiveness and not in a supposed synonymous association between *kāpar* and *kāsâ*. Third, associations with the word *kappōret* are not conclusive because the name is connected to its function related to *kāpar* as a place where purification takes place and not to its structural position.[117] Finally, apart from the likeness between *kāpar* with the Arabic *kafara*, which may have been a later reinterpretation of the Hebrew word, there are no other Semitic comparisons that convey the idea of covering.[118]

The association of the Akkadian and Hebrew words is sometimes made in a more general sense than the concept of wiping off something. Because of the appearance of passages such as Gen 6:14 (where the term refers to Noah's *covering* the ark with pitch) and Babylonian passages that discuss a wiping of a substance on an object, some scholars attempt to broaden the meaning of the Akkadian root to include wiping *on*.[119] They suggest that "the underlying idea of the Accadian [*sic*] root is that of wiping in the widest sense, ranging from cleaning and smearing to wiping away and abolishing."[120] In

---

[115] Levine, *Presence*, 60. Elliott rejects such an assumption on the basis that God is the subject most often, not sacrifice; Elliott, "Atonement," 13–14.

[116] Jacob, *Theology of the Old Testament*, 293.

[117] Levine, *Presence*, 57–58, 63.

[118] Ibid., 59.

[119] *TWOT* (s.v. "כפר") suggests a different root for the two words, but this hardly seems necessary.

[120] G. R. Driver, "Studies in the Vocabulary of the Old Testament," *JTS* 34 (1933): 37; see J. Milgrom, *Leviticus 1–16: A New Translation with Introduction and Commentary*, AB (New York: Doubleday, 1991), 1080.

any case, in the Akkadian "there is hardly a single instance in which covering is necessary, even though it seems sometimes to be possible."[121] The above evidence, however, suggests that the same cannot be said of the Hebrew word, where there seems to be a broader semantic range involving both the primary idea of wiping away and a secondary limited use of covering.

The etymology of the root *kāpar* is indeed helpful, but in the examination one does well to remember the warning of Gerhard von Rad: "Even if it were quite certain that the basic meaning of the root *kāpar* is 'to cover,' the question would still remain open. What is to be covered here, and how is this covering effected? . . .The meaning can no longer be reached by means of its etymology."[122]

The fullest understanding of any word always comes from the way in which it is used, but even here a difficulty remains. Part of the problem of understanding the meaning of *kāpar* may be that Western languages are incapable of expressing the idea in one word or description.[123] Keeping these factors in mind, we must attempt to capture the meaning of *kāpar* with regard to its context. In general, the meanings proposed are centered on whether propitiation (appeasement) or expiation (making amends) is involved, though these are not the only two options.

The idea that the word *kāpar* expresses the act of appeasing or calming a wrathful individual is an old one. Proponents of this view can be found among groups that have very little in common otherwise. For instance, Douglas Judisch, who argues the only reason for not viewing the matter in relation to wrath is a liberal bias, is in essential agreement with the noted liberal Julius Wellhausen on what the original writers intended to communicate through the word.[124] Scholars generally assume that the use of *kāpar* found implementation originally in the social contexts and only later in cultic ref-

---

[121] Driver, "Studies," 37.

[122] von Rad, *Old Testament Theology* 1:262; see D. Judisch, "Propitiation in the Language and Typology of the Old Testament," *CTQ* 48 (1984): 223.

[123] Janowski, *Heilsgeschehen*, 15.

[124] Judisch, "Propitiation," 221–43; J. Wellhausen, *Prolegomena to the History of Israel*, trans. J. Sutherland Black (Edinburgh: Adam and Charles Black, 1885), 81. It should be noted that Wellhausen saw in the term the superstitious perspective of the ancients in how they perceived God and His relationship with the world.

erences. If so, then if one examines its non-cultic occurrences in Hebrew, it should be possible to get an idea of how the word was understood in the cultic texts as well.[125] An examination of these passages reveals that "appeasement" is the clearest understanding of the word.[126]

Objections against the idea that atonement should be understood as meaning appeasement seem strong at first, but fail to convince in the end. First, some argue that appeasement cannot apply in all cases because often God is the subject of the verb and it is not expected that God would have to appease anything.[127] This is only a problem, however, if one is committed to the word meaning the same thing in each context where it is found, though few words function that way. Second, other scholars reason that in the instances where God is not the subject of the verb, the notion of an angry God is nowhere directly expressed in the text.[128] This point hardly seems fair to the evidence since there are specific references where the work of the priest in making atonement offers a "soothing aroma" to God—a statement that clearly suggests appeasement of some sort (Lev 1–6).[129] Finally, still others argue that even if appeasement is the meaning of the word in non-cultic texts, the idea that propitiation is suggested whenever *kāpar* occurs does not allow for the development of understanding the word in Israel, a process the nation would certainly have undergone as it came in contact with the new worldviews and approaches to religion held by neighboring nations.[130] This third conclusion is an assumption based on silence. Given the lack of evidence that would demand such a conclusion, it

---

[125] Judisch, "Propitiation," 221–43.

[126] Ibid.; R. J. Thompson, *Penitence and Sacrifice in Early Israel Outside the Levitical Law* (Leiden: Brill, 1963), 101, 115, 151; P. Garnet, "Atonement Constructions in the Old Testament and the Qumran Scrolls," *EvQ* 46 (1974): 131–63; Levine, *Presence*, 60. See Gen 32:21; Prov 16:14; 2 Sam 21:3 for examples.

[127] Thompson, *Penitence*, 18.

[128] *TDOT*, "כבר."

[129] G. Wenham, "Theology of Sacrifice," in *Sacrifice in the Bible*, ed. R. Beckwith and M. Selman (Grand Rapids: Baker, 1995), 80–81.

[130] Discussion of this development commences below. Although some of his conclusions will be called into question, Garnet's discussion of a development from social to socio-religious to prophetic to Levitical usage is sufficient here to demonstrate that a transition occurred; see Garnet, "Atonement Constructions," 131–63.

seems best to proceed using the comparisons that are evident within the biblical text itself. Therefore, appeasement (propitiation) does seem appropriate, at least on some levels, in relationship to the idea of atonement.[131] This conclusion will become even clearer with an examination of a few of the relevant passages that use the word, followed by an examination of the various interpretations of the concept of expiation.

The passage in Lev 16:33 is important for understanding the meaning of *kāpar* because the word occurs twice, once with a direct object and once with the preposition *'al*. Levine translates the verse, "He shall purify the sanctuary and the tent of meeting and the altar (*kāpar* + direct object), and shall perform expiatory rites with respect to the entire people of the congregation (*kāpar* + *'al*)."[132] The reason direct action on the sanctuary was necessary is that it acts as a magnet of sorts for impurity.[133] Through purification of the sanctuary, expiation then becomes possible. Thus it becomes clear that *kāpar* in this instance at least carries two meanings in one—to *purify* in order to *make amends*.

Perhaps the most important verse for understanding the function of *kāpar* is Lev 17:11. This passage deals directly with the restrictions on eating blood, but indirectly it addresses the issue of the effectiveness of sacrifice. The common rendering of the passage is, "For the life of a creature is in the blood, and I have appointed it to you to make atonement on the altar for your lives, since it is the lifeblood that makes atonement" (HCSB). Though literal in its translation of the Hebrew, it limits one's understanding of the syntactical relations between the different parts and how each phrase affects the other. The idea of blood being equated with life has been addressed above. It is interesting that such an association was solely an Israelite belief in the ancient world.[134] The translation, "the life of a creature is in the blood," is unfortunate in some senses. The statement is actu-

---

[131] T. Fretheim offered a contrasting view in *The Pentateuch* (Nashville: Abingdon, 1996), 129.

[132] Levine, *Presence*, 65.

[133] *EncJud*, "kipper."

[134] McCarthy, "Symbolism," 176.

ally meant to express an equation of blood as life.[135] It is only in this realization that one could explain how the blood could serve as atonement, either as that which performs cleansing or as payment for the life of the worshipper.[136] The translation, "and I have appointed it to you to make atonement on the altar," also misses some aspects of understanding. Because God is the subject of the verb "give" *(nātan)*, the idea expressed is more closely related to bestowal or appointment. In other words, it is a declaration of effectiveness.[137] The construction identified with the word *kāpar* expresses the idea that the work is done on behalf of the individual. The final aspect of the passage to be discussed involves the statement "for your lives." The Hebrew word *nepeš* is used, which suggests that what is taking place is an atonement in order to save the life of the individuals involved—that is, to prevent death. Such a reality in connection with God's righteousness and the presence of a "soothing aroma" suggests that a penalty has indeed been paid.

The word *kappōret* is a derivative from *kāpar*. The *kappōret* was a part of the ark of the covenant made of pure gold. It was of the same dimensions as the ark and was considered the most holy section of the holy of holies since it was the seat of God between or on the wings of the cherubim that were placed above the *kappōret* (Exod 25:22). The term has often been rendered "mercy seat." As mentioned above, the item described with the term has often been used to identify the meaning of *kāpar* as "to cover" since supposedly it referred to the lid or covering of the ark.[138] While this explanation is possible, the word most likely represents its function in the atonement process. Janowski identified the *kappōret* as the spot of God's proximity to His people and the location where atonement occurred.[139] In this way, it is a symbolic representation of the site

---

[135] J. Milgrom, "A Prolegomenon to Leviticus 17:11," *JBL* 90 (1971): 149; see Gen 9:4; Lev 17:14; Deut 12:23; and Jer 2:34.

[136] H. Brichto, "On Slaughter and Sacrifice, Blood and Atonement," *HUCA* 47 (1976): 28.

[137] Milgrom, "Prolegomenon," 150.

[138] H. Gese believed such a concept is fatally flawed because it does not appropriate the description of the ark as a closed chest without a lid (*Essays on Biblical Theology*, trans. Keith Crim [Minneapolis: Augsburg, 1981], 99, n. 3). But such a statement is difficult to defend since the ark clearly contained objects and therefore had to have some kind of lid.

[139] Janowski, *Heilsgeschehen*, 349.

where that which is *other-than* and that which is immanent meet. In other words, it is the place where God's grace was made available and fellowship became possible.[140]

Ludwig Köhler defined expiation as "the removal of the objective cause of disturbance between God and man when the honour of God is offended."[141] In general, the process is usually explained by means of a substitution, purification, or both. The issue of means is usually determined on the basis of either the relation of the word to the etymological idea of "wiping away" or to the consensus translation of *kōper*, the noun form of *kāpar*, referring to a payment or gift.

The association of the idea of expiation with the meaning "wipe away" is usually expressed in terms of a removal of some corrupting influence. Baruch Levine suggested that the motivation behind the need to wipe away was that Yahweh required His environment to remain pure.[142] Others express the act of removal of the blemish in a person by means of a transference that culminated with the cleansing act. Gerhard von Rad stated:

> What was involved in expiation is that in both cases, with persons and objects alike, Jahweh removed the baneful influence of an act. He broke the nexus of sin and calamity; and this was a rule effected by way of channeling the baneful influence of evil into an animal which died vicariously for the man.[143]

His last statement has some relationship to the substitution aspect of expiation that dominates the majority of discussions and which is not too far removed from the meaning of propitiation.

The perception of expiation as effected through a substitution carries with it issues with which one must deal in terms of the meaning of the word *kōper* and the nature of this substitution. There is little doubt that the use of the noun *kōper* carries with it the idea of payment. This relationship has led numerous scholars to associate the general understanding of the use of the root *kāpar* with the idea of paying a ransom.[144] Herbert Brichto accepted the methodology

---

[140] Ibid., 347.
[141] Köhler, *Old Testament Theology*, 214.
[142] Levine, *Presence*, 78.
[143] von Rad, *Old Testament Theology*, 1:271; Gray, *Sacrifice*, 74–76.
[144] See E. Burton, J. Smith, and G. Smith, *Biblical Ideas of Atonement: Their History and Sig-*

of associating the use of *kāpar* with the concept expressed by the noun, but wisely balked at the rendering of this word as "ransom." Instead, he argued that the word is better understood as a legal expression of compensatory payment that restored balance between two parties.[145]

The view of atonement as a payment—and therefore as a substitute for the expected penalty—creates an important issue in understanding the whole process of atonement. If the process suggested by the use of *kāpar* includes substitution, what exactly is being substituted? Is the offering taking on the punishment of the one making the gift, that is, penal substitution, which is not too far removed from propitiation? Or does the offering serve as a cleansing agent, that is, as a representative for the giver regarding his ability to wipe away the guilt, which is functionary substitution? The difference may seem slight, but the issue is critical to how one understands the work of atonement and how it is achieved.

The evangelical approach to the issue has traditionally been that the sacrificial act served as a means of penal substitution in which the animal that was sacrificed underwent the penalty that was due the one making the sacrifice and in doing so appeased the wrath of God.[146] Evangelicals largely base this approach on three grounds: (1) the previously mentioned view that atonement, at least in some sense, involves the appeasement of an angry God; (2) that killing equals punishment; and (3) that the laying on of hands represents the passing on of guilt. Because the first issue has been addressed, only the other two perspectives need examination.

That a sacrifice being killed reveals the nature of the act as a punishment has been commonly assumed or argued in Christian discussions throughout history. This position teaches that the spilling of blood is an event that is most closely associated with death.[147] Such

---

*nificance* (Chicago: University of Chicago Press, 1909), 40; P. Jenson, "The Levitical Sacrificial System," in *Sacrifice in the Bible* (Grand Rapids: Baker, 1995), 38; and Wenham, *Leviticus*, 245.

[145] Brichto, "Sacrifice," 27–28.

[146] For all the succeeding points in favor of this perspective, see Judisch, "Propitiation," 221–43. This has especially been the perspective regarding the atoning work of Christ—an issue which will be addressed below. These issues were first raised for this writer in Culpepper, *Interpreting the Atonement*, 55.

[147] Gese expressed this perception clearly in his illustration of modern literal translations

a position is limited in many ways but is not fatally flawed. First, it fails to recognize that in the clearest biblical explanation of why sacrifice and atonement is effective (Lev 17:11), the passage expresses that it is the life in the blood that makes atonement effective.[148] This is made clearer in the close association of the word *nepeš* with the blood in atonement passages, indicating that life is still present in the blood even after it has been spilled.[149] Second, the meaning cannot be limited to punishment by death because the offering is not always a blood sacrifice.[150] Therefore, it seems that although there is a substitution and the loss of life ultimately occurs (a matter that should not be forgotten), there is an added implication linking the gift to a commitment of one's life as well. A final observation made by opponents to the idea of substitutionary atonement is that the offering cannot be associated with a punishment by death because the sins capable of being atoned for are usually not considered to be serious enough to have been worthy of the death penalty.[151] But this position ignores the biblical teaching that all sin is ultimately both the result of and the cause of death in the world (Gen 2:16–17; 3:1–7,22–24; Rom 5:12–14).

The third perspective, penal substitution, seems incomplete as an explanation for all that is going on in atonement, but it cannot be abandoned. Indeed, there is evidence for it in the practice of the worshipper's laying of hands on the animal to be sacrificed.[152] Eichrodt suggested that the act identified the gift with the giver as it represented the willingness of the worshipper to surrender all that belonged to him. In other words, it signified his obedience to the ordinance and demands of God.[153] Oehler perceived the act as an appointment of the offering to be a mediator before God in or-

that render the Greek phrase that actually reads "blood of Christ" as "death of Christ"; see Gese, *Biblical Theology*, 93.

[148] von Rad, *Old Testament Theology*, 1:270.

[149] Oehler, *Theology of the Old Testament*, 277.

[150] Eichrodt, *Theology of the Old Testament*, 1:165, n. 2.

[151] Ibid., 165. To the further objection that most sins that were punishable by death could not be atoned for, see an important exception in Exod 21:28–32.

[152] The common view that the person was transferring the sin of the people to the animal seems unlikely with the sin/purification offering since the priest would consume part of the meat that was offered.

[153] Eichrodt, *Theology of the Old Testament*, 1:165–6.

der to effect cleansing, thanksgiving, or submission—the end being determined by the type of sacrifice that was offered.[154] Similarly, Gese described the act in terms of delegating participation in the cleansing ritual from the worshipper to his offering.[155] Both the one making the offering and the one accepting it were intimately involved in the process. The worshipper, through identification with the sacrifice, carried out the process whereby a cleansing of the corruption was accomplished. In His assignment of this method, God effectuated the act according to that purpose and subsequently accepted it. Therefore, the concept of penal substitution is broadened to include God's participation in its remedy. Indeed, there are three other connections surrounding the word *kāpar* that will further this idea even more.

When *kāpar* is used with God as its subject and He is not purifying an object, the expression seems best rendered "forgive."[156] This is evidenced by the synonymous usage with words referring to purification, reconciliation, and forgiveness. So it seems that there is some validity to the coining of the English word "atonement" since that unity always follows when this word is employed.[157]

There remains, however, an essential matter about the relationship between atonement *(kāpar)* and forgiveness *(sĕlîḥâ)* that will affect both concepts as they relate to the act of sacrifice. Köhler has argued for a relationship of expiation and propitiation that distinguishes but also links the ideas of wiping away and forgiving. He stated that while expiation and atonement are achieved solely on the basis of the sacrifice, propitiation and forgiveness rest solely within the will of God.[158] His observation is necessary in order to avoid the notion that God is somehow bribed by the offering or limited in how He might act, but he took it too far when he asserted that sacrifice plays no part in forgiveness except in its recognition of the sovereignty of God. Although atonement could occur without an actual sacrifice (see Isa 6:7), the two are still always linked in activity and

---

[154] Oehler, *Theology of the Old Testament*, 274.
[155] Gese, *Biblical Theology*, 105.
[156] *TDOT*, "כפר."
[157] Baab, "God of Redeeming," 140.
[158] Köhler, *Old Testament Theology*, 214–15.

result—in metaphor (the coal applied to Isaiah was taken from the altar) if not in action. Preuss is certainly correct when he argues that forgiveness *(sĕlîḥâ)* was achieved through the cult because of its relationship to atonement. While God's role was still primary in effectuating the forgiveness, the act of atonement mediated the activity of forgiveness.[159]

In a couple of ways, cultic usage of *kāpar* furthers the argument that the activity is effectuated by God's will rather than by some magical power implicit in the sacrificial act. First, people are never used in the direct object position in cultic texts using *kāpar*. Therefore, atonement represents an act that accomplishes something for another.[160] The priest is usually the subject of the verb; however, in some instances God may perform atonement in this sense.[161] The importance of God's action can be seen in the completeness of the preservation He performs. Janowski has written that such passages reveal that not just a part of the man was preserved, but every aspect of his being.[162] Second, even in those passages where God is not the subject of the verb, "in the biblical writer's mind-set *[kāpar]* was not a physical causation for purity, but prerequisite for God to purify."[163] This is important because with God being pictured as both the originator of the call for sacrifice through Moses and the effectuator of the atonement, the sacraments of Israel assume an inscrutable quality and an effectiveness in how they are accomplished.[164] Again, one cannot totally divorce the act from the result achieved, but the recognition that God is the one who makes the sacrifice effective lends itself quite explicitly to the idea that sacrifice has always been grounded in grace, not ritual.

The idea of purity *(ṭohār)* is one that plays an important role in the concept of atonement since it often occurs as a synonym and

[159] H. D. Preuss, *Old Testament Theology,* trans. L. Perdue, OTL (Louisville: Westminster John Knox Press, 1992), 2:179–80; see von Rad, *Old Testament Theology* I, 270; and Jacob, *Theology of the Old Testament,* 295.

[160] Levine, *Presence,* 64.

[161] Ibid., 63.

[162] Janowski, *Heilsgeschehen,* 135.

[163] Levine, *Presence,* 66.

[164] W. Brueggemann, *Theology of the Old Testament: Testimony, Dispute, Advocacy* (Minneapolis: Fortress, 1997), 583.

sometimes expresses the end result of atonement. Levine describes the relationship in terms of impurity being an active, even demonic, force in battle with man and God, while atonement serves as the active destruction of this entity.[165] Though often thought of in a cultic sense, purity played a role in every aspect of Jewish life. Jacob Neusner demonstrated that purity was often imparted to things that had little to do with the cult. Though the divisions of *clean* and *unclean* that were applied to one group (such as animals) were not consistently applied throughout, the concept was a part of every aspect of life—even those with no connection to the temple.[166] Jacob Milgrom suggested that the reason for such a perception was that impurity and sin operated as a type of poisonous vapor that was drawn from all quarters to the tabernacle and the spot where God met His people.[167] Therefore, even in cultic usage *kāpar* took on meaning for how people functioned. It was not simply an external concept, for it involved a life-changing process by which the people sought to preserve fellowship.

Explanations of the word *kāpar* gathered through a linguistic study are many, but the word clearly carries more than one meaning and was multidimensional in terms of the activity that took place. Despite the common expressions relating the process to outward activities, there seems always to have been a constant relation to the inner attitude of the offerer in order to ensure the success of his act. The event could be both preventative and remedial. In terms of its cultic usage, God always effectuated it, regardless of who was the subject of the verb. In all cases, it is the context that determines the intent of the expression. Concerning its influence on sacrifice as an offering for purification, the meaning clearly refers to a decontamination that expects forgiveness but does not establish it. There is a clear intimation in the use of this word that demonstrates that favor (propitiation), forgiveness/purification (expiation), and reconciliation (atonement) are not earned with God, but He grants these. God does not want only sacrifice because it gives the impression

---

[165] Levine, *Presence*, 77–79.

[166] J. Neusner, *The Idea of Purity in Ancient Judaism*, SJLA (Leiden: Brill, 1973), 18–31.

[167] *EncJud*, "kipper."

His favor is gained. What God wants is a heart that loves Him and is therefore obedient to Him as a result of what He alone can do for that person.[168]

The insights from this study allow some preliminary conclusions about the basic meaning behind various contextual applications. It appears that expiation and propitiation work in concert, though there are limitations to the concept of propitiation. Such an association is crucial because a person must be willing to address the seriousness of sin and the relevant passages dealing with God's anger throughout Scripture. Furthermore, if an etymological conclusion is necessary, it would seem that "to wipe off" is the best translation based on the available evidence. As Gese has demonstrated, this root meaning finds affinity with almost all the secondary definitions, and it is easier to explain the Arabic "to cover" as a reinterpretation of "to wipe off" than it is to explain the opposite development.[169] In light of these conclusions, we now move on to a discussion of the Day of Atonement.

## The Day of Atonement

The Day of Atonement, or Yom Kippur, served an essential role in the life of ancient Israel. Even today, it represents the highest holy day in the life of modern Judaism. Indeed, finding this description of ceremonies and rituals in the center of Leviticus and in the center of the Pentateuch clearly reveals its importance for understanding much of the law.[170] Furthermore, it was the only day of fasting the Mosaic law specifically prescribed for the nation of Israel.[171] Therefore, the day deserves an extensive examination.

Before looking at the more crucial aspects of the theological significance of Yom Kippur, it is necessary to identify and understand its elements in a historical setting. Relatively speaking, few elements of debate concern the ceremony itself. What is debated is the purpose of

---

[168] Rowley observed that forgiveness "could not be wrested from God by one whose heart was far from him; but it could be claimed by one who approached him in the right spirit." H. H. Rowley, *Worship in Ancient Israel: Its Forms and Meaning* (Philadelphia: Fortress, 1967), 140.

[169] Gese, *Biblical Theology*, 99, n. 3.

[170] J. Hartley, *Leviticus*, WBC (Waco: Word, 1992), 217.

[171] *IDB*, "Atonement, Day of."

some of the elements for ancient Israel. Two peculiarities of the biblical text make discussion and comprehension of the rites performed on Yom Kippur difficult. First, there are relatively few details that identify certain acts. This is most likely because the text of Leviticus 16 was written for the information of the congregation and not the high priest.[172] Therefore, the writer would have deemed many of the details unnecessary. Second, there is a great deal of repetition in the passage; first the liturgical agenda is listed (Lev 16:3–10) and then it is repeated (vv. 11–28). Despite this factor, there are clearly six separate events in the rite: the preparation of the priest, the casting of the lots, the purification offerings, the goat for Azazel, the whole offerings, and the subsequent responsibilities of the people.

For the most part, Lev. 16:3–10 outlines some of the requirements for the different materials used in the ceremony. Most of these descriptions are simply statements of preparation and choice of materials to be used. Other passages are explanations of what will occur later and will be dealt with in their proper chronological order. However, one important element occurs at the outset and therefore bears immediate discussion—the casting of lots over the goats.

After taking two male goats from the people, the high priest was commanded to cast lots over them. One lot assigned the goat for Yahweh and the other for Azazel *(ʿăzāʾzēl).*[173] Placing both goats before Yahweh, as well as the casting of the lots, makes it clear that the people recognized the entire day as centered around Yahweh. Therefore, regardless of how one translates *ʿăzāʾzēl* (a topic taken up below), these factors make it clear that Yahweh alone received an offering.[174]

The next step in the rite involves a series of sacrifices designed to purify the priest, the holy place, the congregation, and the altar. Each of these activities had their own emphases and variations of meaning; however, the essential nature of purification is seen both in the

---

[172] Hartley, *Leviticus*, 225.

[173] It is here that some translations make the mistake of over-translating. The meaning of Azazel is discussed below, but it should be noted that the translation of the name as "scapegoat" severely limits the interpretive options given to the English reader. Of the major English translations, only the NRSV, ESV, and HCSB do not translate the word but render it "azazel."

[174] Milgrom, *Leviticus 1–16*, 1020.

manner in which the offering is performed and parallel statements of "making atonement" for each of them. In any case, the totality of the purification shows that the designation "Day of Atonement" is appropriate.

The order of the persons and objects purified is logical. If the high priest was to be the actor of each of the individual rites, it makes sense that he would be the first to find cleansing. This was true so that he did not "recontaminate" any of the other objects. Leviticus 16:11 gives the account of the purification/sin offering for the high priest. Based on the words used in the selection of the bull in v. 6 as well as the instructions for the priest's sin-offering given in chap. 4, it is clear that the beast was to be from the priest's own stock. The resulting offering would bring cleansing of the priest as well as some measure of purification to the nation as a whole.[175]

At this point in the liturgy, there is a pause in the sacrifices and a discussion of taking incense and a firepan into the holy place to fill the innermost sanctuary with smoke. The text is clear that the reason for this action was to cover the "throne area" during the subsequent acts of bringing blood into the holy of holies so that the priest did not die. The question that remains, however, is in what sense did the incense prevent death? Two basic approaches have been offered. Each one finds some support in the biblical narrative, but each has its problems in not completely explaining the processes involved.[176]

The first perception of the process is that the smoke hid the priest from the presence of Yahweh. The expression of this opinion comes in different forms. Some have asserted that the priest could not have even seen the mercy seat, lest he die.[177] Others connect the smoke to the previous accounts of Moses on Mount Sinai where he had to shield his eyes out of fear of seeing the majesty of Yahweh.[178] Obscuring the majesty of Yahweh from view is more likely to have

---

[175] A. R. S. Kennedy, *Leviticus and Numbers*, Century Bible (London: Nelson, 1967), 111.

[176] B. Levine has rightly suggested that the incense cloud should not be confused with the cloud of Lev 16:2, which simply represents the presence of God; see Levine, *Leviticus*, JPSTC (Philadelphia: Jewish Publication Society, 1989), 100–1.

[177] J. R. Porter, *Leviticus*. CBC (Cambridge: Cambridge Univ. Press, 1976), 130.

[178] Kennedy, *Leviticus*, 113.

been the intent than obscuring the mercy seat since the seat itself would have been seen when either moving the tabernacle or when the priest first entered the Holy of Holies to bring in the firepan.[179] The second view attempts to define the incense in terms of its description elsewhere. Passages such as Num 17:8–15 and Ps 141:2 reveal incense as some sort of salve to the wrath of Yahweh and as a symbol for the prayers of His people. In this perspective, the smoke from the incense sought to placate Yahweh and allowed for mediation as the priest performed his duties.[180] The problem with this view is the use of the word "cover" to describe the work of the incense.[181] One possible solution is to suggest that the two proposed purposes of the incense are not mutually exclusive. The priest was both prevented from looking upon the majesty of Yahweh, and Yahweh's wrath against the sins of the people was averted.[182] In this way, the biblical references to both "soothing aroma" and covering the seat find meaning.

Twice in the account, in successive verses, the high priest is instructed to enter the holy place to sprinkle blood on the mercy seat, and seven times to sprinkle blood in front of the seat.[183] He was to do this with the blood of the bull sacrificed for himself and with the blood of the goat sacrificed for the people. The explanation given for these actions in v. 16 is that the priest was making atonement for the holy place. While this must certainly be the case, another subtle aspect can be found in the meaning the ancients gave to the blood.

As noted above, for the Israelites the blood represented the life force or essence of the animal. Indeed, it was the most precious part of any living creature. The act of placing the blood could be understood as placing it at the feet of Yahweh as He sat on the mercy seat. As Walther Eichrodt commented, "The meaning of the smearing and sprinkling of the blood is now brought under the aspect of oblation,

---

[179] Milgrom, *Leviticus 1–16*, 1029.

[180] G. Bush, *Notes, Critical and Practical, on the Book of Leviticus* (London: Newman and Ivison, 1852; reprint Minneapolis: K&K, 1981), 158; Oehler, *Theology of the Old Testament*, 311; P. Heinisch, *Theology of the Old Testament*, trans. W. Heidt (Collegeville, MN: Liturgical Press, 1955), 235.

[181] Milgrom, *Leviticus 1–16*, 1029.

[182] Wenham, *Leviticus*, 231; Hartley, *Leviticus*, 239.

[183] Hartley took these actions to be sprinkling of the blood on top of the atonement slate (mercy seat) and against its face; see Hartley, *Leviticus*, 239–40.

which implies the presenting to God of the most valuable offering, namely the life of the animal."[184]

The blood was also sprinkled in other places, such as the altar and the tent itself. There is some debate about the place of the altar mentioned in v. 18. In agreement with most Jewish scholars, R. K. Harrison has seen this as the golden altar within the tent of meeting. His two main arguments for such a view are the close association of the altar with the holy place and the associations of these events with the instructions for sin offerings in Lev 4:7,18.[185] But the most basic sense of the phrase "go out" in v. 18 was to leave the tent, not the holy place. Regardless of which altar was intended, the most likely need for such an act was that the sins throughout the year left a residue on the tent, the holy place, and the altar, which had to be removed and atoned for once a year.[186]

Part of the blood that was sprinkled on the various locations came from the goat sacrificed to Yahweh for the purification of the congregation. In reality, the act of purifying the people was twofold, with both goats playing a part in the atonement. The first goat selected for Yahweh was sacrificed, and his blood was used as a sin offering. In him was the clear fulfillment of the Levitical mandates for expiation and propitiation. On the other hand, the other goat represented a new facet in the rites of the Day of Atonement and finds reference only in this place in the canon.

Leviticus 16:20–22 represents the most debated portion of the passages dealing with the Day of Atonement. The primary reason is the obscure term ʽăzāʼzēl. The word occurs just four times in the OT, all of which are in this chapter of Leviticus. Furthermore, the ritual in which the goat assigned as ʽăzāʼzēl was used has no stated explanation, which leaves much to speculation. In defining this somewhat strange word, scholars have come to four basic interpretations. Each of these has some ancient corollary, and they all have problems either in relation to statements in Leviticus 16 or to other biblical mandates.

---

[184] Eichrodt, *Theology of the Old Testament*, 1:164.

[185] R. K. Harrison, *Leviticus: An Introduction and Commentary*, TOTC (Downers Grove: InterVarsity, 1980), 173.

[186] *ABD*, "Day of Atonement."

One explanation takes the term as an abstract idea in which the goat is said to be "for removal." C. L. Feinberg accepted the definition of Brown, Driver, and Briggs that *ăzā'zēl* meant "entire removal."[187] In this way the goat was given a name that accorded with his duty and purpose of removing sin from the congregation of Israel. A second view builds on this idea of removal, but has a little more etymological support by seeking to divide *ăzā'zēl* into two words, "go away" and "goat," hence the "goat that goes away," usually rendered *scapegoat*. This translation was a favorite for earlier English versions of the Bible, and it finds its ancient support in the Septuagint (*apopompaios*, "carrying away"), Latin Vulgate (*caper emissarius*, "goat sent out"), and the works of many church fathers.[188] One of the problems with this view is that in the verses where it is found, the primary meanings of the prepositions used with it are "for" and "to" *ăzā'zēl*, and this makes it difficult to maintain that the term was descriptive of the goat itself.

The third interpretation explains the meaning of the word in terms of the place to which the goat was to be sent. The previously mentioned prepositions suggest location and not possession. Sidney Hoenig stated this opinion rather curtly and without further explanation when he wrote, "Biblically, *azazel* means 'jagged rocks or precipice.'"[189] Indeed, this was apparently the favorite rabbinic understanding. Despite agreement on that point, interpretations of the place varied from "a rocky precipice" to "hardest of mountains" to "Mount Azaz."[190] The primary problem with this perspective, as well as with the previous two views, is that the word *ăzā'zēl* seems to be in juxtaposition with Yahweh in the passages where it is used. None of these suggestions offers anything that fits in parallel with Yahweh.

---

[187] C. L. Feinberg, "The Scapegoat of Leviticus 16," *BSac* 115 (1958): 331–33. F. Brown, S. R. Driver, and C. A. Briggs, *A Hebrew and English Lexicon of the Old Testament* (Oxford: Clarendon, 1907).

[188] Hartley, *Leviticus*, 237.

[189] S. Hoenig, "The New Qumran Pesher on Azazel," *JQR* 56 (1966): 249. M. Rooker argues that in v. 10 "to the wilderness" is in apposition to "to *'ăzā'zēl*." See *Leviticus*, NAC (Nashville: B&H, 2000), 216–17.

[190] Hartley, *Leviticus*, 237, who quoted numerous rabbis.

The final position on the matter is the most prevalent among modern scholars. This analysis sees in the word *ʿăzāʾzēl* the name of a demon or god that was believed to reside in the wilderness.[191] In defending this thesis, proponents use three lines of argument. (1) Understanding *ʿăzāʾzēl* as the name of a demon makes for a true parallel in the statements coupled with Yahweh. (2) It is commonly known that the ancients viewed the wilderness as the residence of evil (e.g. Isa 13:21). (3) Later pseudepigraphal and Talmudic writings explicitly identify the name "Azazel" as belonging to a principal evil spirit.[192] Objections that an offering for another god specifically contradicts passages such as Exod 20:3 and Lev 17:7 are easily answered with the observation that it was not intended as an offering or a sacrifice. As the recipient and carrier of the sins of the people the goat would be unclean, and therefore unsuitable for any type of offering or sacrifice.[193]

In v. 21, the priest was told to place his hands on the goat, confess the sins of the people, and send the goat into the wilderness. Levine saw in this act an ancient "magic" in which verbally confessing the sins both exposed and trapped them so that they could be exorcised.[194] Milgrom rightly opposed this view on the grounds that confession of sin always carries with it the meaning of releasing sin, not trapping it. He concluded that the straightforward reading of the passage suggests that the priest was transferring the sins of the people to the goat as he sent it into the wilderness.[195]

With the sins imparted to the goat, he was then sent to the wilderness, described in v. 22 as "a desolate land," literally "a land of

---

[191] See R. Helm, "Azazel in Early Jewish Tradition," *AUSS* 32 (1994): 226; D. Wright, *The Disposal of Impurity: Elimination Rites in the Bible and in Hittite and Mesopotamian Literature,* SBLDS (Atlanta: Scholars' Press, 1987), 23; Milgrom, *Leviticus 1–16,* 1020–21; and Hartley, *Leviticus,* 238. H. Tawil's work comparing Azazel to the god Môt, has to overcome too many obstacles and makes too many loose connections for them to be of true value; see Tawil, "Azazel The Prince of the Steppe: A Comparative Study," *ZAW* 92 (1980): 43–59.

[192] Milgrom, *Leviticus 1–16,* 1020–1; Wenham, *Leviticus,* 233.

[193] Hartley, *Leviticus,* 238. Milgrom explains, "Instead of being an offering or a substitute, the goat is simply the vehicle to dispatch Israel's impurities and sins to the wilderness/netherworld." Milgrom, *Leviticus 1–16,* 1021.

[194] Levine, *Leviticus,* 106.

[195] Milgrom, *Leviticus 1–16,* 1042.

cutting off."[196] Again, scholars have had different opinions about the purpose of sending the goat into the wilderness. Some have perceived the act as an expulsion of the demonic,[197] though this hardly fits the circumstances. Others have suggested that the goat acted as a substitute for the people in bearing their sins as he went out to die.[198] The most likely suggestion is that the goat served to separate the sin from the people by taking the sins back to Azazel and thus rendering these sins powerless over the people.[199] Of special importance here is the comparison of this act to that of Lev 14:4–7, where living birds carried away the impurity of the one who once had a skin disease. The wording and the act in both instances hold strong affinities for each other.[200] Again, whatever the reason, it is clear that the biblical writer did not perceive of the goat as a sacrifice to Azazel.

After the release of the goat for Azazel was made, the account returns to the priest, who once again bathed and changed back into his normal clothing. The priest then sacrificed whole burnt offerings for both himself and the people. The instructions for sacrificing the whole burnt offering are found in Leviticus 1 and are examined more below. The explicitly stated reason for the offering was to make atonement for himself and the people. On the other hand, given the previous acts, the nature of the offering could well have held additional praise to Yahweh for His mercy,[201] or it could have represented a promise of complete dedication after the removal of sin. In any case, the offering was completely burned and then the fat from the previous sin offerings was burned as well, thus completing the high priest's work on the day.

---

[196] Wenham, *Leviticus*, 234–35.

[197] Helm, "Azazel," 226.

[198] See Jacob, *Theology of the Old Testament*, 296; Kennedy, *Leviticus*, 113; and Oehler, *Theology of the Old Testament*, 315. Wenham has pointed out that while this was apparent in later Judaism with the casting of the goat over the cliff, there is no suggestion of such an understanding in the Leviticus passage (*Leviticus*, 233–34).

[199] See Hoenig, "Qumran," 249; Milgrom, *Leviticus 1–16*, 1021; and J. Moyer, "Hittite and Israelite Cultic Practices: A Selected Comparison," in *Scripture in Context II: More Essays on the Comparative Method*, ed. W. Hallo and others (Winona Lake, IN: Eisenbrauns, 1983), 34.

[200] P. van Imschoot, *Theology of the Old Testament*, trans. K. Sullivan (New York: Desclee, 1954), 124.

[201] Hartley, *Leviticus*, 244.

One final responsibility of the people is actually discussed in the commands relating to when the day was to be observed. The HCSB, in contrast to other translations that render the phrase "humble yourselves" (NASB), appropriately translates the phrase, "practice self-denial." In this rendering it becomes clear that there were aspects of obedience required from the people on this day beyond the sacrifices of the priest. This hearkens to the biblical references that obedience, not sacrifice, was always the desire of Yahweh.[202] What exactly this denial included is unclear, although fasting was certainly one of the elements.[203]

The ritual of the Day of Atonement was a solemn exercise in obedience. It was the only day of the year when someone could enter the holy of holies. Additionally, the narrative is filled with warnings against uncleanness and wrong actions and threats of impending death if each act was not carried out specifically as stated. The tone for such an understanding is set in Lev 10:1 (the account of the deaths of Nadab and Abihu) and permeates the book, finding expression in the discussion of the day being a Sabbath. Yet the notion that Yahweh is present with the people on this day contributes the concept of grace and fellowship so necessary to the sustenance of the spiritual life sought by all followers of God.[204] The day seems to bring together much of what has already been observed in the Pentateuch regarding worship. This day's rituals, more than perhaps those of any other day, take seriously the nature of sin and affirm the reality that only God can deal with this fatal condition. Not only is the congregation affected by sin, but so are the leaders and the very elements of worship themselves.

The literary ordering of the book of Leviticus seems strange at first. After chap. 10 recounts the story of Nadab and Abihu, the book lists a number of things related to impurity. Instructions about the Day of Atonement follow, beginning with the story of Aaron's sons. Subsequently, the laws concerning holiness are outlined. This structure serves a twofold purpose, revealing the importance of the clean-

---

[202] See 1 Sam 15:22; Pss 40:6, 51:16–17; Isa 1:11; Hos 6:6; Amos 5:21–27; and Mic 6:6–8.

[203] Hartley, *Leviticus*, 242. The other references to the Day of Atonement in Lev 23:26–32 and Num 29:7 also carry this command.

[204] Oehler, *Theology of the Old Testament*, 316–17.

ness of the priest in making offerings and the necessity of atonement before holiness as a way of life can be achieved.[205]

For the Christian, the doctrine of the priesthood of the believer (1 Pet 2:5–9) adds an important element of comparison to the priestly requirements of the OT. That is, the greater message from the Leviticus passage is that the requirements of purity for the high priest also serve as requirements for each priest in the kingdom of God. If there were no other theological relevance to this passage, it would be worth exegeting. Not only do many of the elements of the rite point to the need for purity in the priest, but so does the literary context of the pericope in relation to the event involving Nadab and Abihu.

The fact that every part of the sanctuary had to be atoned for—both the mercy seat inside and the altar outside—reveals the need for purity before God. So do the multiple washings that the different individuals had to endure in meeting God's requirements for purity. Likewise, the shedding of the blood of four innocent animals,[206] the sending away of the live goat, and the strictures against doing any labor are all part of the recognition of the seriousness with which Yahweh takes sin and the necessity that His holiness creates for His people to separate themselves from sin's presence.[207]

To underestimate the influence sin has on God's relationship with His people is to live in direct conflict with the concerns He revealed through the institution of this important day. Sin corrupts everything and requires a serious appraisal of its impact on worship. It is striking how quickly individuals and congregations today enter into a worship event without first considering the effect their sinful lives have on their ability to worship. Indeed, in many evangelical churches it seems that along with the invitation at the end, there should also be an invitation to prepare oneself for worship at the beginning (see Matt 5:23–24; 1 John 1:5–10).

Another theological emphasis in the structure of the pericope is the ability of Yahweh to bring reconciliation, even in the midst of

---

[205] Wenham, *Leviticus*, 227.

[206] I.e., the bull for the High Priest (vv. 3,11), the goat for Yahweh (vv. 9,15), the whole burnt offering for the priest (v. 24), and the whole burnt offering for the people (v. 24).

[207] Ibid., 237; Heinisch, *Theology of the Old Testament*, 236.

great separation. The opposite poles of the goat for Azazel and the goat for Yahweh, as well as the wilderness versus the holy place, serves as a reminder of the lengths Yahweh is willing to go to bring atonement to those whom He loves. Indeed, regarding the distance between the sinner and his redeemer and the variety of means by which that gulf is spanned, there is no other passage in the OT that more clearly expresses God's willingness to overcome than does this one.[208]

There are important theological considerations in some of the requirements and elements of the Day of Atonement. The assignment of the day as a Sabbath and the call to self-denial teach a valuable lesson about the relationship of our possessions to the blessings of God. Saul Berman explained: "The temporary restrictions on consumption imply that we are not to measure the totality of our relationship to God by whether He has provided us with all that we desire to consume."[209] In other words, through this time of self-denial and rest, we gain the ability to contemplate the relationship we have with God and to realize that the measure of God's love for us is found in His willingness to forgive, not in His eagerness to give.

## Sacrifice

God's nature, sacred space, sacred time, and atonement all converge at the final foundation of sacrifice. It is easy when reading through the book of Leviticus to get so preoccupied with all the legislation and particulars of the various offerings and services that one forgets what is actually espoused in the passages—a concern for the everyday realities of life.[210] Without much effort, one might also forget that one of the key realities of sacrifice was that the one bringing the offering took an *active* role in the event and came expecting a significant meeting with God. That each sacrifice required prayer demonstrates both this reality and the more practical conclusion that "sacrifice without prayer is useless."[211] Indeed, the act of of-

---

[208] Jenson, "Levitical Sacrificial System," 34.
[209] S. Berman, "Extended Notion of the Sabbath," *Judaism* 22 (1973): 349.
[210] Wenham, *Leviticus*, 17.
[211] Ibid., 61–62.

fering was—and is—not only significant in terms of the atonement it proclaims and provides but for what it also tells us about God's desires in this earliest of recorded forms of worship (see Gen 4).[212] This latter feature finds special demonstration in the five primary sacrifices outlined in Leviticus 1–6.

## The Whole Burnt Offering (Leviticus 1)

The most basic offering was also the most frequent one—the whole burnt offering *('ōlâ)*. This offering was apparently performed every morning and evening and during the sacred festivals, though it was apparently voluntary as far as the individual was concerned (see Num 15:3). The type of animal offered was determined according to the participant's level of wealth and ranged from a bull to a dove or pigeon. The whole animal was burned on the altar after being cut up by the one giving the sacrifice. The event was costly and significant to the giver, though there is disagreement as to the exact purpose of the offering.

Leviticus lists the offering's purpose as allowing the person to "be accepted by the LORD" (Lev 1:3). Wenham has taken the regularity of the offering, along with its description in Lev 1:3–4, to mean that it functioned as the primary atoning sacrifice in the life of Israel.[213] If one keeps in mind the various ways in which atonement was understood, this may well be the case; however, it seems unlikely that an offering intended for the primary purpose of cleansing someone from sin would be voluntary in nature. Instead, the offering seems to have been more intent on expressing the dedication of the worshipper before God, within which the step of atonement would be necessary.[214]

---

[212] Each of the offerings outlined in Leviticus 1–6 (including the grain offering) carries the implicit, if not explicit, recognition that they play a role in atonement. Furthermore, while some would argue that sacrifices were not part of Israel's early practice in favor of a more ethically centered religious experience of the prophets (Wellhausen, *Prolegomena*, 56–59), Rowley successfully argued that sacrifice was both early and, as in the prophets, defined in terms of conduct, not ritual (Rowley, *Worship in Ancient Israel*, 42).

[213] Wenham, *Leviticus*, 95.

[214] C. F. Keil, *Manual of Biblical Archaeology*, trans. P. Christie (Edinburgh: T and T Clark, 1888), 1:317. Wenham does acknowledge as much when he asserts that the offering expressed an affirmation of faith and obedience (*Leviticus*, 58).

At this point the linking of Abraham's offering of Isaac (which is described as an *ʿōlâ*) and the whole burnt offering's purpose should not be missed. God's challenge to Abraham was more than a command that Abraham sacrifice his beloved son—as significant as that fact is. In Isaac resided not only the status of son, but also the very promises of God. For Abraham to take such a step of faith was to give back to God everything that made Abraham who he was. It was a statement that all that Abraham was belonged to God and that God was worthy of worship not only for what He had granted Him, but simply because of who God is. Furthermore, for many Jews, Isaac's willingness to be offered made all successive burnt offerings effective and meaningful in that they were reminders to God of what Isaac had done, and therefore what the giver was doing.[215] Consequently, the purpose of the whole burnt offering seems to have been the "complete surrender to God by the one making the offering and complete acceptance by God of the worshipper that brought it."[216] Such an offering only found its most complete expression when voluntarily and lovingly given.

## The Grain/Cereal Offering (Leviticus 2)

The grain or cereal offering *(minḥâ)* often occurred in connection with the whole burnt offering and was probably often, though not always, offered at the same time.[217] That the offering is accompanied by the description that it was a "soothing aroma" (Lev 2:2,9,12) clearly designates its propitiatory nature. The offering was a mixture of flour, oil, salt, and incense. The idea that the offering entailed a type of tribute to God as the king is an intriguing one.[218] However, its voluntary status and giving in connection with the produce of the giver suggests a link more closely associated

---

[215] G. Vermes, *Scripture and Tradition in Judaism: Haggadic Studies* (Leiden: Brill, 1961), 193–227.

[216] Ross, *Holiness*, 85; see Kraus, *Worship*, 116.

[217] The Hebrew term מִנְחָה simply means "gift" or "tribute," and finds its translation in Leviticus 2 as "grain offering" primarily from the description that follows. In fact, both offerings brought by Abel and Cain in Genesis 4 are described using this term, as is Jacob's fearful gift to Esau (Gen 32:14).

[218] Wenham, *Leviticus*, 69.

with giving to God the first fruits of everything He had initially provided.[219] As such, the gift was a recognition of gratitude for what had been and a commitment of all that was the person's to give in terms of what would come.

## The Peace Offering (Leviticus 3)

The peace (or fellowship) offering *(šĕlāmîm)*, like the grain offering, is described as a "soothing aroma" before God (Lev 3:5,16). But in contrast to the grain offering, which could only be consumed by the priest or was sometimes burnt whole, the peace offering was consumed by both the one making the offering and the priest. The offering could consist of male or female cattle, sheep, or goats (no birds, probably because of their size), and it also was voluntary (Lev 7:16). Though traditional understanding viewed the offering as a meal consumed by God, the priest, and the giver,[220] more recent interpretations of its purpose and meaning have been somewhat more varied. Schmid has argued that the offering represented a covenant sealing sacrifice.[221] But this approach seems rather redundant and does not seem to fit the contextual status of offering. Based on Ugaritic comparisons, J. C. de Moor has suggested that the offering represented a suit for peace with God from the giver.[222] Indeed, this would explain the "soothing aroma" language and the use of *šĕlāmîm* (related to *šālôm*, "peace"). Finally, Wenham's proposal that the meal represented God's "pledge and [a] physical illustration of all the benefits that may be enjoyed by those at peace with God" also holds merit,[223] but before rendering a decision, perhaps it would be best to revisit the traditional approach.

The objections to God's participation in the meal primarily concern the judgment that such a view of God is too similar to that of the surrounding pagan concepts of deity and would violate God's

---

[219] Ross, *Holiness*, 99.

[220] W. R. Smith, *Lectures on the Religion of the Semites: The Fundamental Institutions* (Edinburgh: A. and C. Black, 1889).

[221] R. Schmid, *Das Bundesopfer in Israel* (Munich: Kösel, 1964).

[222] J. C. de Moor, "The Peace Offering in Ugarit and Israel," in *Schrift en Uitleg: Festschrift W. H. Gispen,* (Kampen: Kok, 1970), 112–17.

[223] Wenham, *Leviticus*, 81.

injunction in Ps 50:12–13 that He does not eat the flesh of bulls.[224] But such objections have two flaws. First, they may be based on an overly literal reading of God's rhetorical question in the Psalm, "Do I eat the flesh of bulls?" The previous lines indicate that His intention is to explain that He cannot be manipulated or bought because He needs nothing from man, since all the earth is His. Therefore, this statement does not even apply to the matter of Israel's being able to hold any kind of symbolic concept of His eating; it only speaks to the people's view that they had some sort of mastery over Him in their sacrifices. Second, and more important, the argument seems to suggest that Israel's worship lacked subtlety and symbolism. On the contrary, it was not required for Israel to think that God literally ate before the people could take part in a meal that represented fellowship and "eating" with Him.[225] Indeed, the power of the image of eating with someone as it reflects on fellowship, peace, and communion is an important one throughout the biblical text (see Ps 23:5; Prov 9:1–9; Luke 13:29). The proposals of de Moor and Wenham, mentioned above, further this imagery without having to abandon the fellowship meal perspective altogether.

## The Sin or Purification Offering (Leviticus 4–5)[226]

The sin or purification offering *(ḥaṭṭāʾt)* is perhaps the most debated offering in OT discussions. The details behind its accomplishment are agreed on. This sacrifice seems to have been distinctly Israelite in origin and conception.[227] When several sacrifices were offered at the same time, the purification offering was offered first (Lev 9; Num 6:11; 2 Chr 29:20–30). Acceptable offerings included

---

[224] Porter, *Leviticus,* 29–30; Wenham, *Leviticus,* 81.

[225] Jenson, "Levitical Sacrificial System," 31. Note the reference to the altar as "the LORD's table" in Mal 1:7, and see discussion in R. A. Taylor and E. R. Clendenen, *Haggai, Malachi,* NAC (Nashville: B&H, 2004), 268–69.

[226] The sin/purification offering is actually only discussed from Lev 4:1 to 5:13, whereas the guilt/reparation offering goes from Lev 5:14 to 6:7. N. Snaith, "Sin-offering and the Guilt-offering," *VT* 15 (1965): 73–80.

[227] See J. Milgrom, "Sin-offering or Purification Offering?" *VT* 21 (1971): 239; and Preuss, *Old Testament Theology,* 2:243. Milgrom's supposition that the purification had little to do with the giver is also erroneous. See N. Zohar, "Repentance and Purification: The Significance and Semantics of חַטָּאת in the Pentateuch," *JBL* 107 (1988): 609–18.

bulls, goats (male or female), lambs (female), and doves or pigeons.[228] It also seems to have been mandatory in nature. But what the offering actually accomplished is somewhat more difficult to discern—hence, the question of what to call it.

The term *ḥaṭṭāʾt* is traditionally translated as "sin offering." But such a translation may be somewhat misleading given the totality of what the offering actually sought to accomplish. Milgrom has suggested that without exception the purpose was merely one of purification, not expiation. In relation to this offering, then, *kāpar* (e.g., Lev 4:20) can mean "purge" and nothing else.[229] Indeed, its uses can hardly be related solely to the expiation of sin. It was implemented in the consecration of the altar and priests (Exod 29:10–14; Lev 8:14–17); consecration of the Levites (Num 8:12); after a woman had given birth (Lev 12:6–8); after a leper had been healed (Lev 14:19); after various contacts with impurity (Lev 15:15,29–30; Num 6:11); after a Nazirite had successfully completed his term of dedication (Num 6:14); and at the new moon (Num 29:6).[230] Therefore, it seems that the better understanding of the word *ḥaṭṭāʾt* would be "purification offering," which was sometimes accomplished in terms of a sin that had been committed. Indeed, it seems clear that the NT writers understood the OT sin offering as more than simply a ritual purification (Rom 8:3; Heb 5:2–3, 13:11–12). The sin offering then allowed for the unimpaired enjoyment of God through the atonement it afforded.[231]

## The Guilt/Reparation Offering (Lev 5–6)

As the last of the primary offerings, the guilt offering *(ʾāšām)* summarizes the relationship between the secular and the sacred nature of the offerings more clearly than the others. As stated earlier, the

---

[228] Wenham found it notable and important that the male lamb was not used. His reasoning was key to his understanding the whole burnt offering as the central atoning sacrifice (and thus the primary picture of Jesus' sacrifice) rather than the purification offering (*Leviticus*, 89). But this perspective views the relationship between the sacrifices of the OT and Christ's sacrifice too tightly since the NT writer's use of the term "sin offering" clearly has in mind the purification offering as well as the whole burnt offering; see discussion below.

[229] Milgrom, *Leviticus 1–16*, 254–55.

[230] R. de Vaux, *Studies in Old Testament Sacrifice* (Cardiff: Univ. of Wales Press, 1964), 95.

[231] Keil, *Biblical Archaeology* I, 299.

other offerings focused on all aspects of life, but it was in the guilt (or perhaps better named "reparations") offering that the civil issue of economic payment for the failures of humans was addressed. In short, besides the required offering, the person making the sacrifice was required to pay the person who had suffered the loss all of the costs incurred, plus an additional 20 percent. Sometimes, the debt owed was to God Himself (Lev 14:12–14; Num 6:9–12). The offering permitted the giving of a male sheep, which has led Wenham to suggest a stronger distinction between this offering and the sin offering than many suppose.[232] However, the description of the crimes involved along with the clear linkage made in the biblical text itself do suggest that the offering was closely linked to the sin offering. In short, the reparation offering suggests that sometimes "I'm sorry" was not, and is not, enough and that there needs to be additional restitution made for the costs incurred to someone for our careless activity. Such recognition advocates both the seriousness of sin and the responsibility to our neighbor, so the offering calls for an outward expression that repentance has taken place.[233]

The offerings outlined by God in the first chapters of Leviticus proclaim not only the need for atonement but also advocate a position of how that atonement then ought to influence our relationship with God and others. The voluntary offerings of the whole burnt offering, the grain offering, and the peace offering reflect aspects of self-giving, thanksgiving, and fellowship that can be regulated, but not mandated, if they are to be sincere and appropriate. The mandatory nature of the sin offering and guilt offering demonstrates a need for purity before God and a responsibility to one's fellow human that is at the heart of the key relationships outlined in the Bible. Worship entails all these factors—responsibility before God that is mandated by His holiness yet also an invitation to give freely and to thank Him sincerely—that can never be coerced. The purpose of all these sacrifices is that we might find real fellowship with Him, which is the final goal of the foundations of worship.

---

[232] Wenham, *Leviticus*, 104–5.
[233] Ross, *Holiness*, 151–52.

## *Foundations in the NT*

The foundations of worship outlined above bear the transition into the NT well. The commandment to love the LORD with all your heart, mind, and strength by avoiding idolatry and by representing God's name well find strong and thorough expression in the NT (Matt 6:24; Col 1:2; 1 Pet 1:2; 2:9–10). The teaching of sacred space is maintained and expanded in its description of every Christian as a walking sanctuary or temple (1 Cor 6:19–20). Christians are called to sacrificial living (Phil 4:18; Heb 13:15–16; 1 Pet 2:5). The nature of God finds expression in the Incarnation in a new, exciting, and thoroughly complete manner in the person and work of Jesus (John 1:1–3,14,18; Phil 2:6–11; Col 2:1–15; Heb 1:1–4). Jesus took on the names of God with power and majesty as both the "I Am" (used many times in John's Gospel; see especially John 8:58; 18:5) and "the Lord" (Luke 3:4; John 1:28; Rom 10:13), not to mention that it is His name Christians are told to call on (1 Cor 1:2). Finally, the foundation of atonement finds its fullest and final expression in the person and work of Jesus (Heb 9:26; 10:12).

## The Christian and Law

At the beginning of this chapter were observations about the Christian's relationship to the law, along with a challenge for the reader to lay aside misconceptions about it that draw stark contrasts with grace—since both grace and law are present in the OT and the NT. Through the examination of the passages perused in this section (most of which would be classified as law), I hope the reader has begun to see the relevance of the principles behind such expressions to their contemporary life and use. The truth and power of Jesus' statement that "all the Law and Prophets depend upon these two commandments" (Matt 22:40) underscores the centrality of that law/grace relationship.

## Jesus and God

The earlier discussion of Judaism's fear (probably developed shortly after the exile) of saying the name Yahweh omitted one important impact on the NT. In view of that fear, when the Jewish translators of the Septuagint came to the divine name, they did not transliterate it into Greek as they typically did with names, but rendered it by the Greek term *kurios*, "lord," which was equivalent to the Hebrew *'ădōnāy*. Being students of the Septuagint, the NT writers' use of *kurios* then seems to be related to their view of the Deity of Christ. That is, when they called Jesus "Lord" *(kurios)*, they were not simply addressing Him with a title (as we might use the title "Boss"); they were identifying Him with the God of the OT—Yahweh. This is abundantly evident when OT passages that use "the LORD" (Yahweh) are applied to Jesus by NT writers.[234] This fact, combined with Jesus' own statements regarding His equality with the Father (John 6:46; 10:20), is fatal to the notion that Christ's deity just reflects late Christian thought.

## Jesus and Atonement

The work and teachings of Jesus Christ created a need for a new community. But this group originated as a Jewish sect and thus carried much of the theological baggage of the Jewish people with them as they dispersed. The church took the ideas and perceptions of the world around them to heart as they sought to explain what had occurred through Christ at Calvary. Studies on the Qumran sect have done much to illuminate the social and religious situation in Palestine during the formative years of the Christian church. Garnet undertook a thorough study of the perceptions that the Qumran community held concerning atonement as it was expressed in their commentaries and teachings. In them one sees the reconfiguration of earlier Levitical ideas of atonement and later expressions into a single concept that, as is shown below, has many affinities with the usage of the NT.

Garnet summarized his discussion by making three observations. First, atonement rituals were considered effective provided they were carried out correctly and were accompanied by repentance.

---

[234] See Matt 3:3, which quotes Isa 40:3, and Rom 10:13, which quotes Joel 2:32. See Thomas's expression, "My Lord and my God!"—probably echoing the Hebrew exclamation of submission evident in some psalms (e.g., Ps 30:12).

Second, it was not possible to buy God's favor. Third, piety could serve as an acceptable substitute in the absence of sacrifice for the accomplishment of atonement.[235] Lang furthered these observations by recognizing that in the Qumran community atonement became even more the prerogative of God. The meanings of atonement expressed at Qumran were usually expressed in terms of God's work, such as His saving power, the Holy Spirit, true counsel, longsuffering, grace, wonderful mysteries, and plentiful forgiveness.[236]

The Day of Atonement represented the centerpiece of the Levitical law. For the writer of the book of Hebrews, the importance of recognizing that Jesus perfectly and completely fulfilled the purposes of this day is that Jesus did not come to destroy but to fulfill the old covenant. In Christ the law found perfection, whereas previously it was incomplete. So perfect was Christ's sacrifice that a new covenant was formed, which was written on human hearts. It was not a temporary solution to be repeated every year, but an eternal salvation that made itself evident every day (see Rom 3:25; Heb 9; 13). Much has been made of comparisons between Jesus and elements of the Day of Atonement. Many see in the goat for Azazel a type for Christ who bore sins for others, who had to die outside the camp, and who bore the sins of people back to their point of origination in the depths of hell.[237] While exegetically speaking some of these points are questionable (such as Jesus' descent into hell), the point is that of all of the sacred events of Scripture, none found expression as fully in the NT as the Day of Atonement—because Christ's death and resurrection was the ultimate Day of Atonement.

In Rom 3:25 Paul wrote that God displayed Christ as a propitiation. The Greek word used here is identical to that employed in the Septuagint in references to the *kappōret*. Many commentators agree that this is the comparison that Paul was making. The comparison invites two conclusions. First, some would argue that since the Septuagint's understanding of this word influenced Paul, he intended

---

[235] P. Garnet, *Salvation and Atonement in the Qumran Scrolls*, WUNT (Tübingen: J. C. B. Mohr, 1977), 117.

[236] *TDOT*, "כפר."

[237] Hartley, *Leviticus*, 245.

Christ's work to be understood as expiation, not propitiation.[238] But as noted above—since expiation wanders very closely to propitiation when it involves the substitution of one for another, and since Paul's overall argument involves at least hostility toward sin by God[239]—one is left with the sense that Christ is the offering through which wrath is averted. Equally significant is that Paul's usage here is the fullest expression of the location where the transcendence and immanence of God meet. For Paul, in this passage at least, Christ serves as that place where grace could be imparted and fellowship restored.[240]

The discussion of the effectiveness of sacrifice being related to the blood/life of the gift and not only to its death has strong implications for the view of Christ's death that one takes. As expressed above, the penal substitution view of atonement, while adequate in the most important regard, does not cover all the matters that are involved in Christ's sacrifice. Christ's sacrifice was not only His receiving the death we deserved, but also His accomplishing the cleansing that we could not achieve.[241] These truths also expand the perception one has of the Father in terms of Christ's work. Instead of only being a wrathful God detached from the event, He also serves to effectuate the event. Instead of only picturing the atonement of Christ as a bridge over the chasm between man and God, we may also see God and man standing next to each other with God effectuating the sacrifice, and man identifying himself with the sacrifice to the end that Christ's blood cleanses the man and puts an end to sin.[242] Indeed, it would be interesting to see the effect on the lives of Christians if they started viewing their salvation as a cleansing from impurity instead of only focusing on an escape from punishment.

---

[238] C. H. Dodd, *The Bible and the Greeks* (London: Hodder and Stoughton, 1954), 94.

[239] S. Travis, "Christ as Bearer of Divine Judgement in Paul's Thought about Atonement," in *Atonement Today*, ed. J. Goldingay (London: Society for Promoting Christian Knowledge, 1995), 27–32.

[240] Janowski, *Heilsgeschehen*, 350.

[241] J. Goldingay, "Old Testament Sacrifice and the Death of Christ," in *Atonement Today*, ed. J. Goldingay (London: Society for Promoting Christian Knowledge, 1995), 10. Goldingay, however, rejected any notion of a penal substitution.

[242] Ibid., 11–13.

# Conclusions

The relationships inherent in Scripture demand principles of interaction that permit someone to act in a way that is both appropriate and beneficial to him. Ironically, these principles that are in fact limitations of a sort are not confining, but freeing. To understand what the other person truly desires in any relationship is a gift beyond expression. In the opening books of the Bible, God established the foundations for understanding and interacting with Him. They represent a precious treasure of revelation that draws us into the heart of One who is otherwise beyond understanding. They set standards of distinction and behavior that aid not only one's relationship with God but with other humans seeking to relate to Him as well.

In this part of the discussion we did not examine the last half of the ten words of the book of Exodus. Perhaps we should have, as the words clearly point to how the relationship God has created between man and Himself impacts the relationship man has with others. However, this topic is better left to the prophets, who expounded these ideas so well. The foundations of relationship merged into the lives of the early Israelites in the narratives of the Former Prophets. Such a fusion plainly illuminates the struggle of how one merges the clear prescriptions of God with the sometimes murky patterns of life and worship. The Latter Prophets delved deeper into the attitudes of worship, thus challenging the reader to find new depths of commitment to the foundations God has outlined. Ultimately, our examination will arrive at the Writings—the final section of the OT where one finds the people gathered together in order to articulate their worship through various expressions. But it is primarily in the relationships and foundations of worship on which everything else rests. One must grapple with these issues in order to appropriately understand what follows.

# Chapter 3
## THE FORMER PROPHETS: PATTERNS OF WORSHIP

Whereas the Pentateuch provides the foundations of worship, the Former Prophets show those foundations expressed in the history of national Israel.[1] Not surprisingly, the Former Prophets demonstrate that Israel continuously had difficulty taking the precepts of the Pentateuch and applying them consistently to their lives. This difficulty is not surprising because, among other reasons, there is always a complexity in relationships that impedes someone putting into action the desires of another. The struggles of communication, appropriateness, and attitude are well understood hurdles to relationships at all levels. As Israel moved into the promised land as described in the book of Joshua, as they worked through the loose confederation represented in the period of the Judges, and as they developed their national structures and institutions as recounted in the books of Samuel and Kings, the nation tried to walk the tender balance between rigid ritualism and unrepresentative freedom. This struggle finds similar expression today from worshippers and churches that ask, "How do we find the pattern of worship that most appropriately weds the seriousness of our endeavor with the joyousness of our experience? What does the Bible have to say about establishing our own patterns of worship?"

In the introduction to this book I outlined some of the problems faced when attempting to use narratives to form theology. An equally important discussion, however, is needed concerning the relationship between history and theology. It is unnecessary to sacrifice historicity for the sake of theology. The fact that these books have been labeled Former Prophets or Deuteronomistic History suggests that the history they relate uses a specific theology as a structure. That some would use this suggestion to undermine the historical veracity

---

[1] The term "Former Prophets" has been selected for the sake of simplicity. These books are often identified in scholarly circles as constituting the Deuteronomistic History. See D. M. Howard Jr., *Joshua*, NAC (Nashville: B&H, 1998), 52–56.

of the text is unconscionable given the fact that all history is viewed through the lens of some theoretical framework.[2] Canonically, the theological grounding of these books allows the texts to serve as bridges between the Pentateuch and the Latter Prophets, and it also permits one to delve into their content in order to ascertain some theological realities concerning the nature of God and our worship of Him.

## Remembrance in Worship

One of the primary vehicles through which the books of the Former Prophets speak is their highlighting of the central feature of remembrance in worship.[3] This factor may even be paramount since at least part of the reason these books exist is that the writers wanted Israel to remember its history with God. Gerhard von Rad proposed years ago that Israel had at its core of belief a credo that amounted to a series of events recounted as an expression of Israel's understanding of God and itself.[4] While acceptance of the entire concept has become passé, there is clearly a relationship between Israel's accounts of history and how the people understand their place in it in connection with God's saving acts. Within the Former Prophets, remembrance as worship finds expression in three general occasions: the setting up of stones, the giving of farewell speeches, and the offering of dedications.

### Altars and Memorials

The pattern of setting up stones appears in two forms in the biblical text: altars and stones of remembrance. The importance of altars in worship goes beyond their specific role in a contemporary act of worship; altars also exist as lasting reminders of God's gracious acts

---

[2] For a good discussion of the relationship between history and theology, see the opening discussion in I. Provan et al., *A Biblical History of Israel* (Louisville: Westminster John Knox Press, 2003).

[3] For a good discussion of remembrance in worship from a slightly different angle than that presented here, see E. Merrill, "Remembering: A Central Theme in Biblical Worship," *JETS* 43 (2000): 27–36.

[4] G. von Rad, *The Problem of the Hexateuch and Other Essays*, trans. E. W. Trueman Dicken (New York: McGraw-Hill, 1966).

and behavior in relationship. That these sites remained important to Israel is noted at various places.[5] Stones of remembrance, on the other hand, apparently functioned solely as permanent narratives among the people as they reflected on the great moments of God's activity in both their collective and individual pasts.

Altars were built at places considered sacred. They served as visual reminders of both an interaction with God and the necessity of response by those receiving the blessing of God's presence. They were meeting places at which the community as a whole could recognize the past deliverance of God and the future expectation of His provision of justice (Josh 8:30–35). Indeed, the people named altars in accordance with the event they recollected. In Joshua, the Reubenites and Gadites named their altar, "It is a witness between us that the LORD is God," reflecting a hope that neither their descendants nor those of the western tribes would forget that they were brothers and worshipped the same God (Josh 22:34). The account in Judges of Gideon's building an altar is a little more enigmatic (Judg 6:24). The immediate context suggests that his naming the altar "Yahweh Shalom" grew out of his being granted well-being *(šālôm)* in the midst of meeting the angel of Yahweh face to face.[6] On the other hand, the narrator's inclusion of the altar's continuing existence suggests that the well-being provided by Yahweh is a reminder to all persons who, like Gideon, have heard the message of God and found themselves lacking and in need of assurance of God's preservation.

The structure of the altar itself, with the presence of the horns, suggests reminders of key elements in one's relationship with God— mercy, justice, and His very presence. The Bible relates the first of

---

[5] See 1 Sam 7:16; 10:17. Among the most interesting of these passages is Amos 5:4–6 where, because of Beersheba's antiquity and importance, it becomes the heart of the argument that the worship site can never replace the worshipped One—an argument to be examined shortly.

[6] This passage is interesting on many levels. Why was Gideon afraid of death at meeting the angel of Yahweh? Such accounts were evident throughout the Pentateuch without such a danger being expressed. In fact, it has been argued that the angel of Yahweh represented the manifestation of Yahweh that allowed for face-to-face meetings devoid of the fear of immediate death. See V. Hirth, *Gottes Boten im Alten Testament*, Theolgische Arbeiten 32 (Berlin: Evangelische Verlagsanstalt, 1975), 83–84. Although Jacob communicated a similar fear in Gen 32:30, if in fact it was the angel of Yahweh he wrestled with, it seems that Gideon's expression describes a struggle in his nature—cowardice versus bravery.

these elements in connection with the custom of holding on to the horns in order to plead for mercy (1 Kgs 1:50–53; 2:28). Additionally, as discussed in the previous chapter, the horns played a key role as the blood was sprinkled on them for certain sacrifices. Such a practice reveals all at once God's mercy (the sin was atoned for), justice (blood was spilled), and presence.[7] Every time the people built or looked on an altar they remembered the comprehensive nature of a relationship with God.

To a greater degree than altars, stones of remembrance highlight an example of remembrance as worship. Building these stones was of some importance—one of Israel's first worship expressions on entering the land was erecting the stones at Gilgal (Josh 4). The account of the general miracle of God bringing Israel across the Jordan became a personal testimony as the story was shared in subsequent generations. These stones served to demonstrate that while God would not always perform such dramatic miracles as He had in those situations, people could remember them[8] and rekindle the fire of faith in God as each Israelite generation recounted what God had done. The drama of the crossing of the Jordan was of such importance and impact to Israel as a whole that each successive generation was to be reminded of the occurrence. This remembrance was not simply on a corporate level, for all parents were to teach the story to their children.

The two Ebenezers (lit. "stone of remembrance") in 1 Samuel (chaps. 4, 7) are additional examples of monumental reminders of God's activity. The Ebenezer of chap. 4 is uncertain in origin, and a question arises as to whether it is a separate entity from the stone of chap. 7. One can say that at least in a literary sense the two are treated separately to bracket the events of the intervening chapters. The first Ebenezer serves as a reminder of what happens when one forgets. Israel at this location forgot who it was and what it was that had brought them to this point in their history. The people's rejection of God's leadership and provision led to a great loss. But its

---

[7] As stated in chapter 2, it is possible that the horns themselves were abstract symbols of God Himself. See H. T. Obbink, "The Horns of the Altar in the Semitic World, Especially in Jahwism," *JBL* 56 (1937): 43–49.

[8] Howard, *Joshua*, 135.

counterpart in 1 Sam 7 was built to demonstrate how far God had brought Israel, both physically and spiritually. It stood as a positive reminder of what happens to people who submit themselves whole-heartedly to the direction of God.

It seems clear that the ancients understood something about human reflection and memory that moderns often forget: memory is an authentic method for present experience.[9] The communication of these memories becomes a conversation between two individuals that forever alters their perceptions of God, reality, and themselves. In Dodd's words, "A conversation between two persons is an event in the lives of both, and in certain circumstances may be an event from which incalculable consequences flow in the world of actual, concrete facts."[10] Therefore, altars and stones of remembrance are useful examples of one component of worship. There are moments in our history of relating to God that create a shared identity between believers but which also call on us for individual reflection. Some miracles are so great that they create an appreciation of God that excludes thoughts of anything else. For Israel one such occurrence was the entry into the land. For Christians today the issue can be as cosmic as the cross or as regional as deliverance through some trial as a church. In each case these events are both corporate and individual.

## Farewell Speeches

Another place that remembrance plays a role in the worship of Israel is in farewell speeches. Of course, Moses' speech in Deuteronomy 33 recounts much about Israel's past and the impact that it might have on his people's future, but it is in the speeches of the Former Prophets where the impact is clearest.

---

[9] C. H. Dodd, *The Bible Today* (Cambridge Univ. Press, 1956), 105. Childs argues as much in his assessment that memory functioned to establish "the continuity of the new generation with the decisive events of the past" and to test "the existing cult in the light of the past historical tradition"; see B. S. Childs, *Memory and Tradition in Israel* (London: SCM Press, 1962), 51.

[10] This quote is especially appropriate in light of Dodd's argument that the recounting of history in the text, known as the communication of the Word of God, constitutes such a conversation. C. H. Dodd, *The Bible Today* (Cambridge: University Press, 1956), 105.

Joshua's speech in Josh 23:1–16 is paradigmatic of farewell addresses. In the midst of his calls for deliverance he reminds his audience three times of God's activities in delivering them. It seems that for Joshua, at least, the encouragement for future obedience is found in the track record of the One for whom obeisance is prescribed. At the heart of his speech is a reminder that the people can know who God is by who He has been. Little could be said to warrant recognition of Yahweh's sovereignty if He had demonstrated that sovereignty in a way that was unresponsive to His covenant promises and stipulations. On the other hand, the fact that God had so thoroughly fulfilled His responsibility to past promises meant that He expected a thorough reaction from those for whom His promises had been fulfilled.

Samuel's speech in 1 Sam 12 is of a slightly different nature than that of Joshua. Whereas Joshua's speech suggests the finality of his activity and service, Samuel's falls at the end of his leadership role, with a continued prophetic role afterwards. Nonetheless, Samuel's speech still represents a farewell address, for it focuses primarily on the transference of leadership from a judge paradigm to a monarchial one. Still, the centerpiece of his speech is a rehearsal of God's past activities. Samuel contrasts Israel's disobedience with Yahweh's steadfastness in a far more harsh tone than the one used by Joshua. Yahweh had continually delivered apostate Israel and brought salvation to a people that had failed to learn from previous mistakes. Remembering deliverance is not only for the purpose of highlighting the value of the One who delivers, but it also serves to train in obedience those who are willing to hear the voices of the sinful ancestor.

David's farewell speech in 2 Sam 23:1–7 once again leads the reader in a new direction. Yet another time, the speech outlines the past activities of Yahweh, but this time as they have found expression in David's behavior.[11] It is here that the activities of God and those of His people are placed in their most surprising manifestation—Yahweh's use of us to carry out His will. This truth is imbed-

---

[11] O. Lete came close to this analysis when he suggested that what David was expressing in his speech is the origin of his dynasty in the charismata of God and the confirming word of the covenant of 2 Samuel 7; see Lete, "David's Farewell Oracle (2 Samuel XXIII 1–7): A Literary Analysis," *VT* 34 (1984): 436.

ded in the previously discussed speeches but finds its most overt expression here. It is not difficult for most to conceive of a sovereign God who is capable of delivering despite His people. It is not difficult for prideful man to assume his accomplishments can be achieved apart from God. What is difficult to fathom is that the sovereign God of the universe would ever deem it proper to use prideful man. In remembering his ministry and monarchy, David outlines his role as the mouthpiece of God and the instrument of His deliverance in the past. Such passages bring in the encouraging elements of the Joshua speech and the warnings of self-glorification voiced by Samuel.[12] All three speeches clearly illustrate that remembering the past puts man in his place and recognizes God in His.

## Dedications

Dedication ceremonies serve as another place where remembering was an element of worship—especially in the dedication of the temple by Solomon (1 Kgs 8:1–65).[13] It is essential to recognize the tension here, as in the other narratives, between how the writer has cast his account of this event and the event itself. In places the immediate context and the broader context merge together quite well, but there are statements in the broader scope that make one painfully aware that this building itself would play a part in exile and destruction. Is God's foreknowledge behind the uneasiness He expressed about the temple being built (2 Sam 7:4–7) and His warnings about the danger of its presence in Israel's midst (1 Kgs 9:7)?[14] One cannot ignore the importance of these factors for how to view the first temple. But in this section the more positive aspect of its portrayal in the immediate setting of its dedication is examined.

The dedication of the temple highlights many of the elements already expressed in relationship to other acts of remembrance. Solomon peppers his prayer with references to Yahweh's deliverance

---

[12] Self-glorification is latent in the idolatry discussed in chapter 2 of this book and in Samuel's charge of forgetting Yahweh (1 Sam 12:9,12).

[13] This passage reflects much about both remembrance and prayer. The latter will be dealt with more below.

[14] J. Goldingay, *Old Testament Theology*, vol. 1, *Israel's Gospel* (Downers Grove: InterVarsity, 2003), 564.

of His people and His past saving acts. Again, a centerpiece of one's faith in God today is His activities of yesterday, but there are some important distinctions addressed in the narrative that push the notion of the relationship of past activities toward present and future ones. The most important of these is the disclosure that worship is related to the place where God's name dwells (1 Kgs 8:16,29).

The importance of the name has already been discussed. That its importance calls for relationship is an unmistakable conclusion. In addition, the use of "My name" in 1 Kgs. 8:16,29 illustrates the fundamental principle of the tension between God's immanence and transcendence in worship that is central to remembrance. A memory, especially a sacred one, communicates forcefully and clearly God's presence with His people. Yet because it is a memory it reinforces the separateness that is a characteristic of God's being. This factor is a word of warning for the use of memory in the worship of God. While God can be understood, appreciated, recognized, and related to through His past activities, His past activities are not Him.

## Replacing God with Something Less

Idolatry takes two basic forms within the biblical narratives— physical and psychological. Physical idolatry is easily identifiable and relates to the actual presence of an object of worship that man constructs. The relationship of idolatry to the worship of false gods seems in many respects a foregone conclusion. But, as illustrated in the discussion of the first two Commandments in chapter 2, the two are not always the same.[15] The pattern of idolatry outlined by the biblical writers communicates much about the essence of true worship and dependence on God alone.

### Physical Idolatry

Physical idolatry seems to have been a struggle for the Israelites from their beginnings. The prototypical story of idolatry is the golden

---

[15] Since this section is dealing with biblical patterns of worship, it does not detail issues of other nations' worship of false gods. Instead, it evaluates only the activities instituted by Israel's leaders and people since they are the ones responsible for a covenant stipulation that is the forerunner of the new covenant of Christianity.

calf incident in Exodus 32, but it is in the era of Former Prophets that rampant manifestations of the practice began. The book of Judges includes overt expressions of idolatry, such as Israel serving the Asherahs (3:7), Gideon making the ephod (8:27), and Micah making idols for Dan (chap. 18). These events are representative of the general apostasy demonstrated in Israel during that period.

The book of 1 Samuel, with Samuel and David as its central characters, has a somewhat more muted discussion of idolatry. Though the book has a few references to Israel's following other gods (1 Sam 7:3; 8:8; 26:19), the only specific reference to idolatry is in the account of David's rescue by Michal, who tricked Saul's men by placing a household idol in David's bed (1 Sam 19:11–17). This event seems to say much about the essence of physical idolatry in Israel and its impact on everyday life. The theological conflict created by the finding of the idol in *David's house* is often not addressed among writers.[16] Some argue that its place there was merely to cast aspersions on the usefulness of idols.[17] Still others note its presence to make a comment about the unfaithfulness of Michal.[18] It must be admitted, however, that this passage is one of those that presents problems for interpretation and application because this idol serves only a utilitarian function in the text and is not commented on by the authoritative narrator. Therefore, any conclusion one makes about its presence has to remain either speculative or general. How and why the idol was kept in David's house is impossible to determine, but that it was there suggests something important about the nature of Israel and the worship of Yahweh alone.

---

[16] That the idol had to have been in David's house already is suggested both by 1 Sam 19:11 and by the recognition that this particular idol would have been sizable (i.e. the size of a man) and therefore hard to move and difficult to slip into the house.

[17] W. Brueggemann, *1–2 Samuel*, INT (Louisville: John Knox Press, 1990), 143; B. Arnold, *1 and 2 Samuel*, NIVAC (Grand Rapids: Zondervan, 2003), 284.

[18] R. Bergen, *1, 2 Samuel*, NAC (Nashville: B&H, 1996), 208. Bergen's observations are based on the fact that only Michal is explicitly linked with the idol. However, since the passage also makes it clear that the idol was in David's house, it seems reasonable, though not absolutely necessary, to suppose that since this is where David clearly slept, he must have been aware of its presence. It must be admitted that the text ultimately makes nothing of the idolatry implied here (either for Michal or David), which is why the discussion undertaken here is tentative in its presentation.

The preexilic world of Israel was saturated with the concepts of polytheism and idolatry. For a person to conceive of a different reality would have been extraordinary, to say the least. And yet, the consistent biblical portrayal is indeed monotheism. The presence of the idol in David's house may be very similar to the NT apostles' inability to conceive of a Messiah who would die a cursed death. Their struggles and unbelief are laid bare for the entire world to see, and they actually highlight the distinctive nature of the Christian message.

One might say the same occurs in the Samuel account. The biblical ideal of monotheism had been definitively established, and yet individuals struggled with it because of the dominating nature of a contrary worldview. Given David's statements elsewhere, *it seems unlikely that he succumbed totally to the notion of polytheism*, but texts such as 1 Sam 19:11–13 might express something of the struggle that he (and others who held a radical, contra-cultural perspective) had in relating the revealed word of God to everyday experiences.

Following 1 & 2 Samuel, 1 & 2 Kings returns in earnest to the problem of idolatry as a practice for both the people and the leadership of Israel and Judah. Solomon was led astray through his marriages to foreign wives. The writer of 1 Kings intimates that with his first foreign policy decision, Solomon caused the downfall of his kingdom: his marriage to the princess from Egypt brought with it foreign gods and the establishment of numerous high places (1 Kgs 3:1; see 11:1–13). Solomon's apparent struggle between the cultural norms of the time and the teaching of Yahweh about his nature is one that numerous kings of Israel and Judah would face.

Perhaps the most famous example of idolatry in 1 & 2 Kings— and in some ways the most important—is the establishment of the golden calves by Jeroboam I at Bethel and Dan (1 Kgs 12:25–33). The reasoning behind the actions of Jeroboam has been the center of some debate among scholars, some suggesting that Jeroboam was in no way seeking to establish an idolatrous religious activity through the erection of these monuments. Rather, some have proposed that he was establishing pedestals on which the invisible Yahweh would sit, with the bulls representing a characteristic of God.[19] The pedestals would thus function similarly to the ark of the covenant on which Yahweh sat and received worship.

There is nothing in the biblical text that would go directly against such an explanation, and this approach is consistent with known practices of the day. Furthermore, it is exactly because he was not setting out to establish an idol that his story is so important to the discussion of the nature and role of idolatry in the life of the people of God. Idolatry is sometimes understood as the sin of setting out to replace God with an alien god, when in fact it seems that the starting place for physical idolatry is sometimes not the replacement of God but the need to see Him for ourselves.[20] Indeed, one could argue that all physical idolatry first begins with psychological idolatry.

## Psychological Idolatry

Physical idolatry is easier for the Western mind to evaluate objectively since few of us have images in our households, but psychological idolatry, the perceptual mind-set that causes one to worship something other than God (sometimes something given to us by Him), has far more application to modern situations. Thus, it is much more difficult to address. Psychological idolatry finds expression when confidence is built on the presence of an object or an activity. In the biblical text, objects often became the source of confidence instead of God. Sadly, this often occurred with the very instruments God had given to the nation to point the people to Him. The transformation of action into a status of idolatry became a problem when the act of worship itself was seen to have some innate power.

Within the Former Prophets there are two items that consistently find themselves the focus of faulty confidence—the ark of the covenant and the tabernacle or temple.[21] Perhaps the clearest example

---

[19] K. Galling, *Biblisches Reallexikon*, HAT (Tübingen: J.C.B. Mohr, 1937), § 202–5.

[20] One need only note the thorough description of Josiah's reforms to understand how prevalent this attitude was (2 Kgs 23:4–27), and it was most apparent in Israel in the veneration of the bronze serpent Moses made (Num 21:4–9) until the time of Hezekiah (2 Kgs 18:4).

[21] The coupling of the tabernacle and temple as one item is not intended to subsume one to the other. Rather it expresses the perspective of the biblical writers who viewed them in very much the same light, even using the same terminology for them (see 1 Sam 1:9; 3:3).

is in 1 Samuel 4. As mentioned above, this account functions as the opening narrative of two incidents involving an Ebenezer. Reflection and remembrance had been turned into manipulation. Israel suffered a defeat at the hands of the Philistines, and a subsequent meeting of the elders determined that what they needed was the ark rather than God. In 1 Sam 4:3 the elders decided, "Let's bring the ark of the LORD's covenant from Shiloh. Then it will go with us and save us from the hand of our enemies." The HCSB makes the interpretative choice here (since Hebrew has no neuter) to render the third masculine pronoun as "it" rather than "he." Such a translation clearly identifies the sought source of victory as being the ark, whereas the Hebrew is more ambiguous.[22] Even if the pronoun is understood solely as masculine and therefore a reference to God, however, the point would change little. The people believed that the presence of the ark would provide victory, either because the ark itself had some innate power or because through the ark Yahweh could be controlled. The fact that the people were relying on corporate memory can hardly be doubted (1 Sam 4:4). The very words of God in Num 7:89 coupled with a shared history of events (Num 10:35–36; Josh 6:1–25) reflect that the use of the ark and presence of God were indeed a significant memory on which Yahweh expected His people to rely. But a memory that has dethroned God becomes a tradition that enthrones man.

The sin of the people was heightened by the accompaniment of the ark into battle by the corrupted priests Phinehas and Hophni, since this demonstrated a willingness to couple worship with sin. Such a coupling belies the true essence of the event: taking the ark into battle mimicked the act of worship prescribed by God but was motivated solely by self-preservation. Since sin at its heart is rooted in an illogical and indefensible attempt at self-preservation, defeat was inevitable. Memory, no matter how strong, cannot replace relationship.[23]

---

[22] It is most likely true from Israel's perspective that Yahweh and the ark were indistinguishable, although it is not necessary to go to Brueggemann's extreme of suggesting that Yahweh lost the battle. W. Brueggemann, *Ichabod Toward Home: The Journey of God's Glory* (Grand Rapids: Eerdmans, 2002), 1–24.

[23] "The sins of Shiloh will not be overcome by mimicking the successes of yesteryear." Arnold, *1–2 Samuel*, 96.

Nearly five hundred years later the cycle would repeat itself in the confidence placed in the temple. Brueggemann is probably correct in seeing the inclusion of the account of the tabernacle/ark (1 Sam 4–7) as a reflection of Israel's demeanor and perceptions about the temple.[24] The implicit relationship between the tabernacle/ark and the temple is made more explicit in the words of the prophets, especially Jeremiah (Jer 7:12–15).[25] As prefaced above, the words of Solomon concerning Yahweh in 1 Kgs 8 reflect an uneasiness about what the temple would become in the mind of the people and His warning of abandonment should He ever be replaced by other gods. That these gods might include the temple itself is borne out in His rejection and defilement of the temple (Ezek 8–9) and in His repeated reflections on the uselessness of the worship taking place there (Isa 1:11–15; Jer 7:21–22).

Ultimately, one of the features of psychological idolatry seems to be that the true focus of worship has become not so much the item that has replaced God, but ourselves. The battle rages where it began: Who will be the sovereign in matters of human existence? Our capacity to transform the very benefits God has granted into elements with which we will replace Him knows few boundaries. When such things occurred in Israel, however, God's righteousness and justice were manifested as He allowed His people's defeat.

This feature manifests itself to an even greater extent in the second type of psychological idolatry—when the act of worship replaces the One worshipped. When acts of worship become the focus of confidence and commitment, the situation is intriguing, to say the least. It seems quite clear from the evidence of manuals on divination and other religious practices that humanity has always placed a high level of confidence in its ability to control its own destiny. In the Former Prophets, the warnings of the Pentateuch about divination (Deut 18:10–11), rash vows (Lev 27; Deut 23:21–23 ),[26] and

---

[24] Brueggemann, *Ichabod*, 12–13.

[25] The temple sermon in Jeremiah 7 makes the most striking of the comparisons between the temple and the ark in Jeremiah's appeal to history in vv. 12–15.

[26] It should be noted that the former passage here is often understood as an "out" by which people who have been dedicated in a rash manner by someone might be released from the vow's obligation. See D. Block, *Judges, Ruth,* NAC (Nashville: B&H, 1999), 377.

false piety (Exod 32:9; 33:3,5; 34:9; Deut 9:6,13; 10:16; 31:27)[27] find expression as both consequence and specific judgment.

The rash vows uttered by Jephthah (Judg 11:30–31) and Saul (1 Sam 14:24) both seem to be attempts to manipulate their situations through the transformation of their battle into a holy war. Jephthah's words to the Lord are some of the most debated in Scripture: "If You will hand over the Ammonites to me, whatever comes out of the doors of my house to greet me when I return in peace from the Ammonites will belong to the LORD, and I will offer it as a burnt offering." Did he have in mind an animal or a person? Did he actually sacrifice his daughter or simply dedicate her to the local altar? The discussion is ongoing and the differences of opinion do not fall along any noticeable line of religious demarcation.[28]

Although definitive interpretations of Jephthah's actions are impossible, it is likely that Jephthah intended human sacrifice and that he, indeed, carried out his vow by sacrificing his daughter.[29] Jephthah was a master negotiator in form but not in content. It has long been recognized that his points in negotiation with the king of the Ammonites are an inaccurate conflation of the Moabites, Ammonites, and Amorites.[30] Likewise, the vow to God was rash and

---

[27] The Hebrew words behind the commonly translated "stiff-necked people" (עַם־קְשֵׁה־עֹרֶף) reveal a disposition of difficulty and refusal to be subject to any outside authority. Contextually, they seem to express a lack of authentic worship before God despite His worth as One to be worshipped.

[28] For a concise but fairly thorough survey of the various opinions concerning the matter, at least up to 1986, see D. Marcus, *Jephthah and His Vow* (Lubbock: Texas Tech Univ. Press, 1986). Although D. Gunn overstated the abandonment of the non-sacrificial view of Jephthah's actions, his discussion of the debate through the centuries is both vivid and evocative; see Gunn, *Judges*, BB (Malden, MA: Blackwell Publishing, 2005), 147–53.

[29] Although Iron Age floor plans suggest numerous ways in which an animal may be said to dwell in a house, the text seems less ambiguous in its assertions than is sometimes proposed. M. Bal, *Death and Dissymmetry: The Politics of Coherence in the Book of Judges* (Chicago: Univ. of Chicago Press, 1988), 45. For examples of Iron Age construction contemporary with Jephthah's era, see H. K. Beebe, "Ancient Palestinian Dwellings," BA 31 (1968): 50–58.

[30] Characteristic of many is the attempt by O. Eissfeldt to argue that this was the result of a later addition of extraneous materials; see Eissfeldt, *Die Quellen des Richterbuches* (Leipzig: J. C. Hinrichs'sche Buchhandlung, 1925), 26. But I believe that the errors are Jephthah's, rather than the biblical text's, and that the speech reveals an attitude of boisterousness and a lack of concern for detail that ultimately fails him in his dealings with Yahweh. Block similarly argued, though with a slightly different conclusion, that Jephthah's "theology is fundamentally syncretistic, so ideological compromises . . . are not surprising" (*Judges, Ruth*, 362).

riddled with ambiguity and a forced convergence of various streams of theological thought. His opening words are filled with first person singular pronouns and his expectation of deliverance through the guarantee of a sacred gift are simply further expressions of a mindset that confused Yahweh with the gods of surrounding nations. [31] In short, Jephthah's conflation of the gods of foreign nations likely carried over to the God of Israel as well.

Obvious comparisons to Abraham and Isaac are both necessary and appropriate, not in commending the actions of Jephthah but in further condemning him. Whereas Abraham's actions were rooted in a loving expression of dedication and trust and were met with confirming words from Yahweh, Jephthah's actions were rooted in ignorance and self-preservation and were met with silence from God. Jephthah is the extreme example of what happens when one brings together self-centeredness, ignorance of the precepts of God, and supposed worship of Yahweh.

There seems to be general agreement among scholars that Saul's oath in 1 Sam 14:24 is of a normal and pious form.[32] The problem was not with the speech's form[33] but with Saul's purpose and timing, as demonstrated by the contextual evidence. McCarter rightly argued that in its present form it demonstrates Saul's presumptuous

---

[31] See R. Boling, *Judges*, AB (Garden City: Doubleday, 1975), 207–10. For an opposing evaluation, see J. A. Soggin, *Judges*, OTL (Philadelphia: Westminster Press, 1981), 215–16. Block viewed these characteristics as representative of calculation (Block, *Judges, Ruth*, 367), but they seem to be more a natural outgrowth of an inner perspective reminiscent of the old saying that *character is what comes out when pressure is applied.*

[32] See G. von Rad, *Holy War in Ancient Israel*, trans. M. Dawn (Grand Rapids: Eerdmans, 1991), 42; and R. P. Gordon, *1 & 2 Samuel: A Commentary* (Exeter: Paternoster Press, 1986), 138–39. The opening phrase of v. 24 contains a fairly significant textual variant: The MT simply reads, "for Saul had placed the troops under an oath"; whereas the LXX reads, "Saul committed a serious blunder that day by causing the troops to take this oath" (author's translation). But this might help the argument being made here since the latter rendition seems unlikely on the basis that one is hard pressed to demonstrate how or why the MT version would have come into being out of the LXX, while the LXX reading seems more like an editorial comment. This view is against P. K. McCarter, *1 Samuel*, AB (Garden City: Doubleday, 1980), 245–49.

[33] E.g., J. Conrad saw the form as an example of the staid traditionalism of the past in contrast to the new immediacy and commonality of religion as expressed by Jonathan and David. He argued that the author was obviously advocating a movement to the latter, despite the fact that it was the traditionalistic religious rules that would be the final judge of Saul's activities in the next chapter (*Die junge Generation in alten Testament* [Stuttgart: Calwer, 1970], 71).

and rash character and that the vow was designed to garner Yahweh's favor.[34]

An array of evidence supports the opinion that the vow was inappropriate. First, the vow was taken when victory was already evident. Second, the presence of a priest from the disgraced line of Eli (Ahijah, his lineage being listed back to Eli makes this point; see 1 Sam 14:3) cast the religious tone and direction of all the involved events in a bad light. Third, the victorious and truly pious Jonathan reflected on the vow as his father bringing "trouble to the land."[35] Finally, the outcome of the vow was that following the victory, the Israelites ate meat with blood in it because they were famished from having been inappropriately stopped from consuming the honey that was readily available. The convergence of its pious form and its improper expression lead one to the natural conclusion that the goal of this act of worship was to advance the participant rather than to express the value of the sovereign God.

Whether this idolatry takes the form of a physical image or, more likely, is expressed in presumptions about divine prerogatives, it is the essence of humanity's hubris and the cause of its biggest collapses. No doubt this self-worship played a significant role in idolatry becoming the image used by the Latter Prophets for any form of immorality (Jer 2:4–25; Ezek 23:25–49). Those of us today who see in ourselves sophistication and piety that would never stoop to serve a carved image must watch ourselves carefully lest we fall into the more subtle sin of worshipping ourselves. Such sin is at the heart of so much that is said about how one desires to "do worship." It is not the form that gets us where we want to be; it is humbly submitting ourselves to the God that we seek to worship and understanding His ways that will take us there (see 1 Sam 15:23).

## The Essentials: Service and Distinctiveness Introduced

Of all the expressions of worship and theological emphases that one could draw from in the Former Prophets, the two central con-

---

[34] McCarter, *1 Samuel*, 251.

[35] That Jonathan was the one assigned guilt by the lots in v. 42 should not be understood as the vindication of Saul. Rather, it is the final event in a list of many in the narrative that both emphasizes the seriousness of vows and the unforeseen consequences of making a rash and foolish one.

cepts seem to be the grouping of service and distinctiveness (or separateness). Both advocate the essential matter of relating worship as life and worship as event, though one works from life to event and the other from event to life. Service relates the importance of recognizing that one's actions outside of sacred time and space have implications for how well one can worship within those spheres that are dedicated to God. On the other hand, distinctiveness demands that because one is a holy person, set apart by God during the worship event, one is also called to life that is itself divergent from how everyone else is living. These two patterns express both the juxtaposition of life and worship and the struggle created in life as one attempts to bring the black and white of God's laws into the grayness that the world offers. There is a realism in the texts as the individuals in them recognize the struggle of being God's people without conceding defeat on any level. The effort exists because the laws of God are not viewed with skepticism but through the eyes of faith, so they indeed can find application in one's life.

Yet there is also an expectation in the midst of this obedience to never forget that one is in a relationship with God and with other men and women, relationships that require genuine interaction with both parties. Indeed, one could argue that these two topics function as the theological and practical bridge between the mandates of the Pentateuch and the exhortations of the Latter Prophets. All lives truly committed to Yahweh seek to walk this fine line between observing His commands and recognizing the relational aspect of all that takes place in our communications with the world at enmity with Him and also with those who are His.

## Service—All Our Lives before God

The account of Saul's failure in 1 Sam 15:1–9 is one of the most examined texts of all the narratives about the troubled king. The contrast between Saul's assurance that he had "carried out the LORD's instructions" (15:13) and Samuel's question, "Does the LORD take pleasure in burnt offerings and sacrifices as much as in obeying the LORD?" (15:22) is rich fodder for both sermons and monographs.

The present question centers on possible implications of the text for worship.

When Samuel questioned Saul, he made a statement (15:13) that would become a prophetic credo of sorts. It would find restatement among many of the preexilic prophets and would become the center of debate in scholarly circles regarding the relationship of the prophet to the priest or cult.[36] The Qumran community used Habakkuk to argue that the Jerusalem cult was corrupt and their withdrawal from it justified.[37] During the Reformation, John Calvin suggested such texts demonstrated the primacy of the law over one's life since the prophets' rejection of the Israelite cult was merely an attempt to draw the people back to recognition of the superiority of God's divine edicts.[38] In today's culture it has become somewhat fashionable, especially among those in the free church tradition, to denigrate a more liturgical approach through the utterance of an "obedience rather than sacrifice" mantra. The questions that scholars have asked and the answers that have been offered are today at the center of the debate about service and worship.

The scholarly debate over the relationship between the prophet and the cult began with Wellhausen's and Duhm's claim that the former preceded the latter, but Norman Snaith brought the perspective of antagonism between the two to the forefront.[39] Snaith argued

---

[36] While most of the discussion centers on the prophetic words found in Hos 6:6; Amos 5:21–25; Isa 1:11–15; Mic 6:6–8; and Jer 7:21–22, the fact that the origin of the debate begins here with Samuel's correction of Saul suggests that this is the appropriate place for this discussion.

[37] J. Baumgarten, "Sacrifice and Worship Among the Jewish Sectarians of the Dead Sea," HTR 46 (1953): 153–54.

[38] J. Calvin, Commentary on the Book of the Prophet Isaiah, vol. 1, Isaiah 1–16, trans. W. Pringle (Edinburgh: Calvin Translation Society, 1850), 55–57.

[39] J. Wellhausen (Prolegomena to the History of Israel, trans. J. S. Black [Edinburgh: Adam and Charles Black, 1885], 56–59) considered the evidence that the writing prophets preceded the Levitical law codes to be compelling. Using passages such as Jer 7:22 and Amos 5:25, he concluded that the prophets looked back to the wilderness period as a golden age of sorts that was bereft of any sacrificial system. In relation to the sacrificial system then, the prophetic complaints are to be understood as an assessment of the failure of the priests to follow the prophetic Torah and the priestly desire to confuse and mislead the people into a superstitious system of sacrifice. Roughly contemporary with Wellhausen's work, B. Duhm, Die Theologie der Propheten als Grundlage für die innere Entwicklungsgeschichte der israelitischen Religion (Bonn: Adolph Marcus, 1875), argues that the prophetic work was the foundation of the development of Israel's religion.

that the concern of the prophets for the cult was centered on the fact that the Israelites were learning a sacrificial system from their contact with the Canaanites, and therefore it was an intrusion into true Yahwistic religion.[40] The argument followed that the result of this antagonism between the prophets and the priests was a heightening of the debate in terms of two competing religions.[41] Skinner went so far as to posit that man's relationship to God could not be based on both obedience and sacrifice since the two were incompatible.[42] Christopher North furthered this understanding by rejecting any type of comparative idea between sacrifice and obedience and suggesting that the prophets' views of the cult were not simply that it was unessential, but that it was a hindrance and religion was better off without it.[43]

Were this line of thinking allowed to continue, the results would not only be a contradictory biblical text, but the centrality of sacrifice in Christian worship would ultimately lose its place. Fortunately, comparative studies of other ancient Near Eastern texts served as a necessary corrective to the overzealous claims of the preceding generations. In 1935, Aubrey Johnson made some preliminary remarks concerning the role of the prophet in the worship of Israel.[44] Nine years later he followed his work with a more thorough discussion of the cultic prophet. Through philological comparisons for the terms applied to the prophets in the Bible, he suggested that the prophet *(nābî')* functioned in much the same way as priest and seer in a role of consultant and instigator of worship.[45] While his theory was

[40] N. Snaith, *Mercy and Sacrifice: A Study of the Book of Hosea* (London: SCM Press, 1953), 90–91.

[41] Some such as G. Oehler more appropriately perceived the statements as comparative. In other words, the prophets did not reject sacrifice as ineffective completely; they simply saw the spiritual life as the better way; see Oehler, *Theology of the Old Testament*, trans. George Day (New York: Funk & Wagnalls, 1883), 452; also H. W. Wolff, *Joel and Amos*, trans. W. Janzen and others, Her (Philadelphia: Fortress, 1977), 264–65.

[42] J. Skinner, *Prophecy and Religion: Studies in the Life of Jeremiah* (Cambridge: Cambridge Univ. Press, 1922), 182.

[43] C. North, "Some Outstanding Old Testament Problems: Sacrifice in the Old Testament," *ExpTim* 47 (1935–1936): 252.

[44] A. Johnson, "The Prophet in Israelite Worship," *ExpTim* 47 (1935–1936): 312–19.

[45] A. Johnson, *The Cultic Prophet in Ancient Israel* (Cardiff: Univ. of Wales Press Board, 1944), 21–25. These scholars are capable of accepting non-cultic prophets, but they see the primary picture of prophets as being cult personnel. Disagreement remains as to which canonical

subsequently modified and its original form is seen as overzealous, his work and others who drew on his conclusions served as a necessary step toward a more appropriate view of the relationship between the prophet and the cult. Johnson himself offered a rationale for the prophetic statements that would later become the standard explanation: the prophets' denunciations were based on corruption and abuses of the cult, not a rejection of the cult itself.[46] But it was not until the canonical structure of the OT was given due consideration that appropriate answers concerning the relationship of the two entities were finally explained.

Adam Welch argued that the prophetic determination of sacrifice as being detrimental was illogical. He suggested that the prophetic materials never rejected the religious practices in which they originated, but sought only to bring life, vitality, and genuineness to the acts. In other words, the priests served a static role, but the prophets a dynamic one.[47] Works subsequent to that of Welch have illustrated many difficulties in the perception of the prophet against the cult itself. First, the thought of a person in the eighth and seventh centuries BC conceiving of a religion void of sacrifice and ritual is inconsistent with every known piece of evidence in the development of religious understandings.[48] Second, the structure of the canon itself, with the prophetic sermons apparently based on their interpretation of the Torah's prescriptions and penalties, suggests a consistency between the cultic perceptions of the Levitical law and that of the prophets.[49] Third, the prophets' positive statements relating to Zion, the temple, and cultic festivals illustrate their commitment to maintenance of the elements of the cult.[50]

---

prophets were cultic in the strict sense of the word. See the discussion in J. Lindblom, *Prophecy in Ancient Israel* (Oxford: Basil Blackwell, 1962), 184–85, 207–10.

[46] Johnson, *The Cultic Prophet*, 29–30.

[47] A. Welch, *Prophet and Priest in Old Israel* (New York: Macmillan, 1953), 30–32, 77.

[48] K. Roubos, *Profetie en Cultus in Israël. Achtergrond en Betekenis van Enige Profetische Uitspraken Inzake de Cultus* (Wageningen: H. Veenman en Zonen, 1956), 120–21.

[49] R. Clements, *Old Testament Theology: A Fresh Approach* (Atlanta: John Knox Press, 1978), 124–25.

[50] Roubos, *Profetie en Cultus*, 25–43. See Amos 1:2; 2:11; 7:17 (reference to unclean indicates acceptance of concept of ritual purity); Hos 3:4–5; Isa 2:2–5; 6:7, 29:1–8; 30:27–33; Mic 1:2; 2:10 (uncleanness brings destruction); and Jer 17:24–27; 33:10–11.

In short, the prophets meant to correct abuses they observed in the cult and not to denigrate the cult itself. While many scholars have suggested this approach, none have put it quite so well as Abraham Heschel:

> Of course, the prophets did not condemn the practice of sacrifice itself; otherwise, we should have to conclude that Isaiah intended to discourage the practice of prayer (Isa 1:14–15). They did, however, claim that deeds of injustice vitiate both sacrifice and prayer. Men may not drown the cries of the oppressed with the noise of hymns, nor buy off the Lord with increased offerings. The prophets disparaged the cult when it became a substitute for righteousness. It is precisely the implied recognition of the value of the cult that lends force to their insistence that there is something far more precious than sacrifice.[51]

In other words, if sacrifice was not precious to begin with, how could the prophets use it as a point of comparison to demonstrate the greatness of righteousness? Roubos expanded such a concept by illustrating that because the cult was set and static, the prophetic warnings against it were designed to maintain the element of God's grace by demonstrating that He was never constrained by any human device. He is the owner of the temple, not simply its occupant.[52] This understanding of the prophetic charge also aids in giving a balance to how one views the obedience demanded. One should not place in the mouths of prophets, who were rejecting one form of legalism, mandates that create another.[53]

When examining the words of Samuel and his successors, one must be careful to recognize that it is not the methodology of the worship practice that is in question but the relationship of the act itself to everything else in one's life. Saul's failure in 1 Samuel 15 was more of the same from chaps. 13–14—he never correctly established the lines between his actions as king and his place as a servant of Yahweh. He blurred distinctions that he should have drawn between

---

[51] A. Heschel, *The Prophets* (New York: Harper & Row, 1962), 2:196; see R. Albertz, *A History of Israelite Religion in the Old Testament Period*, vol. 1, *From the Beginnings to the End of the Monarchy*, trans. J. Bowden, OTL (Louisville: Westminster John Knox Press, 1994), 171; and G. von Rad, *Old Testament Theology*, vol. 2, *The Theology of Israel's Prophetic Traditions*, trans. D. M. G. Stalker, OTL (New York: Harper & Row, 1965), 4.

[52] Roubos, *Profetie en Cultus*, 122.

[53] G. von Rad, *The Message of the Prophets*, trans. D. M. G. Stalker (New York: Harper & Row, 1962), 154–55.

the sacred and the profane and failed to connect his sinfulness with his relationship to God. To our generation that is so enraptured in the experiential, Saul serves as a stern warning to understand theological distinctions, to seek God's definitions rather than our own, and to recognize that worship takes place as much, maybe more, in our daily actions as it does in any event in which we take part.

## Distinctiveness—Holy Lives before Men

It is fitting to discuss distinctiveness and holiness of lifestyle at this point since it is in the narratives surrounding Saul that the matter of the mixing of the profane and sacred finds its most overt expression. Furthermore, the warnings of the previous section on service will help the reader understand that the argument of this section is not for another form of legalism, but for distinctiveness in one's life and in the worship in which we take part. Saul's actions in 1 Samuel 15 reflect his failure to observe the regulations of the ḥērem—instructions from God regarding the annihilation of the Canaanite peoples (Deut 7:1–11; 20:16–18). Regarding the mandate for distinctiveness, no teaching or set of narratives more thoroughly advocates such a position as those surrounding the ḥērem.[54]

Before discussing the relationship of the ḥērem to Christian worship, it is helpful to discuss the relationship between the command and Christianity itself. It is safe to say that few elements within the OT law and narratives have caused as much consternation and questioning as this command. For some, it is a law and act to be cast aside as representing the ancient superstitions and prelogical thoughts of the Israelite people.[55] Others view it as inconsequential and unimportant as the outgrowth of a sovereign right. For this lat-

---

[54] This noun, often translated "the ban," is derived from the verb form חָרַם. The word is ambiguous in meaning and so most likely has a wide semantic range that is largely dependent on context for intended meaning in any given text. While its basic meaning is "to dedicate," the level of that dedication can vary in degrees, from simply setting something aside to annihilation of it. See *TDOT*, "חָרַם ḥāram; חֵרֶם ḥērem."

[55] For instance, T. Mafico wrote: "The Israelites regarded other nations and their idol gods as enemies of Yahweh. For this reason the Israelites were not shocked by the callous cruelty they exhibited by killing men and women, young and old, ox and sheep, camel and ass (1 Sam 15:3; Josh 11:40)" (*ABD*, "Ethics, Old Testament"). J. Barr called the command "morally offensive"; see Barr, *Biblical Faith and Natural Theology* (Oxford: Clarendon, 1993), 218.

ter group, time and distance permit the matter to be looked at rather forensically and God as "excused" because it is His right to do as He pleases. The latter is problematic because the argument sacrifices God's righteousness at the expense of His sovereignty.[56] The former fails to take seriously the source of the command in the mind and words of God and has led to less than satisfactory responses for those who accept the command as being from God.

The subject of sacred violence is one that has taken many different directions over the past several decades. One particular writer, René Girard, challenged perspectives on violence and its place in the ancient mind-set and text. Girard's intriguing hermeneutic and philosophical perspective have sent many scholars scurrying to find a way to apply his approach to the various biblical texts and issues.[57] Essentially, Girard built his case around the proposition that humanity is mired in cyclical violence as an outgrowth of imitation-induced-envy. As civilization progressed, man sought to placate or dampen this violent tendency through a process known as *scapegoating*—someone is blamed for evil and punished, which soothes the violent tendencies of the group.[58] Girard argued, however, that what is distinctive about Judaism and Christianity is that their texts reflect a view of the scapegoat as one who is innocent. Such a portrayal shatters the cycle of violence and brings humanity from a realization that such violence is senseless to a place of peace.[59] The perspective of the texts, according to Girard, is so counter-cultural that it must be divine. Indeed, on the surface this argument seems to be a victorious apologetic for the distinctiveness of the gospel.

---

[56] This is a position some are all too ready to accept. Although dealing with the origin of sin, the notable quote of R. C. Sproul Jr. concerning God's absolute sovereignty illustrates the mind-set of some: "God desired for man to fall into sin. I am not accusing God of sinning: I am suggesting that God created sin"; see Sproul, *Almighty Over All: Understanding the Sovereignty of God* (Grand Rapids: Baker, 1999), 54.

[57] Indeed, the conferences, discussion groups, and literary works on Girard's theories have been a regular fixture since the early 1990s—the most persistent and developed of these being the Colloquium on Violence and Religion. See W. Swartley, ed., *Violence Renounced: René Girard, Biblical Studies, and Peacemaking*, Studies in Peace and Scripture 4 (Telford, PA: Pandora Press, 2000).

[58] R. Girard, *The Scapegoat*, trans. Y. Frecero (Baltimore: Johns Hopkins University Press, 1984).

[59] Ibid., 189.

Unfortunately, Girard's presuppositional foundation suffers at many points and fails to deal adequately with the issue of violence in the biblical text. First, Girard viewed sacrifice and its origins within the realm of anthropology—that is, their source was humanity instead of God.[60] As a result, he claimed that while the OT text radically demonstrates God's introduction of Himself into the thought and practices of man, it is also riddled with misconceptions about God that persist in the writings and stories that are not overcome until the Gospels.[61] Such an approach again leaves the interpreter picking and choosing which parts of the OT he would like to use and which ones he can assign to unnecessary, antiquated thinking. This approach ultimately leaves one without much of the Hebrew text to interpret.[62] Second, Girard's view of humanity's capacity to change based on reason has not been borne out by experience. His thoughts are reminiscent of the pre-World War I optimism of the likes of Herbert Spencer that collapsed under the weight of evidence about what man can do to man.[63] Third, his premise of a nonviolent God robs ancient Israel of one of its primary understandings of Yahweh—the divine Warrior.[64] Indeed, numerous narratives,

---

[60] R. Girard, *Things Hidden Since the Foundation of the World,* trans. S. Bann and M. Metteer (Stanford: Stanford University Press, 1987; reprint London: Continuum, 2003), 154; idem, *Violence and the Sacred,* trans. P. Gregory (Baltimore: Johns Hopkins University Press, 1979; reprint London: Continuum, 2005), 272.

[61] Ibid., 157–58. Certainly Schroeder went too far in his accusations of Girard as Marcionite, one who engendered a view of the OT individuals as barbaric and as provoking anti-Semitism; see C. Schroeder, "'Standing in the Breach': Turning Away the Wrath of God," *Int* 52 (1998): 17. But Girard's repeated references to sacrifice as a great pillar of *primitive* religion (*Things Hidden,* 154), to the *absurdity* of the sacrificial pact as somehow representative of God (ibid., 182), and to his desire to distinguish texts that support his claim of a nonviolent God as divine and those which do not as *harmful* and *unfortunate* (ibid., 155–58), to name a few, leave little doubt that he saw the OT system as something less than God's revealed word.

[62] For instance, M. Hardin identified the church fathers as failures for not recognizing that "there is no wholesale takeover of the Hebrew Scriptures in the NT," and he subsequently proposed expunging such inappropriate materials; see Hardin, "The Biblical Testaments as a Marriage of Convienience [*sic*]: Rene Girard and Biblical Interpretation," Presentation to the Colloquium on Violence and Religion, AAR/SBL Annual Meeting, 1990.

[63] Girard denies teaching that the world is getting less violent (*The Girard Reader* [New York: Crossroad, 1996], 274), his words clearly place a hope in human reason since he argued that as time progresses it becomes easier to convince people of the senselessness of violence (*The Scapegoat,* 201).

[64] Though ultimately skeptical of its origin in factuality and critical of its stance, J. J. Collins argued cogently that violence was indeed at the heart of Israel's conception of God; see Collins,

psalms, and prophetic utterances would have to be wholly abandoned if Girard's perception of God is accurate.[65] Finally, by removing the nature of sacrifice from the realm of actually performing *neither* expiation nor propitiation in relation to God, Girard has left humanity without a solution to its most significant problem—sin. It seems that Girard believed man's primary problem is ignorance and that the solution is enlightenment.[66] In contrast, Scripture declares that man's problem is sin, which is at the heart of one's understanding of God's wrath (and grace) and is also the starting point for understanding the *ḥērem* in a Christian context.

The relationship of the *ḥērem* to the practice of sacrifice has been somewhat debated. Though some scholars, such as Milgrom, have described the relationship as almost a one-to-one reality, there was distinctiveness in the nature of the "offerings" that ought to caution one against seeing the relationship so holistically.[67] That is, simply because the word *ḥērem*, or one of its derivatives, was used in a passage does not demand it was always in reference to the same thing.[68] Passages such as Lev 27:21,28 and Num 18:14 apparently refer to objects dedicated to Yahweh that were already a part of Israel's possessions, were therefore sacred, and could survive or be sacrificed. On the other hand, those that were under the ban in Deuteronomy 7; 20; Joshua 6; and 1 Samuel 15 were objects or persons that were

---

"The Zeal of Phinehas and the Legitimization of Violence," *JBL* 122 (2003): 3–21; see L. Morris, *The Apostolic Preaching of the Cross* (Grand Rapids: Eerdmans, 1956), 156.

[65] See Gen 19:14; Exod 15:3; 2 Chr 32:21; Ps 94:23; Isa 42:13; Jer 20:11; 51:11; Lam 2:8; Ezek 25:7; Amos 9:8; Zeph 2:5; 3:17. That these images are applied to Christ in Apocalyptic texts (2 Thess 2:8; Rev 19:21) was explained by Girard as being non-divine in origin and only illustrative of the mimetic crisis (*Things Hidden*, 185–90). He further argued that the sword Jesus said he brought in Matt 10:34 was a stripping away of mythological layers of religious thought that protected the persecutors and led the world towards resolution; see Girard, *I See Satan Fall Like Lightning* (Maryknoll, NY: Orbis Books, 1999), 174.

[66] Girard, *Things Hidden*, 201. He had suggested earlier that reconciliation with God can take place unreservedly and with no sacrificial intermediary through the rules of the kingdom; ibid., 183.

[67] J. Milgrom, "Profane Slaughter and a Formulaic Key to the Composition of Deuteronomy," *HUCA* 47 (1976): 1–17.

[68] Milgrom argued that since "the devoted thing" in Lev 27:28; Num 18:14; Ezek 44:29 was to be sacrificed, that Saul's actions in 1 Samuel 15 were a correct interpretation of laws surrounding the practice (ibid., 8). But one is hard pressed beyond the use of a common word to see in the context of these passages why it is necessary to make a correlation between that which was חרם because it had been dedicated to God and that which was חרם and under "the ban."

profane and therefore dedicated to God through destruction (not sacrifice), so they served a different purpose in the theology and life of Israel.

If we are even to begin to understand the place of the *ḥērem* in the Christian canon, we must begin with sin and its relationship to God's command. Gen 15:16 illuminates it: "In the fourth generation they will return here, for the iniquity of the Amorites has not yet reached its full measure." These words from God to Abram express both the centrality of sin in God's removal of the inhabitants of Canaan and His forbearance in delaying the activity. The implicit intent was that once sin reached its full measure, recovery was not an option and so only destruction remained. God echoed the same sentiment in Mal 4:6 when He threatened the same fate as the Canaanites should Israel not respond to the word of Elijah who was to come. The *ḥērem* did not grow out of a capricious act of God but was His response to people who were completely at odds with God's worldview, people who had apparently reached the point of no return.

A close companion to understanding the relationship of sin to the *ḥērem* is the necessary comprehension of corporate responsibility in OT perspectives. H. Wheeler Robinson made proposals early in the twentieth century that had a significant impact on understanding the relationship of the community as a whole to the individual in ancient Israelite thought. In many ways his theory falls apart because it is largely based on unfounded anthropological conclusions.[69] Nevertheless, the sin and punishment of Achan and his family (Joshua 7), the sense in which the sinfulness of the people also makes Isaiah sinful (Isa 6:5), and the interplay of sin and redemption of that sin evident in the Suffering Servant passages (Isaiah 53) all mean that Israel could view a group in light of the whole and vice versa, a realization that can hardly be denied.[70] Consequently,

---

[69] The 1980 release of Robinson's seminal works by Fortress has an introduction that appropriately outlines the deficiencies. See H. W. Robinson, *Corporate Personality in Ancient Israel* (Philadelphia: Fortress, 1980); also J. W. Rogerson, *Anthropology and the Old Testament*, 2d edition (Sheffield: JSOT Press, 1984), 55–59.

[70] Wheeler highlighted Gen 4:15,24; Exod 20:5; Deut 21:1–9, 25:5–10; Joshua 7; and 2 Samuel 21 as examples of this viewpoint, though there are others—including some in the NT (1 Corinthians 12; 15; Eph 4:16).

the near loss of a perspective of corporate responsibility in favor of the individualism prevalent today has created a major gap between the present and the biblical world. We must overcome this gap to see that the biblical perspective of a group as an organism in itself is partly behind the holistic command of the *ḥērem*, as the actions of some reap consequences for the whole.

Another key aspect of the *ḥērem* is that God made the command in order to preserve and protect Israel—not only through averting a bad influence, but also by confirming Israel's righteousness. God specifically stated in Deut 7:3–6 that His purpose in the command was to protect Israel from the influence of the Canaanites, a caution borne out by Israel's acceptance of such practices after its failure to fully carry out His commands (Judg 3:5–6; 1 Kgs 9:20–21). Positively, since the Israelites viewed God as a righteous judge and His perceptions of their righteousness played a role in whether they won or lost,[71] their victory at Jericho and in other situations served the function of reinforcing the value of righteousness. Furthermore, the encouragement to remain holy in the passages shows that the *ḥērem* was as much or more of an expression of Israel's devotion to God as it was a focus on the sinfulness of the Canaanites.[72]

Awareness of the multilayered status of revelation is also important to explain the rationale behind the *ḥērem*. God worked in history to reveal Himself to His people in a manner that is both consistent with His character and cognizant of the worldview of the people He addressed.[73] While we must certainly recognize the difference that the Incarnation makes and the finality that it offers, if all Scripture is inspired it will not do to label earlier revelation as somehow erroneous in how it portrays God. At the same time, the fact that God has chosen to reveal Himself to a specific era and people cannot be ignored as one seeks to explain events—God is indeed a God of history. It is axiomatic that cultures of different times and geographical settings

---

[71] R. Good, "The Just War in Ancient Israel," *JBL* 104 (1985): 385–400.

[72] Goldingay, *Old Testament Theology*, 501.

[73] The specific phraseology chosen here in contrast to "progressive revelation" is intended to express a distinction from the latter term by avoiding an appraisal of the earlier revelation as somehow inferior to the later ones. See the discussion of the authority of the OT in the Introduction.

understand their own relationship to reality differently. The world of the ancient Near East understood the realm of the gods as one in which military victory secured the position of a god as supreme. The biblical material alters, but does not abandon, such conceptions in what it teaches about Israel by acknowledging the juridical nature of warfare as Yahweh expressed His judgment over the nations and their gods.[74] Yes, there is a relativity to this concept, but it does not reside in whether the activity is morally right or wrong, but in the worldviews of the people being addressed. God knows and responds to the views of mankind, and in that light He reveals principles for His people that are completely consistent with His attributes. In other words, Yahweh used warfare as a tool to express His essence to Israel and to the nations in a manner that did not contradict His nature but also recognized their perspectives.

In attempting to understand the *ḥērem* one must also keep in mind the demonstration of God's grace even in the midst of His wrath. In particular, the story of Rahab portrays this truth. We must be careful not to read into the story a plan or strategy for converting the heathen,[75] although we might be tempted to travel in that direction, given Rahab's words to the spies:

> Before the men fell asleep, she went up on the roof and said to them, "I know that the LORD has given you this land and that dread of you has fallen on us, and everyone who lives in the land is panicking because of you. For we have heard how the LORD dried up the waters of the Red Sea before you when you came out of Egypt, *and what you did to Sihon and Og, the two Amorite kings you completely destroyed across the Jordan.* When we heard this, we lost heart, and everyone's courage failed because of you, *for the LORD your God is God in heaven above and on earth below.* Now please swear

---

[74] Good wrote that "war was conceived as a judicial activity. By this we mean that war was interpreted as the expression of *legal* judgment of Yahweh made for the purpose of resolving a dispute between Israel and neighboring states" ("The Just War," 387; emphasis in original).

[75] J. Milgrom argued that religious conversion was neither attested in ancient Israel nor possible prior to the second temple period; see Milgrom, "Religious Conversion and the Revolt Model for the Formation of Ancient Israel," *JBL* 101 (1982): 169. But his premise is built on an unwarranted division of the texts and a notion that the *ḥērem* texts were designed to undermine the legitimacy of the Davidic line. This supposition seems strange given the text's survival past the dissolution of the Northern Kingdom, who are the only ones who would have had such a motive, and given their inclusion in the canonical text of the pro-Davidic south. While this discussion argues that God's command did not have conversion as its motivation, Rahab's decision can hardly be described as anything less.

to me by the Lord that you will also show kindness to my family, because I showed kindness to you. Give me a sure sign that you will spare the lives of my father, mother, brothers, sisters, and all who belong to them, and save us from death (Josh 2:8–13, emphasis added).

However, taking the position that God intended to use the command to kill as a means of winning over the Canaanites would logically lead to the conclusion that conversion at the point of the sword has legitimacy in Scripture. Such a conclusion would be wrong on several accounts that require elucidation here.

The observation already made that warfare was a means of proclaiming the greatness and justice of a god in the ancient Near East does not necessarily lead to the conclusion that Yahweh would use them in terms of converting other nations. The method of conversion implemented in Scripture is always expressed in terms of benign persuasion, not vicious intimidation. It has been demonstrated above that God's sovereignty is evocative, not coercive. Why then would He implement a policy of severe coercion for His people to use towards other nations that He was not willing to employ Himself?

Furthermore, the basic supposition behind the concept of a multi-layered status of revelation is that it portrays a principle, but not necessarily actions, that are repeatable. The principle of the *ḥērem* is found both in the need to purge the sacred from the profane as God's holy people and in His standing as a just and righteous God. To apply the *method* today in a world that does not conceive of gods in the same way would actually be going against the *principle*. In other words, today such a method would actually indicate a people who are profaned through violence and a God who is neither just nor righteous. Therefore, the *ḥērem* is a non-repeatable event.

Finally, the consistent primary admonition of the *ḥērem* texts has been one of concern for maintaining Israel's holy position before God, not other nations' conversion. Therefore, Rahab and her family represent the exception to the law (grace), not the basis of it. She is the picture of God's graciousness, not the result of coerced conversion. The wondrous grace of Yahweh in preserving someone condemned to death under the *ḥērem*, when coupled with the Genesis 15 passage, demonstrates that He is indeed slow to anger and quick to forgive, but He will not leave the guilty unpunished (Num 14:18). The depth of His gracious activity is heightened all the more with the realization that not only were Rahab and her family spared, but she was also brought into David's lineage and ultimately into the Messiah's (Matt 1:5; Heb 11:31).

Such grace is thoroughly consistent with God's nature, but so too is the wrath that is demonstrated in the original command. One must recognize that wrath is one of the most frequently expressed divine actions in the OT and is viewed as essential to God's just and holy character.[76] Wrath in the OT is not malicious hatred and has nothing evil in its expression; instead, it is "the manifestation of the displeasure of God's unsearchable greatness."[77] As an expression of His character and essence, wrath is inextricable from Him in present theology, nor is it surprising that it is present in the NT as well (John 3:36; Rom 1:18; Eph 5:6; Rev 6:16–17). Indeed, while it is thoroughly appropriate to talk about the cross as the ultimate expression of God's love (Rom 5:8), it is additionally appropriate to speak of it as the ultimate expression of God's wrath (Isa 53:4–10; 2 Cor 5:21).[78] It does little good to attempt to quantify God's love or wrath in comparison to each other since God is the perfect expression of both. In His wrath we find our responsibility and His righteousness. In His love we find hope and grace. Neither without the other means anything.

No doubt the questions and issues will persist. Neither the short treatment given here nor the countless essays, sermons, and monographs on the issue will address the sensibilities of those who see in this command and texts evidence to bolster their belief that "the Bible, for all the wisdom it contains, is no infallible guide in ethical matters."[79] Certainly the final answer lies beyond our comprehension, leaving us to acknowledge that we must simply trust God

---

[76] E. Jacob, *Theology of the Old Testament*, trans. A. Heathcote and P. Allcock (New York: Harper & Brothers, 1958), 114. L. Morris identified twenty Hebrew words in 580 places that referred to God's wrath; see Morris, *Apostolic Preaching*, 131.

[77] W. Eichrodt, *Theology of the Old Testament*, OTL (Philadelphia: Westminster Press, 1961), 1:261.

[78] The innocence of the one who had the sins lain on Him by Yahweh is especially germane to the question at hand.

[79] Collins, "Phinehas," 20.

with that which is beyond us. Perhaps we must simply relegate the concept as a doctrine to a spiritual realm of purging the profane elements of life from the sacred spheres of operation. What we can say about the *ḥērem* command is that it was tempered by grace, centered in concern for those who were God's, and consistent with the revealed nature of God throughout the Scriptures.

Having addressed, at least provisionally, the consistency of the *ḥērem* command with the evangelical worldview, it now seems appropriate to examine the role such passages as those involving Jericho and Saul play in our understanding of patterns in worship. What might surprise us is that these events are portrayed as ones of worship in the biblical text. As such, they have something to say about the distinctiveness that God calls His people to as they live and come before Him in worship—Jericho in a mostly positive sense, and Saul as a negative example.

Israel's approach to Jericho, the instructions given to them by Yahweh, and the carrying out of those instructions have an almost liturgical feel to them as God hands the city over to Israel. So it is not surprising to find scholars who connect the story to a worship event, or even as a new creation in which God brought order and security into a chaotic world.[80] The *ḥērem* reminds Israel, and ultimately us, that the land and all the earth are Yahweh's and that their acquisition is a gift from Him.[81] Since everything is God's, and He has won the victory, He gets the spoils.[82] Expressing thankfulness by devoting ourselves, our victories, and our possessions to God is at the heart of much that constitutes worship. Though the manner and method are non-repeatable, the principle and intention remain.

Saul's failure with the Amalekites resided primarily in two spheres—his double-mindedness and his self-interest. Saul's double-mindedness rested in his failure to recognize that the profane could not be confused with the sacred. Saul is reminiscent of Cain in this passage in that he brought a sacrifice that cost him little or

---

[80] The former description can be found in Goldingay, *Old Testament Theology*, 492–94, and the latter in P. Stern, *Biblical Herem: A Window on Israel's Religious Experience* (Atlanta: Scholars' Press, 1991), 218.

[81] Goldingay, *Old Testament Theology*, 495.

[82] J. Creach, *Joshua*, INT (Louisville: John Knox Press, 2003), 75–76.

nothing.[83] As objects that were under the *ḥērem*, they already belonged to God, so they were not his to give in the sense one might give an offering. Further, as objects under the *ḥērem*, they were items that were profane and unworthy to be brought into the realm of sacrifice where only the best could be offered.[84] Instead, they had to be dedicated through destruction. The tension here is significant. The *ḥērem* demands recognition that although everything is God's, He requires distinctions to be drawn in how we bring them before Him. Since God is holy and requires His people to be holy, mixing the holy with the profane is yet another example of man placing his priorities above God's. As the story of Rahab illustrates, the measure is not a call to ethnic purity, nor is it an encouragement to ignore one's responsibility to a lost world. Instead, the *ḥērem* at this point manifestly calls for purity of attitude and the true meaning of *distinctiveness*. In short, there is a difference in how the people of God carry out a task and how the pagan world does.

Saul expressed self-interest in much the same way as Achan in the book of Joshua—he placed a higher priority on his desires and those of his people than God's. As Creach put it, the *ḥērem* is actually about the values of two worlds. The command makes it clear that one cannot profit at the expense of faith.[85] Things that rival God in our hearts cannot be instruments of worship before Him. Worship by definition is the commitment to God's principles and precepts and a recognition that we give what He seeks—not what we desire when we worship—without compromise and without reservation.

## Prayer—The Conversation of Worship

The patterns of service and distinctiveness advocate a portrayal of the life of the person of God to the world. But it is in the pattern of prayer that one finds the resources to be able to accomplish such tasks. For prayer, at its heart, is one of God's most effective methods of altering human perspective and also granting access to His power.

---

[83] See the discussion of the nature of Cain's sacrifice above (chapter 1).

[84] See the response to Milgrom's objections ("Profane Slaughter," 8) to such a proposal above (n. 67).

[85] Creach, *Joshua*, 75.

It is the communication of the created with the Creator, "communication" reflecting the fact that it is a two-way event. It is an opportunity for humans to bring their needs and their praises before the only One who can meet them and who is worthy of them.

In the Former Prophets there are numerous waters one could navigate within the goal of discussing prayer. Dealing adequately with prayer could well fill its own volume, as few narratives proceed without the mentioning of a prayer being offered in some manner. This is as it should be in texts designed to explicate the rich variety of ways that God effects change and moves along human history. Unfortunately, time and space provide the opportunity for only a passing examination of this important pattern in the life of those who are God's. The prayer of Solomon in 1 Kings 8 provides a special insight not only into the king's views of God but also into the very nature of prayer itself. The petition of Hannah in 1 Samuel 1 is a prototypical example of someone who took a severe situation to the One she knew was sovereign and able to meet her needs. Hannah's subsequent prayer in 1 Samuel 2 offers insights into how intimately God is involved in the lives of His people and serves as one of the purest forms of adoration and thanks in Scripture.

On what basis does one approach God in prayer? Or to put it another way, what gives any person the notion that as a lowly fallen creature, he has the ability and right to go before a holy righteous Creator with his or her needs? Certainly, the doctrine of man as the image of God has something to say about this question. The opening chapter of this book concludes that being created in the image of God reflects our status as representatives of God to each other and the world. A similar conclusion is that God's creation of humans in His image means we must not attempt to return the favor and create images of Him, as the second Commandment clearly forbids. Also, in light of the second Commandment's concern about God's vastness and eminence, we have also recognized that being created in the image of God is granted by Him as a special status of relationship as a result of both His condescension and our elevation. Clearly, such a creation is empowering while at the same time humbling.[86]

---

[86] D. McBride, "Divine Protocol: Genesis 1:1–2:3 as Prologue to the Pentateuch," in *God*

There is an enabling for prayer made possible by the relationship that exists in being created in God's image, for no other creature has been granted that privilege.[87] Along with this enablement, however, comes a stricture of personal responsibility. Because the challenge of reflecting God is all encompassing—not limited to religious aspects but to every instance of life—there are clear links between how one lives and the prayers that one is able to pray (see Jer 11:14; Matt 6:1–18). Solomon expressed all of these factors in his prayer at the dedication of the temple in 1 Kings 8.

The actual prayer of Solomon at the dedication of the temple appears in 1 Kgs 8:22–53. But Solomon's opening and closing remarks are important for understanding both his intention and the theological underpinnings that directed his prayer in the posture he prayed it. This then sets a framework for discussing his prayer as including all of 1 Kgs 8:14–61.

The event makes important contributions to many theological discussions, but none as overwhelmingly as what it has to say about prayer. Solomon's prayer transforms the image of the temple from being a house solely dedicated to sacrifice to being a house of prayer.[88] He makes this point forcefully by omitting any discussion of sacrifice in his prayer and by offering the prayer in the presence of the altar (1 Kgs 8:22). This would have reminded Israel of its covenant benefits and responsibilities.[89] Furthermore, this transformation highlights the central role that prayer has always played in Israel's thought and theology.[90] Interestingly, the bases for Solomon's prayer, both implicit and explicit, allow one to peruse the theol-

---

*Who Creates: Essays in Honor of W. Sibley Towner*, ed. W. Brown and D. McBride (Grand Rapids: Eerdmans, 2000), 16.

[87] M. Thompson, *I Have Heard Your Prayer: The Old Testament and Prayer* (Peterborough, UK: Epworth Press, 1996), 4.

[88] S. Balentine, *Prayer in the Hebrew Bible: The Drama of Divine-Human Dialogue* (Minneapolis: Fortress, 1993), 50.

[89] Ibid., 85–86.

[90] The common notion among scholarship that Solomon's prayer was redacted during the exilic era in order to downplay the importance of sacrifice for a people who could not perform them is unnecessary and unwarranted. The temple dedication concluded with exorbitant sacrifices and, as noted above, each sacrifice required the presence of prayer from the earliest appearance of them in Israel's cult. Therefore, the theological connection of prayer and the altar of God would not be too difficult of a leap for someone in Solomon's place to make.

ogy behind why one can pray.[91] This is true because in many ways Solomon's prayer is actually "a prayer *about* prayer."[92]

The theological content of Solomon's prayer is easily identifiable and dividable into sections that integrate with each other, so that they represent more than just the concepts associated with them. Such an amalgamation of thought and insight demonstrates the interweaving of life and practice in a way that a discourse on such interrelatedness never could. There are three theological foundations in the accompanying texts that speak clearly about how to approach God in prayer: the reputation of God (1 Kgs 8:15–19a,21–23), the promises of God (1 Kgs 8:19b–20,24–26,53–61), and the character of God (1 Kgs 8:27–52).

The reputation of God as a basis for assurance in prayer is grounded firmly in Israel's view of history. As mentioned above, the aspect of remembrance for Israel was a significant function of its worship. Through understanding how God related to previous generations, one builds a confidence and understanding in how He relates to us. Solomon's primary focus was on God's relationship with his father, David. Such emphasis is not surprising since that is the association with which Solomon would have had the most direct affinity and the one that would most thoroughly impact his own life and reign. But Solomon also drew from Israel's collective history, primarily the exodus, as a means of understanding one's relationship with God that is central to prayer. His utilization of the "name" theology to illustrate Yahweh's closeness, yet separateness and freedom, most clearly suggests a link to the "I am" passage in Exodus 3.[93]

The "I am" statement, regardless of how one renders it, is best understood in relational terms. For God to be able to say, "I am who I was," "I am who I will be," or "I will be who I was," all of which are

---

[91] The discussion of Solomon's prayer by P. House (*1–2 Kings*, NAC [Nashville: B&H, 1995], 143–44) served as a catalyst for many of the points found in this section. House identified four reasons for Solomon's confidence in the prayer: (1) God has revealed himself in the past; (2) God has a covenant with Israel; (3) God promised the temple would be built; and (4) God's character is consistent with such a confidence.

[92] G. Savran, "1 and 2 Kings," in *The Literary Guide to the Bible*, ed. R. Alter and F. Kermode (Cambridge: Belknap, 1987), 157.

[93] R. Nelson's discussion of the "name theology" is illuminating, though he does not draw a direct connection to Exodus 3 (*First and Second Kings*, INT [Atlanta: John Knox Press, 1987], 59).

legitimate renderings of the sentence, is for God to say, in essence, if you want to know Me, notice how I have acted in the past. Such a revelation calls for confidence not only in present concerns but in future hopes—for God will always be who He has been.[94] Solomon built off this perspective as he drew Israel together in relationship to the temple. The building that stood before the people had to be understood in light of the previous events of not only Sinai (where God revealed and bound himself to Israel), but of Shiloh (where God judged the people for making the ark more important than him). In short, the consistency of God's reputation gives power and meaning to God's promises that also find expression in the prayer.

Dealing with the promises of God is always a perilous undertaking. These expressions in Scripture of God's provision for people or for a person are always a desirable commodity to be claimed by modern readers. Whether it is passages like Prov 22:6, which are limited by their genre, or ones like Jer 29:11, which are limited by their historical context, people often inappropriately transform comments from the Scripture into promises for themselves. Therefore, when one is writing a theology that is attempting to bridge the gaps between the ancient world and the present, there is a certain trepidation that comes into play when raising questions about promises.

The promises of Yahweh that Solomon highlights are all covenant expressions made between God and Israel. It seems appropriate to pause for a moment to focus on the idea of covenant since it has significant implications for prayer in particular and worship in general. The Hebrew word for covenant is *běrît*, but beyond this fact there are few areas of agreement among scholars. At least four roots have been identified as the basis for *běrît*, with meanings such as "bind," "between," "eat," and "select."[95] James Barr was correct in his conclusion that the term is probably one of extreme antiquity and is not derived from another word, and so it has a meaning that can only be derived from the information in the OT.[96] In the OT the

---

[94] R. Abba, "The Divine Name Yahweh," *JBL* 80 (1961): 325–28.

[95] W. Zimmerli, *Old Testament Theology in Outline* (Atlanta: John Knox Press, 1978), 49.

[96] J. Barr, "Some Semantic Notes on Covenant," in *Beiträge zur alttestamentlichen Theologie: Festschrift für Walther Zimmerli zum 70. Geburtstag*, ed. H. Donner et al. (Göttingen: Vandenhoeck und Ruprecht, 1977), 35.

term appears in connection with the ideas of "a binding agreement" (Neh 9:38 [Hb. 10:1] *'ămānâ*) and "law" (Deut 29:21 [Hb. 29:20] *tôrâ*). Such observations, however, offer little to explain exactly what is meant.

The topic of ancient Near Eastern parallels to the concept of covenant is as debated and convoluted as are the etymological arguments. George Mendenhall began the conversation through his comparisons of the biblical covenant idea to Hittite treaties. He argued that as the Hittite king consolidated his sovereignty over a country by means of a treaty that prescribed proper behavior, Israel was bound together by God in a similar manner.[97] While this approach has held sway over much of the scholarship done on the issue, objections have arisen about various elements of the idea.[98] The various treaties may have something to say about the form that the covenant took in the OT, but it does not necessarily follow that there is a comparison to be made about the exact nature of the stipulations contained in both.[99] Such is especially true when one looks at the Abrahamic and Davidic covenants that contain few, if any, regulations on the human participants and focus primarily on the promises of God.

So what can be said about the idea of covenant? First, the parallel covenantal expressions of the OT suggest a legal context for understanding the function of covenants. That is, they convey a relationship that is both binding and regulated. The power and force of this legal agreement resided solely in the promises of God.[100] It is because He is immutable and righteous that Israel could find confidence in the promises—not because the people were somehow worthy of it. Second, the covenant made between God and Israel was one of free choice to which both parties acceded—God for no expressed reason, and Israel because it would have been foolish to turn it down.[101] Third, it may be helpful to divide the covenants of

---

[97] G. Mendenhall, *Law and Covenant in Israel* (Pittsburgh: The Biblical Colloquium, 1955), 24–27.

[98] Most notably, E. Nicholson argued that the theory "yielded little of value"; see Nicholson, *God and His People: Covenant and Theology in the Old Testament* (Oxford: Clarendon, 1986), 71.

[99] J. Bright, *Covenant and Promises* (Philadelphia: Westminster Press, 1976), 43.

[100] See C. Barth, *God with Us* (Grand Rapids: Eerdmans, 1991), 52.

[101] Nicholson, *God and His People*, vii-viii.

the OT into separate intentions and results. Some of the covenants seem to be more administrative in that they offer direction and order (such as the Sinaitic covenant). Other covenants are more promissory and carry with them the simple aspect of what God will do in the future with the people to whom He relates (such as the Noahic and Davidic covenants).[102] It is necessary to note, however, that at the heart of all the covenants is the desire for relationship. Even those that are promissory in nature make their promises for the sake of expanding the people's capacity for service in a meaningful and enlightening way.

All the covenants of the Bible emphasize a God who provides for His people in extravagant and wonderful ways and who expects them in return to acknowledge that He alone is God.[103] Only the Noahic covenant can be said to be universal in its application and meaning.[104] The others find expression specifically to Israel or to sub-groups within Israel. This is not to say that they do not have application outside the context of historical Israel, but only that when one looks at the statements of Solomon about his expectations of God's interaction, one needs to keep in mind that his exposition was primarily based on promises that God made to him and his people, who are in a unique relationship with Him. As Christians who also receive promises in our covenant with God, we, like Solomon, can find confidence in the application of that covenant and expectations for our behavior in it. We can move forward confident in tomorrow because of who God has been in the past, including who He was for Solomon and Israel in relation to the temple.

The section of the Solomonic prayer that focuses on the character of God is derived directly from His covenant promises. Solomon outlines seven occasions on which one might approach the Temple to pray (vv. 31–51). Of these seven occasions, almost all of them

---

[102] See T. McComiskey, *The Covenants of Promise: A Theology of the Old Testament Covenants* (Grand Rapids: Baker, 1985).

[103] A. Jepsen, "Berith, Ein Beitrag zur Theologie der Exilszeit," in *Verbanung und Heimkehr, Wilheim Rudolph zum 70. Geburtstag*, ed. A. Kusskhe (Tübingen: Mohr, 1961), 161–79.

[104] The supposed idea of an Adamic covenant finds no support in the biblical material. As W. T. Conner put it, "somebody has well said that the [Adamic] covenant originated in Holland rather than in the Garden of Eden"; see Conner, *The Gospel and Redemption* (Nashville: Broadman Press, 1945), 29–30.

were dire and dangerous situations. In fact, five of the seven situations arose directly from the covenant stipulations of Deuteronomy 28.[105] But beyond the covenant aspect of each one, the occasions themselves serve to portray God as great and incomparable yet intimately involved in the lives of His people.[106] These situations also serve to underline the interplay of the various theological concepts that explain how we should understand God and His relationship to His people. There is a tension that must always be maintained between God's grace and His justice. Nowhere is that more true than in prayer, where people must never be presumptuous about receiving what they desire, and yet they must not forget the lavish grace of God when boldly going before Him in prayer.

Hannah's petition in 1 Samuel 1 represents one of the most personal reflections of prayer in Scripture. Hannah portrayed her prayer as "pouring out my heart before the LORD" (1 Sam 1:15). The intimate nature of her prayer is reflected in an almost universal concept of need for God and commitment to God that few people have not found themselves expressing at one time or another. Without a doubt Hannah's prayer provides an opportunity to examine the depths of sorrow that sometimes drives us to our knees in a way few texts can. This is true both because of the clearly human elements in its content and because the sorrow is clearly tempered by hope and trust.[107]

The setting for Hannah's prayer is significant for understanding its content and theology. Hannah was the first wife of Elkanah and had not been able to have children. Elkanah's second wife Peninnah had given him both sons and daughters. The rivalry was apparently considerable—the text states that Hannah received special treatment from Elkanah and that Peninnah continuously taunted her severely because she was without children. Her childless status would

---

[105] Nelson, *First and Second Kings*, 53.

[106] Thompson, *I Have Heard*, 186.

[107] This is not to say that other laments do not have value. But the laments in Psalms and in Lamentations are often anonymous (or at least decontextualized) or are firmly rooted in a national dilemma. Hannah's lament is distinctly individualistic in expression, though the resulting birth would have national implications. Those implications that are probably behind the preservation of the event are adequately explained by Thompson (*I Have Heard*, 26) and P. Miscall (*1 Samuel: A Literary Reading* [Bloomington, IN: Indiana Univ. Press, 1986], 11).

have carried with it the added weight of the perception that she was cursed.[108] The text relates several times that it was Yahweh who had prevented her from conceiving (1 Sam 1:5–6), which is consistent with the biblical perspective of God as intimately involved in all aspects of human life. Finally, it is quite ironic that her prayer for God to have pity on her misery took place at a yearly trek to the sanctuary to sacrifice and celebrate before God for His provision in their lives. This ironic twist only augments the tension created by her rivalry with Peninnah, her apparently cursed status, and her belief that Yahweh was responsible for her miserable state. Accepting the lack of provision in an area of life held so important to both one's self and one's culture is acutely more difficult during such times of celebration of God's provision in so many other spheres. Indeed, Hannah was apparently so overwhelmed by the experience that she did not even notice the presence of the chief priest Eli as she began to pray.[109]

The recorded portion of Hannah's prayer is rather brief: "LORD of Hosts, if You will take notice of Your servant's affliction, remember and not forget me, and give Your servant a son, I will give him to the LORD all the days of his life, and his hair will never be cut (1 Sam 1:11). There is certainly more to the prayer than these words, as the prayer probably followed the normal conventions of laments at the time.[110] But it is these words that the writer revealed, so it is these words that we must examine. To be certain, the major motivating factor for the inclusion of these specific words was to emphasize the dedicated and special nature of the birth and life of Samuel.[111] Beyond this factor, there was also the belief that since there was

---

[108] P. Miller, *They Cried to the Lord: The Form and Theology of Biblical Prayer* (Minneapolis: Fortress, 1994), 237.

[109] J. Baldwin, *1 and 2 Samuel*, TOTC (Leicester: Inter-Varsity, 1988), 52.

[110] Miller, *They Cried*, 237–38.

[111] The claim that the text originally served as a birth narrative for Saul rather than Samuel is a topic beyond the interests of this text. The repeated use of the verb שׁאל "to ask," from which the name Saul is derived, is instructive of the writer's purpose, namely, contrasting Saul with both Samuel and David. Further, there are strong grammatical and theological reasons for viewing the text as a birth narrative of Samuel from the outset. See P. K. McCarter, *I Samuel*, AB (Garden City: Doubleday, 1980), 62; and J. Ackerman, "Who Can Stand before YHWH, This Holy God? A Reading of 1 Samuel 1–15," *Proof* 11 (1991): 3–4.

a theological cause for her distress (that is, "the LORD had kept Hannah from conceiving"), there must also be a theological answer to her distress (that is, "LORD of Hosts, if You will take notice of Your servant's affliction, remember and not forget me . . ."). The language is covenantal in force and reminiscent of the reflections in Exod 2:24–25.

In an age centered on scientific explanations for so much, it might seem easy enough to interpret God's active hand on our lives as old-fashioned superstition, or at the very least, as over-theologizing a physical problem. Such thinking is antithetical to a Christian world-view that understands the supernatural element in life and that knows God—who created everything—is certainly capable of altering the contents of His creation as His will sees fit. On the other hand, to go the route of those who eschew medical treatment in general because of an expressed faith that God will "take care of it" certainly oversteps the intention of passages such as this one. In the end, it is Hannah's desperation that characterized the approach she took. She found herself in a difficult situation that was beyond human intervention. Miller put it well: "Her bitter weeping is evoked by God's withholding of her greatest need, and neither the absence of any reason for that nor a theological analysis of her sterility could alleviate her suffering."[112] In short, in situations such as Hannah's there is little that reason or even medicine can offer a person. The only remedy for such hopelessness is the intervention of God Himself, for no one else can offer the help He can. Nothing else will ever produce the hope He does. Such a realization is both the starting point and the denouement of *all* prayer. Notice that the woman who left the celebration distraught returned with a confidence that transformed her very countenance—even before she learned she was pregnant (1 Sam 1:18).[113]

Another distinctive feature of Hannah's prayer that is important for understanding the relationship between prayer and other matters of worship is her use of the name for God, *yhwh ṣĕbāʾôt*, "LORD of Hosts." This narrative is the first place that the name appears

---

[112] Miller, *They Cried*, 238.
[113] Baldwin, *1 and 2 Samuel*, 53.

canonically. The general explanation concerning its meaning is that it was linked to Yahweh's status as the commander of His armies (or "hosts") who do His bidding—whether they be heavenly bodies (Neh 9:6; Isa 40:26), humans (1 Sam 17:45), or angels (1 Kgs 22:19). The name was also clearly related to Yahweh's status as the majestic King of all the universe (Ps 24:9; Zech 14:16) and Creator of all that is (Jer 10:16).[114] But the use of the name is not some magical incantation whereby Hannah intended to incur God's favor. Had it been, one might expect the use of *yhwh yir'eh*, "Yahweh will see/provide" (see Gen 22:14) or *'ēl rŏ'î*, "the God who will see" (see Gen 16:13). Instead, Hannah used the name that was associated with the region and that was already a part of her worship (see 1 Sam 1:3)—that is, she went to God in prayer reflecting on Him as she knew and related to Him. Prayer, being a relational conversation between two persons, can only reflect the intimacy between those two people in the names by which they know each other. It is not an opportunity for manipulation or self-service.

This last observation draws one into the question of whether Hannah's vow represented some sort of bargaining with God. H. W. Hertzberg observed, "Her pledge to consecrate the longed-for boy to the service of the sanctuary is meant to make the Lord willing to fulfill her requests."[115] The human tendency in dire situations such as Hannah's is to resort to bargaining, and it must be admitted that her motives were probably mixed in this regard.[116] But Hannah's whole demeanor in the prayer and afterward was one of total submission and servanthood to Yahweh and His representative.[117] A person with this perspective would hardly have presumed that such an offer would earn God's favor. Additionally, her use of "LORD of Hosts" as a salutation, with its monarchial and creator background, suggests

---

[114] *TWOT*, "צְבָאוֹת"; Baldwin, *1 and 2 Samuel*, 51.

[115] H. W. Hertzberg, *I & II Samuel*, 2d edition, trans. J. S. Bowden, OTL (London: SCM Press, 1960), 25.

[116] Baldwin, *1 and 2 Samuel*, 50.

[117] Note Hannah's repeated use of the word אָמָה ("maid-servant, female slave") and its synonym שִׁפְחָה, which has the same meaning ("female slave, maid-servant"; KB³, "אָמָה", and "שִׁפְחָה"). She used אָמָה three times in the prayer itself (HCSB substitutes the 1cs pronoun for one of these) and once in responding to Eli in v. 16 (again HCSB substitutes "me"). She used שִׁפְחָה in 1:18.

recognition of Yahweh's status as owner of everything. How could one bargain in offering something to the one who already owns everything? Instead, the vow seems more a recognition that any child born through her barren womb would by nature be a gracious gift from Yahweh, and therefore he could function only in service to Him.[118]

If Hannah's prayer of petition plumbs the depths of the desperate person before God, her prayer of praise scales the heights of the person before God in thanksgiving and adoration. The prayer (1 Sam 2:1–10) is often called the "Song of Hannah" because of its form and structure. But the narrative introduction to the words of praise identify them as the activity of "praying" *(pālal)*, so it seems safe to address her communication this way (1 Sam 2:1). Baldwin addressed the relationship well when she asserted: "Homemade prayers still echo phraseology familiar from worship."[119] In other words, in praying to God in thanksgiving Hannah used the terms, expressions, and forms that she had always associated with praising God. This does not diminish the power or feeling behind the words. Rather, it accentuates the fact that in our most energized moments of worship (or even other exchanges) it is quite appropriate to express words and ideas that have come to mean so much to us in previous experiences.[120]

Hannah's prayer was one of complete adoration and thanks. There was not a single request in it anywhere![121] The words reflect on a God who is intimately involved in the lives of everyday people, but who is Himself beyond the confines of Shiloh or even Israel. He is, in fact, the God of all creation—from the depths of Sheol to the heights of the highest heavens.[122] The fact that she had just delivered Samuel

---

[118] Baldwin, *1 and 2 Samuel*, 52.

[119] Ibid., 56.

[120] This explanation also answers the seeming detachment of the terminology in the prayer from the events that immediately preceded it (such as the references to "bows of warriors"). Balentine's suggestion that such terms functioned to draw the prayer from an individual deliverance to a national deliverance (Balentine, *Prayer*, 219) may well represent why it is included in the text, but it seems unnecessary in terms of explaining why Hannah herself might have uttered such words.

[121] Thompson, *I Have Heard*, 27–28.

[122] Miscall, *1 Samuel*, 15.

to the service of Yahweh moments before says something more about the power of sacrificial giving. Hannah's joy was not only grounded in the fact that God answered her prayer but also in the comprehensiveness of ecstasy that came from a person who had found God to be worthy of praise simply because of who He is.[123] Hannah realized in experience what she had suspected in theology: "Her God controlled the providential ordering of the world, and therefore she need have no anxiety."[124]

In Solomon's prayer are many of the theological underpinnings and expressions important to understanding how prayer works. In Hannah's two prayers are examples of experiencing God at the two poles of human experience: unrelenting sorrow and unspeakable joy. No doubt the vast majority of prayers are somewhere between these two poles. Yet this may be one of those rare occasions where it is the extremes of a situation that best characterize its nature and function. Like Hannah, all those who pray must find a willingness to go to God, holding nothing back in either sorrow or joy, for only in full disclosure will one find the relief that only God can offer. His answer may not be as dramatic or as aligned with our desires as Hannah's was,[125] but if we remember that prayer is a conversation so we can listen for God's response, there will no doubt be a transformation of spirit that only He can render.

## Patterns in the NT

> Therefore since we also have such a large cloud of witnesses surrounding us, let us lay aside every weight and the sin that so easily ensnares us, and run with endurance the race that lies before us, keeping our eyes on Jesus, the source and perfecter of our faith, who for the joy that lay before Him endured a cross and despised the shame, and has sat down at the right hand of God's throne. For consider Him who endured such hostility from sinners against Himself, so that you won't grow weary and lose heart (Heb 12:1–3).

Worship as a way of life and as an expression at a specific event or time often grows out of remembering the saints of old. They walked

---

[123] Baldwin, *1 and 2 Samuel*, 56.
[124] Ibid.
[125] Clearly, her request was in line with the broader will of God, though she could not know this when she prayed.

a path before our God that can teach us much. It also grows out of our relationship with Jesus Christ. The writer of Hebrews encapsulated much of what has been said about patterns of worship. Remembrance is one key to the sustenance and strengthening of our walk. To model ourselves after the source and perfecter of our faith, we must lay aside the trap of self-interest so characteristic of idolatry, looking towards the goal of being a distinctive people committed to the service of our Lord, who ignored the shame of His path for the sake of His people. With the fervor and passion of the OT prophets, the writer of Hebrews admonished believers to endure, mindful that the indwelling Spirit and the transformed life are what make such a commitment and journey possible in the end.

## Remembrance

It would be difficult to identify a service with more pathos yet joy, remembrance yet foresight, and universality yet individualism than the Lord's Supper. Jesus' instruction in Luke 22:19 that we carry out this act in remembrance of Him established the principle of remembrance around the central event of human history—the cross of Christ (see 1 Cor 11:24–25). Countless Christians through the centuries have taken part in this sacred and significant ceremony, mindful to reflect the event in the way it was taught to them and to explain it to their children as they also grow and the faith becomes their own. The corporate memory of the cross of Christ experienced in this one event transcends cultures, eras, and continents, and it invites us into the realization that we are not alone in our sorrows, joys, and journeys.

The final speeches of Jesus and Paul, like those of Joshua and David, leave us with reflections of whom we represent and where our worship ought to lead. Jesus reminded us that the goal of all we do is to introduce others to a life-changing relationship with the Triune God, and He promised that He would always be with us (Matt 28:18–20). Indeed, it is the power and encouragement of the examples throughout both the OT and the NT of God's presence that so overpoweringly bridge the gulf between what has happened in the past and what will happen in the future. Paul's farewell discourses are many. He encouraged the church to guard the faith (Gal 6:1–16; Phil 4:8–9), guard our fidelity (Col 4:2–6; 2 Tim 4:1–4), and guard the fellowship (2 Cor 13:11–14; Rom 16:17–18). This establishes the direction that our service and distinctiveness should go as we come together as a community of faith. As seemingly the last words Paul left with the churches to whom he ministered, they represent Paul's primary desires for who we would be as a covenant people.

## Idolatry

The NT is quite clear that an idol is nothing to those who are in Christ (1 Cor 8:4–6), yet we are continually warned against idolatry (1 Cor 10:14; Gal 5:20; 1 Pet 4:3; 1 John 5:21). There is little question that the NT world was much more like the OT world regarding the presence of physical idols than the Western world is today. There was still a struggle because of the prevalence of idolatry in the surrounding religions from which many new Christians arrived in faith, and this manifested itself in a struggle for how Christians ought to relate to these matters (see 1 Corinthians 8). Paul advocated a radical position of freedom before God that is balanced with responsibility before one's fellow man. In the worship wars of the present where a style of worship itself has become an idol before which too many of us bow, we would do well to heed the warnings of the apostle as we seek to express our freedom and yet build up our brothers in Christ.

Paul himself took the position that self-interest and self-promotion are forms of idolatry: "Therefore, put to death whatever in you is worldly: sexual immorality, impurity, lust, evil desire, and greed, which is idolatry" (Col 3:5). Colossians 3 advocates selflessness and submission of our desires to God's. It is not surprising that Paul's injunctions to such behavior climax with instructions involving worship and its role: "Let the message about the Messiah dwell richly among you, teaching and admonishing one another in all wisdom, and singing psalms, hymns, and spiritual songs, with gratitude in your hearts to God" (vv. 15–16). A person who has not set aside self in the presence of the Other will never find the ability to worship in any meaningful sense of the word.

## Service, Distinctiveness, and Prayer

That the NT advocates obedience to the laws of Christ can hardly be questioned (see Rom 6:16; 2 Cor 9:13; Jas 2, 4; 1 Pet 1:22). And the laws of Christ are encapsulated in his mandates to "Love the Lord your God with all your heart, with all your soul, with all your mind, and with all your strength," and to "Love your neighbor as yourself" (Mark 12:29–31), which is the very essence of the convergence of worship with service and distinctiveness. To love God the way Jesus advocated is the heart of worship. It mandates a purging of the profane in our commitments as we come into the sacred. To love God in this way results in a distinctiveness that avoids our being confused with a world that does not know Him. Because the instruction is irrevocably coupled with loving our neighbor, we see an insoluble correlation between worship and service that NT writers are no less likely to point out than those of the OT (see Matt 25:34–40; Rom 12:9–21; 2 Cor 9:6–15; 5:13–26; Jas 2:14–17; 1 Pet 4:7–11).

The instructions in the NT regarding the basis of prayer are also built on our special relationship with God as well as His reputation, His promises, and His character. The narratives of the NT also promote an understanding that the prayers of our spiritual forbears motivate our prayers as well, since God is indeed faithful and consistent (Acts 12:1–10; 21:5). The covenant afforded us through Christ is accentuated with a promise of access to God unparalleled in other religions (Hebrews 4). Indeed, God's status as our loving Father is at the foundation of both how and why we pray (Matt 6:5–13).

Concerning the practice of prayer, the NT writers instruct believers about prayer in ways that are reflective of the lessons of prayer found in the narrative of the life of Hannah. They promoted prayer as a constant reality in life (Rom 12:12; Phil 4:6; 1 Thess 5:16–22). They taught that the intense prayer of the righteous can accomplish many things (Jas 5:15). Even in the most difficult and trying of situations, the first response they advocated is that of prayer (Rom 8:18–27; Eph 6:18–19). In fact, in the extremes of both joy and sorrow, their instructions are to pray (Jas 5:13). Indeed, did not the Savior Himself pray in the midst of His most trying and difficult experience (Mark 14:32–42, esp. vv. 33–34)?

Hannah's prayer of praise is mirrored in the NT by Mary's prayer (Luke 1:46–55). Each woman faced an experience in which God filled a womb that by all accounts should not have held a baby. Of course, Mary's conceiving a child when she was a virgin was different than Hannah's situation—Hannah had been married and barren for years—but in both events the child's birth occurred by God's control and power as He manifested Himself in history and life. Thus, both women became "testifiers to the impossibilities and wonders that cannot be figured out."[126] This is the power of prayer. It accomplishes what nothing else can—not only in transforming the reality of the world, but also in elevating humans from mere observers of God's activities to being participants in His divine majesty.

## Conclusions

The struggles in the Former Prophets to find a means of applying the foundations outlined in the Pentateuch continue today. Walking the fine line between legalism and licentiousness is a difficult path to navigate: the former undermines our task and elevates ourselves, while the latter may feel good but has no grounding in mandates to service. Developing a pattern of worship involves more than establishing a way of carrying out a task. It requires a holistic look at one's life in service to others and one's position before God. It requires openness, not only to what God wants to do in the future but to what He has already done in the past. Most of all, it requires a transformed heart that only Christ can bring as we walk the path He has already authored and journeyed on before us.

---

[126] Miller, *They Cried*, 243.

# Chapter 4

## *THE LATTER PROPHETS: ATTITUDES IN WORSHIP*

Why does one worship God? Already we have seen in the words of Samuel that worship must arise from an attitude of selflessness and the recognition of our place of lowliness before an awesome God who demands much from us. This understanding deepens as one examines the approaches of the Latter Prophets. Behind their robust proclamations and sometimes even quizzical actions is an advocacy of a position before God in service and appreciation that stretches the imagination, constrains the heart, and increases our understanding of OT worship as it relates to how we view worship in today's church. The prophets challenge us to evaluate not so much the *how* of worship as discussed in the previous chapters, but the *why*. They call us to evaluate and change, where necessary, our own attitudes about worship.

## The Prophets and Prophetic Texts

The prophets and their texts present special problems in interpretation, especially for the evangelical.[1] This fact is true because of the way the office of prophet has become associated primarily with prediction. The rich variety and distinctiveness present in each prophet is often lost as interpreters seek to unlock or discover a unified picture of what the prophets would have us understand about where the world is heading. Topics such as the prophets and worship are then left to others who would simply see in their expressions an opportunity to reconstruct the social conditions of the perceived battle between the prophets and the priests. Before moving on to discuss the prophet and worship, therefore, it is helpful to appraise the office of the prophet and to further develop methodologies for interpreting the prophetic texts.

---

[1] Certain portions of the text that follows here and the sections involving Micah below are from the writer's previously published article, "Micah as a Case Study for Preaching and Teaching the Prophets," *SwJT* 46 (2003): 77–94. Used by permission.

## The Prophet

The previous chapter of this book discussed the perceived antipathy between the prophet and the cult, but our observations left open the question of exactly how the prophet would have behaved in relation to the cult. As mentioned before, Aubrey Johnson made a strong case for the role of the prophet as being primarily cultic in nature.[2] He made three observations based on the content of the biblical material. First, the common expressions in the statements of the canonical prophets in which both priests and prophets were addressed in connection with the cult suggest the prophet's role in worship (Isa 28:7; Jer 4:9; 8:1; 13:13; 14:18; Hos 4:4; Mic 3:11; Zeph 3:3). Second, the numerous speeches made at the sanctuary indicate the possibility of the prophets being responsible for teaching there (Jeremiah 7, 26; Zech 7:1–3; Amos 7). Finally, there is at least one reference implying that there were living quarters for prophets in the temple (Jer 35:4).

Because Johnson attempted to make his theory of the cultic prophet universally applicable to the biblical prophets, scholarship in general has rejected his concept of the cultic prophet. But scholars still recognize that some prophets did serve a function in the temple.[3] H. H. Rowley correctly defined the problem of labeling the canonical prophets as cultic when he wrote, "If the term 'cultic prophet' is to be given any meaning, it must denote a person who took some defined part in the official services of the shrine, and not merely a person who spoke to groups of people in the Temple court."[4] In other words, simply because a prophet made appearances in a sacred precinct does not necessarily mean that he was a part of the worship services held there. The term "cult prophet" should be utilized only in those instances where it is clearly established in the passage that a prophet had a role in the temple services. Among

---

[2] A. Johnson, *The Cultic Prophet in Ancient Israel* (Cardiff: Univ. of Wales Press Board, 1944), 51–53.

[3] H. H. Rowley, *Worship in Ancient Israel: Its Forms and Meaning* (Philadelphia: Fortress, 1967), 151, 157.

[4] Ibid., 159.

the writing prophets, Habakkuk[5] and Joel[6] are the two most regularly identified as cultic prophets. Other prophets clearly preached at noted sanctuaries and religious sites (see Amos 7; Jer 7, 26), but their exact relationship to the services held at those locations is less clear.

Perhaps a better place to gain an understanding of the role of the prophet resides in the terms applied to them throughout the biblical material. The three primary terms are "prophet" *(nābî')*, "seer" *(ḥōzeh)*, and "seer" *(rō'eh)*. The distinction between the latter two seems inconsequential or unknown at this distance, and they are both used synonymously with the first.[7] It would seem that the distinction between the first and the last two resides solely in the fact that *nābî'* denotes the office, while the other two suggest a method of revelation and may in fact be terms used of the prophet prior to the institutionalization of the cult (see 1 Sam 9:9). The type of sight suggested by the contextual usage of "seer" in relation to the prophets ranges from simply functioning as a prophet (Amos 7:12; Isa 30:10; applied to false prophets in Zech 10:2) to visionary experiences of the extraordinary sort (Num 12:6; Dan 10:7–8).

The term *nābî'* is far more difficult to interpret and more debated as to its exact meaning and intention than the other words for prophet. Some scholars link the word to the Hebrew word for "gushing forth" *(nābaʿ)*, which leads them to the conclusion that the prophet is one who spouts words ecstatically under divine inspiration.[8] Others argue for an origin in the Akkadian root meaning "to call"

---

[5] First proposed by S. Mowinckel because of the liturgy found in the book of Habakkuk *(Psalmenstudien III* [Kristiana: Dybwad, 1922], 27–29), the concept has more recently been argued by J. D. W. Watts *(Joel, Obadiah, Jonah, Nahum, Habakkuk and Zephaniah,* CBC [Cambridge: Cambridge Univ. Press, 1975]).

[6] G. Ahlström, *Joel and the Temple Cult of Jerusalem,* VTSup 21 (Leiden: Brill, 1971), 130–37.

[7] All three terms are used in one passage in 1 Chr 29:29. Compare Gad's description in this passage with his description in 2 Sam 24:11.

[8] G. Oehler, *Theology of the Old Testament,* trans. G. Day (New York: Funk & Wagnalls, 1883), 363. R. Wilson goes a different route, but also determines that to act like a prophet meant to sometimes exhibit ecstatic behavior; see Wilson, "Prophecy and Ecstasy: A Reexamination," *JBL* 98 (1979): 321–37.

and suppose that the word means "one who is called by God" or "one who calls out."[9] Since both of these options have good evidence for and against them, most scholars are resigned to simply suggest that the origin of the word is lost to us. The meaning of the word then is best located in how it is used in the OT.[10]

The clearest explanation of the meaning of *nābî'* is found in Exod 7:1: "See, I have made you like God to Pharaoh, and Aaron your brother will be your prophet [*nābî'*]." Aaron functioned as Moses' mouthpiece or spokesperson (Exod 4:14–16), and he was a mediator between Moses and Pharaoh both in signs and words (Exod 7:2,9–10). Indeed, the prophet is best known for the expression, "the LORD says/said."[11] As a messenger from God, it should not be surprising that the prophet also took the people's needs back to Yahweh. At many places the prophetic role is directly linked with praying for someone else (Gen 20:7; Jer 37:3, 42:2–4; Ezek 22:30; Amos 7:2,5). Thus, the prophet was a spokesperson who both declared the very words of Yahweh and who took the people's needs back to Him.[12] What exactly the whole gambit of the term *nābî'* entailed has probably been lost to us, but one can be certain that prophets were held with varying degrees of esteem by the populace and that the components of their office were similarly complex and varied.[13]

---

[9] W. F. Albright, "The Archaeological Background of the Hebrew Prophets of the Eighth Century," *JBR* 8 (1940): 131–36.

[10] H. E. Freeman, *An Introduction to the Old Testament Prophets* (Chicago: Moody Press, 1968), 37–39.

[11] The phrase "the LORD says" or "The word of the LORD came to/through" occurs in every prophetic book except Habakkuk, and even Habakkuk was ordered to write down the vision that God gave him (Hab 2:2).

[12] A. G. Auld ("Prophets Through the Looking Glass: Between Writings and Moses," *JSOT* 27 [1983]: 3–23), proposed that נָבִיא was a word with only negative connotations until the exile. But this view has been dealt with adequately elsewhere; see T. Overholt, "Prophecy in History: The Social Reality of Intermediation," *JSOT* 48 (1990): 3–29.

[13] G. von Rad has argued that many of the issues surrounding the meaning of נָבִיא would be settled if scholarship had a "keener awareness" of the variety with which most of the concepts regarding the various components of the prophetic office were held in antiquity; see von Rad, *The Message of the Prophets*, trans. D. M. G. Stalker (London: SCM Press, 1968), 30.

## The Prophetic Texts

As already mentioned, the appropriation of prophetic texts in the evangelical church today suffers at various points. Misuses of the text are either internal (within the text) or external (within the interpreter). As with other biblical areas, the internal difficulties spring from the gaps between the modern and ancient worlds. But these gaps seem more common and acute in the prophetic texts. Whether it is the ambiguity of the symbolism of Ezekiel or the lack of a coherent ordering of the oracles as represented in Jeremiah, there is a foreignness to the materials that is often difficult to overcome. One might be able to find a way to relate to the other forms of literature in the Bible because of similar modern examples, but there is no directly comparative modern genre to the prophetic materials.[14] Furthermore, the prophetic materials find meaningful expression in the totality of God's revelation and maintain the historical particularity of the individual prophet, which makes their scope difficult to comprehend. As Willem VanGemeren wrote, "An exploration of the prophetic word requires an openness to the whole revelation of God in both the OT and the NT, to the cultural context of the prophets, to the prophetic language, metaphors, and forms of speech, as well as to the canonical importance of the prophetic message."[15]

The external difficulties arise from improper presuppositions that people have about the prophetic materials. Some approach them with an ease and carelessness that prevents them from seeking outside help. Eschewing scholarly aid in interpreting any biblical material is illogical, but it is especially dangerous with texts as dependent on historical background as are the prophets.[16] This is not to say

---

[14] J. S. Duvall and J. D. Hays, *Grasping God's Word* (Grand Rapids: Zondervan, 2001), 357.

[15] W. VanGemeren, *Interpreting the Prophetic Word: An Introduction to the Prophetic Literature of the Old Testament* (Grand Rapids: Zondervan, 1990), 71.

[16] Every interpreter of the English text already depends on the expert who has evaluated the ancient cultures, examined the various linguistic relations, and determined the best possible translation of the biblical text. For one then to move to the interpretative process without consulting the experts for how those same issues impact interpretation makes little sense; see J. Goldingay, *Models for Interpretation of Scripture* (Grand Rapids: Eerdmans, 1995), 169. This fact also illustrates the need for serious interpreters of Scripture at every level to gain training in the background and languages of the Bible in order to avoid being overly dependent on scholarship and to be able to discern for themselves the appropriateness of a viewpoint.

that all scholarly opinions are of equal value, for they must also be built on proper perspectives about the nature of prophetic materials as supernatural in force and character. Other interpreters of the prophetic texts fail because they do not allow the prophets to speak for themselves. This principle finds expression both in the need to maintain the historical particularity of the text and in the requirement that any exegete of the prophetic material also knows and understands the various forms of prophetic writings. The list of genres and subgenres in the prophets is staggering. Without an understanding of what each of these entails, one may indeed come away with a faulty interpretation.[17]

Probably more so than with any other biblical genre, maintaining the historical particularity of a prophetic statement is a principle that has been lost in many circles today. Because of apologetic interests, some interpreters have abandoned the historical approach in favor of a solely predictive concern in dealing with these texts. That is, if one can demonstrate enough fulfilled predictions, the Bible is proven to be authentic.[18] Of course, there is nothing inherently wrong with an apologetic concern in relation to the prophets, nor is there a lack of fulfilled predictions in the Bible. But when this becomes an end in itself, the Word loses its power to speak to the myriad of concerns that God sought to address through the prophets. Others have forsaken the principle of historical particularity in favor of eschatological presentations of the prophets. The recent turn of the millennium and events in the Middle East often drive a desire to make the Bible speak directly to modern realities.[19] The impact is felt when teachers and preachers either skirt the prophets in order to avoid a discussion of the end times or become immersed

---

[17] As J. Green put it (*How to Read Prophecy* [Downers Grove: InterVarsity, 1984], 25), an uninformed reader is in danger of twisting the text to his own ends and becoming like the lovesick person who turns every "Hello" from the object of his affection into an "I Love You."

[18] To recognize the validity of this statement, one need only open any study Bible for its charts of fulfilled predictions or notice that nearly every apologetics discussion includes a section on the topic.

[19] The desire I am addressing about the Bible speaking to people today is not the necessary and appropriate recognition of the Word being a living word and thus applicable to the Christian life. Rather, I am specifically addressing the goal of some who suggest that prophetic passages were designed to outline our present or near future experience.

in the eschatological discussion to the point of ignoring other elements of the prophetic message. The former is disconcerting since it means that a significant portion of the canon is lost to our churches and membership.[20] The latter is troubling because only one percent of the prophetic material relates to events yet to come.[21] This means that a purely eschatological approach either misrepresents or ignores large portions of the prophetic message. Eschatology is important, and its role in one's understanding of worship is examined below, but it is not primary to the prophetic concern.[22]

In contrast to many of the popular approaches to the prophetic materials, the prophets themselves seem to require their readers to pay attention to the historical context of their expressions. Repeatedly within the prophets there is an intentional expression of authorship, setting, date, and audience. Indeed, "It is striking that the scriptural material that most overtly claims a divine origin is also the material that most consistently draws attention to its own historical background and thus to the need to understand it against its background."[23] A historical approach to the prophets establishes a broad foundation for further understanding, allowing the distinctive voice of each prophet to be heard even when one is considering their overall view on a particular topic.

The prophets were not a homogenous unit. Each prophet had his own emphases, interests, and methods for addressing the concerns of his time and place. Their backgrounds varied from the agrarian (Micah) to the decidedly urban (Isaiah); from the priestly (Ezekiel) to the nobility (Zephaniah); and from the very young (Jeremiah) to the very old (Haggai).[24] Their ministries spanned from c. 760 BC (Amos) to c. 450 BC (Malachi). Therefore, their forms of speech and the issues they address also varied widely, making it difficult to

---

[20] The body of OT prophetic books is slightly longer than the NT.

[21] G. Fee and D. Stuart, *How to Read the Bible for All Its Worth*, 3d ed. (Grand Rapids: Zondervan, 2003), 182.

[22] For a discussion of the role that prediction can play in the exhortations of the prophets, see E. R. Clendenen, "Malachi," in R. A. Taylor and E. R. Clendenen, *Haggai, Malachi*, NAC (Nashville: B&H, 2004), 221–22.

[23] Goldingay, *Models for Interpreting*, 167.

[24] These conclusions are drawn from the prophet's own descriptions (see Isa 7:3; 22:15; 37:2; Jer 1:6; Ezek 1:1; 4:14; Mic 1:1; Zeph 1:1; Hag 2:3.

link their thought into one cohesive view on any topic, including worship.

On the other hand, the office of the prophet has certain institutions and concerns that are consistently found in the individual works: a heightened sense of justice, a divine compulsion to service, and a central position in the political and social development of the country.[25] Therefore, a cohesive evaluation of the prophetic materials is possible, as long as one maintains the uniqueness of each man and his ministry.

## The Essentials: Service and Distinctiveness Revisited

The prophetic credo that "obedience is better than sacrifice" echoes in numerous ways throughout the prophetic materials (Isa 1:11–15; Jer 7:21–22; Hos 6:4–6; Amos 5:21–24; Mic 6:6–8). The call for an acknowledgment of the superiority of obedience over sacrifice was not a unique expression in the ancient Near East. The Egyptian proverbs found in *The Instruction for King Meri-Ka-Re* include the following statement: "More acceptable is the character of one upright of heart than the ox of the evil doer."[26] The idea that a god would be more interested in righteous acts than in simple ceremony should not be surprising. What is different is the matter of relational worship the Bible advocates in contrast to that of Israel's neighbors. Therefore, while the association this maxim relates between the prophet and the cult has been discussed above, there is something more relational to be discovered in the prophetic texts than what has already been identified. The individual texts express perceptions about worship and obedience that are helpful to visit as

---

[25] These conclusions are established within the texts themselves and also through comparative studies with other ancient Near Eastern nations. See J. Blenkinsopp, *A History of Prophecy in Israel*, rev. ed. (Louisville: Westminster John Knox, 1996), 26–48; W. F. Albright, *Samuel and the Beginnings of the Prophetic Movement* (Cincinnati: Hebrew Union College Press, 1961); R. Clements, *Prophecy and Covenant*, SBT 43 (London: SCM Press, 1965); T. Overholt, *Channels of Prophecy: The Social Dynamics of Prophetic Activity* (Minneapolis: Fortress, 1989); and D. Petersen, *The Roles of Israel's Prophets*, ed. D. Clines and others, JSOTSup 17 (Sheffield: JSOT, 1981).

[26] Although Meri-Ka-Re was a king of the Middle Kingdom Tenth Dynasty of Egypt (c. 2130–2040 BC), the extant texts come from the New Kingdom Eighteenth Dynasty (c. 1570–1305 BC), so the ancient provenance of the work is unclear. *ANET*, 414–18.

one attempts to gain a more complete understanding of the connection of worship as an event and as a lifestyle.

## Meeting God Versus Trampling His Courts (Isa 1:11–15)

Isaiah 1:11–15 includes statements such as, "I have had enough of burnt offerings and rams," and "Stop bringing useless offerings." In this passage Yahweh rejects the sacrifice, incense, festival observances (such as New Moon and Sabbath), and prayer of the worshippers of Judah.[27] As already indicated, such messages from the prophets should not be understood as a rejection of the institutions themselves but as a desire for genuine worship. In the case of Isaiah, the content itself advocates such a position. First, Isaiah's inclusion of prayer in that which is rejected demonstrates that even the practice most clearly representative of attitude over ritual throughout the biblical material is not desired. Second, linking iniquity with the festivals at the end of v. 13 makes the nature of the problem explicit: God detests the coupling of a life of sin with the event of worship. Worship ought to advocate a challenge and require a change from iniquity to obedience. When it does not, it becomes something insipid and unworthy of God's attentions and focus. A religion that leaves the violence and injustice mentioned in the closing part of this passage unaddressed may be many things, but it is not pleasing to Yahweh.[28]

Isaiah's expressions about worship are punctuated by a somewhat anomalous construction in his summary of the people's activity. Verse 12 opens with the elongated "When you come to appear before me" instead of the more common "when you come before me." It is possible that this is simply a stylistic feature, but the inclusion of the verb *rā'â* in the passive voice ("appear"="be seen")

---

[27] Some have tried to differentiate between each aspect in relation to their acceptance before God. For instance, R. Clements (*Isaiah 1–39*, NCB [Grand Rapids: Eerdmans, 1980], 32–34) argued that incense alone was rejected in and of itself, whereas the other elements were rejected only because of the insincerity of the worshippers. While such conclusions are possible, it seems that the context would suggest that all of them were rejected because of the attitude of the people.

[28] J. Oswalt, *The Book or Isaiah, Chapters 1–39*, NICOT (Grand Rapids: Eerdmans, 1986), 95–97.

may suggest something else is going on. Isaiah was likely emphasizing that their actions were solely for the purpose of being seen.
John Oswalt characterized this as expressing the people's desire to
be seen, or, in other words, a careful examination of the procedures
of worship when, in fact, God desires careful examination of one's
motivation for worship.[29] Indeed, Isaiah took the observation in this
direction when he characterized the people's activity before God as
trampling God's courts. The focus here is the distinction between
actually meeting God and simply coming into the place where He
resides. Ultimately, the conclusion must be that coming before God
for any other reason than truly meeting Him is wasted energy and
time—and God has no use for such worship.

## God Versus What He Has Given (Jeremiah 7)

It is no surprise that in the midst of their discussions of the true
nature of worship the prophets would eventually come to the matter
of idolatry. Though this topic has been dealt with above, Jeremiah's
discussion of the futility of worship when it turns the worship instruments themselves into rivals of God deserves some attention.
Jeremiah's use of this phenomenon of faulty substitution in the context of useless worship highlights the fact that if a person is not
all God's he is not God's at all. The people had turned the temple
into their focus of trust in order to conceal every kind of sin imag-
inable.[30] Jeremiah refers to the "Queen of Heaven" (implying that
Yahweh had a consort) as an example of insincere syncretic worship. His contemporary Ezekiel was somewhat more graphic in his
description of events taking place at the temple at that time (Ezekiel
8–9). In any case, such worship epitomizes a heart that is not wholly
God's. Perhaps this is one reason Jeremiah focused so much on the
whole burnt offering in his dismissals. An offering that is designed
to express complete dedication means little when it is given in the
midst of such divided loyalties. Therefore, it makes more sense to
consume for oneself that which would have been offered to God (Jer
7:21).

---

[29] Ibid., 95.
[30] J. A. Thompson, *The Book of Jeremiah,* NICOT (Grand Rapids: Eerdmans, 1980), 286–87.

Before leaving Jeremiah, it serves us well to look at the case that the prophet makes against the practices of the people. He uses a threefold argument based upon conscience, logic, and history to demonstrate that such reliance on the temple was an affront to God. Like Amos years earlier, Jeremiah began by advocating to the people the connection between the worship they performed and their treatment of the oppressed (Jer 7:3–8). He pulled at their conscience in an attempt to get them to see that there is little resemblance between what they think they are accomplishing and what they are actually doing. He then appealed to reason to ask if one can commit sins that are an affront to nearly all of the Ten Commandments and still expect to be safe (Jer 7:9–11). Finally, he invited his listeners back to Shiloh where the people had put their confidence in the ark instead of Yahweh and as a result this holy place had been destroyed (Jer 7:12–15). In short, through Jeremiah God called the people to a holistic view of their existence and presence before Him—both in the present and in the past. For each group is intrinsically tied to that which has gone before, for good and for bad. To ignore one's past is to lose a vital means God uses to shape the present.

## Loyalty to God Versus Temporary Allegiance (Hos 6:4–6)

The primary verse regarding the negative position of Hosea toward faulty worship is Hos 6:6. As with previous passages, scholarship has viewed the verse in one of two ways: (1) a negation of God's desire for sacrifice in light of His concern for *hesed*;[31] (2) a comparative with sacrifice being of less value than *hesed*.[32] Grammatically speaking, both are possible, but the evidence above and the translation of the verse in the Septuagint suggest that the latter is the better interpretation.

What is *hesed*? The word itself is represented with a variety of meanings in English translations. In Hosea 6 it has been rendered "loyalty" (HCSB), "mercy" (LXX, KJV, NIV), "goodness" (ASV), "steadfast love" (NRSV, ESV), "faithful love" (NJB), and "love" (NLT). Nelson Glueck carried out the preeminent study of the word

---

[31] See H. W. Wolff, *Hosea*, trans. G. Stansell, Her (Philadelphia: Fortress, 1974), 105.

[32] H. H. Rowley, *The Unity of the Bible* (Philadelphia: Westminster Press, 1953), 40, n. 1.

and concluded that the primary idea expressed by the word is that of faithfulness to the covenant.[33] Subsequent writers have critiqued his work with varying degrees of success. Perhaps the most telling criticism came through H. J. Stoebe, who pointed out that Glueck's emphasis on obligation could not be maintained since there were numerous places in the Bible where *hesed* is said to be present without any sense of obligation on the part of the person granting it (see Gen 24:29; 2 Sam 2:5; 1 Kgs 3:6).[34] One proposal says the term has nuances of help or assistance freely given, while another claims that the word expresses some sort of faithful love.[35] Apparently *hesed* has a wide semantic range, which makes the meaning difficult to identify with any precision. It also allows the word to be used to illustrate a number of truths related to mercy, kindness, and love with a condition of loyalty— whether covenantal or freely offered—at its foundation.

The Israelites interpreted their religion through the milieu of their neighbors, and ritual meant everything. What one did beyond that was unimportant. But Hosea reminded them that God is not like the gods of other nations. He has placed requirements on Israel that extended well beyond the worship event and has mandated realities concerning worship as lifestyle.[36] In this oracle, Hosea contrasted the attitude and accompanying actions of God with those of Israel—to a devastating effect. Whereas God's *hesed* is "like the rising sun, which increases in strength as day advances; theirs is like the morning cloud which vanishes quickly."[37] God openly expressed frustration at the transient nature of Israel's commitment to Him and rhetorically wondered what to do with His unfaithful people. The people believed that some mechanistic application of the biblical precepts for worship protected their future, but God informed them that lacking the weightier matters of *hesed* they were only par-

---

[33] N. Glueck, *Hesed in the Bible* (Hoboken, NJ: Ktav Publishing House, 1968).

[34] *THAT,* "חסד."

[35] For the former, see K. D. Sakenfeld, *The Meaning of Hesed in the Hebrew Bible: A New Inquiry* (Eugene, OR: Wipf & Stock Publishers, 2002); for the latter see *TWOT,* "חסד."

[36] D. Stuart, *Hosea–Jonah,* WBC (Waco: Word, 1987), 110.

[37] F. Andersen and D. N. Freedman, *Hosea: A New Translation with Introduction and Commentary,* AB (Garden City: Doubleday, 1980), 427.

tially fulfilling the covenant. As in other places throughout the biblical text, God viewed partial fulfillment of covenant expectations as no fulfillment at all (Josh 24:15; Matt 23:1–36; Rev 3:15–16).[38] Likewise, worship that does not give full allegiance to God is not worship at all.

## Justice and Righteousness: The Prerequisite for and Result of Worship (Amos 5:4–27)

Amos's final charge in the oracle regarding the nature of worship in Amos 5 is perhaps the best-known section of his writings. His summation that Israel must "let justice flow like water, and righteousness, like an unfailing stream" (Amos 5:24) properly became the hallmark passage for the civil rights movement under Martin Luther King Jr., who understood the close link between believing faith and the practice of justice. The Christian who proclaims a love for God and yet neglects his brother represents neither biblical Christianity as a lifestyle nor biblical worship as an event. Amos's exposition of the relationship between belief and practice remains among the most poignant and important texts for illustrating the inextricable link between worship and lifestyle.

Amos 5:25 is often used to suggest that Israel did not participate in a sacrificial system prior to their appearance in the land. Some have suggested Jeremiah used Amos's words in his own defense of this concept (Jer 7:22).[39] In general, this understanding of Amos's statements is built on the idea that a "no" answer is expected when Amos asks his question. As a continuing examination of some of the issues related to the matter at hand, it is enough here to make two other observations about the issue of sacrifice taking place in pre-national Israel. First, Sidney Jellicoe argued that if sacrifice was not present during the wanderings, why did Hosea, who was the prophet most interested in the period, not make something out of such a fact?[40] Though this is an argument from silence, given Hosea's keen interest both in history and syncretism with Canaanite religion, it does seem

---

[38] Stuart, *Hosea–Joel*, 113.

[39] S. Jellicoe, "The Prophets and the Cultus," *ExpTim* 60 (1949): 258.

[40] Ibid., 257.

odd that he would not have used a pre-Canaanite period to illustrate how things could be without such syncretism. Second, there is a precedent for questions posed in this way to be understood as expecting an affirmative answer (1 Sam 2:27).[41] Since Amos followed the question by asserting what Israel was known to have done in the period, this may be the case here. If so, Amos was illustrating that Israel incorrectly looked to sacrifices as being primary in the early period. Such ordering of the situation is wrong, just as the ordering of other gods before Yahweh is wrong. Sacrifices are to be brought, but God commanded justice and obedience first.

That Amos had some animosity toward the cult can hardly be doubted. Numerous times he called the people to avoid the cultic centers and to focus on justice (Amos 3:14; 5:4–7; 9:1–4). His expressions in 5:21 contain some of the strongest negative words in Scripture about God's disposition toward something. God said that He hated *(sānē')* their feasts. This word expresses an emotional attitude and enunciates an unequivocal desire to have nothing to do with the feasts.[42] In parallel usage, Amos chose the word "despise" *(mā'as)*, which suggests a complete rejection of the object it addresses.[43] His complaint, however, was not with the sites themselves but with what they represented. Remembering that Amos's concern throughout his work was social injustice, it seems apparent that his attack on the cult would have something to do with the cult's relationship to such abuses. The cult as a large landholder was a large drain on the economic life of Israel. Either directly or indirectly, the shrines were responsible for the plight of many of the oppressed individuals in his community—so Amos had to include them in his call for repentance.[44]

But even more pointedly, Amos focused on the worshipper's role in activities of injustice and unrighteousness. The compartmentalization of the festivals and assemblies away from the immoral life that the people were living was more representative of a Baal cult

---

[41] E. Lucas, "Sacrifice in the Prophets," in *Sacrifice in the Bible,* ed. R. Beckwith and M. Selman (Grand Rapids: Baker, 1995), 62.

[42] *TWOT,* "שָׂנֵא."

[43] *TWOT,* "מָאַס."

[44] Blenkinsopp, *History of Prophecy,* 81.

than that of Yahweh. The two words "justice" and "righteousness" form a hendiadys, so that Amos is advocating a justice that is righteousness, a justice on which society ought to be founded.[45] Without justice, worship itself becomes abhorrent to God.[46] Therefore, while Amos did not emphasize the rampant problem of syncretism,[47] he was clearly so disgusted by the practices of religion held in the North that he viewed the whole of its content as false. Their lifestyle belied the fact that although they may have believed themselves to be worshippers of Yahweh, they actually worshipped false gods.[48]

Amos was perhaps the earliest of the prophetic books, and it is striking that such an early text has such a strong disposition toward the proper relationship between worship and lifestyle. As is already clear, the later prophets would take up the position advocated by Amos and adapt it to their own situations, but few made the relationship as explicit as Amos did in this text. Amos was unambiguous in his expression that worship cannot occur if righteousness has not been a part of the life of the practitioner. Likewise, he posited that without appropriate worship focused on the true God and His precepts, the only result is oppression and cruelty.

## Actions Will Eventually Mimic Attitude (Malachi)

The book of Malachi is last in order, both canonically and chronologically. It presents the final appraisal of the relationship between attitude and action in worship through prophetic disputation, in which the writer discloses a charge followed by an objection, which is then responded to with a restatement of the charge and further evidence supporting the accusation. The book is generally thought to contain a series of disputations carefully centered on the topic of

---

[45] M. Weiss, "Concerning Amos' Repudiation of the Cult," in *Pomegranates and Golden Bells: Studies in Biblical, Jewish, and Near Eastern Ritual, Law, and Literature in Honor of Jacob Milgrom,* ed. D. P. Wright and others (Winona Lake: Eisenbrauns, 1995), 209.

[46] Ibid., 204.

[47] This fact has been used by more than one scholar to erroneously suggest that Amos had no problems with the golden calves of Bethel and Dan; see J. Wellhausen, *Die Kleinen Propheten,* 3d ed. (Berlin: G. Reimer, 1898), 92; and T. K. Cheyne, *Hosea: With Notes and Introduction,* Cambridge Bible (Cambridge: Cambridge Univ. Press, 1884), 24.

[48] L. B. Paton, "Did Amos Approve of the Calf-Worship at Bethel?" *JBL* 13 (1894): 89–90.

the people's relationship with God. The prophet characterizes the realities of worship within which His people find themselves.

Even more than the other postexilic prophets, Malachi's words are reminiscent of his preexilic predecessors. He described polluted offerings and demonstrable contempt for God. However, there is a noticeable shift in the activities of the people themselves. Whereas the preexilic prophets once addressed a people who were fervent in their activities but who lacked the necessary basis in the orientation of their hearts, Malachi found himself addressing people who had lost enthusiasm in the realm of both action and attitudes. He then illustrated that eventually this mind-set would catch up with someone so that even the procedures that once seemed so fervent would diminish into meaningless and backward activities.

The starting point for Malachi's discussion is the matter of election. He contrasted Israel's standing and status with that of Edom in order to emphasize God's love, graciousness and favor—a foundation that serves as the platform for making God's case against the unfaithfulness of Israel. Because Israel had been granted so many resources and favors by God, their infidelity in worship could not be tolerated.[49]

Malachi's reflections find their perspective from the third Commandment (Exod 20:7). He specifically mentions that the people held God's name in contempt *(bāzâ, Mal 1:6)* because they went beyond simply not bringing the best but proceeded to bring that which even the heathen governor would not accept.[50] The comparison could not be stronger. A heart that forgets the grace of God and therefore the One to whom so much is owed—who gives out of ritual instead of righteousness—eventually brings Him gifts that even those who do not know Him would not offer. Worship itself is a gift and a privilege. To turn it into a wearisome endeavor devoid of the realization that it is a meeting with the Creator is a crime that reaps its own rewards in an event and a lifestyle that are anything but stimulating.

---

[49] C. C. Torrey, "The Prophecy of 'Malachi.'" *JBL* 17 (1898): 13.
[50] Clendenen, "Malachi," 268–70.

Malachi contains the most often used text about tithing and thus the matter of giving (Mal 3:10), so a brief discussion of tithing as it relates to the Christian is in order. The verse states:

> "Bring the full 10 percent into the storehouse so that there may be food in My house. Test Me in this way," says the LORD of Hosts. "See if I will not open the floodgates of heaven and pour out a blessing for you without measure."

This is perhaps the best-known reference in Scripture to tithing's potential benefits. Unfortunately, more often than not it is utilized devoid of both its historical and literary contexts. The prophet Malachi addressed people who had returned from exile with great expectations but who found themselves in a somewhat more precarious situation than they had anticipated. The temple had been rebuilt, and life under Persian domination—while highly preferable in comparison to life in Babylon—was difficult and depressing. Nehemiah's contemporary account describes a people who found themselves strangers in their own land and who were somewhat religiously apathetic. Haggai records that the people suffered under a drought (Hag 1:10) and that only a special movement from God had resulted in their renewed focus and completion of the temple (Hag 1:14). Early in his book Malachi recorded that they were a people who had forgotten that they were loved by God (Mal 1:2). Furthermore, there can be little doubt that the taxes the Persians required of their vassals were significant and draining on the economic well-being of many individuals. Into this setting, Malachi stepped forward to issue his challenge regarding the tithe. He did so not from some detached theology of reward and punishment but in the context of a covenantal expectation on the part of God.

The context is important to consider as one approaches the contents of Mal 3:8–12. The imagery of "opening the floodgates of heaven" and "rebuking the devourer" reflect God's promise of restoration from the hardships of drought and locust. In the law of

Moses, God promised the people of Israel that their failures regarding the covenant would lead to their land turning into "falling dust" (Deut 28:15–24). The prophet Joel painted a vivid picture of locusts as an invading army from God sent to devour the produce of the land (Joel 1:4; also 2:25) as punishment for the sins of the people against the covenant.[51] So the matter of tithing becomes a clear allusion to a specific portion of failure about the more general covenant. But again, the emphasis is one of relationship so that what Malachi is advocating is a question of trust in God rather than trust in one's own means.[52] The confrontation is all the more striking in light of the economic hardships the people were under through taxation. Malachi was asking for an authentic step of faith in God with whom one has a relationship, not faith in the reward and punishment of tithing. To understand the challenge in terms related primarily to tithing is to turn this act into the very thing that all the prophets had been arguing against—idolatry. Like the ark and the temple of previous generations, the tithe was merely a pointer to a relationship, not the means of manipulating God. Furthermore, Malachi expresses here that the tithe is indicative of whether one gratefully views his life as God's gift.[53] To see Mal 3:10 as referring only to the action of tithing in light of its intended purpose as a reminder of the covenant, and more particularly the relationship that the covenant represents, amounts to a misunderstanding and a trivializing of the text. Such a conclusion is important to the topic of the Christian and the tithe, but it still does not answer the overall matter of the role of the tithe in Christian experience and practice.

Tithing in the Christian church has a long history. The imposition of the obligatory tithe on parishioners during the medieval era led to

---

[51] Notwithstanding Stuart's strong arguments for viewing the locusts of Joel as an invading human army (Stuart, *Hosea–Jonah*, 232–35; also D. A. Garrett, *Hosea, Joel*, NAC [Nashville: B&H, 1977], 298–301), the most natural reading of the text is that the reference is to the creature, though they are certainly viewed as part of a supernatural invasion at the behest of God. This is made obvious through the descriptions of the various stages of locust development in Joel 1:4, the reference to the darkening sky in Joel 2:10, and the distinctively singular focus on the destruction of herbage in Joel 1:7; 2:3.

[52] J. O'Brien, *Nahum, Habakkuk, Zephaniah, Haggai, Zechariah, Malachi*, AOTC (Nashville: Abingdon, 2004), 308, 310.

[53] Clendenen, "Malachi," 236–38, 414. Also see the same author's excursus on the issue of the tithe, pp. 429–33.

more than one revolt and was the source of constant frustration on the part of those who were required to pay an amount they did not have. Since the Reformation, the practice of the voluntary tithe to support the church and its work has focused upon a slightly different set of values as the questions have changed into the ones that now remain: What is the standard of giving that the tithe suggests? How does it find expression alongside the more fervent calls for sacrifice outlined in the NT? For people who draw the strongest distinctions between the old and new covenants, the answer is that the tithe is a requirement of Israel, not the church.[54] But others have argued that since the tithe preceded Israel, was a part of religious exercises outside of Israel, and was never refuted by Jesus or Paul, then the tithe still remains a part of Christian practice.[55] Perhaps an examination of exactly what the word "tithe" means in the OT will help.

The primary texts relating to the tithe in the OT are in the Pentateuch (see Lev 27:30–33; Num 18:21–32; Deut 14:22–29). Generally speaking, scholars have understood these texts to refer to a single tithing custom or institution.[56] Though this approach is made somewhat difficult by the varying instructions in the three texts, Neh 10:37–38 [Hb. vv. 38–39] seems to indicate that there was only one prescribed tithe taken in the OT era.[57] As McConville suggested, each law gives only a partial picture of the regulations involving the tithe as they each assume both the presence and the regulations of the others.[58] The passage in Leviticus outlines the

[54] R. C. Stedman, "Giving under Grace, Part 1," *BSac* 107 (1950): 321–28.

[55] G. Salstrand, *The Tithe: The Minimum Standard for Christian Giving* (Grand Rapids: Baker, 1971). H. Lansdell, one of the most consistent proponents of the tithe in Christianity, once made his case by suggesting that Cain's sin was not rightly dividing his gift (that is, he did not bring a tithe); however, his translation of the LXX from which his conclusion is drawn is highly suspect since it omits certain words and adds others; see Lansdell, *The Sacred Tenth: Studies in Tithe Giving Ancient and Modern* (London: SPCK Press, 1906; reprint Grand Rapids: Baker Books, 1955), 1:41. All references are to the original printing.

[56] M. Tate, "Tithing: Legalism or Benchmark?" *RevExp* 70 (1973): 155–56; G. McConville, *Law and Theology in Deuteronomy*, JSOTSup 33 (Sheffield: JSOT Press, 1984), 74. In contrast, Lansdell argued that these three refer to three separate tithes and that the Israelite was actually required to give 20 percent each year and an additional 10 percent every third year; see Lansdell, *The Tithe in Scripture* (London: SPCK Press, 1908), 36.

[57] Later rabbinic writings do identify more than one tithe, but this seems to be a later understanding in an attempt to deal with varying instructions in the Pentateuchal passages.

[58] McConville, *Law and Theology*, 77.

materials that can be offered and the nature of the tithe, Numbers clearly enunciates the provision of the tithes for the Levites and their right to be supported, and Deuteronomy expresses the theology of the tithe and the added feature of the consumption of part of the tithe by the one giving the gift. Therefore, the practice of the tithe in Israel involved a yearly gift given to the temple, with the gifts of every third year kept in the community for the care of the poor and oppressed. [59] Theologically then, the law was a reminder of Israel's holy status before God and that its enjoyment of the rewards of that status was a consequence of their election. Therefore, the tithe had relational implications regarding recognition of both God's position and all that belonged to Him. Because it demanded recognition of God's ownership of all the land and was genuinely costly, the tithe functioned effectively in putting God first in the giver's life. Because the participant was allowed to consume part of the tithe, he was reminded that "the enjoyment of the benefits of the land depends upon readiness to relinquish them."[60] The prioritizing of God as first also helped the people to understand their role in the treatment and care of others and forced them to be outward looking. Such an emphasis is probably one of the primary reasons Malachi chose the gift as an illustration of the entirety of the covenant in his discourse.[61]

Through the study of Malachi's language in its historical and literary contexts, today's church receives both a warning and an opportunity. Too often sermons on tithing turn into messages that affect only the most vulnerable in the church, those who are superstitious or anxious and can be manipulated into giving.[62] As a result, the sermon turns the tithe into the opposite of one of its intended purposes—an aid in relief from oppression (Deut 14:28–30). The Malachi text should not be understood as a challenge to cease preaching on giving or even on tithing. Rather, one should enter

---

[59] Ibid., 69, 82–83.

[60] Ibid., 80–83.

[61] It is instructive to realize as well that the word tithe (מַעֲשֵׂר) may sometimes refer only generally to a gift and not necessarily to an exact 10 percent. J. Baumgarten ("On the Non-literal Use of maʿsēr/dekatē," JBL 103 [1984]: 246) understands the use here in Malachi that way since it is placed in parallel with "contributions."

[62] E. Flynn, "Beware the Tithing Team," TToday 40 (1983): 195–96.

into such moments in the life of the church cognizant of the fact that "the revolutionary interpretation of possessions by Jesus is not adequately expressed through tithing."[63] The call for the Christian is sacrificial giving after the pattern of the widow (Mark 12:41–44). Malachi himself advocated recognition that our resources are not the basis of our confidence, but God's resources are. Thus, tithing can serve a liberating function when addressed in the right spirit, possibly serving as a benchmark rather than a divine law devoid of grace. It ought to be addressed from the perspective of the joy and strength that it imbues, rather than the too often expressed motivation of the perceived "needs of the church."[64]

The concept of obedience rather than sacrifice opens many avenues of discussion about the relationship of lifestyle and worship. From the prophetic perspective, there can be no distinction between the two. The compartmentalization of life that is so common today would be impossible from the prophets' point of view. Their focus on the worship event maintains an advocacy of the supremacy and uniqueness of God. They call on individuals to meet God when one comes to worship, to adore Him alone and not the objects that He has furnished, and to be completely devoted and loyal to Him rather than as a passing disposition. The prophets remind us to consider the inseparable relationship between our ability to worship God and to practice righteousness. A life of righteous commitment nourishes episodes of humble adoration. The practice of true worship leads a person to a clearer understanding of his role in the world. The Creator, whose presence at the center of all reality forms the means by which enjoyment in life becomes possible, has marvelously established this cycle for the greatest possible outcome for those who adhere to it. These realizations find further expression in the realization that attitude and action also are intertwined and that what a person brings to worship in attitude also impacts what he takes from worship.

---

[63] Tate, "Tithing," 159.
[64] Ibid., 161.

## What We Bring to Worship

The Latter Prophets, though they lived in different times and addressed specific issues of their day, generally agreed about what one brings to worship. They carried an established view of worship as being interwoven with one's life. In order for an event to even be defined as worship, they understood that certain attitudes had to be present at its inception and certain actions discernable at its conclusion.

### Who is Worship For? (Amos 4:4–5)

This section concerns first the essentials needed for worship to begin and then what is needed when it concludes. Perhaps the most fundamental attitude at the inception of worship is an acknowledgment of who is being worshipped. In a world where churches are increasingly focused on getting people in the door, we can lose the element of worship as a function of congregational gatherings. The meetings become a matter of preference, rather than a matter of focus. Both those who favor the contemporary style of worship and those who prefer the traditional can be guilty of such idolatry. Indeed, while it is usually the churches attempting innovative forms of worship and style that are accused of being too seeker-sensitive and not sensitive enough to God, they do not stand alone in their self-centered perspectives on how a service should be conducted.

The prophet Amos faced a similar situation. The sacred places were full to capacity and religion was on the minds of most. He described the commitment to the forms of worship as exorbitant and unquestionably fervent in action. However, he noted quite clearly that what was taking place was not pleasing to God. In fact, he said that such "worship" amounted to rebellion and sin in the eyes of God. A closer examination shows what it was about their activity that made it sinful.

The message of Amos 4:4–5 is best understood through an examination of the vocabulary. In general the attack is twofold. Amos's identification of Israel's sinful actions at the sanctuaries is demonstrated in his substitution of "you" for "me" and "your" for "my" in the discussions of religious regulations.[65] That is, the manner in which the offerings were being brought had nothing to do with a concern for what God desired, but merely reflected the desires, whims, and feelings of the participants. Amos also made his point by exaggerating the frequency of their gifts to the sanctuary. He requested that the sacrifice be brought every morning, but he did not refer to the offering that would have functioned in this way (the whole burnt offering, *ʿōlâ*), but rather to the generic term for sacrifice *(zebaḥ)*, which is usually associated with the peace offering and only necessary once a year (1 Sam 1).[66] He further sarcastically requested that the tithe, which is to be brought yearly, be brought instead every third day. Such apparent mockery of what the people were doing demonstrated that Amos was attacking the religiosity of his listeners as insincere and from false motivations. Worship was used as a means of legitimizing the current political and social status of the worshippers, and Amos was not fooled by the religiosity of his contemporaries.[67]

When worship ceases to be about God, it ceases to be about anything and turns into a rebellious activity because there is no longer a place in the life of the individual for God to receive the honor due to Him.

---

[65] R. J. Thompson, *Penitence and Sacrifice in Early Israel Outside the Levitical Law* (Leiden: Brill, 1963), 169.

[66] Blenkinsopp, *History of Prophecy*, 81.

[67] Ibid. A side issue unimportant to the point being made here but significant for understanding the development of the sacrificial system in Israel is the mention of the three various offerings throughout the passage. Scholars commonly assume that the first form of sacrifice to develop was the slaughter sacrifice, referred to as the זֶבַח (B. Levine, *In the Presence of the Lord: A Study of Cult and Some Cultic Terms in Ancient Israel*, SJLA [Leiden: Brill, 1974], 3). They further suppose that from this one sacrifice, the cultic institutions of Israel developed numerous, more well-defined, sacrifices that found their expression in the priestly texts of the Bible, especially Lev 1–7. Amos's use of all three offerings here is detrimental to a late developing priestly text and pushes the development of Levitical sacrificial laws to a period much earlier than most scholars are willing to admit. Indeed, the traditional ascription of them to the Mosaic era hardly seems out of the question in light of texts such as this one.

## Bringing Our Best to Worship (Micah 6:6–8)

Normally the oracle in Micah 6:6–8 would be interpreted along-side other passages on the relationship of obedience and sacrifice, but a closer examination of it suggests that it serves a slightly different function than the other texts. Micah's tone was less strident than those of his colleagues, so he was not as negative toward the cult as the other prophets. Instead, his emphasis was purely one of comparison in which he advocated that people must bring their best when coming to worship. In this instance, Micah did not tear down the practices of the people, but used them to illustrate a better way. It is quite easy to suggest something is better after demolishing that to which it is being compared in one manner or another. But here Micah highlighted the extravagant gifts to show how powerful and special God's desires are.

One might ask, why do I make this distinction for Micah and not the other prophets? First, as pointed out above, the prophets were able to make their comparisons only because they held sacrifice in such high regard. Second, Micah was devoid of any of the negative verbs describing God as despising the people's offerings as in the other prophets. Finally, Micah's opening question in 6:6 suggests that he was making a comparative evaluation of what would be best to bring before Yahweh. A detailed examination of the passage makes this apparent.

The specific verses in question fall within the interpretative context of Mic 6:1–8, as determined through the introductory refrain. The first verse opens with a call to listen and is followed by verses that relate the connection between God's past actions and His present expectations concerning Israel. Since v. 9 also opens with the command to listen, it is clear that the prophet is moving on to a new list of circumstances and evaluations, thus establishing the closure of the passage at v. 8.

Micah's rehearsal of the mighty acts of God in chronological succession is significant. The passage progresses from the deliverance out of Egypt at the exodus, through the protection God offered against Balak on the threshold of the promised land, and concludes at the miraculous crossing of the Jordan as Israel moved from Shittim to Gilgal. Since Micah's ministry as a whole took place during the wearisome and complex years when Judah sought direction for dealing with the oppression inflicted by Assyria, this recitation seems to have the purpose of reminding the people of Judah about Yahweh's faithfulness to His covenant. That is, Micah outlined the evidence for God's demonstration of *hesed*.

Micah's comparison in Mic 6:6–8 of what Judah was willing to offer and what God desired is compelling both in style and argument. Micah took on the role of the people of Judah in his list of things they were willing to offer. What is most striking is that he did not characterize their offerings as menial or unimpressive. Instead of identifying the crowd as a group disinterested in pleasing God, Micah portrayed them as committed but misdirected. He started with the whole burnt offering. As previously discussed, this offering was special because the entire animal was given to God; no part of the animal went to the participant or the priest. In short, it was the most costly of the sacrifices. Next, Micah discussed the offering of a yearling. This is significant because any calf seven days old or older was eligible for sacrifice, yet the people were willing to offer a yearling, which was most costly because a year's worth of food and time went into its care.[68] Micah then moved to great quantities of goods—thousands upon thousands of rivers of oil are suggested, reminiscent of Solomon's gifts at the dedication of the temple (1 Kgs 8:62). Finally, the worshippers expressed their willingness even to offer their children, if God wanted them. At this point it is important to recognize that there is little warrant to the suggestion that such sacrifices were taking place in Judah, for the practices of Ahaz and Manasseh along these lines (2 Kgs 16:3; 21:6) do not necessarily mean that it was common among the people. This is especially true given the fact that the stated reasons for the offerings are antithetical to the motivations of child sacrifice elsewhere in the area.[69] Instead, the expression is best understood as one final plea to determine

---

[68] L. C. Allen, *The Books of Joel, Obadiah, Jonah and Micah*, NICOT (Grand Rapids: Eerdmans, 1976), 370.

[69] Ibid.

what it takes to please God, obviously remembering the actions of Abraham.

In relating what God desired from Judah, Micah focused on three requirements: to "act justly" (lit., "do/carry out justice") to "love faithfulness," and to "walk humbly." The word "justice" *(mišpāṭ)*, represents the central message of the prophets. The command counters a variety of situations from perjury and bribery to basic mistreatment and oppression.[70] The term "faithfulness" *(ḥesed)* often expresses covenantal love. It is divine in origin and denotes the actions of kindness, loyalty, mercy, love, and unmitigated devotion. The requirement to "walk humbly" uses a term *(haṣnēaʿ)* whose root occurs elsewhere only in Prov 11:12 ("with *humility* comes wisdom"). It is not the usual term for humility, however, and may refer rather to wise or careful behavior.[71] H. J. Stoebe proposes that it "signifies a walk with God that insightfully recognizes God's attentions and that affirms the consequences for one's behavior."[72] It suggests a pattern of life characterized *not* by the self-effacement one normally associates with humility, but by careful and measured conduct.[73] The construction and syntactical relationship of the three phrases suggest that Micah was not relating three separate requirements, but ascending models of behavior from the specific to the general. Micah called for an adoption of the "specific requirement to do justice which is a way of loving mercy, which in turn is a manifestation of walking humbly with God."[74]

Because the genre has characteristics of an oracle of judgment expressed in terms of a covenant lawsuit, certain expectations grew about where Micah was taking his audience. Oracles of judgment almost always end with a judgment sentence; its absence here creates three possibilities. The first is that Micah built a case that continues into vv. 9–16 where the judgment is then outlined.[75] While

---

[70] KB[3], "מִשְׁפָּט."

[71] K. Barker and W. Bailey, *Micah, Nahum, Habakkuk, Zephaniah*, NAC (Nashville: B&H, 1999), 114.

[72] *TLOT*, "צנע *ṣnʿ* be careful."

[73] See J. L. Mays, *Micah: A Commentary*, OTL (Philadelphia: Westminster Press, 1976), 142.

[74] Mays, *Micah*, 142.

[75] Barker and Bailey, *Micah, Nahum, Habakkuk, Zephaniah*, 116–20.

this approach has the advantage of completing the pattern for this type of literature, it seems that Micah purposely distinguished between the case of vv. 1–8 and that of vv. 9–16. A second possibility is that the judgment is implicit in Judah's present situation or that the case speaks for itself and Judah is invited to judge itself. Such an approach, however, seems rather obtuse and difficult to defend in light of Micah's clear use of judgment expressions elsewhere. A third and more likely reason for the omission is that the purpose of the lawsuit is not to exact judgment on Judah, but to bring her to repentance.[76] This approach has the added advantage of the alteration in structure being a further picture of the portrayal of Yahweh already manifest in the passage. In other words, Yahweh did not function as an unrelenting judge but is Himself abundant in justice, covenantal love, and self-sacrifice.

The summation of the text grows directly out of the conclusions of the previous sections. Micah was interested in moving his audience from a position of living with a disconnect between worship and lifestyle to a recognition that secular life impacts spiritual life. His methodology was as ingenious as his message was radical. Instead of tearing down the practices of Judah and their concerns for pleasing God, he utilized their ardent desire to please and sought to redirect their energies. He accomplished this task through three distinctive steps. First, Micah established a paradigm of justice and covenant commitment through outlining Yahweh's past actions. Secondly, he utilized vivid and costly comparisons in order to illustrate that the better gift before God is a disposition and attitude of self-sacrifice. Finally, he drew these two concepts together by stating that the ability to accomplish what he asked comes from linking oneself to the covenant keeper Himself—Yahweh. The better attitude that Micah desired his people to bring to worship is the emulation of God Himself.

Like his colleagues, Micah drew on the need for one to recognize the relationship between lifestyle and worship. However, Micah's approach differs in that his emphasis was on self-sacrifice and emulation of Yahweh as a means to achieving that goal. Micah was able

---

[76] Allen, *Joel, Obadiah, Jonah and Micah*, 363.

to achieve a careful balance between the call for putting one's own desires to the side and for still recognizing the call to act justly and seek justice for others.

This emphasis is necessary for a modern church that is often committed to either justice for others or introspective examination of our life before God, but seldom both. Micah's mandate grew out of the intrinsic value that the Bible places on the whole person. Whereas the modern expression of "walking with God" usually focuses either on the spiritual state of the heart or on observable behavior, the Bible rejects that dichotomy and recognizes that without attention to both, one's service to God is incomplete. Micah's message also illustrates the means by which one can accomplish a life of worship before God—careful consideration of and commitment to connecting oneself to the Creator. We cannot accomplish the task of godly living merely by redirecting our efforts toward doing what is right; rather, only by latching ourselves to God's side and walking with Him can we succeed. Churches in my own denomination often underemphasize the indwelling of the Holy Spirit and His work in this regard. But if one is ever going to be successful in worship or life, the process begins with attaching oneself to the only One with the resources to make such an endeavor possible.

## God Simply for Who He Is (Habakkuk 3)

Inherent in Abraham's offering of Isaac (Genesis 22) is the worship of God for who He is. Implicit in Hannah's prayers is the same recognition. The psalm of Habakkuk, however, is the most explicit of the three in recognizing God for who He is. The point where the prophet began his book, what he described as transpiring in relation to Jerusalem, and the contrasts he drew between these events and his disposition toward Yahweh demonstrate that Habakkuk was being torn from his theological moorings of how he believed God ought to act (Hab 1:2; 1:12–2:1) and found himself reintroduced to the idea of who God is and how He acts.

Those who have been through a personal theological crisis similar to the loss experienced by Habakkuk will find significant affinity with this passage. Others who have not experienced such a crisis need to understand that Habakkuk found himself at a juncture in life in which everything he had ever believed precious was destroyed. He wrote his book around the time of the destruction of Jerusalem and the temple. Like most Judeans, he held the temple and the city in high regard and apparently viewed them in some sense as inviolable (comparable to Isaiah). As such, the destruction, even in light of the corruption in the city, was a significant blow to his worldview and his understanding of God. It is not too surprising, then, that Habakkuk alone among the prophets began his book with questions of theodicy and the seeming disinterest of God in the plight of Jerusalem. God's responses amount to a promise that things were about to get worse (Hab 1:5–11) and that Habakkuk should do his job of proclamation and leave the details to God (Hab 2:2–5). After proclaiming the woes of judgment on those who sin (Hab 2:6–20), Habakkuk concluded with a psalm. He drew together his present situation with his knowledge of God's past actions, which enabled him to reformulate his puzzlement at God's actions. Eventually, he praised the One who is worthy of praise, regardless of what happens.[77]

The national appeal that one would expect from Habakkuk became very personal at the beginning where he appealed to God to remember mercy even when demonstrating His wrath. It is clear that for Habakkuk, the events of destruction are costly and hurtful to him personally.[78] Such a realization speaks volumes against those who would view the prophets as somehow detached from the events that they proclaimed and witnessed, that somehow they participated in their duties with either glee at the prospect of people receiving their deserved punishments or with a disinterested measure of stoicism. These men and women proclaimed their messages at high personal costs, not only materially but also theologically. Their struggle to understand all that was occurring and to cope with the

---

[77] J. Bruckner, *Jonah, Nahum, Habakkuk, Zephaniah*, NIVAC (Grand Rapids: Zondervan, 2004), 258.

[78] M. Sweeney cast the entire speech in the light of deserved punishment (*The Twelve Prophets*, vol. 2, *Micah, Nahum, Habakkuk, Zephaniah, Haggai, Zechariah, Malachi*, Berit Olam [Collegeville, MN: Liturgical Press, 2000], 487), but that hardly seems the direction that Habakkuk took the discussion given the clear expressions of personal impact.

ensuing loss serves well as a model and a comfort for those today
who face similar struggles, whether or not the struggle occurs in
relation to a direct ministry crisis or is more personal.

Much of the psalm is in the form of the hero epic.[79] But the usual
rehearsal of the hero's great deeds finds expression not with a human but with Yahweh. The imagery begins with the event that most
OT recollections of the great acts of God are drawn to—the exodus.
This immensely gracious and powerful act of God forever categorized Him as a deliverer from oppression and situations of immense
loss. To say that God comes from Teman and Paran is to link Him
to His revelation of presence through His divine name, Yahweh.
For it is in these precincts that He responded to Moses with the
"I Am" statement. One knows who God is by who He has been, and
Habakkuk's rehearsal of Yahweh's past greatness was sufficient to
ensure him of the future, even in the midst of great collapse.

The final movements of the psalm are the most poignant and conspicuous of the song. Habakkuk reflected on the majesty and power
of God as nature itself acknowledges the presence of Yahweh, and
even the mountains quiver at His approach (3:9–13a). He expressed
his confidence in the fact that God would defeat wickedness and
be vindicated ultimately in His actions (3:13b–15). But Habakkuk
knew that the loss would be severe and costly. The images in 3:16–
17 reflect loss of not only material goods but also national identity
and worldview, for each of the listed losses is a symbol of Israel and
its status before God. Habakkuk related the strongest of responses to
these events, demonstrating that he was utterly destroyed and seemingly incapable of wading through these difficult days until God's
restoration occurred.

Despite all this loss—national identity, personal security, and
even the way he viewed the world itself—Habakkuk concluded with
words of triumph and resolution. He never described God as capricious in His acts, evil in His intents, or unconnected to the suf-
ferings of His people. Though Habakkuk was undone and in some
sense lost, he knew that his God was his salvation and would cause
him to stand (3:18–19).

[79] R. D. Patterson, "The Psalm of Habakkuk," *GTJ* 8 (1987): 178–85.

From where does such confidence come? It comes from an underlying knowledge that to love God only for what He has given is to love what He has given more than Him.[80] When one truly knows God's activities and His heart, it becomes possible to worship and adore Him with confidence simply because He is God. Habakkuk used the genre of psalm in order to allow his song to become that of the nation and ultimately of all who experience loss. His expressions of survival certainly would have resonated most clearly with his contemporaries, but anyone who finds himself singing this song of confidence should also be moved from recognition of God's greatness in what He has granted to an acknowledgment of His greatness in who He is.[81]

## Prayer as an Offering (Hos 14:2)

We have looked at prayer already, but the passage in Hos 14:2 is so remarkable in its conception of prayer as a form of sacrifice that we must consider it. In the HCSB the passage reads: "Take words of repentance with you and return to the Lord. Say to Him: 'Forgive all our sin and accept what is good, so that we may repay You with praise from our lips.'" The last phrase literally reads, "and we will pay you with the bulls of our lips." As the imagery is clearly that of sacrifice, this passage has generally been interpreted as expressing a desire for a new beginning.[82] The words being assessed as a sacrifice are acceptable only when they can be presented as representative for past actions and future commitment.[83] In this way, the prophet made

---

[80] An objection might be raised at this point about distinguishing what God has done from who He is. As seen below, there is a close link between thanksgiving and praise, between praising God for what He has done and for who He is. But in a manner similar to the traditional wedding vows, "for better or worse," there comes a point at which the realities surrounding the one being loved fade into the background in favor of the person himself (or herself). Ultimately, a maturing relationship with God finds expression in moving beyond all that He has done to focusing simply on who He is.

[81] F. Andersen's conclusion that "Habakkuk is recording an experienced fact, not expressing an unrealized hope, and certainly not stating a general truth" is appreciated in its emphasis on the certainty of the reality of Habakkuk's experience, but seems to go too far in neglecting the universal implications of the psalmic genre; see Andersen, *Habakkuk: A New Translation with Introduction and Commentary*, AB (New York: Doubleday, 2001), 350.

[82] Wolff, *Hosea*, 234.

[83] Stuart, *Hosea–Jonah*, 213.

clear that at the heart of all his expressions concerning the nature of true worship and relationship with God is a call for confession and repentance. This is the crux of the attitude to be brought to all worship. Apart from confession and repentance we cannot enter into worship, and apart from the accompanying commitment of personal worship and service, worship has not been achieved.[84] Herein resides the bridge into what one takes from worship.

## What We Take From Worship

In many ways, what one takes from worship is as important as what one brings to it, but not in the sense of benefits received, though there are many. Rather, it is in the sense that whenever a meaningful exchange has taken place, transformation also occurs. Even in the most menial relationships, change happens when two persons communicate. How much more should we expect transformation from a meeting with the Creator of the universe? But one should be careful not to confuse good feelings with a worship experience. Worship is not about how one feels; it is about serving God and subjecting oneself to His direction. This is not to say that worship should be emotionless. Emotions do play a part in the experience because emotions are a part of who we are. We bring all that we are before God in worship, and an exchange on the most personal of levels takes place. But the meeting may not always result in solely positive expressions and emotions. This is clear not only in the laments that the next chapter examines, but in other events and practices already discussed. Whether it is the self-denial that occurred in conjunction with Yom Kippur (Lev 16:29) or the uneasiness and blatant terror expressed by worshippers (Exod 20:18; Hab 3:16), there can be a negative aspect to true worship.

### The Negative and Positive Aspects
### of Meeting God (Isa 6:1–7)

Isaiah's temple vision has been the subject of great interest for interpreters including those who focus on worship. In fact, some have

---

[84] Anderson and Freedman, *Hosea*, 645.

seen in these verses a pattern of a specific liturgy to be reproduced in a worship event. Such occasions can either be the most meaningful moments in the life of a church or some of the most painful to sit through. The difference in the outcome is directly dependent on the attitude with which the worshipper approaches God and the willingness of the leaders to follow the guidance of the Holy Spirit in its preparation. This work does not attempt to outline such a methodology, but it is clear that Isaiah's vision is one of the most clearly enunciated worship experiences in Scripture and thus deserves close scrutiny, particularly in relation to the numerous references to negative truths in this special text.

Isaiah 6 begins with a reference to the death of King Uzziah. Why Isaiah marked the outset of the narrative in such a way has been the subject of debate. Some consider it a simple marker of time, with no specific meaning other than setting an event within the sphere of history.[85] Or Isaiah may have begun with Uzziah's death to suggest that the experience was part of some significant worship event in the life of Israel.[86] Perhaps the world setting was the referent as Israel entered into this difficult time with a resurgent Assyria, and the prophet was making it clear that their reliance had to be on the true King of the universe instead of the temporal king of Israel.[87] Possibly Isaiah saw in the slow and alienated death of the king (2 Kgs 15:5) a picture of what might happen to Israel if they did not heed God's word of judgment.[88]

But there seems to be a more personal motive in addition to all the above. According to ancient tradition, Isaiah was Uzziah's first cousin. Additionally, the biblical narratives describe Uzziah as a good king who had a lengthy reign (2 Kgs 15:1–3; 2 Chr 26:3–15). Only toward the end of his reign was he cursed with a skin disease

---

[85] H. Wildberger, *Isaiah 1–12: A Commentary*, trans. T. Trapp (Minneapolis: Fortress, 1991), 259–60; see von Rad, *Old Testament Theology*, vol. 2, *The Theology of Israel's Prophetic Traditions*, trans. D. M. G. Stalker, OTL (New York: Harper & Row, 1965), 363.

[86] H. Ringgren proposed a link to Jotham's coronation (*The Prophetical Conception of Holiness* [Uppsala: Lundequistska Bokhandeln, 1948], 26).

[87] Oswalt, *Isaiah 1–39*, 176–77; against J. A. Motyer, *The Prophecy of Isaiah: An Introduction and Commentary* (Downers Grove: InterVarsity, 1993), 75.

[88] Motyer, *Isaiah*, 75. Similarly J. Watts noted that the marker illustrates the timing of God's choice to send Judah into exile (*Isaiah 1–33*, WBC [Waco: Word, 1985], 73).

of some sort. The affliction was apparently a result of misdeeds in the temple (2 Chr 26:16–23). The loss of his cousin, the only king he had ever known, would have been a time of personal crisis for the prophet. It is possible this played a role in his entrance into the temple precincts. Perhaps he went in to utter a lament and to seek answers, or perhaps he went simply to reflect on all that had transpired in the last several years. Whatever the reason, the event represented a significant moment of loss and change in his life.

The negative aspects of the vision continue with his description of the throne room or council of God. He hears the seraphim singing "Holy, Holy, Holy" (Isa 6:3), a super-superlative meant to express a holiness that is far beyond human thought.[89] While other gods might be called holy by their followers, only Yahweh is deserving of the appellation afforded him here—He is *the* holy one.[90] The mystery and necessary wariness suggested by the term "holy" *(qādôš)* is furthered by its coupling with the glory *(kābôd)* of God. The glory of God in the OT is generally understood as a manifestation of His holiness. It almost always calls for a sense of dread and fear, primarily because it reflects the meeting of the profane with the absolute holiness of God. Such is the case here where Isaiah described his plight as ruined *(nidmêtî,* "I am ruined"), a word which has a meaning related to silence so that Isaiah expressed severe despair. As von Rad wrote, "At this direct encounter with supreme holiness and in this atmosphere of sheer adoration, Isaiah became conscious of his own sinfulness and was appalled."[91]

One wonders at how easily today's churchgoers enter into God's presence in worship. When the biblical record is so clear that "for the finite, the mortal, the incomplete, and the fallible to encounter the Infinite, the Eternal, the Self-consistent, and the Infallible is to know the futility and hopelessness of one's existence."[92] To meet a holy God is to feel unsettled and disarmed. The experience could never be wholly positive, yet if one remains in this negative sphere for long, it can only be because one has no hope of atonement.

[89] Motyer, *Isaiah*, 77.
[90] Oswalt, *Isaiah 1–39*, 181.
[91] von Rad, *The Message of the Prophets*, 43.
[92] Oswalt, *Isaiah 1–39*, 182.

The narrative of Isa 6:6–7 is distinctive in its careful use of the word "atonement" *(kāpar)*. The act of the seraphim placing the hot coal on the lips is related to atonement. One should not miss the point that although no sacrifice is directly mentioned, the coal used does come from the altar where sacrifices were made.[93] Further, the event reveals two types of atonement in both ritual cleansing and removal of sin, something previously only having occurred on Yom Kippur.[94] This use of the word in reference to Isaiah's consecration by a coal from the altar suggests both a recognition of the efficacy of the altar when properly related to God and a notification of the prophet's submission to ritual in his being set apart for use by God.[95] Furthermore, the reference to atonement illustrates the word's relation to consecration. The event furthers the understanding of the importance of forgiveness in the worship experience and the fact that such cleansing is often an explicit part of preparing a person for God's use.

What happened to Isaiah inevitably raises the issue of whether or not his experience falls into the genre of a call narrative. Some reject such a classification because of Isaiah's ready acceptance of the invitation. Mordecai Kaplan suggested that the fact that an invitation—not a command—was given leads one to the proposal that this was not a call but simply a response to a moment of grief or despair about the failure of his preaching.[96] John Watts objected to referring to the passage as a call narrative insofar as it was not an inaugural experience, though he saw elements of such narratives in it.[97] Similarly, Christopher Seitz was hesitant to identify it as a call and saw it more as an event of distinction in Isaiah's experience that drew him away from sinful Israel and allowed him to do what they could not.[98]

[93] Thompson, *Penitence*, 175.

[94] J. Milgrom, *Leviticus 1–16: A New Translation with Introduction and Commentary*, AB (New York: Doubleday, 1991), 1084.

[95] O. Kaiser, *Isaiah 1–12: A Commentary*, 2d ed., OTL (Philadelphia: Westminster, 1983), 81.

[96] M. Kaplan, "Isaiah 6:1–11," *JBL* 45 (1926): 251–52; see H. L. Ginsberg, "Introduction," in *The Book of Isaiah: A New Translation* (Philadelphia: Jewish Publication Society, 1972), 16–18.

[97] Watts, *Isaiah 1–33*, 70–72.

[98] C. Seitz, *Isaiah 1–39*, INT (Louisville: John Knox Press, 1993), 54–56; also G. V. Smith, *Isaiah 1–39*, NAC (Nashville: B&H, 2007), 183–84.

Kaplan's position is the most ardently expressed against identifying the text as a call narrative, though other writers have joined him.[99] His supposition that we cannot consider it a call narrative since God offered an option is not convincing. One might reflect that the reason an option was given is that the form of the event was a meeting of the heavenly council in which a question of this sort was always put forward.[100] Strangely, Victor Matthews may have been attempting to address the need for a demand from God instead of an offer when he proposed a prior call to service and suggested that Isaiah's words in v. 5 were a demurral to escape service and the cleansing by the seraphim was God's command to go.[101] But since no command was expressed, this seems unlikely. Rather it seems best to simply acknowledge that there was no such demurral on Isaiah's part, and that this was a place where his call was to be distinguished from that of Jeremiah and Moses.[102] The location of the narrative in Isaiah 6 rather than at the book's beginning is intended to be determinative of his mission. It represents a twofold intention of demonstrating the doom to come while also presenting the idea that in the same way Isaiah had been rescued and cleansed, Israel could also be reconciled with God.[103]

In summary, Isaiah's experience should be considered a call. His acceptance of service is an extreme blessing from God and a key element that all participants should be taking away from a worship experience in one degree or another. This is true because those who have experienced the holiness of God and have received His unmerited favor and deliverance are repeatedly left with the sense that there is much that can be done for God.[104] Isaiah's narrative expresses his response to Yahweh's offer as immediate and brief, using among the fewest words possible in Hebrew to say, "Here I am,

---

[99] See O. Steck, "Bemerkungen zu Jesaja 6," *BZ* 16 (1972): 188–206; and K. Koch, *The Prophets*, vol. 1, *The Assyrian Period,* trans. M. Kohl (Philadelphia: Fortress, 1983), 113.

[100] Wildberger, *Isaiah 1–12*, 270.

[101] V. Matthews, *Social World of the Hebrew Prophets* (Peabody: Hendrickson, 2001), 82–83.

[102] J. Lindblom, *Prophecy in Ancient Israel* (Oxford: Basil Blackwell, 1962), 186.

[103] P. Ackroyd, "Isaiah I–XII: Presentation of a Prophet," in *Congress Volume: Göttingen 1977,* VTSup 29 (Leiden: Brill, 1978), 16–48.

[104] Oswalt, *Isaiah 1–39*, 186.

send me."[105] That Isaiah's call happened in the midst of, or as the culmination of, a worship experience demonstrates the close link between worship and calling. The implications of this link between worship and calling will be highlighted more later. But since not all call experiences are the same, a perusal of the various call narratives of the prophets is in order.

## The Call to Service

The same kind of call that the prophets received cannot be experienced by every believer. While every believer in the face of God's grace is challenged to service and ministry, there is a distinctiveness to the call to vocational ministry throughout Scripture that is vital to recognize. Still, it is appropriate to include discussion of the call here because it is often in the corporate experience of worship that the worshipper realizes and almost always submits to the call to ministry as a vocation. Indeed, at least one of the prophetic call narratives (see below) finds expression within a corporate worship experience, and every one of them can legitimately be described as an individual worship event. This reality heightens the irony and the problem all the more that so many churches now omit the call to ministry from their invitation, if they have an invitation at all. Worship without an invitation to commitment hardly seems representative of one of the clear directions that worship takes in Scripture.

A prophet's experience of the divine call was not wholly unique, even though it often occurred in a one-on-one setting with God. Whereas each call had its own individual emphases and perspectives, there was also in both form and content a clear link to other Israelite religious traditions and experiences. The prophets realized they were carrying on a long-standing duty held by previous prophets and that the call also occurred in connection with other cultic terminology and experiences.[106] Their calling was that aspect of their experience with God in which they achieved legitimacy and the authority to proclaim their message.[107]

---

[105] von Rad, *The Message of the Prophets*, 43.
[106] R. Clements, *Prophecy and Tradition* (Atlanta: John Knox Press, 1975), 37–40.
[107] Lindblom, *Prophecy*, 182.

One particular prophet's call merits special attention. Amos's story is quite different in many respects from that of his colleagues. Some even suggest that his words in Amos 7:14 indicate he was not a prophet at all.[108] However, Amos seemed to be objecting not to his vocation as a prophet but to what kind of prophet Amaziah was accusing him of being. He was not a cultic prophet who was linked to the altars and who fed off the income that such religious sites provided. He was not a leech to the false religion of the North. Therefore, Amaziah's words were false and disruptive to Amos's prophesying, which God Himself told him to do.[109] The most distinctive element of his report in the chapter is that he expressed his call in terms of a seeming momentary diversion from his usual employment.

More than the other prophets, Amos expressed his call in stark contrast from who he was when he received his call—a herdsman and keeper of sycamore figs. His call seemed somewhat unexpected to him. Furthermore, information about his ministry suggests that it only lasted about a year.[110] While it is always dangerous to draw conclusions from silence, the overall tone of the record may indicate that he probably returned to his former occupation at the end of his stint.

Amos's example may illustrate that there are individuals who are called into vocational ministry but not necessarily for their entire lives. Without a doubt there have been ministries and churches severely hurt because a minister who believed God was releasing him from the call to ministry stayed because he had earlier been told that to surrender to the call meant that he had to remain in vocational ministry for the rest of his life. We need to be cautious: one should pray as much about leaving the ministry as one does about entering it, but it does seem possible that God has temporary purposes for individuals in service to Him. The person surrendering needs to be ready to commit to a lifetime, but the individual serving before God

---

[108] J. Morgenstern, *Amos Studies*, vol. 1 (Cincinnati: Hebrew Union College, 1941), 30–31.

[109] Lindblom, *Prophecy*, 183–85. Lindblom also suggested that such a realization makes the translation of the verb in Amos' rejoinder of Amaziah—"I *was* not a prophet" instead of the more traditional "I *am* not a prophet"—unnecessary. Indeed, Amos's words of confrontation only make sense and carry weight in rebuttal if he is speaking of his present condition.

[110] Stuart, *Hosea–Jonah*, 284.

must always be ready to go wherever God leads him or her—even if that means out of vocation ministry.

To understand the prophetic call, it is necessary to step out of the prophetic books back into the Pentateuch. Exodus describes the call of Moses, and subsequent prophets looked to his call (Exod 3–4) to understand their own.[111] That Moses was the prototypical prophet finds expression in Deut 34:10 and in the numerous similarities of the components of his call with the extended call narratives of Isaiah, Jeremiah, and Ezekiel. Describing his call and noting the theology behind it make understanding the calls of those who came later a bit easier.

Moses' call to intercede on behalf of Israel and to serve as God's spokesman classifies him as a prophet in the most basic sense. This realization would logically draw us to the burning bush incident as we seek to identify elements of his call experience. Since no call takes place in a vacuum, it is necessary to take a brief look at the biblical descriptions of his life leading up to his call (Exod 2–4). Some conclusions concerning the discussion between Yahweh and Moses at the burning bush are largely affected by insights gained through a perusal of the first two periods of his life.

Following a command by Pharaoh that every infant Hebrew male should be cast into the river (Exod 1:22), the narrative begins with an account of the birth of a baby boy to Levite parents. Fearing for the child's life and perhaps assuming that an uncertain fate was better than a sure death, the infant's mother laid him in a basket made of reeds, which she then placed on the waters of the Nile.[112] His crying attracted the attention of Pharaoh's daughter, who commanded her servants to bring her the basket. She took the child into her family's household, and he grew into a man who intervened on behalf of the oppressed. First, he killed an Egyptian in order to save a Hebrew man's life, and then he delivered the Midianite shepherdesses from the brigands. The former event led him into the desert where he performed the latter. While in the desert, he married the

---

[111] Matthews, *Social World*, 39; W. Holladay, "The Background of Jeremiah's Self-Understanding: Moses, Samuel, and Psalm 22," *JBL* 83 (1964): 155–57.

[112] M. Noth, *Exodus: A Commentary*, trans. J S. Bowden, OTL (Philadelphia: Westminster, 1962), 25–26.

daughter of a Midianite priest named Jethro and became a shepherd. At this time he received his call from the Lord. Features of each stage teach important lessons about the total picture of calling that will also manifest themselves in the calls of the later Prophets.

The first feature, which is clear throughout each event, is *protection*. From the birth of a child into a world that sought his death to his discovery by a relative of the very person who had made the death decree, the narrative serves well to develop an undeniable feel of concern for how the story might end, yet throughout there are clues about God's ultimate purpose. The basket in which the child was placed (Exod 2:3) is literally an "ark" *(tēbâ)*. The only other place this word occurs in Scripture is in the narrative of Noah and the flood (Gen 6:14). It seems more than coincidence that the same word for the vehicle of salvation in Genesis was used in describing the instrument that would carry this infant boy.[113] The daughter of Pharaoh, aware of the child's ethnic origin, had pity on him and determined to save him despite Pharaoh's command. The story then relates that through the maneuvering of the baby's sister, the princess allowed the child to be weaned by his own mother, who was even paid for her efforts. Even in the events surrounding his flight to Midian there is a real sense of protection. The words of the Hebrew man asking if Moses would kill him too, though somewhat shocking to Moses, reveal God's ability to disclose to Moses from an entirely unexpected source that his life was in danger.[114]

The section of narrative involving the actual call also reflects protection, this time through God's granting of authority. This has already been suggested above in the manner that God revealed His name to Moses. But there are other features that also reflect this au-

---

[113] U. Cassuto, *A Commentary on the Book of Exodus*, trans. Israel Abrahams (Jerusalem: Magnes Press, 1967), 18. The narrative is a familiar one to the ancient Near East. Comparisons have been made to Herodotus's account of the childhood of Cyrus, but the most striking comparisons are to the story of Sargon, King of Akkad. The similar nature of the events is probably best understood as arising out of the most common manner of abandoning a child in the ancient Near East. See R. A. Cole, *Exodus: An Introduction and Commentary*, TOTC (Downers Grove: InterVarsity, 1973), 57; and L. Boadt, "Divine Wonders Never Cease: The Birth of Moses in God's Plan of Exodus," in *Preaching Biblical Texts*, ed. F. Holmgrem and H. Schaalman (Grand Rapids: Eerdmans, 1995), 55–56. For an English translation of the Sargon story, see *ANET*, 119.

[114] Cassuto, *Exodus*, 23.

thoritative prerogative. George Coats, for instance, sought to demonstrate that even in the rod one could see the necessity of man's actions coupled with God's authority as essential to the success of any endeavor.[115] The passage also reveals that what Moses experienced at the burning bush was indeed a theophany—a supernatural appearance of God that accompanied extraordinary natural phenomena for the purpose of conveying a message.[116] Fire occurs elsewhere as representing the very presence of God Himself.[117] That God chose to work through this revelation and through the "angel of Yahweh" has implications in the authority granted to Moses but also as a protective means of revelation. In light of the nature of the fire, while other texts may indicate a difference between this angel and Yahweh, it seems clear that in this particular reference the entity is God Himself, with the eponym used to maintain necessary distance from the divine nature.[118]

The second facet of the call apparent in this narrative is that of *preparation*. An examination of the interplay of both Moses' initial upbringing by his own Hebrew mother and the secondary training he gained in the house of Pharaoh are essential to understanding this feature of his preparation for the ministry he would undertake. Moses' training in his mother's house would most likely have consisted of instruction in the faith of his people. During these formative years he might have been introduced to stories of Abraham, Isaac, and Jacob and came to understand the notion of the "God of the Fathers."[119] These lessons may explain identification with his people and knowledge of those characters during later episodes.

Moses' training in Pharaoh's court is probably best explained through policies instituted by Thutmose III (c. 1500 BC).[120] It is

[115] G. Coats, *Moses: Heroic Man, Man of God* (Sheffield: Sheffield Academic Press, 1988), 68.

[116] As distinguished from an epiphany in which God appears to render aid and there seems to be little extraordinary phenomena involved. See C. Westermann, *Elements of Old Testament Theology* (Atlanta: John Knox Press, 1982), 25–26, 57–61.

[117] Cassuto, *Exodus*, 31; R. Clements, *Exodus*, CBC (Cambridge: University Press, 1972), 20; J. Durham, *Exodus*, WBC (Waco: Word, 1987), 31.

[118] Clements, *Exodus*, 20. M. Buber (*Moses: The Revelation and the Covenant* [New York: Harper & Row, 1958], 39) helpfully suggested that the angel of Yahweh represents that part of God that can be safely perceived.

[119] Cole, *Exodus*, 58.

[120] There are some isolated instances of similar policies in the Old and Middle Empires. A.

well-known from Thutmose's military annals that he instituted a policy in which the sons of foreign leaders were taken to Egypt, educated in their schools, and taught to fear and revere Egypt. Later, these leaders were placed on the thrones of their home kingdoms as rulers who were acceptable to both the natives of their lands and to Egypt.[121] The situation that may have given rise to the acceptance of Moses into the house of Pharaoh and his training seems fairly apparent, but exactly what that education included is less clear. Alan Cole claimed that only Solomon, Nehemiah, and Daniel could claim training of similar value to that of Moses.[122] James Boice suggested that the subject matter would have included areas in which Egypt was known to have had expertise—mathematics, astronomy, architecture, music, medicine, and writing.[123] Charles Pfeiffer concurred and added to the list the study of wisdom literature (see Acts 7:22).[124] It is difficult to say for certain that all of these features would have been a part of his training, but it seems likely that at the very least he would have learned the knowledge and skills necessary for leadership.[125]

As Moses shepherded Jethro's flocks, he would have developed an intricate knowledge of the desert. Knowledge of the topography and the effect rainfall had on the lower regions during the "wet" season would have been necessary for him to survive and to protect his sheep against loss. Further, being aware that there were only four major water supply centers in the Sinai area, Moses would have had to learn how to space out his movement and travel to avoid running out of water.[126] Another aspect of life in Midian would be knowledge

---

Erman, *Life in Ancient Egypt,* trans. H. M. Tirad (New York: Dover, 1971), 77–78.

[121] G. Kelm, *Escape to Conflict: A Biblical and Archaeological Approach to the Hebrew Exodus and Settlement* (Fort Worth: IAR Publications, 1991), 27. See S. Quirke and J. Spencer, *The British Museum Book of Ancient Egypt* (New York: Thames & Hudson, 1992), 41. For an English translation of the Thutmose annals referred to here, see *ANET,* 239. This policy was carried out from the time of Thutmose III (c. 1500 BC) to the end of the New Kingdom (c. 1100 BC).

[122] Cole, *Exodus,* 59.

[123] J. M. Boice, *Ordinary Men Called By God: Abraham, Moses, and David* (Wheaton: Victor Books, 1982), 55.

[124] C. Pfeiffer, *Egypt and the Exodus* (Grand Rapids: Baker, 1964), 43.

[125] This matter might include the study of law, such as the Code of Hammurabi, which is known to have been a favorite of Egyptian scribes; see Cole, *Exodus,* 59.

[126] Kelm, *Escape to Conflict,* 9–11.

of major trade routes. The shepherds and tradesmen of the Sinai Peninsula held to specific treks and paths as they moved through the area. There is no indication that the Bedouin of the region ever traveled outside already determined markers and paths. Also, Moses would have learned the patterns of migration that are, even today, necessary to maintain an adequate food supply. Moses' work and life in Midian provided him an opportunity to gain familiarity with a region where any group exiting Egypt and approaching the Levant would have had to spend a considerable amount of time.[127]

Moses' repeated questioning as he stood before God and God's patience in answering express something significant about God's preparation of Moses. William Alston revealed that many commonly held suppositions about the nature of God might require reevaluation in light of the knowledge gained from this pericope, which seemingly involves a genuine give-and-take dialogue on the part of God.[128] Indeed, there is much to gain about our understanding of God's preparation of man through an examination of this section of Scripture.

Moses' initial response to the presence of God was "Here I am." However, after learning of God's desire for him the statement quickly shifted to a question: "Who am I?" Numerous explanations have been offered for this question, usually relating to God's preparation of Moses for the task that lay before him. Cole saw in the question the residual effects of an earlier nervous breakdown that led to paralysis caused by complete self-distrust.[129] Others, more appropriately, understood the response to be a natural reply from a man who had been living the life of a shepherd but who was asked to approach the leader of the greatest empire on the face of the earth and to de-

---

[127] During the middle part of the twentieth century, scholars commonly suggested that Moses gained his knowledge of Yahweh and the religion that became Israel's from Jethro, his father-in-law, the Midianite priest. But more recent scholarship has rejected this "Kenite hypothesis" on the bases that it did not take into account pre-canonical structures of the story and that it went far beyond any demonstrable evidence. See B. S. Childs, *Exodus: A Commentary*, OTL (London: SCM Press, 1974), 322–23.

[128] W. Alston, "Divine-Human Dialogue and the Nature of God," *FaiPhil* 2 (1985): 5–20.

[129] Cole, *Exodus*, 68. Similarly, D. Zeligs (*Moses: A Psychodynamic Study* [New York: Human Sciences Press, 1986], 63) understood this reply to be the result of a lack of self-identity on the part of Moses.

mand obedience.[130] Moses needed one final act of preparation, and God provided it in a way that is both surprising and enduring.

God's answer to Moses' dilemma essentially ignored his complaint and focused on directing his attention from himself to God. God sought to reassure Moses by getting him to recognize that the struggle and success of the operation rested with Yahweh, not with Moses' abilities and efforts. As further assurance, God promised Moses a sign in the fact that Israel would worship God at the very place Moses stood before Him, Mount Sinai, which in 3:1 is called "Horeb, the mountain of God." In essence, God said that the sign would be that Israel would take part in what Moses was experiencing. [131] Cassuto described the sign in a similar way but also argued for a more immediate application. For him the sign need not rest on the completion of the task. Moses merely needed to contemplate God's statements and imagine Israel on a mountain, away from the natural path to Canaan and some distance from Egypt, for him to realize that the mission would be a success.[132] Such a visualization was only possible because of the insights Moses held into who God had been with Abraham, Isaac, and Jacob. The sign would be the actuality of the event, but the promise of such from a God known to keep His promises itself carries a strong note of assurance.

As a "down payment" on this sign, God gave Moses three others. His throwing down of the rod signified a subjugation of the religious hierarchy of Egypt.[133] Though the Egyptians were able to enchant snakes to the point that they became as stiff as a staff, Moses did the miracle of making a staff a snake. The miracle of the hand turned leprous and then cleansed carried with it meanings that reveal both God's power in the healing of an incurable disease and Moses' faith and courage in repeatedly accepting the severe malady. God's third miracle was the polluting of the Nile by turning it to blood. Without a doubt, this sign intended to communicate Yahweh's power over the gods of Egypt, especially the god of the Nile. Because the Nile was a deity to the people of Egypt, Yahweh's ability to destroy it and

---

[130] Childs, *Exodus*, 74; Cassuto, *Exodus*, 36.

[131] Durham, *Exodus*, 33.

[132] Cassuto, *Exodus*, 36.

[133] F. B. Meyer, *Moses: The Servant of God* (Grand Rapids: Zondervan, 1953), 38.

rob it of its fertility indicated His superiority.[134] These miracles serve both to confirm Moses as God's prophet and to demonstrate God's ability to accomplish what He has promised. This assurance is the final step in preparing Moses for the task before him.

Behind the events and actions of each person involved in the Moses narrative, one can recognize a unifying movement that culminates in the preparation of a man now qualified to accomplish the monumental task of delivering God's people from oppression. From the beginning of the story, despite being discovered by one from whom certain death would have been expected, the infant Moses was placed in a situation in which he received both the religious training of his Hebrew ancestry and the administrative training of the schools in Egypt.[135] In summary, "God's creative work in Moses' life to that point shaped a human being with endowments suited for the tasks ahead."[136]

The third aspect of the call is the *person* that God wanted to use. Moses' life and call reveal that he was indeed the person needed for the task. The killing of the Egyptian reveals Moses' concern for the plight of the oppressed. Justice was important to him, and he revealed great courage in his actions. When Moses saw the Egyptian "beating" (Hb. *nākâ*) the Hebrew (Exod 2:11), Moses "struck" (same Hb. verb) the Egyptian so that he died (v. 12). The repetition of the verb communicates the principle of retributive justice.[137] The lessons of his origin and heritage as a Hebrew that must have been taught him by his mother were not forgotten. Here was a man who had some degree of power but who never let that blind him to who he truly was.[138] Moses' actions against the shepherds in defense of the women represents once more his role as a fighter for the oppressed and protector of the weak (Exod 2:17).

---

[134] Cassuto, *Exodus*, 47–48; C. F. Keil, and F. Delitzsch, *Commentary on the Old Testament*, vol. 1, *The Pentateuch*, trans. J. Martin (Grand Rapids: Eerdmans, 1949), 450; Meyer, *Moses*, 38.

[135] Durham, *Exodus*, 16; Boadt, "Divine Wonders," 50.

[136] T. Fretheim, *Exodus*, INT (Louisville: Westminster John Knox, 1991), 56.

[137] This is not to say that Moses' actions were completely appropriate. D. Stuart points out the reality that premeditation was involved in the killing, and so there is very much a sense in which Moses is lost in knowing how to respond to the injustice he sees (*Exodus*, NAC [Nashville: B&H, 2006], 95).

[138] Buber, *Moses*, 36–37; Cassuto, *Exodus*, 22.

The questions Moses asked God reveal much about who he was and why God called him. Therefore, they also say something integral about the nature of God's call, not only to the prophets who came later but also to the church today. Some see in Moses' statements the acts of a coward, while others see a natural reaction to the immense task that he was asked to undertake.[139] Childs is probably correct in his assessment that the beauty and interest of the narrative lie in the fact that there is a mixture of both legitimate and unworthy responses by Moses to the call of God.[140] Fretheim perceptively observed that Moses' questions, while indeed displaying a lack of ambition, also reveal the very characteristic—single-mindedness—that Yahweh recognized in him as part of His decision to call Moses to the task at hand. According to Fretheim, the fact that Moses could stand in the midst of the wondrous sight, fully recognizing that he was before Yahweh, and still bring questions and complaints reveals that Moses was precisely the man God needed to be able to stand before mighty Pharaoh and announce that he must release the Israelites. In other words, if God could get Moses to accept His call and recognize how important it was to be the spokesman for Israel, He had a person who would pester Pharaoh until he gave in.[141] So often people worry about changing their personalities to fit what they perceive as the proper one for service, when in fact this text demonstrates that even those characteristics that we might view as negative can be used by God. Moses' single-mindedness is obstinacy when refusing God's directions, but is passionate commitment when utilized by God.

Now we can return to the account of the burning bush. Moses' questions quickly transformed into excuses and refusals. God was still patient, but the tempo has quickened and the time for Moses' replies has ended. He has to either accept the call or refuse it.[142] Moses initially chose to refuse and to request that God would send someone else. God's response to Moses' plea was anger. The reasons for the anger are somewhat hidden because one must resort to

---

[139] Fretheim, *Exodus*, 58; Buber, *Moses*, 47.
[140] Childs, *Exodus*, 73.
[141] Fretheim, *Exodus*, 58.
[142] Childs, *Exodus*, 79.

precarious anthropopathisms in order to make suppositions. Some suggest the response to be the result of frustration from the fact that God had answered every objection and Moses was still unwilling to go. Others see in the anger a tone of disappointment because He must now resort to accomplishing His task in a way that is less desirable.[143] But one must be careful in evaluating God's actions so as not to constrain God by our own emotions and feelings concerning the event. It was Moses, not God, who lost in the exchange, since it is clear from the way the narrative abruptly ends that the matter is no longer up for discussion. Moses as the commissioned one will go; yet God did not ignore Moses' questions and plight: He not only provides Aaron but He also once again gently reminded Moses of His presence with him—which is the true source of his ability—by encouraging him to take up his rod as he goes.[144]

All three of the elements present in Moses' call grow out of a theology of God's providence. As illustrated in Genesis 1, this sovereignty is not coercive but evocative. Man is a free agent, yet God is sovereign. How both these elements coexist is somewhat of a mystery; but this is no more mysterious than the Trinity in which God is both three Persons and yet one God, or in the Incarnation in which Jesus Christ is both fully God and fully man.

But today Christians for some reason feel it necessary to argue over whether our freedom or God's sovereignty ought to receive the greater emphasis. As with the other mysteries, the overemphasis of either side leads down the road to loss of important biblical concepts and to indefensible division. The narrative of Moses' call reflects a God who protects and prepares. But God also works in relationship with the individual's personality, moving and directing it—but not overriding or obliterating it. James H. Kennedy eloquently summarized the interrelatedness of the responsibilities of both parties: "It is God's prerogative to provide the talent; it is man's part to perform the task. It is man's privilege to dedicate all that he has received; it

---

[143] Keil and Delitzsch, *The Pentateuch*, 451; Fretheim, *Exodus*, 73.
[144] Childs, *Exodus*, 79.

is God's pleasure to consecrate all that he has given."[145] These same features are evident in the other prophets also.

Isaiah's call and its implications for worship have been part of this book's previous discussion. What remains is an application of the descriptions in the book of Isaiah to the event of his calling. Like Moses, Isaiah's background played a significant role in his ministry. He might very well have been of noble blood, as noted above. He apparently had access to even the most private of the king's chambers (2 Kgs 20:1), and much of his preaching took place in the king's court. Such social standing also would have contributed to a literacy that may account for the second half of his book being called among the most beautiful and skillfully written in the entire Bible.[146] He rarely expressed doubt and articulated an assuredness of his positions that few other prophets displayed. The call itself reveals his confidence through the absence of any demurral once a call was put forward. That the event in the temple further prepared him for his ministry is finally clear in his distinctive use of "holy." Whereas other prophets spoke of God's holiness in relation to His anger and wrath (Jer 23:9; Ezek 43:8; Joel 2:1), Isaiah added to this perspective the view that the Holy One is the Redeemer (Isa 10:20; 12:6; 29:19; 30:15).[147] One can reasonably surmise that such usage grew out of his call experience where God's holiness went side by side with the redemption and the forgiveness that he gave Isaiah.

The call of Jeremiah (Jer 1:4–10) probably has the most affinity of all the prophetic calls with that of Moses. William Holladay demonstrated that Moses did, in fact, function prototypically for Jeremiah in his complaint about speaking followed by God's provision and in the prominent role of his mother in his early ministry.[148] Further,

---

[145] J. H. Kennedy, *The Commission of Moses and the Christian Calling* (Grand Rapids: Eerdmans, 1964), 67.

[146] Though highly debated, the opinion here is that Isaiah ben Amoz is responsible for the whole of the book of Isaiah; see Oswalt, *Isaiah 1–39*, 17–23; Motyer, *Isaiah*, 13–34.

[147] Only Hosea comes close to this concept (Hos 11:9). This emphasis is highlighted all the more by the fact that Isaiah among all the prophets was committed to the appellation of God as "The Holy One of Israel." He used the adjectival form of "holy" more than all the rest of the OT writers put together (Motyer, *Isaiah*, 17) and the full phrase 29 times, as compared to five times in the rest of the OT.

[148] Holladay, "Background of Jeremiah," 155–157.

both would intercede for the whole nation and introduce a new covenant to the people.[149] Elsewhere, Holladay explained that Jeremiah likely saw himself as the fulfillment of Deut 18:18: "I will raise up for them a prophet like you from among their brothers. I will put My words in his mouth, and he will tell them everything I command him."[150] Jeremiah's connection to Moses makes it clear that there is much one can understand about his own call from those who are his spiritual ancestors.

Jeremiah's call contained the elements of protection (Jer 1:8) and preparation (Jer 1:5,9). God responded to the objections that Jeremiah raised with the same patience and redirection that he had offered to Moses (Jer 1:7). But because of the person Jeremiah was, there was a distinct difference in how the call itself is manifested. There is nothing visionary in God's call; instead, it is primarily auditory in nature. The comments were simple and restrained. The experience was much more of an intellectual exchange with greater theological reflection and less imagery. Even in the visions that immediately followed the call, there was a sense in which they were very static.[151] The opening words of his call in v. 5 contain three words (*yāda‘*, "to know," *qādaš*, "to sanctify," and *nātan*, "to give, appoint") that emphasize the distinctiveness and intimate nature of his call. Such expressions would indeed be important for one as young as Jeremiah.

Ezekiel's call (Ezekiel 1–3) is the longest call narrative in the Scripture. It is generally divided into the throne vision (Ezekiel 1), the commissioning (Ezek 2:1–3:15), and the call of the watchman (Ezek 3:16–27). Ezekiel's status as the only prophet to function entirely in his office outside the land of Israel no doubt played a role in how his call transpired.[152] From the perspective of his recipients, and probably to some degree even in his own mind, his presence in the exile marked him as a cursed man under the punishment

---

[149] Ibid., 163–64.

[150] W. Holladay, "Jeremiah and Moses," *JBL* 85 (1966): 17–27.

[151] von Rad, *The Message of the Prophets*, 45. Lindblom's statement (*Prophecy*, 189) that the call certainly had to be ecstatic and visionary seems unnecessary and is hardly evidenced in the text.

[152] R. Wilson, "Prophecy in Crisis: The Call of Ezekiel," in *Interpreting the Prophets*, ed. J. Mays and P. Achtemeier (Philadelphia: Fortress, 1987), 169.

of God. The throne vision alleviates much of that perspective by highlighting the fact that Yahweh is on his throne, even in the midst of the exile in Babylon. This separation from the promised land apparently also serves as the background for the opening reference to the "thirtieth year." Scholars are now nearly unanimous in the view that this year marker is in some way a reference to both his priestly and his prophetic role (see Numbers 4).[153] That year was an important milestone for this priest who was separated from the temple and unable to seek consecration.[154] Further, because of his status as a priest, there is nothing anthropomorphic in Ezekiel's concept of Yahweh in his call; Yahweh's glory is the emphasis.[155] That it is also linked to his prophetic calling serves to further emphasize the totality of God's responsiveness to who we are when he issues a call.

There is significant discussion as to whether Ezekiel received any sort of preparation for his prophetic duties. Gerhard von Rad suggested that since there is no discussion of Ezekiel's transition from a status of un-called to that of serving, neither personal endowment nor faith played a role in preparing the man who would serve.[156] But this observation seems not to take in the full range of evidence, for apart from the implicit process in the first prophetic signs as rites of passage into the prophetic role,[157] his empowerment by the Spirit (Ezek 2:2) and the consumption of the scroll (Ezek 3:1–3) are clearly preparatory in nature. The former hearkens back to the judges when such an empowerment was the very basis for their activity and success, and the latter is tantamount to God's placing His words in Jeremiah's mouth and giving Ezekiel the message he is to proclaim.[158]

---

[153] J. E. Miller, "The Thirtieth Year" *RB* 99 (1992): 499–503.

[154] M. Odell, "You Are What You Eat: Ezekiel and the Scroll," *JBL* 117 (1998): 239.

[155] Matthews, *Social World*, 133.

[156] von Rad, *Old Testament Theology* 2, 58.

[157] Odell, "What You Eat," 235–48.

[158] See E. Davis, "Swallowing Hard, Reflections on Ezekiel's Dumbness," in *Signs and Wonders: Biblical Texts in Literary Focus*, ed. J. C. Exum, SemeiaSt 18 (Atlanta: Scholars' Press, 1989), 217–37; W. Zimmerli, *Ezekiel 1*, trans. R. Clements, Her (Philadelphia: Fortress, 1979), 106; and Lindblom, *Prophecy*, 189. Contrast Odell who argued that the swallowing is the consumption of the judgment or fate of the people itself. Ezekiel was the priest eating the sin offering, taking away the sin of the people and absolving it (Odell, "What You Eat," 244).

The distinctiveness of each call is directly attributable to the distinctiveness of each prophet. This in itself should say something about the need for responsiveness from each individual in the call. For if the matter solely rested in God's decree, there would be no need for a distinct approach to each man. For Moses, God was the fire that would lead him and the people through the wilderness. For Isaiah, he was the Holy One of Israel who is both separated from Israel and yet bound to His people through covenant. For Jeremiah, God was simple and discreet, even gentle; yet God was intimately involved in Jeremiah's life. For Ezekiel God was the eminently enthroned One in the midst of the exile and separation. For each man's needs and outlook there was a unique response from God to draw them into His service.

The same is true today as God draws and calls people. Such a conclusion should help alleviate the tendency by many to question their calling because it was not expressed the way another's was. Different individuals should expect different calls. But beyond this, the calling also takes into account God's protection and preparation as the person carries out the task he has been assigned—and with an authority that is only found when such a call exists.[159]

What one takes away from worship is no more centered in self than what one ought to bring to worship. The confidence of the prophets in their calling should not be confused with a confidence that they would be a "success." Repeatedly, God's words in the calling accounts highlight that though the prophet goes, no one will respond (Isa 6:9–13, Jer 1:19; Ezek 3:18–21). Indeed, it seems that from a biblical perspective God's call is to faithful execution of His expectations, not to success as man would define it. Furthermore, in an event dedicated to the praise and adoration of God and the

---

[159] One further note on the authority of the modern minister. The call is important for authority, but there is a distinction between the prophet and the preacher that must be recognized—the source of his authority to say what he says. Whereas the prophet spoke the words of God through inspiration, preachers expound on the Word of God through illumination. The distinction is important because when a prophet brought judgment on a challenger, he was doing so because the person was not only challenging him, but God. Too often preachers use such texts and arrogantly suppose that the preacher too is above being questioned. But a preacher's authority to say what he says is only present to the degree to which he has faithfully exegeted the Scriptures.

humility of the worshipper, the only thing one can truly take away is a deeper understanding of his responsibility before God. It would seem then that the oft-mentioned appraisal of an event as a place where "real worship" took place is an empty refrain if the one saying it is not driven to a manifestly more substantial commitment to God's message and ministry. For some, this means a pledge to vocation ministry; for others, something else. But in a world heading toward its culmination, there is a need for such dedication to play a significant role in all worship events.

## A New Attitude: Worship and the Last Days

The emphasis on eschatology that has surfaced over the last several decades is not too surprising given the turn of the millennium. In the rush to lay out the last events and to emphasize the imminence of Christ's return, it can be easy to forget that at the center of the end time perspective of the Bible is the doctrine of worship. This is made clear in the centrality of the temple precincts to "final events" (Isa 2:2–4; Ezekiel 40–46; Mic 4:1–5; Zech 14:20–21). This emphasis is probably the outgrowth of the nature of eschatology, which is a "dimension of belief that history moves in a direction, that this direction is set by God, and that God acts within history to insure his direction."[160] Such belief is the heart of worship not only because it puts God at the center of history, but also because such a belief has the ability to transform attitudes by reemphasizing justice, transformation, and hope.

### The Restoration of Justice (The Day of Yahweh)

The Day of Yahweh terminology in the prophets is complex and considerable. Beyond the specific use of the exact phrase "the Day of Yahweh," there are at least eight other synonymous expressions, the most prevalent of these being "in that day" which occurs approximately two hundred times.[161] The place of the day in the cultic

---

[160] P. R. Davies, "Eschatology in the Book of Daniel," *JSOT* 17 (1980): 33.

[161] Other phrases are "Day belonging to Yahweh" (Isa 2:12; Ezek 30:3; Zech 14:1); "Day of Yahweh's Wrath" (Ezek 7:19; Zeph 1:18); "Day of Yahweh's Anger" (Zeph 2:2–3; Lam 2:22); "Day of Yahweh's Sacrifice" (Zeph 1:8); "Day of Vengeance" (Jer 46:10; Isa 34:8; 61:2; 63:4);

activity of Israel remains a debated issue. Sigmund Mowinckel has identified a cultic Day of Yahweh service that reaffirmed hope for successive generations in the ultimate Day of Yahweh when God would be enthroned and favorable conditions would be instituted.[162] Although this is possible, it does not appear to be likely in light of the lack of any biblical or historical evidence that points to such a day. Still, the day served a purpose in the worship perspective of Israel in that it played a vital part in Israel's view of election and their expectation that Yahweh would ultimately keep the covenant promises He had made.[163]

The day is not always described as a positive experience, and it is clear from the texts that there was more than one Day of Yahweh in the minds of the prophets.[164] Amos describes it as a day of darkness when Israel is judged and destruction occurs (Amos 5:18–20). Similarly, the book of Lamentations looks back on the temple's destruction as an expression of the day (Lam 1:12; 2:1). Apparently, for the prophets the day was more about Yahweh's enemies than Israel's. Therefore, when Israel was in good standing with God, the people would enjoy His blessing. When they were not, they would incur His wrath. Whether or not the prophetic concept was a correction of a long-standing tradition concerning the day of Yahweh or a transformation of it, the point seems to be clear that the day serves as a time when Yahweh annihilates His enemies.[165] Therefore, this day is a day of justice. This theme is a significant function of the transformative power of worship since it reminds us that our present state of experienced injustice is not the final state we will see (see Ps 73:17).[166]

"Day of His Burning Anger" (Lam 1:12); "Day of His Anger" (Lam 2:1); and "Day of tumult, trampling, and bewilderment" (Isa 22:5).

[162] Mowinckel, *Psalmenstudien* II, 229.

[163] Clements, *Prophecy and Covenant*, 108–9.

[164] This latter fact is most clearly demonstrated by the use of the day in reference to past events (see Lam 1:12; 2:1).

[165] von Rad, "The Origin of the Day of Yahweh," *JSS* 4 (1959): 97–108.

[166] Some may object that for the Christian grace is a more appropriate focus than justice. The role of grace in salvation is a key matter in the issue of worship. That we all do not get what is deserved is a source of great joy. But God's attribute of righteousness as well as His repeated reflections on the distinction between the righteous and the unrighteous, even in the NT (Matt 25:31–46), does render justice a suitable subject in worship.

## The Transformation Towards Holiness

Another eschatological expectation that functions significantly in worship is that of transformation toward holiness. The centrality of holiness to the matter of worship has already been emphasized above in numerous ways. But what the prophets do with this concept is to expand it into a universal by identifying God's purpose of ultimately renovating that which was formerly profaned into that which is His. Two of the most outstanding expressions of this purpose are Ezekiel's and Zephaniah's new Jerusalem.

Ezekiel's new Jerusalem (Ezekiel 40–47) at the end of his ministry directly contrasts with the Jerusalem he inspects at the beginning (Ezekiel 8–11). His journey to Israel for a second tour was designed to juxtapose the restoration with the destruction. As such, Ezekiel's vision amounted to an "ideal revision of the institutions of the new Israel that would ensure the permanence of the restoration."[167] God will transform Israel from the failure that it had been to the success that only He could render. This conversion will only be possible with God on His throne (Ezek 34:7–16) and with His abiding presence in the midst of his people, thus the new name of the city as *yhwh šāmmâ* ("Yahweh Is There"; 48:35).[168]

For Zephaniah (Zeph 14:20–21), the transformation begins with Jerusalem and Yahweh's enthronement there, but it moves outward to encompass the whole world (see Isaiah 65). Whereas it was the Canaanites who had polluted the land (Exod 34:11–16; Lev 18:2–5; Deut 7:1–6), there would no longer be a Canaanite present.[169] God will transform even the most simple pots and horses' bells into objects that are holy to him. The meaning could not be clearer. The entire world will be transformed and drawn into holiness and worship of God,[170] not in the sense of a non-distinguishing salvation

---

[167] M. Greenberg, "The Design and Themes of Ezekiel's Program of Restoration," in *Interpreting the Prophets,* ed. J. Mays and P. Achtemeier (Philadelphia: Fortress, 1987), 235.

[168] Ibid., 216; Matthews, *Social World,* 143.

[169] That a double entendre is present here with reference to the Canaanite and the merchant (both are proper translations of the Hebrew) is clear in the indications of the holiness of the entire land and not simply the temple; see M. Boda, *Haggai, Zechariah,* NIVAC (Grand Rapids: Zondervan, 2004), 529.

[170] O'Brien, *Nahum–Malachi,* 283–84.

but through transformation of those who are His and expulsion of all that are not (see Mal 1:11,14b). But here the emphasis is not on the justice of God as much as it is on His grace and the capacity of that grace to turn even the most common realities into new elements before Him.

## The Restitution of Hope

Closely related to the concept of the transformation toward holiness, though nuanced in a slightly different direction, are the prophetic expressions of the restitution of hope. The most jolting of these to their context is Amos 9:11–15, though other passages also speak of this restoration (Isaiah 7–12; 44; Jeremiah 30–31; Joel 3:1,17–21; Nah 2:2; Zeph 2:7; 3:9–20). Amos's message was the doom of Israel and the fact that its destiny would be severe and complete destruction. Yet at the end of his message the situation transformed into one of bountiful hope and grace. Israel will once again be under Davidic rule (Amos 9:11–12). The harvest will be such that while the harvesters were still working, the planters for the next season will begin their work (Amos 9:13). Ultimately, the people who were to be the brunt of Yahweh's judgment and not even allowed to live in their houses (Amos 3:15; 6:11) will one day find security in the land and never be uprooted again (Amos 9:14–15). These expressions reveal that the prophets had a concept of an event in their future in which a radical transition would be made and their fortunes would be renewed.[171] Such is the source of hope and subsequently a cause for worship. This hope is primarily centered in a messianic reality since the Messiah will be there to usher in much of what is mentioned in these promises.

There is much that could be said at this point about the Messiah. While it is tempting to follow the direction of looking at the role of the king in the cult (a topic for the next chapter), the study here will be limited to the hope offered through the radical transformation the Messiah will bring in His nature and essence. The passage in Mic 5:2 illustrates this prophetic hope concerning a Messiah: "Bethlehem

---

[171] Clements, *Prophecy and Covenant,* 113–14.

Ephrathah, you are small among the clans of Judah; One will come from you to be ruler over Israel for Me. His origin is from antiquity, from eternity."

It is quite easy with such a passage to jump immediately to the birth of Christ and speak only of its fulfillment. This is especially true given Matthew's use of the oracle in Matt 2:6.[172] But if one is too quick to make the connection or is resigned to seeing only that relationship and import in Micah's statement, much is lost. First, as stated previously, to limit the passage only to a prediction-fulfillment level is to limit God's ability to express His nature as history progresses.[173] In contrast to such an approach, a recognition of the voice of God to Israel in the days of Micah reveals a God responsive to His people's needs and involved in resolving their problems. Second, the coupling of this passage with the Assyrian approach with which Micah dealt suggests a call on the part of Micah for the people to turn away from self-reliance and recognize that victory comes only from God.[174] This emphasis has already been seen as essential to worship. The messianic context of the passage simply reinforces this. Finally, if one jumps too quickly to the passage's fulfillment in the NT, he misses the main idea being addressed here: the radical change the Messiah would be from the kings of Israel.

Micah emphatically stated that the Jerusalem monarchy was devoid of power and legitimacy, but reliance upon God, typified by the monarch born in Bethlehem, would result in victory.[175] He made a clear statement about an illegitimate versus a legitimate monarchy,

---

[172] The issue of the NT's use of the OT, including Matthew's slight alteration of the Micah passage, is beyond the scope of this book. For discussion of the issue in general and Matthew's use of Micah in particular, see E. E. Ellis, *Prophecy and Hermeneutic in Early Christianity* (Grand Rapids: Baker, 1993); and D. Baker, *Two Testaments, One Bible,* rev. ed. (Downers Grove: InterVarsity, 1991).

[173] See VanGemeren, *Interpreting the Prophetic Word,* 80–82.

[174] Whether or not Mic 5:5–6 is an oracle of salvation (applicable to the Messianic era) or a nationalistic song of victory that Micah disputed is an unsettled issue. See H. W. Wolff, *Micah: A Commentary,* trans. G. Stansell (Minneapolis: Fortress, 1990), 147, with Allen, *Joel, Obadiah, Jonah and Micah,* 347–48.

[175] The link to Jesus at this point is significant because the power base in Jerusalem that Micah addressed was the same kind that Matthew addressed in Christ's birth narrative. C. Blomberg (*Matthew,* NAC [Nashville: B&H, 1992], 63–64) compared the corrupt Jerusalem establishment with the new Bethlehem king, though he did not draw Micah's similar position into his interpretation.

highlighting the declaration in his allusionary jump past the lineage of David to David himself. Both Micah (Mic 5:2) and Isaiah (Isa 11:1) make a radical assessment of the future messianic King that anticipates how He should be understood further than that of earlier messianic expectations (Amos 9). For them, it is not enough that the future Messiah be a descendant of David. Such individuals had proven themselves to be less than satisfactory. Instead, the One who is to come would arise outside of the corrupt influences of the royal house; He would be from humble beginnings.[176] He would sprout from the shoot of Jesse and would be born in the city that gave birth to David. In short, He would not simply be a descendant of David; He would be a new David![177] The eschatological hope of a new David, then, is as radical a transition as is the new Israel. Both are built on the fact that men had failed in the covenant promises, but God would be faithful to His.

Eschatology rightfully serves a purpose as an emphatic part of worship in evangelical churches. While it is possible to become overly enamored with it and forget that there is more to the biblical revelation than just eschatology, there is much about the subject that instills and reinforces the emphases of worship. In a world devoid of justice, the stress placed on the topic in the end-time perspective of the prophets both reassures and challenges. That God is just is cause for adoration, but it is also a challenge to emulate Him in this way and to see His will done on earth as it is in heaven. To a world mired in darkness and corruption, the transformation toward holiness anticipated in the biblical texts is a source of great joy and confidence. For the hopeless, the instillation of hope via the new creation awaiting the King of the universe to take His throne generates a freedom of expression unlike much else.

---

[176] Oswalt, *Isaiah 1–39*, 278–79.

[177] This jump may be the result of a prophetic contemplation of the nature of the messianic promise in light of their need to admit there would be an end to the physical reign of David's line at the onset of the Exile, something not seemingly expressed in God's promise to David in 2 Sam 7:8-15.

## *Attitudes in the NT*

It is a truism among evangelicals that the NT is focused on the attitudes behind our actions. Hopefully, this perusal through the prophets has established if only in some small way that the same is true of the OT. The foundation of worship is relationship. For any relationship to work there has to be a proper attitude or disposition toward the other person. The OT prophets highlighted attitude by emphasizing its superiority to, though not exclusion of, actions. They accentuated the necessity to bring one's best to worship, since doing less reveals that no worth is being ascribed to the One who is supposedly being adored. They highlighted that all worship ultimately leads to a response and that what one really should hope to take away from worship is a deeper commitment to the God being served. Finally, they stressed that eschatology is a great source of worship because of what it says about God and where He is taking the world. As with previously outlined aspects of worship in the OT, these attitudes are also found in the NT.

### Obedience Is Still Better Than Sacrifice

The NT emphasizes the true nature of worship in its mandates and instructions as being service before both God and man. Jesus reminded the Pharisees of the prophetic credo that mercy is preferable to sacrifice in His defense of His ministry to the oppressed and lost (Matt 9:13). The gathering together of the corporate body for any purpose can never be divorced from the requirement for outreach. Worship should never be viewed as solely an internal focus between God and man. Its implications and effects go outside this vertical relationship to speak to horizontal ones as well. While there is much to be said for keeping a worship event focused on God, one loses his way if he forgets that God's desire is for relationship with *all* people. Indeed, an experience that has little to no impact on the world around the participants cannot be said to be worship from a biblical perspective.

In the same way that the prophets emphasized the interaction of righteousness and justice with worship, Christ proclaimed that those who were His would practice them too (Matt 25:31–46). Jesus' expulsion of the money changers from the temple while quoting the words of Jeremiah in His temple sermon (Matt 21:13; Mark 11:17; Luke 19:46) suggests that He also understood the thievery and oppression inherent in their activities as antithetical to worship. James followed Christ's lead when he proclaimed: "Pure and undefiled religion before our God and Father is this: to look after orphans and widows in their distress and to keep oneself unstained by the world" (Jas 1:27). John similarly merged ethics and theology in his teaching that true followers of Christ demonstrate the same concern through loving the Father *and* the Father's children (1 John 4:7–5:4).[178] The association of worship with righteousness and justice is so inextricable that if one is missing, the other cannot exist either.

## All That We Are Is All We Need Bring

Micah challenged his readers to "walk humbly" (Mic 6:8), which means to "walk with careful and measured conduct as an expression of worship before God." Paul also encouraged his recipients to "pay careful attention" to their walk and to make the most of their time, as they walked before God (Eph 5:15–17). In both contexts the focus is on complete commitment to God as opposed to other things that compete for one's attention. Also, both contexts place their injunction in direct contact with worship terminology. As has been demonstrated, Micah did this in connection with services related to an altar; similarly, Paul continued his instruction with an encouragement to make music, to give thanks, and to submit to one another in the fear of Christ (Eph 5:19–21).

In Rom 12:1–2 Paul gave his clearest instructions about the topic of bringing all that one is to God in worship and service. This passage serves as practical council at the end of Paul's theological exposition. As a bridge into further pragmatic instructions, it serves to highlight the demanding work of human relationships as one lives out his commitment before God, a work that is so demanding that Paul used sacrificial language as his metaphor to describe it.[179] But

[178] S. Smalley, *1, 2, 3 John*, WBC (Waco: Word, 1984), 270–72.
[179] J. D. G. Dunn, *Romans 9–16*, WBC (Waco: Word, 1988), 715–17.

he made the sacrifice distinctive through the use of three adjectives to portray it. For Paul, the sacrifice that is the Christian life is "living" in that it is a lasting righteousness; it is "holy" in that it is a dedicated service to God; and it is "pleasing" because it is what God always desires.[180] It results in "spiritual" or true worship because it combines the reality of an inner attitude at the worship event with a life of action that is characterized by the same selflessness. Käsemann brilliantly commented on the interaction between worship and life: "Either the whole of Christian life is worship and the gatherings and sacramental acts of the community provide instruction for this, or these gatherings and acts lead in fact to absurdity."[181]

Confession before God can be a somewhat sensitive topic for those of us who believe in the full efficacy of Christ's sacrifice. Therefore, the link between confession of sin and worship in Hosea 14 might seem like a matter for a different age. But 1 John highlights the fact that we cannot avoid the presence of sin in the world and that even Christians struggle with it (see 1:5–10). Consequently, just as Hosea had done some eight centuries earlier, John reminded his readers of the necessity to acknowledge their sin before God, and in doing so to have authentic fellowship with God and his people.[182] Therefore, since Jesus forever settled at the cross our need for atonement, we are able to truly give God everything we are in worship. But John made clear that Christians continue to sin and that it must be dealt with in confession. The juxtaposition of these two truths serves as a source of great joy when one, like Isaiah, finds himself purified before the holy God.

## The Call Remains the Same

In an enlightening examination of the commission formula in the NT, Terence Mullins advocated that the call narratives present in the OT bear a conspicuous resemblance to those of the NT in form, content, and theology.[183] He identified 37 accounts in the NT of a

---

[180] D. J. Moo, *The Epistle to the Romans*, NICNT (Grand Rapids: Eerdmans, 1996), 751.

[181] E. Käsemann, *Commentary on Romans*, trans. G. Bromiley (London: SCM Press, 1980), 327.

[182] Smalley, *1, 2, 3 John*, 30, 41.

[183] T. Y. Mullins, "NT Commission Forms, Especially in Luke–Acts," *JBL* 95 (1976): 603–

specific commission.[184] Like those in the OT they vary depending on who is being commissioned. The person was prepared through the expression of the authority of the individual who made the calling and brought from a perspective of loss and bewilderment to one of commitment. As in both OT and early NT times, one knows he is ready for service when called simply because it is God who does the calling. Calls to service logically arise from the recognition of the debt owed to the One who has transformed us. But a call is more than an obligation, for it represents a privilege of serving the Creator of the universe and the Creator of one's new heart.

## To Be Heavenly Minded

The gospel itself is eschatological in nature. In the same way that each individual is transformed and made holy as a new creature, so will all creation be transformed and made holy one day. Revelation 21 describes this final transformation. Like those of the OT, these images describe a situation of peace and security that is almost completely antithetical to that of the present creation.[185] The Father sits on the throne in power and majesty, and this is the occasion for moving away from the past in order to make all things new (Rev 21:5).[186] This new creation removes the distinction between the profane and the holy. In reflections reminiscent of those of Zech 14:20, there is no sacred space because everything is sacred in the presence of God and the Lamb.[187] For "in the transcendent city of God, unqualified holiness, the nature of God himself, will prevail."[188] Such is the hope of the Christian—the unmitigated presence of God at the center of everything. Such is the nature of true worship; this new creation is

---

614.

[184] Six are in Matthew (14:22–33; 17:1–8; 28:1–8,9–10,11–15,16–20), two in Mark (11:1–10; 16:17–20), ten in Luke (1:5–25,26–38; 2:8–18; 5:1–11; 7:20–28; 10:1–17; 15:11–31; 22:7–13,14–38; 24:36–53), one in John (20:19–21), seventeen in Acts (1:1–12; 7:30–36; 9:1–8,9–29; 10:1–8,9–29,30–33; 11:4–17; 12:6–10; 13:1–3; 16:24–34; 22:6–11,12–16,17–21; 23:11; 26:12–20; 27:21–26), and one in Revelation (1:10–20). Mullins, "Commission Forms," 605–6.

[185] G. K. Beale, *The Book of Revelation*, NIGTC (Grand Rapids: Eerdmans, 1999), 1048–49.

[186] R. Mounce, *The Book of Revelation*, rev. ed., NICNT (Grand Rapids: Eerdmans, 1998), 384.

[187] Beale, *Revelation*, 1091.

[188] M. E. Boring, *Revelation*, INT (Louisville: John Knox Press, 1989), 222.

nothing less than the praise of the whole world for a God worthy of as much, simply because of who He is.[189]

## Conclusions

Oliver Wendell Holmes once quipped: "Every calling is great, when greatly pursued." His emphasis was on the fact that even the mundane can be transformed by a great attitude. How much more does the emphasis exist to pursue the greater callings of life with attitudes appropriate to their nature? Of the greater callings in life, the most foundational is worship and adoration of the sovereign King of the universe. The prophets understood this and highlighted the various ways and means for a proper attitude to find expression. The prophetic stress on the interconnection between everyday life and events within the sacred precincts, coupled with their identification of God's ultimate purpose in creation, results in a holistic presentation of the essentials of the attitudes behind worship. Their emphases reflect the fact that the worship that someone brings is about the entire self that gives comprehensive adoration in every moment of time to the One who is thoroughly worthy of it.

The Pentateuch and the Prophets have much to say about the expectations of God in both the worship event and worship as a lifestyle. We have examined both guidelines and examples in these biblical texts to arrive at a conclusion about the wholeness of worship in the life of the person of God. As attention turns to the Writings in the next chapter, the examples of Israel's worship become predominant in the biblical texts. The ways that the inspired text describes how the people approached God in their worship are, like the examples already examined, illuminative of what God desires. But they also represent the clearest opportunity for us to see worship as it ought to exists, even individually experienced. Indeed, from the wisdom literature to the Book of Psalms, the examples of worship in the Writings represent the most personally involving section of Scripture.

---

[189] Beale, *Revelation*, 1095.

# Chapter 5
## *THE WRITINGS: EXPRESSIONS OF WORSHIP*

The Writings, particularly the book of Psalms, represents the portion of the OT canon most directly applicable to Christian worship. Indeed, even in those moments when Christians have felt it necessary to limit what portions of the Scripture they print, Psalms has usually been included. Passages in Psalms have had contemporary tunes applied to them throughout Christian history. They have been sung by groups ranging from the staid conservativism of liturgically minded congregations to the effusive freedom of some of the more radical bands of Christian contemporary music. But the usefulness of the Writings to worship should not be limited to Psalms alone. Wisdom literature is specifically grounded in a spirit of worship, and the historical texts (Ezra–Nehemiah, 1, 2 Chronicles) are rooted in concerns centered on a unity of focus so worship might be achieved. Since wisdom literature is scarcely dealt with in worship contexts, the intention is to spend much of this chapter on it. Of course, no work that claims to be a theology of worship can ignore Psalms. The present goal is to outline the theology of the various expressions of worship found in the Writings, drawing comparisons where possible to that which has already been presented. In this way, this chapter will exemplify and illustrate how theology and worship must interact if either is ever going to find its ultimate purpose.

### *Interpreting Psalms and Other Writings*

Interpreting each section of the materials under consideration has been the starting point of each of the previous discussions. This approach works because one's theology cannot be divorced from one's hermeneutic. This axiom is no less true in Psalms and other writings where the starting point of interpretation can take the exegete in wildly different directions about the conclusions that can be drawn from their contents. As with previous endeavors, the methodology is principle-centered and genre-driven in its observations. With the book of Psalms, however, a stated ambiguity about the notion of a single meaning must be expressed. This is true because psalms are a musically-oriented genre that is intended to speak to the heart, and more than any other part of the Scripture they call on their interpreters and readers to make the text their own in both expression and in meaning. Therefore, while the remarks that follow are not expressly Christological in their declaration, the reader should recognize that Christology is behind them. In fact, I presuppose that a Christian can scarcely read the psalms without foundationally and explicitly thinking of the Savior. As one meditates on the issues of instruction, sorrow, and praise that are represented in the various songs, one is immediately driven to the One who was the greatest Rabbi, the Man of Sorrows, and the awesome Lord of the universe—even more so than in other sections of the OT. Yet there is value at looking at the psalms merely in terms of their expressiveness in worship, so this is the primary approach that is taken.

The work of form critic Hermann Gunkel drastically changed the way scholars interpret the psalms, even in evangelical circles. Gunkel's work began with the idea that regularly occurring events in any particular culture, such as religious observances and the communication that takes place during them, tend to take on stable forms or structure over time. Therefore, identifying these patterns or forms would result in a better understanding of how the psalms had been used in Israel's worship. This *Sitz im Leben* ("situation in life") could then serve as a medium through which the variations, expressions, and intentions of each song could be identified and interpreted.[1] Since historical indicators frequently found in prose sections of Scripture are generally missing in the psalms, this methodology allowed for a consistency of conclusions longed for by scholars. Additionally, this method as applied to the psalms had great affinity with what became an accepted means of dealing with songs in modern life by classifying them according to the style they represented and their role in expression—whether secular or religious.[2]

---

[1] See H. Gunkel, *Psalms: A Form-Critical Introduction,* trans. T. Horner (Philadelphia: Fortress, 1967).

[2] Most hymnals classify their songs according to where the song most appropriately fits in a worship service or church calendar. Similarly, radio stations are usually identified by their format—that is, by the style of music they play.

Gunkel's method had some drawbacks. Some were almost immediately acknowledged, while others only manifested themselves over time. For instance, the method had the often-unhelpful side effect of leading to the suggestion of hypothetical rituals where a certain class of psalms might find expression, even if there were no explicit evidence of these rituals in the biblical text. For instance, one festival proposal was a re-enthronement ritual in which the king would take part in a drama of sorts whereby his legitimacy as king and servant of Yahweh would be reemphasized (generally associated with Psalms 2 and 110). Second, since most psalms are hybrids of the various genres the writers drew on, interest has more recently shifted from the broader literary structures to the components of that genre.[3] This means that the presence of a multiplicity of expressions within nearly every psalm suggests that Gunkel's groupings could only be held in the most general way. To be sure, each type of psalm has an underlying pattern, but one must not forget that each individual psalm also has a distinctiveness in both content and theology that cannot be ignored.[4] Third, Gunkel did not see some of the psalms in terms of the community but chose to distinguish between personal feelings or experiences and cultic practices.[5] Such a dichotomy was understandable in light of the misconceptions about the human development of cultic institutions in contrast to the perceived prophetic notion of personal piety. But this dichotomy left many of the psalms without a clear perspective in which they could be understood and applied. Finally, even in the distinguishing of certain psalms as individual and others as corporate, there are matters of whether such an attempt was even possible. For in a collection of works deemed sacred by a group as a whole, the question of how a so-called individual psalm might operate and continue in services is a reasonable one. It is unclear whether or not there were indeed opportunities of service at the

---

[3] S. Terrien, *The Psalms: Strophic Structure and Theological Commentary*, ECC (Grand Rapids: Eerdmans, 2003), 41–42.

[4] R. Davidson, *The Vitality of Worship: A Commentary on the Book of Psalms* (Grand Rapids: Eerdmans, 1998), 5.

[5] S. Mowinckel, *The Psalms in Israel's Worship*, vol. 1, trans. D. R. Ap-Thomas (Oxford: Blackwell, 1962), 29–30.

temple for an individual to function in a manner formal enough to warrant psalms dedicated to these services. Coincidentally, the so-called "individual" psalms may have simply always been corporate; perhaps they were used in a manner similar to the practice of the singular "I" in corporate hymns today.

The failings of Gunkel's specific approach are significant, but his general perspective on the psalms as belonging to categories is extremely helpful in interpreting them. This is true because—just as a modern worshipper might misrepresent the meaning of a song simply by misclassifying its genre—people often find themselves understanding a psalm in a certain way only to be dismayed when they find out its intent is in the opposite direction. Further, in a theological work such as this, it is necessary to focus on types for the sake of clarity and succinctness. Like previous genres, the psalms are first and foremost relational, so if someone is going to maximize the role of the psalms in worship, knowing the general genres and what they say about relationship is essential. Whether they are teaching, lamenting, or praising, the psalms express a belief in the God who is in partnership and relationship with humanity. This is an outgrowth of the fact that life is complex, and so is the God with whom we communicate as we experience life's ups and downs. A person's relationship with God is dynamic; therefore, praising Him must be as well.

When dealing with wisdom literature, the simple imperative of interpretation is to remember that it is for the development of wisdom and is not promissory in nature, except in the most general of ways. The outcomes are motivational and commonsensical, not guarantees of cause and effect. The speculative wisdom of Job and Ecclesiastes[6] is intended to force consideration of the foundations of much wisdom thought, though both end up being extremely ortho-

---

[6] Two genres of ancient wisdom literature are often recognized, based on purpose and literary method. One is didactic or practical, usually in the form of lessons from authority figures like elders or parents. The biblical book of Proverbs represents this genre. The other is called speculative or reflective wisdom, represented by Job and Ecclesiastes. This type addresses the most challenging issues of life through a reflective or discursive style, often relying on observation. See A. E. Hill, "Non-Proverbial Wisdom," in *Cracking Old Testament Codes* (ed. D. B. Sandy and R. L. Giese Jr.; Nashville: B&H, 1995), 256–57; A. E. Hill and J. H. Walton, *A Survey of the Old Testament* (2d ed.; Grand Rapids: Zondervan, 2000), 320–21.

dox in their conclusions. The proverbs must be read holistically and in relation to the other wisdom texts if they are going to be understood appropriately. This is appropriate because the proverbs themselves advocate it (Prov 22:18) and because a simple comparison of certain proverbs suggests it is necessary (Prov 26:4–5). A warning in the other direction is important as well. One should not fall into the trap of seeing them merely in terms of the wisdom of the ancient Near East or of wisdom in general. The propositions put forward in the pages of Scripture are countercultural in many ways since they are instructions for the wise from God's perspective, which is often at odds with human perception.[7]

## Wisdom and Worship

Wisdom *(ḥokmâ)* means "masterful understanding" and involves internalization of a concept or, more accurately, a way of life.[8] Generally speaking, wisdom is merely the art of success without any notable ethical stance. Solomon's marriage to the princess of Egypt (1 Kgs 3:1) could be called wise in many respects since it created an important alliance, improved trade possibilities, and provided him with Gezer as her dowry (1 Kgs 9:15); but it was unrighteousness that would undo his entire kingdom and stance before God (1 Kgs 11:4).[9] Therefore, it is significant that in the books directly assigned to the advocacy of wisdom, righteousness plays such a significant role in their presentations. This conclusion may be the first link between wisdom and worship.

## Worship Is Where Wisdom Begins (Wisdom's Credo)

"The fear of the LORD is the beginning of knowledge" (Prov 1:7). This is wisdom's credo, finding expression in nearly every place wisdom is presented as either a foundation for a narrative or as a

---

[7] B. Waltke, *The Book of Proverbs, Chapters 1–15*, NICOT (Grand Rapids: Eerdmans, 2004), 56–57.

[8] Ibid., 76–78.

[9] One may debate whether the decision was then truly wise based on the outcome, but there is little debate that such a practice was categorized as such throughout human history.

paradigm to be pursued. This credo must be understood in its totality, as opposed to its component parts, or it cannot be understood at all. Bruce Waltke divides the fear spoken of here into rational or objective and nonrational or emotional. The former is present in the synonymous use of the phrase with God's instructions and commands, while the latter refers simply to the response of fear, reverence, or awe before Yahweh.[10]

The expression "the fear of Yahweh" had its origin in worship. Specifically, it was an attitude of worship that was fundamental to finding wisdom, which subsequently became the theological framework through which wisdom itself was understood.[11] Gerhard von Rad saw this introduction to worship as late since he believed wisdom was originally secular in nature,[12] but Leo Perdue demonstrated that the connection between such worship and wisdom existed from wisdom literature's earliest expressions.[13] This may also explain why the statement in Prov 1:7 is distinctive to the Bible among all the wisdom literature of the ancient Near East.[14] Whereas wisdom was fundamentally a secular institution in the surrounding cultures, it was rooted in the worship of Yahweh in Israel.

The fear expressed in the phrase is different from the fear prescribed and described in other locations (Gen 28:17; Lev 25:17; Judg 6:22). In wisdom literature fear does not seem to be linked with holiness but is expressive only of reverential submission to the creator of wisdom.[15] Therefore, fear is more relational in its emphasis and consequentially has "man as the image of God" theology at its heart. In other words, because man is at the same time like the Creator and yet distinct from him, the individual best understands his Creator through the convergence of the observation of the world with worship. Worship and analysis work side by side, even feeding off each other. Worship involves experiencing God, and wisdom is estab-

---

[10] Waltke, *Proverbs 1–15*, 100–1.

[11] G. von Rad, *Wisdom in Israel*, trans. J. D. Martin (Nashville: Abingdon, 1972), 53–73.

[12] G. von Rad, *Old Testament Theology*, vol. 1, *The Theology of Israel's Traditions*, trans. D. M. G. Stalker, OTL (New York: Harper & Row, 1965), 418–41.

[13] L. Perdue, *Proverbs*, INT (Louisville: John Knox Press, 2000), 75. See Leo Perdue, *Wisdom and Cult*, SBLDS 30 (Missoula: Scholars' Press, 1977).

[14] Waltke, *Proverbs 1–15*, 180.

[15] Perdue, *Proverbs*, 76–77.

lished on the premise that experience feeds knowledge. Ultimately, the knowledge of the source of wisdom logically leads to more wisdom. This may explain the dual intention of the writer of Proverbs in describing this fear as the "beginning" *(rē'šît)* of wisdom. It is the beginning because it is foundational to arriving at an understanding of the world.[16] But it is also the beginning because it is the *best* means through which wisdom might be acquired.[17] Waltke summarized the idea well when he wrote: "What the alphabet is to reading, notes to reading music, and numerals to mathematics, the fear of the Lord is to attaining the revealed knowledge of this book."[18]

The book of Proverbs clearly understands worship and wisdom as two sides of the same coin. It refers specifically to the fear of Yahweh nearly 20 times in its 31 chapters. This and the fact that wisdom entails mastery of life lead one to the inescapable conclusion that the one who would truly desire to master life must begin with worship of the One who created it and placed things in order. This is no doubt why the Scripture considers the one who says there is no God as the ultimate fool; this person is the complete antithesis of those who are wise (Pss 14:1; 53:1 [Hb. 53:2]).

## Wisdom and Worship Are Where We Recognize Our Place (Job)

People often misunderstand the book of Job precisely because they fail to recognize its character as wisdom literature. Of special importance to the issue of its role in wisdom, as well as its implications for worship, are the final speeches of Yahweh and Job. In these climactic speeches, one finds the thrust of the book and also further reflections on the interrelatedness of worship and wisdom. The conclusions the interpreter draws about both, however, are directly dependent on understanding their intent. Do God's words—"Who is this who obscures My counsel with ignorant words?" (Job 38:2)—contain an accusation of sin that should be repented of, or something far more gentle and didactic? When Job responded—"Therefore I

---

[16] Waltke, *Proverbs 1–15*, 180–81.
[17] Perdue, *Proverbs*, 74.
[18] Waltke, *Proverbs 1–15*, 181.

take back my words and repent in dust and ashes," (Job 42:6)—was he expressing remorse over some sin, or simply reflecting the notion of a lesson learned?

The problem is exacerbated by the difficulty of translating these phrases, especially Job's final response. Though most come close to the rendering of the HCSB offered here, some go in the exact opposite direction. While few take John Curtis' translation seriously— "Therefore I feel loathing contempt and revulsion toward you, O God; and I am sorry for frail man" [19]—it does demonstrate both the difficulty of the meaning of the words and the connection between what someone thinks is going on in the book and how he reads it. The word translated "repent" *(nāḥam)* has a semantic range including changing course, recanting, and repentance. The "dust and ashes" can either be an expression of the activity of mourning in repentance, or modifiers identifying Job's lowly status as a human (see Gen 18:27; Job 30:19).[20] While it may be logical to suggest that Job's response is one of total abasement and repentance, the nature of the work as wisdom literature, the lack of any clear accusation of sin by Yahweh, and the repeated expressions of Job's blamelessness (HCSB "perfect integrity") and correct conduct, both before his speeches (Job 1:1,8, 2:3) and after (Job 42:7) suggest a different reading is in order.[21]

In light of the evidence, it would seem that Yahweh's question in Job 38:2 presupposes humanity's limitations in regard to wisdom. He did not reprove Job but addressed him as a teacher, grounded

[19] J. Curtis, "On Job's Response to Yahweh," *JBL* 98 (1979): 510. His translation can be removed from the realm of the plausible on two accounts. First, the linguistic support for it is limited at best (see W. Morrow, "Consolation, Rejection, and Repentance in Job 42:6," *JBL* 105 [1986]: 214). Second, as Curtis himself admitted, it renders the prose and poetic sections as so diametrically opposed that the former can only serve as a deliberate deception of the content of the latter, added by a subsequent writer. Regardless of how one views the compositional history of the book and the origin of the prose and poetic passages, the idea that a redactor would construct a work in this manner is illogical, not to mention irreverent.

[20] The association of ashes with repentance is drawn primarily from this Joban text and their use in the practice of mourning (Esth 4:1–3; Ezek 27:30). See J. Hartley, *Job*, NICOT (Grand Rapids: Eerdmans, 1988), 535–37.

[21] F. Andersen rightly observed that the view that Job was repenting of sin would cause the entire argument of the book to collapse (*Job*, TOTC [Downers Grove: InterVarsity, 1976], 268–69, 292; see Hartley, *Job*, 535–36; against B. L. Newell, "Job: Repentant or Rebellious," *WTJ* 46 [1984]: 298–316).

in His concern for Job's well-being.[22] Wisdom is largely based on experience. Since man will never be able to possess the history or perspective that Yahweh has, the opportunity to sit at the feet of this master Teacher and learn represents a unique opportunity that cannot be ignored.[23]

The wisdom God shared is at once dismissive of some conventional wisdom and yet still built on previous revelations. "One expects a word which establishes a position within which one may *stand*,"[24] and this is what He delivered. Job moved in the wrong direction in his defense of his innocence, for he has implied that God is unjust when in fact Job simply does not have all the information. Yahweh's speeches are firmly grounded in the image of God theology as they demonstrate the tension of participating in some ways with Him and yet not being Him. Though humans have no capacity for victory over Leviathan and Behemoth (Job 40:7–41:34) and no creative abilities (Job 38), we are capable of relating to God and hearing and responding to His counsel. This is manifest in the fact that Yahweh's words in Job 38 are in the genre of a hymn of praise, which allows Job, and ultimately us, to find agreement and erudition.[25] There is something of value in us that affords us the privilege of direct communication with the Creator, yet there is still much that distinguishes us from Him. The question of how one takes seriously the issue of justice as reflecting God's justice without reducing His concept to ours is very much at the center of the book's argument.[26] But the underlying presupposition behind the answers offered is that through both wisdom and worship one learns and experiences the nature of his standing before God.

Job's earlier words reflected on his smallness before God and God's enormity. Job spoke some of the most powerful words in the book when he observed that all the matters that man can document in Yahweh's revelation of Himself are "but the fringes of His ways"

---

[22] See Hartley, *Job*, 487.
[23] See Andersen, *Job*, 269.
[24] G. Janzen, *Job*, INT (Atlanta: John Knox Press, 1985), 226. Emphasis in original.
[25] See Hartley, *Job*, 488–89.
[26] See Janzen, *Job*, 242.

(26:14).[27] Similarly, in his initial response to Yahweh's speeches (40:4) Job selected a word to describe himself that is antonymic to God's majestic glory when he referred to himself as "insignificant" *(qālal)*.[28] This word is important because it suggests that only a person with such circumspect consideration of himself could receive the instruction he does in the manner he does. Again, this illustrates the intimate relationship between the fear of Yahweh, worship, and the righteous life of humility for those who seek a meaningful relationship with God.

## Wisdom and Worship as a Universal Call (Eccl 12:13–14)

Like Job, Ecclesiastes is a difficult book. The debates of authorship and the place of such an apparently pessimistic book in the orthodox canon serve as the primary focal points for much of the discussion. Yet for our purposes, it is sufficient to focus solely on the last two verses of the book. This is true because regardless of where one lands on other matters of interpretation, these passages are viewed almost universally as the summation of all that is argued in the book.[29] Tremper Longman's translation (without supplying a verb since the Hebrew doesn't have one) of the first words of v. 13—"The end of the matter"—serves well to point out the emphatic nature of the statement. The writer seems to be communicating that what is about to be said is the point of everything else that has been said:[30] "Fear God and keep His commands" (Eccl 12:13).

---

[27] See Andersen, *Job*, 215–19); Hartley, *Job*, 368.

[28] M. Tsevat, "The Meaning of the Book of Job," *HUCA* 37 (1966): 91. It has been rightly observed that Job is somewhat ambiguously reserved in this initial response. His words can be read either as submission or as a strategic reserve that allows him to mull over his own positions without submission. This is what forces Yahweh's continued questioning. Janzen, *Job*, 243; Hartley, *Job*, 517–18.

[29] For instance, T. Longman drew contrasts to the rest of the book in these words, while W. Brown took a comparative perspective. Both agree that these words represent a summation of thought that one is to take away from the text. See Longman, *Ecclesiastes*, NICOT (Grand Rapids: Eerdmans, 1998), 281–82; Brown, *Ecclesiastes*, INT (Louisville: John Knox Press, 2000), 118.

[30] Longman, *Ecclesiastes*, 281–82.

The writer of Ecclesiastes ends where Proverbs starts—with the fear of Yahweh. His point is that life is best lived through establishing and maintaining a right relationship with God. Every element of life, good and bad, must lead one back to God and to worshipping Him alone.[31] What is most striking about the charge, however, is not the directive itself, which appears elsewhere; rather, it is the focus of the charge—all humanity. The phrase "because this is for all humanity" in the HCSB may simply mean that this is the most important thing a man or woman could do.[32]

On the other hand, based on three things, it is possible that there is a universal aspect here. First, this is the most straightforward reading of the syntax and words of the sentence. Longman considers that it may be an idiom. But while idiomatic phrases are rampant in wisdom literature, there is nothing in the phraseology here that requires an idiomatic interpretation. Second, wisdom literature as a rule is universal in focus, especially in Scripture (see Prov 1:2–6). No other genre found in Scripture has as many parallel expressions and texts in the ancient Near East as does wisdom literature. Third, there is clearly an emphasis on eschatological judgment in the verse that follows: "For God will bring every act to judgment, including every hidden thing, whether good or evil" (Eccl 12:14). This in itself draws the perspective outside of merely a covenantal framework into a perspective of universal need. The primeval prologue introduced the idea that worship was the ultimate purpose for all creatures, but most of the texts discussed since then have focused solely on the covenant people. Ecclesiastes returns now to the initial premise by demonstrating the futility of any human endeavor if it is not cast firstly, even solely, in the knowledge of God. This knowledge cannot be acquired through books; it only comes from relationship with God. The book advocates the use of Scripture as pointing to God's agenda in life and not man's.[33] In many ways, it is the prototypical book that argues for a life of worship.

---

[31] See Brown, *Ecclesiastes*, 136–37.

[32] See Longman, *Ecclesiastes*, 282, who translates "for this is the whole duty of humanity," supplying the word "duty," which is not in the Hebrew.

[33] See I. Provan, *Ecclesiastes, Song of Songs*, NIVAC (Grand Rapids: Zondervan, 2001), 231–33.

There was a close relationship in biblical wisdom circles between wisdom and worship. This manifested itself often in the use of wisdom stock materials in the development of psalms (see Psalm 111).[34] Further, since wisdom sages drew together faith and rational inquiry, the wisdom texts themselves assert that worship is necessary. This means that since Yahweh is Creator and Sustainer of the order that permits wisdom to function, He is worthy of worship and awe in the mind of the sage.[35] This perspective has implications for daily life since wisdom is the search for mastery of life. It also has implications for missions and evangelism since wisdom calls for all humanity to partake in the wonder that is God. Wisdom has suggestions for worship since relationship and knowledge are at the heart of both wisdom and worship.

## The Horizontal Features of Worship

The book of Psalms is known to have comprised Israel's expressions of worship, at least since the time of the second temple. Many within the evangelical camp would move their formation, and perhaps even the present form and editing, to an earlier period. It seems evident in light of Ugaritic comparisons and some of the content of the psalms, even apart from the superscriptions, that many of the texts can be identified as early in composition. It also seems apparent, however, based on the Dead Sea scrolls and other evidence, that their compilation continued well up to the time of Christ. Such an understanding is significant, because it is likely that an increasing emphasis on the written word, especially the need and desire to explain the text in worship, took place in the postexilic era (see Nehemiah 8).[36] Therefore, one would expect both the content of the

---

[34] M. E. Thomas, "Psalms 1 and 112 As a Paradigm for the Comparison of Wisdom Motifs in the Psalms," *JETS* 29 (1986): 16; Terrien, *Psalms*, 55–58. Though viewing the process as occurring later than is historically necessary, Mowinckel's expression of the interplay of wisdom scribes and psalmists is helpful (*The Psalms in Israel's Worship* II, trans. D. R. Ap-Thomas [Oxford: Blackwell, 1962], 104–5.

[35] Perdue, *Proverbs*, 10.

[36] This is not to suggest that only in the postexilic era was the written word important in the worship and life of Israel (see Exod 24:4–12 and the countless references to the Law of Moses throughout the Old Testament). I only suggest that because of the dispersion of Israel, a change in worldview, and the variety of languages common in Israel in the postexilic era, the written

psalms and their ordering would take on an instructional feel as well. Early scholarly approaches to interpreting Psalms identified much about the form of certain individual psalms in their instructional intent.[37] More recent techniques have attempted to look at the psalms collectively as one book with its own flow and development.[38] These techniques have also determined that instruction plays a key role in the intention of the arrangement of the book as a whole. Indeed, instruction serves a significant purpose in the structures, function, and forms of the book of Psalms, individually and collectively.

## Psalms Teach Through Their Structures

As with any literature, the constructions that comprise the psalms' content must be understood in order for proper interpretation to take place. However, the structures that constitute the psalms go beyond this normal purpose. The genres are not only important in interpreting their content because they help one correctly classify the relationship of the words in them; they are also significant since the structures themselves proclaim a message. For instance, parallelism is the distinctive feature of Hebrew poetry. A person can learn much about what is being said by understanding how this poetic form impacts the relationship of phrases in Hebrew poetry. Whereas previous generations attempted to identify the types of parallelism in the poetic sections of the Hebrew Scriptures, a more succinct yet flexible system has recently emerged. This approach simply describes parallelism as a subsequent line relating to a previous line through an expressed commonality of support by means of completion, expansion, and restatement.[39] This definition indicates that restated phrases, sometimes in antithetical expressions, are not trying to make two separate points but a single emphatic one. Beyond this important syntactical element, however, is what the structure of

word would take on a heightened importance and use in all of Israel's worship. Therefore, it seems logical to suppose that a shift occurred in how the written word was presented as well.

[37] Mowinckel, *Psalms in Israel's Worship* II, 104–25.

[38] B. S. Childs, *Introduction to the Old Testament as Scripture* (Philadelphia: Fortress, 1979), 513–15.

[39] P. Miller, *Interpreting the Psalms* (Philadelphia: Fortress, 1986), 33; J. Kugel, *The Idea of Biblical Poetry* (New Haven: Yale University Press, 1981).

parallelism itself says about worship and instruction. The repetition and emphasis inherent in parallelism underscores the importance of both institutions, for worship itself is significant and the statements describing it demand reiteration. Since instruction needs to be clear, the repetitive poetic structure reinforces, clarifies, and teaches concepts in a manner that is at once conducive to both memorization and aesthetics.

Sometimes the content provokes further understanding through the emotive power of the genre, in addition to the structural framework of the words themselves. Simile and metaphor serve this purpose in the book of Psalms, as often the imagery chosen enhances the power of the expression and direction of the writer. When referring to the power that words have over a person, simply stating the obvious would be sufficient to get the idea across. But the psalmist-poet goes beyond the obvious because there is a desire to evoke a passion, not simply share information. The psalmist wrote: "Hide me from the scheming of the wicked, . . .who sharpen their tongues like swords and aim bitter words like arrows" (Ps 64:2–4 [Hb. vv. 3–5]). This comparison of his enemy's words to weapons only heightens the experience, allowing readers to *feel* the impact as they hear the lesson.[40] Such powerful metaphors convey a truth that could never be expressed otherwise, but it is crucial to recognize that the form is also limiting in what can be taken from the imagery. The same factor that makes the metaphors powerfully emotive makes them limited in the contribution they can make in other areas.

## Psalms Teach Through Their Functions

The book of Psalms teaches through its function in the worship of Israel. The underlying theme of Psalms as a whole is that God is in control of the universe. Since the psalms were used in Israel's worship, this theme would drive and develop not only the way the people understood them but also the role of cultic personnel. The place of the king in worship is particularly significant. Although from earliest times a king would perform sacrifices (2 Sam 6:13,17–

---

[40] See Miller, *Interpreting the Psalms*, 82.

18; 24:25; 1 Kgs 3:4,15; 8:64), his role as the anointed representative of the people and mediator pushed him in other directions as well.[41] In fact, eventually the king became the governing figure in the religion of Israel.[42] The lesson for Israel in his functionary role was brought home through the king's juxtaposition with Yahweh throughout Psalms. The king's presence and power taught important lessons about Yahweh's presence and power. The whole structure worked together as a paradoxical meeting of transcendence and presence.[43] Therefore, one cannot too quickly diminish the role of the king in the psalms, as his presence alongside Yahweh enhanced, rather than diminished, his position. The people were to learn confidence in Yahweh alone; the king was to serve as the example for the rest of them.[44]

Another place where Psalms as a whole functioned in a didactic role was in how worship as a whole was understood. The book of Psalms interspersed the notions of righteous living with expressions of the immeasurable worth of God so that the people rightly viewed worship. Nowhere is this more evident than in the so-called entrance psalms (Psalms 15, 24), but it was by no means limited to them. The question, "Who may enter worship?"—which was made explicit in Psalm 24—clearly echoes the sentiments of the prophets. The response that only those with "clean hands and a pure heart" (Ps 24:4) may do so advocates "a life which will express in outward actions the inner motivation which controls the will and the conscience, an inner motivation which is rooted in total allegiance to the one God."[45] Thus, the psalms functioned to monitor sacred space and to reinforce the notion that such space did actually exist.[46]

---

[41] See Mowinckel, *Psalms in Israel's Worship I*, 57; H. Ringgren, *Israelite Religion*, trans D. Green (Philadelphia: Fortress, 1966), 59; A. Johnson, "The Role of the King in the Jerusalem Cultus," in *The Labyrinth*, ed. S. H. Hooke (London: SPCK, 1935), 77.

[42] See Ringgren, *Israelite Religion*, 59; H.-J. Kraus, *Theology of the Psalms*, trans. K. Crim (Minneapolis: Augsburg Press, 1986), 111–23.

[43] T. Longman made this observation implicitly in suggesting that royal psalms fit well under the category of hymns; see Longman, *How to Read the Psalms* (Downers Grove: InterVarsity Press, 1988), 34; see also Terrien, *Psalms*, 48.

[44] J. Grant, *The King as Exemplar: The Function of Deuteronomy's Kingship Law in the Shaping of the Book of Psalms*, SBLAB 17 (Atlanta: Society of Biblical Literature, 2004), 59–60.

[45] Davidson, *Vitality of Worship*, 86.

[46] See J. Crenshaw, *The Psalms: An Introduction* (Grand Rapids: Eerdmans, 2001), 158–67.

This coupling of the righteous life with worship while concurrently distinguishing special times and places for the activity of worship is the pattern established in Leviticus. It is a lesson worth repeating.

## Psalms Teach through Their Form

Perhaps the clearest way in which Psalms teaches is through the form that some individual psalms take. Specifically, there is a genre of "wisdom" or "didactic" psalms. Early discussions rejected the category designated as wisdom psalms based on the lack of identifiable forms that might characterize the type.[47] For instance, both Gunkel and Mowinckel argued against the classification, though both recognized certain psalms demonstrated a dependence on wisdom material.[48] Von Rad identified a group of psalms invested in the wisdom tradition but viewed them as distinguished from cultically oriented psalms.[49] This means that these psalms played little if any role in the cultic practice of Israel. Such an approach is far too minimalistic. As there are, indeed, psalms driven by a poet's intention of passing on life's lessons under the rubric of submission to Yahweh's ways, the reality of wisdom psalms seems an inescapable conclusion, though how one defines and uses them is still very much up in the air.[50] That they played a role in the cult of Israel is certain through the axiomatic purpose that "we are informed by the Bible so that we know God better."[51] In light of the foregoing observations on the interaction of the sage and the cult and the presence of psalms that explicitly focus on wisdom, it is difficult to imagine that the Israelite cultic structure did not participate in endeavors such as wisdom.

Concerning the criteria for how to identify a wisdom psalm, it would seem that specificity may actually be harmful to the process.[52]

---

[47] Currently, the strongest proponent of this position about wisdom psalm nomenclature is J. Crenshaw; see Crenshaw, "Wisdom Psalms?" *CurBS* 8 (2000): 15.

[48] Gunkel, *Introduction*, 305,327; Mowinckel, *Psalms in Israel's Worship* II, 105–6.

[49] von Rad, *Wisdom in Israel*, 48.

[50] See J. K. Kuntz, "Reclaiming Biblical Wisdom Psalms: A Response To Crenshaw," *CBR* 1 (2003): 152–53.

[51] Longman, How to *Read the Psalms*, 76.

[52] R. N. Whybray wanted more specificity outlined before he was willing to submit to the idea of a wisdom psalm category ("The Wisdom Psalms," in *Wisdom in Ancient Israel*, ed. J. Day and others [Cambridge: Cambridge University Press, 1995], 159–60); however, that is exactly

Wisdom itself is a matter of style and universal content. Wisdom psalms include questioning the presence and purpose of retribution, drawing distinctions between the wicked and the righteous ways of life, and giving advice on how a person should conduct his life; all driven primarily by wisdom's credo.[53] The wisdom psalm (sometimes referred to as a "torah psalm") focuses on piety driven by commitment to the teachings of Yahweh and meditation on them, whether that reflection took place in the worship event or in life in general. This religious perspective is distinguished from legalism because prayer and praise drive it, not regulations on every aspect of life.[54] This is where the true power of the wisdom psalm exists. On the one hand, it focuses on the instruction of God necessary for a proper lifestyle because it is wisdom literature. On the other hand, it constrains the restrictive power of the law by categorizing it in the realm of praise and adoration determined by its status as a psalm.

Psalm 1 represents a place where the three aspects of how the psalms teach converge. It contrasts the two paths of conduct—one that leads to the successful and happy life and one that leads to nothingness and failure. This psalm specifically connects reflection on the experiences of Israel's past with the desire and drive to a fortunate future.[55] Through both these explicit connections and the more implicit suggestion of the centrality of the fear of Yahweh, the psalm bears the primary markers of the wisdom psalm form. But the psalm also furthers these premises in its internal structure and function in Psalms as a whole.

Psalm 1 is one of those literary works that proclaims its message not only in the words it contains but also in the way it structures them. For example, in contrasting the way of the wicked with that of the righteous it employs the images of tree and chaff. These similes in themselves carry the weight of the imagery by expressing the strength and permanence of the righteous versus the weakness and

---

what needs to be lost in this case because ambiguity in the relationship of wisdom and the psalms is where the power of the interrelatedness of worship and wisdom exists.

[53] See R. E. Murphy, "A Consideration of the Classification, 'Wisdom Psalms'," in *Congress Volume: Bonn 1962*, VTSup 9 (Leiden: Brill, 1963): 159–60.

[54] See J. L. Mays, "The Place of the Torah-Psalms in the Psalter," *JBL* 106 (1987): 12.

[55] Ibid., 4.

irregularity of being unrighteous. The structure goes even further to highlight this reality in the quantity of words and phrases that describe the two elements. There is much said about the tree. It is eternally refreshed, it bears fruit, it does not wither, and it has success in every endeavor. In contrast, the only thing that can be said about the chaff is that it blows away. The abundance of words applied to the tree and the insignificant amount applied to the chaff further illustrate that the righteous life is abundant, but the wicked life leads to nothing.[56]

The probable function of Psalm 1 in Israel's worship has come more into focus as scholars have moved toward viewing Psalms as both individual works and a collective whole forming one book. This psalm seems to have been deliberately composed to serve as the introductory psalm to the book of Psalms.[57] Its place serves to illustrate that the psalms themselves are *torah*. They are instructions into every element of one's life before God.[58] There is a reordering of the emphases as the priority of righteousness before worship that served as the primary means of expression in the Prophets and elsewhere is turned around, so that here worship becomes a tool for instruction in outside life. The matter of obedience inherent in the content of this psalms proclaims that the privilege of worship and praise inform the obedient life and vice versa.[59]

There is little question that the book of Psalms views instruction as an integral part of worship. It would seem that proclamation, therefore, has always been a divinely intended part of worship. This realization has two implications for worship today. First, it corrects the notion that worship is linked solely with singing in the Scriptures. The identification of the song leader as the worship

---

[56] See Miller, *Interpreting the Psalms*, 82.

[57] D. Kidner, *Psalms 1–72: An Introduction and Commentary on Books I and II of the Psalms*, TOTC (Downers Grove: InterVarsity, 1973), 47.

[58] See Grant, *The King as Exemplar*, 53. G. H. Wilson took this supposition to extremes by removing the book of Psalms from any experience of corporate worship and seeing it solely as didactic—"to be *meditated over* rather than to be *recited from*" (*The Editing of the Hebrew Psalter*, SBLDS 76 [Atlanta: Scholars' Press, 1985], 206–7). But this position is too dependent on the old scholarly perspective of separating reflective possibilities from corporate worship expressions.

[59] See W. Brueggemann, "Bounded by Obedience and Praise: The Psalms as Canon," *JSOT* 50 (1991): 64–66.

leader in many evangelical churches reinforces the idea that worship is tied up in the practice of singing and that this is what takes place prior to the preaching. The psalms themselves, that portion of Scripture most clearly musical, proclaim a different truth. Their starting point is in the matter of instruction and teaching, and they advocate the idea that instruction must take place even in music. Both the pastor and the music leader need to work in unison to ensure that all the service is instructional in some sense and uncompromising in the message that it proclaims.

The centrality of instruction as advocated by the psalms has a second contemporary implication. Music leaders, writers, and performers need to become better versed in theology. It is not enough to be able to construct a tune and lyrics that are aesthetically pleasing and emotionally evocative. Music must be immersed in proper theology precisely because it has a power to instruct and evoke in a manner that few mediums can. The struggle exists in the fact that since lyrics are often built around metaphor and simile, imprecision is the norm rather than the exception. For the writer or leader who has had only a passing introduction to the content and theology of worship, there is a greater danger of presenting content that is less than ideal.

In short, the compartmentalization of the act of worship itself can be as dangerous and damaging as separating worship as event from worship as lifestyle. Focusing on instruction does not mean the abandonment of praise and thanksgiving. In fact, there needs to be more of an inclusion of both these elements in preaching. Evangelical preachers often seem oblivious to the fact that the presence of both was abundant in the teaching of the biblical saints (Dan 2:23; Hab 3:3; 1 Cor 1:4; Phil 1:3; 1 Thess 5:23–24; Heb 1:1–4). Focusing on instruction simply advocates that everything done in worship should teach something. Then we may ask, Will those lessons be accidental? Or will the Holy Spirit direct the entire service in the same way He directs the preparation of the message? No doubt the Spirit will move and instruct where He wills, but this does not mean that leaders are excused from participating in the divine working (see Phil 2:12–13).

## Expressions of Exhortation

Closely related to the instructional expressions of worship are the exhortative expressions. The difference is primarily one of form and emphasis. Whereas instructional expressions originate with an emphasis toward the mind that then feeds and grows out of worship, exhortative elements simply encourage postures or practices in the act of worship itself. The phenomenon involves concentration on fellow worshippers as one praises Yahweh (see Ps 96:4). Interestingly, of all the hymns, Psalm 8 is the only one in the entire book of Psalms that is "composed completely as direct address to God."[60] This illustrates that distinguishing between horizontal and vertical elements in the biblical texts is not an uncomplicated endeavor. Indeed, it will be seen below that sometimes the phrase that was intended as an exhortation to fellow worshippers becomes an articulation of honor to the One being worshipped.

The first exhortation in the book of Psalms involves a challenge or charge to the congregant to follow a path of life that leads to a blessed state (Ps 1:1). The common term for these texts is "beatitudes." Some have argued that the "blessed is/are" expression also designates the psalm in which it is found as a wisdom psalm. While it is true that such terminology is in wisdom psalms and in wisdom materials (see Prov 3:13; 8:32; 8:34; 14:21; 16:20; 20:7; 28:14), it is not in any sense a determining factor for such an identification.[61] What is important to realize is that these beatitudes cannot be confused with a static state of happiness. They are a constant call to action for those who would serve and worship God.[62] The word behind these beatitudes is *'ašar* (inflected as *'ašrê*, a particle of state), not *bārak* which is the Hebrew verb meaning "bless." The distinction primarily resides in the fact that "the blessing *[bārak]* invokes God's beneficent support of life, while the beatitude *['ašrê]* points to and commends the conduct and character that enjoy it."[63]

---

[60] J. L. Mays, *Psalms*, INT (Louisville: John Knox Press, 1994), 65.

[61] See Whybray, "The Wisdom Psalms," 159. No doubt some of the psalms that are perused in this section ought to be classified as wisdom psalms, but the intent here is to look at a specific phrase or injunction rather than the psalm as a whole.

[62] See Terrien, *Psalms*, 71.

[63] Mays, *Psalms*, 41. The LXX translators utilized the same Greek word in their translation

The word *ʾašrê* comes from a root meaning "to go forward," "walk on," or "march steadily." It is an encouragement to walk out boldly into a new path of service.[64] As a status, it might suggest a person who is to be "envied with desire."[65] It seems to be placed at key points and transitions throughout Psalms, suggesting its key role in the merger of worship as event and worship as lifestyle (see Psalms 1; 41; 89; 106).[66] Thus, it is intended to express an enhancement of both the religious and secular life.[67] Because the word is always followed by a duty of man in order to find fulfillment, there is little doubt that it was intended to be exhortative in nature. Not surprisingly, the types of activities it enjoined are centered on relational aspects of the worshipper's life with both man and God.

The beatitudes encourage worshippers to observe a pattern of life that pleases God in all aspects. The initial beatitude in Psalm 1 sets the stage for the entire book of Psalms in this light. The psalms put this sanction forward in a variety of ways. In some places, the focus is on how a person can worship Yahweh in his life. There are perspectives advocating the practice of integrity and mercy on behalf of the oppressed and desperate (Pss 41:1 [Hb. v. 2], 106:3), for being fruitful and multiplying, and for simply fearing Yahweh (Pss 112:1; 128:1). In other places, the beatitude centers on worship as an event as the satisfied ones are those who lift up Yahweh's praises and take part in His sacred festivals (Pss 84:4 [Hb. v. 5]; 89:15 [Hb. v. 16]). But the most striking beatitudes are those that simply express a holistic concern for right relationship with God. In these passages the blessed are those whom Yahweh has called unto Himself (Ps 65:4 [Hb. v. 5]) and those who have Yahweh as the center of their life's focus (Pss 34:8 [Hb. v. 9]; 40:4 [Hb. v. 5]; 84:5,12 [Hb. vv. 6,13]; 119:1–2; 146:5). Probably the most evangelistic of all these is Psalm 32 where the double beatitude (vv. 1–2) and triplet of synonymous blessings—transgressions forgiven, sin covered, guilt not charged—

---

of the word אַשְׁרֵי that Jesus used in his beatitudes (see Matt. 5:3–11).

[64] Terrien, *Psalms*, 71.

[65] *TWOT*, "אָשַׁר."

[66] *TDOT*, "אָשַׁר."

[67] Terrien, *Psalms*, 833.

emphatically state that "the pardon of God is the first and principal basis of the life of the people of God."[68]

A second kind of exhortative expression of worship involves calls to praise Yahweh. In these expressions resides a specific Hebrew word that has lost its place in encouraging fellow worshippers and has instead been turned into an emphatic expression of supreme praise: "Hallelujah!" (e.g., Ps 104:35; 106:1,48). It seems that modern readers have taken the exclamation point at the end of English translations and have mistaken them as expressing force, when in fact they are intended to relate a command to praise. The word *halĕlû-yāh* is an imperative plural verb (*halĕlû*, "you must praise") appended to a shortened form of the name Yahweh *(yāh)*. The first occurrence of the word is in Psalm 104, which is thoroughly appropriate given that psalm's focus on the providence of God in the activities of man. The command to praise is the crescendo of the book of Psalms since the last five psalms are dominated by the word and concept. Other hymns that do not use "hallelujah" may still begin with a *call* to praise using another synonymous verb in the imperative plural, summoning the assembled community to praise Yahweh (e.g., *ydh* in Ps 33:2, *zmr* in Ps 66:1 [Hb. 66:2], and *rwʿ* in Ps 100:1). To the one whose life has been altered by the power and majesty of God, there is no other place that one can go than to His praise. But praising God alone has never been the apex of worship, for joy seeks company, and those who are most driven to His praise find themselves calling in their neighbors to join them.

There is another charge for fellow worshippers to praise Yahweh that requires special attention. Throughout the book of Psalms there are calls to bless *(bārak)* Yahweh. Blessing someone is to request aid for them. Since God Himself, however, is the source of all blessing, the charge to bless Him serves more as a recognition of His already evident claim to strength and glory.[69] It is a call to praise Him based on the memory of who He has been in the past and who He will continue to be in the future. The call to bless Yahweh is closely linked with blessings announced on people in the book of Psalms because

---

[68] Mays, *Psalms*, 146.

[69] F. Horst, "Segen und Segenshandlugen in der Bibel," *EvT* 7 (1947–48): 31.

in the Scriptures one calls for the granting of God's blessings on another because of the good the other has done. When calling on others to bless Yahweh, it amounts to praise for the good that He is. But beyond this it is also an encouragement for other people of God to seek the continuation of God's intervention in their lives.[70] Worship must convey clearly and unequivocally every part of what God has done in the lives of those who are His "from the central act of salvation to the furthest limits of God's blessings. In this way it will correspond to our intercessions, which have the same center and the same limits."[71] The psalmists' skill at interlacing the horizontal and vertical aspects of worship is a reality that stretches the imagination and stirs the heart.

The third form of exhortative practices in the book of Psalms is in the blessing of others. Blessings have lost their emphasis in the modern culture because we have lost a sense of the power of words. Too often, individuals express a benediction such as Paul's in 2 Cor 13:13 ("May the grace of Our Lord Jesus Christ, and the love of God, and the fellowship of the Holy Spirit, be with us all, evermore, Amen.") without stopping to think of the potency of the words. In the biblical text, stated blessings are more prevalent in the narrative areas of Scripture (especially Genesis and Deuteronomy).[72] The blessings in other parts of the Scripture include fertility (Gen 1:22,28; 9:1; 24:35); victory (Gen 24:60; Numbers 23); and sometimes spiritual transformation (Isa 11:2). While they are usually not exhortative in expression, they certainly are in purpose. They serve as a means of communicating vital power and are the essence of what allows life to function and operate. In worship the blessing was the climactic event, bringing security and increase to the community and to individuals.[73] Since God alone bestows the blessing, the expression from the human mediator serves as an exhortation to move in Yahweh's direction.[74]

---

[70] C. Westermann, *Blessing in the Bible and the Life of the Church*, trans. K. Crim (Philadelphia: Fortress, 1978), 50.

[71] Ibid., 112.

[72] Ibid., 29.

[73] Mowinckel, *Psalmenstudien* V (Kristiana: Dybwad, 1924).

[74] Horst, "Segen und Segenshandlugen," 26

In the book of Psalms, blessings played a significant role in moving the congregation toward a spirit of worship as a whole. They are conspicuously present in the Songs of Ascent (Psalms 120–134) in which it seems each of the songs was a response following the priestly blessing. The journey itself functioned, therefore, as a blessing.[75] Blessing from God was the preeminent gift one could receive, as it was blessing that enhanced life and brought it to abundance (see Ps 134:3).[76] The desire, as the blessings were sung, was for God's favor and power to envelop the entire group. This would then lead immediately into praising God (see Psalm 67). It is here that one sees the clearest expression of the purpose of the horizontal sanction for the blessing of the members of the congregation—it directly leads to praising God which in turn leads to reaching the nations![77]

One cannot separate praising and adoring God from encouraging fellow worshippers to also participate in the praise and adoration. Worship is about fellowship and relationship—with God foremost, but also in some ways with fellow humans. One cannot worship when human relationships are broken and divided. The exhortations in the book of Psalms turn this premise over and examine the more positive possibility that when human relationships are encouraging and supportive, worship will be enhanced all the more.

## Sorrow Has Its Place In Worship

One of the most prevalent forms of worship expressions in the biblical material is the lament.[78] It is probably the manifestation of worship in the biblical record that is most unlike modern worship. Whereas contemporary worship services revel in the positive, almost to the point of ignoring the sorrows of life, ancient worship recognized the wholeness of life and the emotions it elicits as part of what a person brings before God. True, the cross has permanently transformed reality so that praise ought to be the major expression of life. But the presence of so many laments can hardly be attributed

---

[75] L. J. Liebreich, "The Songs of Ascents and the Priestly Blessing," *JBL* 74 (1955): 33–36.

[76] Terrien, *Psalms*, 854; Mays, *Psalms*, 403.

[77] Mays, *Psalms*, 224.

[78] Depending on how one divides the psalms, lament may in fact be the most prevalent form of psalm in the book of Psalms.

merely to the pre-resurrection status of the participants. Their presence also in the Christian canon prevents one from viewing them solely in this light. Rather, their presence points to two realities that require the modern church to adjust and transform accordingly.

The first contributing factor is the disparity between how Eastern and Western cultures view emotions. One of the main reasons for the omission of expressions of sorrow in worship today is an aversion for any form of emotion in the Western tradition. The ancients had no such misconceptions about emotion. In the West, emotion often plays one of two roles in worship—it is either removed altogether or becomes all that is expressed. Anyone who has spent time in cultures less influenced by the negative cultural perspective on emotions can attest to the presence of more lament forms of hymnology and prayer than those evident in the Western tradition. Even those denominations that express aversion for charismatic manifestations demonstrate a far more expressive form of worship, both jovial and mournful, than their Western counterparts. This is not to say that their forms of expression are superior, only that the Western church needs to be aware of those elements that may contribute to its inability to fully participate in all aspects of worship that the biblical material views as significant and to adjust accordingly. As Longman put it, these laments "teach us that our emotions are grounded in our faith, our covenant faith. This contradicts our mistaken belief that emotions are something over which we have no control."[79]

A more important reflection of their presence has to do with the unity of life and worship that is implicit in the biblical worldview but that is often missing today. Laments arose from individual or corporate crises. These crises could be as personal as sickness (Psalms 6; 88) or as corporate as an invading army (Psalms 44; 60). They could be as public as a criminal trial (Psalm 22) or as private as secret sin (Psalms 38; 51). The artistry of the writer is clear and meaningful in these Psalms as these opposing forces were often personified in the psalmic genre or characterized as death itself. Whatever the specific source of crisis, the biblical writers viewed the matter as under the purview of God. No matter was too small or too negative to take

---

[79] Longman, *How to Read the Psalms*, 81.

before Him. Clearly implicit in this supposition is a trust that He is both willing and able to deal with whatever concerns His people. Worship then must deal honestly with needs and pain. The imagery used in Psalms in such a wide variety of circumstances is a vivid reminder of the strength and power of God—which is even stronger than death (Pss 16:10; 49:15 [Hb. v. 16])—and His commitment to never abandon those in relationship with Him.[80]

One of the subgenres of lament most difficult to understand and to appropriate into modern worship is that of the imprecatory psalm. The requests for vengeance and the presence of glee at the enemy's potential destruction seem very much at odds with the NT advocacy of forgiving one's enemies and loving those who persecute you (Matt 5:43–44; Luke 6:27). No place is the disparity more evident than in Ps 137:8–9 in its address to "Daughter Babylon": "Happy is the one who pays you back what you have done to us. Happy is he who takes your little ones and dashes them against the rocks." Therefore, this psalm is the center of the discussion that follows.

Concerning the place of these psalms in Christian ministry and worship, various approaches have been implemented. Some have suggested that it is not proper for Christians to use these psalms.[81] The rationale for such a position varies from viewing them as the residue of antiquity to being an outgrowth of natural feelings.[82] Exegetes holding this position propose that the expressions are sinful and that repeating them would be tantamount to blasphemy. That these passages are part of the inspired canon prevents such a position for evangelicals, but questions as to how one might appropriate them still remain.

Some attempt to understand and employ the texts via psychological application. They argue that these psalms represent a biblical

---

[80] H. Ringgren, *The Faith of the Psalmists* (London: SCM Press, 1963). 74–75.

[81] For a good discussion of the various difficulties people have with these Psalms, see J. G. Vos, "The Ethical Problem of the Imprecatory Psalms," *WTJ* 4 (1942): 123–26.

[82] R. Kittel, *The Scientific Study of the Old Testament*, trans. J. C. Hughes (New York: Harcourt, Brace & Company, 1958), 143; P. Craigie, *Psalms 1–50*, vol. 19 of *Word Biblical Commentary* (Waco: Word Books, 1983), 41–42. See C. S. Lewis, *Reflections on the Psalms* (New York: Harcourt, Brace & Company, 1958), 22.

way of moving through the process of anger.[83] Through expressions of anger, the psalmist is able to get past the unhealthy and improper feelings that anger represents back to a place where God can use him.

While much may be contributed to counseling through biblical texts, their place in the genre of a worship event suggests this approach is far removed from their purpose. This is evident by the fact that many imprecatory psalms, such as Psalm 137, express no resolution. Therefore, viewing them as the first step toward healing, even though they are themselves improper, leads one to the conclusion that the revelation here is either incomplete or erroneous. Surely if that were the purpose, then every psalm in question would somehow make such a journey of personal reconciliation apparent.

A somewhat more popular approach is to view the imprecatory psalms as a response to sin by one's enemies. Thus, the psalmist was seeking to preserve and protect both his position in the covenant and Yahweh's holiness when the imprecations were expressed.[84] The concern for holiness is an essential thought of the biblical text; however, this perspective in relationship to these passages is far too limited and in many ways leaves open the question of the appropriateness of such expressions in Christian worship.[85] What's more, this position seemingly ignores the personal nature of many of the imprecations and attempts to draw firm doctrinal positions from language that is vague and often hyperbolic.

A third line of attack in proposing a manner in which Christians might utilize these psalms is through spiritualizing them. Building off the NT teaching that our "battle is not against flesh and blood" (Eph 6:12), this approach suggests that the focus of such psalms for the church ought to be toward either a more general expression of evil or toward the spiritual forces behind that evil. Often this train of thought suggests that these psalms represent an eschatological perspective when all evil will be done away with and justice will

---

[83] S. Carney, "God Damn God: A Reflection on Expressing Anger in Prayer," *BTB* 13 (1983): 90–99.

[84] C. Laney, "A Fresh Look at the Imprecatory Psalms," *BSac* 138 (1981): 41–43.

[85] Interestingly, Laney, after defending their presence in the Old Testament, goes on to say that these psalms are improper for use by those in the church age (Laney, "A Fresh Look," 44).

become the norm of life.[86] This approach has the strength of cross references in the eschatological materials of Scripture that indeed view the end in this light and also rightly place the emphasis on God's actions rather than on human actions. But we need to carefully define eschatology as relating to both the *now* and the *not yet* if this approach is applied.

James Mays did a masterful job of interpreting Psalm 137 in light of its genre, its purpose, and its place as *Christian* worship.[87] He observed that the expressions of vv. 8–9 are indeed wish prayers and that "there is no evading the passionate pain and anger that animates these prayers. They call for the accounts in the books to be balanced. *But they are not to be reduced to a personal desire for savage revenge.*"[88] The psalmists were indeed driven by their passion for both God and His place of occupancy, and they seek not only vengeance but also the reign of Yahweh as manifested in people's lives in the present. One cannot help but be reminded of the words of the model prayer, "Your kingdom come. Your will be done on earth as it is in heaven" (Matt 6:10).

In many ways, songs such as these enliven one's appreciation of the tension of one who lives in a world in conflict with God's will. The struggle of everyday life is a real one for the faithful. It is one of pain and sorrow. Anger at sin, and grief over our temporary confinement to a fallen world—all these are necessary reflections with which all Christians must grapple. No other place in Scripture allows us to reflect in such a personal way as do these psalms. But like the psalmists, we must remember that the outcome of such desires and wishes are left in the hands of God and not our own. To whom else can we turn with such desires and in whom else can resolution be found? If it is truly fellowship with Him that drives our passions, then it is submission to His will that must direct our speech and thoughts.

The church today too often is a place where the façade of happiness at all costs must be maintained. The one place where people

---

[86] Longman, *How to Read the Psalms*, 139–40.
[87] Mays, *Psalms*, 423–24.
[88] Ibid., 424. Emphasis added.

ought to be able to bring their grief and struggles has become the one place where it is improper to show sadness. Indeed, even churches that are critical of the so-called health and wealth gospel often imply by their attitudes that those who are hurting are somehow defective in faith. People are often left with the idea that sorrow is restricted to the counseling session or interpersonal relationships since worship is only for the happy. How far removed from the biblical perspective of sorrow is a church with such an outlook in its worship services? Worship should provide an outlet for meeting God with all that a person is. This does not occur in terms of pyschologizing messages and self-help directives, but in an openness to sorrow and struggle that both acknowledges their reality and points one toward the hope that God can and will repair the damage.[89]

## Thanks and Praise

Conventionally, scholarship has distinguished psalms of thanksgiving from hymns (or psalms of praise). More recently, psalms of thanksgiving have come to be viewed in closer relationship with hymns. Some describe the former as a subset of the latter, while others distinguish the two by calling the first psalms of declarative praise and the second psalms of descriptive praise.[90] The psalms of declarative praise or songs of thanksgiving normally contain an explicit reference to thanksgiving *(tôdâ)*. They express gratitude for particular acts of rescue from a plight in which the individual or nation was ensnared. The deliverance might have been from sickness (Psalm 30; 116) or from enemies (Psalm 92; 118). The resolution of such crises has transformed the psalmist's perspective and allowed him to see in God's work an opportunity for a fresh start.[91] They may be corporate expressions of thanks for a bountiful harvest (Psalm 67) or from some unknown moment of deliverance (Psalm

[89] These observations should not be read as an appraisal of the appropriateness of counseling, nor as an advocacy that one forego such counseling in favor of simply going to church more. Rather, the focus here is on what a church acknowledges, addresses, and allows in its worship service that facilitates the meeting of all aspects of life before God.

[90] Terrien, *Psalms*, 43; C. Westermann, *Praise and Lament in the Psalms*, trans. K. R. Crim and R. N. Soulen (Atlanta: Westminster John Knox, 1981), 25–30.

[91] Davidson, *Vitality of Worship*, 104.

124). This last psalm includes imagery from the act of creation (Ps 124:4–9), which is more of a hallmark of simple praise than a marker of thanksgiving—hence, the identification of the genre with that of hymn.

Hymns *(tĕhillâ)* tend to be more removed from dynamic contact with God's actions in history than are songs of thanksgiving. They are not a reaction to a particular or direct experience with God. Hymns, like songs of thanksgiving, draw significantly on remembrance and telling the story of God's activities, but they are more reflective of the nature and character of God as the One who has acted in history rather than of the event itself. While songs of thanksgiving tend to be more emotive, occasionally including elements of lament, the song of praise has a contemplative depth that comes from time, reflection, and growth. As mentioned above, hymns often include exhortation to the congregation to praise Yahweh for His being. Themes included in hymns are the creation of man (Psalms 8; 104), God's might and mercy (Psalm 113), and His rule over history (Psalms 78; 105). There is always a careful distinction between seeing God's interactions in history and fully associating Him with His creation. Sometimes the use of name theology (Ps 8:1 [Hb. v. 1]) makes this distinction, and sometimes statements that distinguish Him from how creation behaves are the means (Ps 147:10).[92]

Both the hymns and the psalms of thanksgiving are firmly grounded in history. The idea of many today that one might be able to maintain a theology of God while removing Him from supernatural acts within history is antithetical to all that the biblical record suggests, whether the interpreter finds himself in the narratives or the hymns. God is bound to His people and His people to Him through the events of history; His acts in this realm are the basis for Israel's self-identity and their entire concept of Him.[93] The challenge for modern worship leaders is to produce and present history in such a way that the congregant appreciates this important concept as they evaluate their place before God. Such information should not be limited solely to the history of the biblical world (as important and absent as

---

[92] Mays, *Psalms*, 65.
[93] Kraus, *Theology of the Psalms*, 175–76.

that is in the modern church), but should also concern history and issues that are closer chronologically to the modern worshipper. The current church ignores its history since the time of Christ to its own detriment, not simply because of the danger of repeating past mistakes, but also as a source of worship of the God who has directed and preserved His people through it.

## One God, One People

The postexilic histories of 1–2 Chronicles, Ezra, and Nehemiah record a story of God's faithful restoration of His people and their struggle to find themselves again after years of separation from the land of promise. The question of the common origin of these books remains a matter of significant scholarly debate. For our present purposes it is enough to acknowledge that at the very least, the evidence demands that the writer or writers of these four books in their final form intended them to be read as a single entity.[94] Many themes pervade these texts as they tell and retell events of Israel's history with different emphases from those of the writer or writers of 1–2 Samuel and 1–2 Kings. Whereas the writer or writers of the Samuel and Kings material often focused on the mistakes of the past in order to explain the sorry state of the present, the Chronicler looked to the history of Israel in order to outline a hopeful commitment to its future. In particular, the emphasis of unity seems to be a guiding presupposition and emphasis of the Chronicler.

## Unity in Identity

When one thinks of 1–2 Chronicles, often the first thing that comes to mind is the genealogies that dominate the first nine chapters of 1 Chronicles. These long and sometimes taxing genealogies serve an important purpose of expressing inclusiveness and unity. The writer also focused on the name "Israel" instead of "Jacob" and

[94] S. S. Tuell, *First and Second Chronicles*, INT (Louisville: John Knox Press, 2001), 8–9; P. Ackroyd, "Chronicles–Ezra–Nehemiah: the Concept of Unity," *ZAW* 100 Supp (1988): 189–201. The term "Chronicler" is used for the biblical author in the discussion that follows to avoid redundancy and clumsiness of expression. It is not intended to assume single authorship of the books in question.

highlighted the term "all Israel," even in those events of the past when only a tribe or two were involved (2 Chr 24:5). The intention seems to have been to suggest that those groups who were previously lost and divided had been brought together again. Therefore, the remnant of the faithful served not to exclude but to represent the group to which all are welcomed if they would but return (2 Chr 13:4–12).[95]

This focus on "all Israel" finds some of its most important expressions in texts related to the cult. J. A. Thompson said, "The repeated thrust of the Chronicler's work was that north and south, 'all Israel,' ought to be and finally would be one in a unity based on their common worship of Yahweh centered in the Jerusalem Temple."[96] This unity of worship is grounded in the word ḥesed, God's continual and faithful love to the people (1 Chr 16:34,41; 2 Chr 5:13; 7:3,6; 20:21).[97] The stipulations of Deuteronomy 12–26 required application in their present situation, for Yahweh had not completed His work with the people. Their presence in a restored Israel suggested a hope for God's beneficial provision and development to be fully realized. Indeed, the last words in the Hebrew canon are those of 2 Chronicles: "Whoever among you of His people may go up, and may the LORD his God be with him" (2 Chr 36:23). What a poignant reminder that no people are ever abandoned who belong to Yahweh!

Additionally, the specific cultic texts express a formally equivalent version of the worship of postexilic Israel with that of preexilic Israel. The Chronicler went to great pains to express the continuity of the present generation with previous ones in terms of their worship. The altar (Ezra 3:3), temple (Ezra 5; 6:7), clergy (Neh 12:24,45), and cult (Ezra 3:3; Neh 8:14) are all referred to in terms not only reminiscent of the ancient views but also identical to them in many ways.[98] The customs and practices of the past and the strict adherence to the law outlined in these texts could have easily become a

---

[95] H. G. M. Williamson, *1 and 2 Chronicles*, NCB (Grand Rapids: Eerdmans, 1982), 24–26; S. McKenzie, *1–2 Chronicles*, AOTC (Nashville: Abingdon, 2004), 50–51.

[96] J. A. Thompson, *1, 2 Chronicles*, NAC (Nashville: B&H, 1994), 35.

[97] McKenzie, *1–2 Chronicles*, 58.

[98] D. J. Clines, *Ezra, Nehemiah, Esther*, NCB (Grand Rapids: Eerdmans, 1984), 25.

legalistic journey that was completely antithetical to the prescripts and positions of the prophets discussed above. But these first adherents to the old ways avoided this path that it seemed their successors would slip into (see Malachi) through an emphasis and heartfelt expression of joy as they carried them out (Ezra 3:11,13; 6:16,22; Neh 12:27).[99] Moreover, within the clear liturgical patterns of the worship services, there seems to have been a freedom for some that only advances the concept of unity further.

## Unity in Purpose

In Ezra 3 the reestablishment of worship following the return from exile is outlined in terms that relate a mixture of styles in worship that is both striking and commendable. In the text there is a clear program that diminishes the principal players of the time through the absence of identifiers that would relate them as leaders. Biblical readers know both Joshua and Zerubbabel (Ezra 3:2) as the key leaders of Israel at the people's initial return. From other texts we know that Joshua was the high priest (Hag 1:1,12,14; Zech 3:1) and that Zerubbabel was both the governor of Judah and the heir to David's throne (Hag 1:1; 2:21–23; Matt 1:12; Luke 3:27). So it is striking that in Ezra 3:2,8 neither is recognized by their office. Instead, the writer groups them with others almost equally in relation to the work to be carried out on the temple. This style seems to be the outgrowth of a desire to highlight and emphasize the entire people in the rebuilding of the temple and the worship that immediately followed.[100] As the description of the ceremonies begins, the Chronicler furthered this emphasis on unity through the mixed discussion of the service that transpired. Certain practices such as the blowing of trumpets (see Num 10:1–10) and the presence of the sons of Asaph, the levitical musicians, clearly reflect a traditional, liturgical order of service. Other practices, such as the refrain from the psalms, the shout of victory (see 1 Sam 4:5), the tears of joy, and especially the freewill offering were far more spontaneous and

---

[99] Clines, *Ezra, Nehemiah, Esther,* 29; Williamson, *1 and 2 Chronicles,* 30–31.

[100] L. Grabbe, *Ezra–Nehemiah* (London: Routledge, 1998), 16; M. Throntveit, *Ezra–Nehemiah,* INT (Louisville: John Knox Press, 1992), 24.

free in appearance.[101] The unity of the people extended to a freedom of response that was not constrained by tradition or concern over correctness.

There is clearly an emphasis on both joy *and* freedom expressed in the text and event.[102] The people had toiled many years in the dispersion of the Babylonian captivity. Their newfound unity and cohesion found expression largely in the worship that expressed their desire to be a people committed to praising the same God. Moreover, their concord was the direct result of a hope in the future consummation of God's promises. Though they lived at a time when they were under the control of a foreign power and were standing near a building that had only its foundations visible, they had a convinced elation that allowed them to express gratitude to God even when, by all appearances, there was not yet anything for which to thank Him.[103]

It is interesting that at the end of the story of Israel in the OT, the biblical text emphasizes that worship both proceeds from and ushers in unity. In this unity the people found that the commonality of the God they worshipped was more important than the circumstances which could so easily separate them—a unity born in their common history and their future hopes; a unity that allowed them immense freedom to express their joy and gratitude to God in a way that was both liturgically framed and articulated and yet absent from

---

[101] Clines, *Ezra, Nehemiah, Esther,* 67. H. G. M. Williamson may be correct in his supposition that the quotation of the psalm was more the invention of the Chronicler as a summary of the type of refrain that was used (see Pss 100:4–5; 106:1; 107:1; 118:1; 136:1) (*Ezra, Nehemiah,* WBC [Waco: Word, 1985], 48). But it just as likely that the people in the excitement of the moment drew from numerous psalms as they related the event to the worship they already knew (see the discussion of Hannah's prayer/song above). That the tears cried by the elders were tears of joy because the work on the temple was finally proceeding seems more plausible than the idea that they were sorrowful at its appearance (see Clines, *Ezra, Nehemiah, Esther,* 71–72). This seems true for three reasons. (1) The passage often used to support the sorrow viewpoint (Hag 2:3) refers to events that were much later since the events in Haggai took place in 520 BC and Ezra 3 in 537 BC. (2) Since only the foundations had been repaired at this point and the text relates the new temple to the previous one (Ezra 5:15; 6:3; see Clines, *Ezra, Nehemiah, Esther,* 91), it is difficult to assume the elders would conceive that what was being built was less than what existed before. (3) The whole flow of the text is joyous, and it is difficult to imagine that the Chronicler who has spent so much time outlining continuity with the past would emphasize the opposite here.

[102] Williamson, *Ezra, Nehemiah,* 51.

[103] Clines, *Ezra, Nehemiah, Esther,* 72.

a set pattern for how worship ought to be done. In the midst of an era of Church history where worship often divides, the expressions of unity in the worship of ancient Israel serve as a clarion call to let the focus on God inherent in His praise pull together those who are called by His name.

## Expressions in the New Testament

As stated in the introduction to this section, the Writings represent the part of the OT revelation that can most directly and easily be assimilated into Christian worship. Therefore, it should not be surprising to find direct quotations, allusions, or echoes of the Writings, especially the book of Psalms, throughout the NT. But the goal of this section is not to examine the NT's use of the Writings. Rather, the focus, as with the other chapters above, is to demonstrate that many of the expressions and realities espoused in the OT are furthered and strengthened through their presence in the NT as well.

## Wisdom and Worship in the New Testament

The NT writers were as committed to the pursuit of godly wisdom as their predecessors. Indeed, one continuing perspective on Jesus in scholarship has been in the role of sage or wise man.[104] The fact that He taught in parables that required special insight and explanation is enough to classify Him in this light (Matt 13:10–13; Mark 4:34). The typological association of Jesus with the personification of wisdom (Proverbs 8) only serves to further this perspective (1 Cor 8:6; Col 1:15–17; Rev 3:14). This view of Jesus played a part in how His disciples would understand their own roles. The disciples patterned their ministries after His so that through their teaching and worship one can find expressions of wisdom throughout the NT witness.

As a previous section of this chapter has stated, the book of Proverbs relates a countercultural wisdom that opposed how a

---

[104] Although T. Y. Mullins' "humanization" of Jesus went so far as to practically remove him from the realm of the divine, his short article on the NT's use of wisdom materials is helpful in identifying basic links in seeing Jesus as a sage. see Mullins, "Jewish Wisdom Literature in the NT," *JBL* 68 (1949): 335–39.

person might logically live his life if all he was seeking was success. Similarly, Paul drew distinctions between God's wisdom and man's (see James 3:15–17). Paul challenged his congregations to understand that God had made the world's wisdom foolish (1 Cor 1:20). He demonstrated this by living a life directed and committed to that wisdom (2 Cor 1:12). In a world at enmity with the high calling of Christ, there is nothing more laudable to pursue than wisdom in how one might walk in triumph (Col 1:21–28; also John 15:11–18). For Paul, this wisdom extended into every area of life.

Paul, especially in the book of Colossians, used a method of explication and argumentation reminiscent of the wisdom teachers of his day and of the OT. He began his book with exhortations to wisdom (1:28) in juxtaposition to the hymns regarding the majesty and greatness of Jesus (1:15–20), a method employed in Psalms also. He continued his emphasis on wisdom through phrases that synonymously advocate the fear of Yahweh as the basis for all activity (1:10; 2:6; 3:17). He concluded his argument with practical expressions for how to live an ordered life in both everyday living (3:18–4:1) and participation in the life of the church (4:2–18).[105] In fact, this pattern of theological exposition and praise followed by practical instruction is evident in many of Paul's epistles. The implications could not be clearer: all life must be lived under the agenda of worship, for it is God to whom all must go if wisdom is ever to be achieved (see Jas 1:2–7).

## Instruction and Worship in the New Testament

It seems almost unnecessary to say that the NT emphasizes instruction in worship. The status of the Epistles as the primary text of evangelical sermons is evidence enough that such is a foregone conclusion in many churches today. Indeed, such an emphasis for the Epistles seems to go back to the biblical era itself. The fact that the letters were addressed to the whole church at a specific location may be evidence enough to suggest that they were employed in such a manner. But there are also texts that clearly outline the rite: "I charge

[105] A. Lincoln, "The Household Code and Wisdom Mode of Colossians," *JSNT* 74 (1999): 93–112.

you by the Lord that this letter be read to all the brothers" (1 Thess 5:27); "And when this letter has been read among you, have it read also in the church of the Laodiceans" (Col 3:16). Further, Peter clearly equated Paul's letters with Scripture when he stated that they need to be handled carefully, lest people twist their content as they do with other biblical texts (2 Pet 3:15–16). Finally, Hebrews is particularly instructive on this matter since it "possesses an especially strong oral, sermonic quality" and the writer "employed language in ways that would have aural impact when spoken aloud to a group gathered for worship."[106] Therefore, the instructional nature of NT worship seems secure as a presuppositional position through which to appreciate its contents.

## Exhortation and Worship in the NT

For evangelicals, inclusion of both exhortative and instructive passages is a common practice. However, the nuanced manner in which the NT sometimes expresses exhortation may be somewhat more unfamiliar to today's worshipper. It is true that the sermons of Jesus and the Epistles are full of commands and encouragements to walk a certain path or to hold on to the faith. But it is also true that as in the OT, the NT expresses exhortation via beatitudes, blessings, and hallelujahs.

Jesus' beatitudes occur at the beginning of His teaching ministry (Matt 5:3–10; Luke 6:20–22) and therefore serve in some ways as a framework for all that follows. There is a longstanding debate among scholars about whether the beatitudes represent patterns of behavior to be followed or simply reflect hope of what the kingdom will represent in the eschaton.[107] But this struggle too restrictively defines eschatology. If one views the promises of Scripture regarding the end through the tension of the now and not yet aspects that

---

[106] T. Long, *Hebrews*, INT (Louisville: John Knox, 1997), 5. Ellingworth rightly notes that this style should not be seen as distinguishing it too broadly from the other Epistles, because it is likely that the uniqueness simply resides in the writer's extraordinary oral skills that simply came through in the writing. P. Ellingworth, *The Epistle to the Hebrews*, NIGTC (Grand Rapids: Eerdmans, 1993), 62.

[107] R. Guelich, "The Matthean Beatitudes: 'Entrance-Requirements' or Eschatological Blessings?" *JBL* 95 (1976): 415–34.

seem to predominate its contents, one would expect there to be ethical dimensions to the texts. The exhortative nature of the beatitudes can therefore not be excluded since Jesus explained the nature of those who will make up His kingdom. The beatitudes, then, represent declarations of encouragement toward behavior that is pleasing to God and that is transformative of both society as a whole and the individual person practicing them.[108]

Blessing in the NT is grounded in the saving activity of Jesus (Acts 3:25–26; Gal 3:8–9; Eph 1:3). In Rom 15:29 the expression "blessing of Christ," in a manner very reminiscent of the OT concept of blessing, relates the fact that the "proclamation of the gospel brings about growth, prosperity, and strengthening of the community."[109] The blessing as part of the letter and worship emphasizes that Paul, in ministering to the church at Rome, would also be ministered to and encouraged by their blessings.[110] Paul's perception and practice were also manifested in his greetings to the churches to which he wrote. Despite Westermann's hesitancy to derive conclusions about Christian worship from such blessings,[111] it is difficult to imagine they did not play such a role given the tradition of blessing formulas and the context of the early church in relationship to the synagogue where such practices are known to have taken place. The charges from Paul to the churches include guarding the unity of the fellowship (2 Cor 13:11–14), guarding the faith of the church (Gal 6:11–16), and guarding our walk (Eph 6:18–20). Such an emphasis on the protection and the continued health of believers and the church as a whole suggests strongly their exhortative essence.

The word "hallelujah" is brought into the NT through transliteration only in the book of Revelation (Rev 19:1,3,4,6). Here, as in the OT, the word represents an invitation or command to join in the praise of God. The uses of it are clearly related as an outgrowth of God's activity in defeating the enemy and His status as ruling the world. As such all are invited to worship and praise Him.[112] The

---

[108] C. H. Dodd, More NT Studies (Grand Rapids: Eerdmans, 1968), 1–10.

[109] Westermann, Blessing, 82, 99.

[110] D. J. Moo, The Epistle to the Romans, NICNT (Grand Rapids: Eerdmans, 1996), 907.

[111] Westermann, Blessing, 96–97.

[112] G. K. Beale, The Book of Revelation, NIGTC (Grand Rapids: Eerdmans, 1999), 926–31.

book of Revelation also includes a blessing of God that clearly expresses His grandeur and majesty (Rev 7:12). Evidently, the encouragement imbued through the praise of God and participation in that praise functions in such a way as to offer hope in even the most difficult of situations. Can those of us in less trying times than those represented by John's immediate audience afford not to encourage each other in like manner (see Heb 10:25)?

## Sorrow and Worship in the New Testament

We often view sorrow as antithetical to the Christian life and perspective. Yet, until the time when the presence of sin is removed from the created order completely, it is a reality with which the faithful must deal. The cross has changed the way suffering is viewed for the Christian, not that its intensity is denied or even reduced. Rather, it changes the view one has of suffering by understanding that it is not the final word and that there is hope beyond all that someone experiences here (Rom 8:18–21).[113] Still, there are reflections of true sorrow being expressed in the NT in the context of worship, primarily in the recorded prayers, that bear examination.

The prayers of Jesus relating to His crucifixion are similar to, and sometimes quote from, the lament psalms. His cry of dereliction while on the cross is unquestionably drawn from Ps 22:1 [Hb. v. 2]. This was not only a cry of pain (though it certainly was this), but was also a reflection of the principles of power made complete in weakness and of submission to the will of God.[114] Further, the use of Psalm 22 throughout the Gospels clearly indicates that "Jesus took on himself in detail the suffering that befell individuals in Israel in the Old Testament."[115] His death was not only a healing of sin, but a response to suffering. Knowing that Christ has been through such suffering grants us a new foundation on which to stand as we deal with suffering.[116] He did not deny his suffering, but He did not

---

[113] Moo, *Romans*, 511.

[114] P. Miller, *They Cried to the Lord: The Form and Theology of Biblical Prayer* (Minneapolis: Fortress, 1994), 323–24.

[115] Kraus, *Theology of the Psalms*, 190.

[116] Mays, *Psalms*, 114.

succumb to it either. Instead, He victoriously and finally placed it in the hands of the Father (Luke 23:46; John 19:30).

The prayers of Jesus, the ultimate Sufferer, clearly appear in the NT in the context of full submission to the will of God (see Matt 26:42; John 12:27–28).[117] This is not fatalism or a claim that Jesus ignored the pain that He felt. Even with His foreknowledge of what was to transpire, Jesus returned three times to pray for deliverance from the cup. Likewise, Paul pleaded with God three times to have his thorn in the flesh removed (2 Cor 12:8–10), only to be told that the deliverance he sought came not in the mighty act but in the perfecting strength granted in the midst of suffering.[118] Like the psalmists centuries before, NT expressions of grief and sorrow found authentic expression and longing for relief. Also like the psalmists, the NT practitioners understood that the only One to whom such longings can appropriately be expressed is the One who legitimately understands, sustains, and heals.

## *Praise and Worship in the New Testament*

The NT texts are replete with expressions of praise to God for who He is and what He has done. The number of texts identified as possible hymns or hymn fragments in the Epistles alone is staggering. Like the psalms, these hymns are built on either the near (Phil 2:5–11) or distant (Col 1:15–20) acts of God, though the focus is often on Jesus as the second Person of the Trinity. The hymns function in their contexts as serving different purposes. Some exalt Christ and His majesty so that the recipients can find confidence to emulate Him and also know they will be sustained (Eph 2:14–16; Phil 2:5–11).[119] Others announce His greatness in order to present a theological basis for the claims, instructions, or charges proposed in the teaching (1 Tim 3:16; Titus 3:4–7).[120] The hymns of Revelation serve as a rejoinder to the saints about where their commitment and honor belong. They remind us that there is no room for compro-

---

[117] Miller, *They Cried*, 322.
[118] Ibid., 323.
[119] G. Hawthorne, *Philippians*, WBC (Waco: Word, 1983), 76–79.
[120] G. Knight, *The Pastoral Epistles*, NIGTC (Grand Rapids: Eerdmans, 1992), 186.

mise in a world that is in complete opposition to the will of God.[121] Whatever their purpose, their presence demonstrates the same reality that hymns did in the psalms. The past activities of Christ must be the subject of reflection in the church.

## Unity and Worship in the New Testament

The sacrificial emphasis of the NT is the basis for the proclamation of unity in its pages. In Romans, Paul advocated relationships in worship practices that recognize the freedom of the new dispensation and the concern for others that is, at its heart, nothing more than a demand for subordination of self (Romans 14). In Ephesians, Paul's reflections on unity in worship are somewhat loftier, since unity's foundation is the oneness of the God who is worshipped and served and who is an exemplar for the church that serves Him (Ephesians 4). The diversity of gifts, talents, and perspectives that makes up the church cannot be used to divide it, because it is the *one* God who has brought those realities into existence. What the people of Israel following the exile experienced, Paul advocated in his instructions to conformity in orthodoxy and to understanding what the church ought to be—but he also taught freedom in the matters that are secondary in nature.

## Conclusion

The expressions of worship represented in the Writings give dramatic manifestation to the gathering of the people of God with whom they worship. This book has undertaken an exposition of precepts and principles behind OT and NT worship events and texts to better understand the experience of the relationship of Creator and created. The present chapter has demonstrated how the worship event was given its most explicit voice as the musicians, philosophers, and theologians of ancient Israel took their turn. As texts that are related more as words about God than words from God, the Writings communicate in a way that goes right to the heart of the

---

[121] R. Morton, "Glory to God and to the Lamb: John's Use of Jewish and Hellenistic/Roman Themes in Formatting His Theology in Revelation 4–5," *JSNT* 83 (2001): 89–109.

reader. Yet because they are inspired texts, they convey the truth of God that goes beyond the mere aesthetic value of other great reflections on the divine.

To the lessons from these expressions that have already been offered above it seems appropriate to add one more: the matter of the surrounding nations' influence on the expressions of Israel's worship. Previous discussion hinted that Israel drew on the religious practices of its neighbors. Apparently, in places God led the Israelite sages to incorporate non-Israelite works into their own Scriptures (see Prov 30:1; 31:1), though it must be expressed that even in these cases the origin of the truth and the content of these passages must have been God Himself. Further, some of the Psalms seem to utilize the common theological language of other nations (e.g., Psalm 29), as they both praise Yahweh and disclose the falsehood of foreign religions.

The relationship of the expressions of worship, though, is most clearly seen in the forms of the psalms. There are clear formulaic similarities between the biblical expressions and those of Israel's neighbors. That the movement of formula sometimes went from the other nations to Israel seems apparent when the other nation's text has an earlier provenance than the earliest date likely for the biblical text. Some have chosen to explain the commonality of expressions as the result of a common human experience of seeking to reach out to something greater than ourselves.[122] Perhaps that explanation is valid, but there may very well also be a reflection of cultural relevance in this practice. As Israel developed its cult under the guidance of Yahweh and His chosen leadership, there would have already been a familiarity with certain forms and expressions among the people. To introduce a totally new way of worship and experience would have no doubt been difficult and in some ways damaging. Instead, God chose to work in common forms to speak as clearly and as meaningfully as possible to those who served Him. That is, God was culturally relevant in his forms of expression, though one would have to admit that God likely had a hand in moving the other

---

[122] Miller, *They Cried*, 31.

cultures in their expressions as part of his preparation for what He would do with Israel.

There is a need for cultural relevance in worship. This statement is not a call for a specific style of worship, for sometimes the traditional style speaks more clearly to the surrounding culture than a contemporary style would. Neither does it express willingness to compromise on content as one reaches out. As the people of Israel adopted the forms of expression of their neighbors, they also adapted the theology out of which those forms originated to be appropriate to both orthodoxy and the more general viewpoints of God that orthodoxy maintained. For instance, both monotheistic emphases and relational factors play a role in distinguishing Israel's hymnal, the book of Psalms, from that of their neighbors. The God praised in Israel's worship was always the same God, and He is praised in the context of specific acts of relationship, not vague expressions of what it means to be a god. To know one's culture and to respond accordingly is the mandate of evangelism; to do so solely in the context of the truth about God and His relationship to man is the demand of orthodoxy.

# Conclusion
## *WHERE DO WE GO FROM HERE?*

As James Muilenburg wrote, in the OT worship is not "a flight into the dim unknown, to timelessness, or to a presence that disturbs and elates one in ecstasy." Rather, it is "a holy meeting in which God grants forgiveness, comfort, and guidance, and where the worshipper responds in praise, often reciting God's great redemptive acts."[1] There is a genuineness about the OT that is almost palpable as one moves through its contents. Whether it is the blatant emotional expressions or the grounding in history that lies beneath everything it says, the texts have a way of connecting with the modern reader that few pieces of literature can match. Perhaps this is why the terminology "living word" is so often applied to the Scriptures. Certainly this connection results from the text being the very words of God poured out before us through the lives of numerous men and women in biblical history. Whatever the source of this capacity to speak so clearly today, there can be little doubt that these scriptural reflections on worship are some of the greatest manifestations of the OT's relevance for the modern reader. The worship of Israel speaks plainly to a world that often struggles with the subject. The use of the material in a way that honors God and impacts lives then becomes the duty of all who peruse the biblical presentation. Hopefully, this book has, in some small way, facilitated such an understanding of the text and has been able to accomplish the other tasks that it set out to do as well.

Obviously one of the primary goals of this book was to bring theology back into worship without necessarily promoting a specific system. Any work of this sort will certainly have a model or conception of God's workings that drives it, but I have tried to bind my observations primarily to the biblical record rather than some agenda-driven system that must defend certain precepts and principles. This is by no means the first book to attempt a biblical theology of worship, nor is it the first to suggest that all conceptions about worship

---

[1] J. Muilenburg, *The Way of Israel* (New York: Harper, 1961), 107–8.

must be driven by a proper theology. But on an issue so central to all that we are as Christians, there is scarcely the chance of saying too much about what the Bible contributes to the subject.

Methodologically, I have sought to demonstrate the way a proper hermeneutical method must drive theology. The reason I devoted space in each chapter to describing the method applied to the various genres was not only an outgrowth of my desire to allow the reader to know from where I drew certain conclusions; it was also an attempt to demonstrate the importance of history and language to arriving at sound conclusions in a postmodern world that is quickly abandoning both disciplines. Matters in my approach that are sometimes classified as modernist unapologetically drive the subject matter of this book. However, the argumentation is also fundamentally motivated by key presuppositions that hearken back to premodernity—namely, the trustworthiness of the original texts and the divine nature of its expressions. Since this work was not a philosophy of hermeneutics in its conception, I could not address such topics directly. I could merely demonstrate the present approach's aptness in application. The degree to which I have achieved my goal will only be measurable on an individual basis in the responses of those who read it.

Another goal of this work has to do with the nature of the OT itself. As stated in the introduction, there is still a widely disseminated undercurrent of dismissiveness toward the OT in much of evangelicalism today. This text has attempted to show that, in fact, there is a unified message of the Bible that encompasses both the OT and the NT. God has always been a God of grace, just as He has always had certain expectations for those people who would call themselves His. The abrogation of nearly two-thirds of the biblical canon through either neglect or outright dismissal does not represent well the belief that one is a "person of the book" as many evangelicals claim to be.

On the other hand, there is a distinctiveness about the OT we simply cannot ignore either. In several places throughout this book is the observation that application of the biblical content can only be accomplished through the principles they present. Sometimes when the NT speaks on a matter, it takes a text originally applied to physical human realities and applies it more spiritually. Other times it looks at the principle behind an activity rather than the activity itself. But in each case in this book, the OT was allowed to speak first, hearing what God has said in the past so that we can better understand what He wants us to do in the present and the future. The supposition behind such an approach is that if it was important enough for Him to say it in the past, it is important enough for us to hear it today.

What all these goals amount to is an ultimate aspiration to know both our God and ourselves better. Repeatedly addressed was the theme that knowing who God was in the past has direct implications for knowing who He is today. Therefore, attention was drawn to His attributes, actions, and expressed desires whenever possible. This approach rests upon the supposition that language does in fact dependably portray a reality and is more than simply an *accepted* utterance of truth; it is in fact *the truth* in declaration. In short, the religious speech of Israel does not simply approximate in its descriptions of God, it actually describes Him.[2] Simply because language cannot express all that God is should not compel us to suggest that what it is able to express is less than accurate. We cannot think of all that is God, but we can think of Him correctly. Such was the goal of this work. Furthermore, to correctly see God is also to correctly see ourselves. Only in the light of His surpassing greatness and mercy can we come close to seeing both the implicit limitedness and imputed value that is mankind.

There are many directions I could have traveled in this book but purposefully avoided. I unapologetically view those directions as outside the purposes and focus of the book. Of these, I will address here only the matters of secondary materials and tone. Those familiar with the subject of worship and the various studies that have been undertaken over the years no doubt recognized the absence of many of these works in the previous discussions. I do not mean

---

[2] Against W. Brueggemann, *Theology of the Old Testament: Testimony, Dispute, Advocacy* (Minneapolis: Fortress, 1997), 121–22; see G. von Rad, *Old Testament Theology*, vol. 2, *The Theology of Israel's Prophetic Traditions*, trans. D. M. G. Stalker (New York: Harper & Row, 1965), 353.

their exclusion as a slight on those studies, and many of them are in the bibliographical material at the end of the book. Rather, from the outset I have endeavored to make this book more about the biblical material itself rather than about the modern setting and discussions of it. Therefore, even though many of the other works on the topic do a masterful job of dealing with the biblical materials, I perceived them as a group as dealing more with the popular discussion of the issue than with the biblical material itself.

Concerning the tone of the work, there was a constant struggle in writing to find the best path between academic assessment and exhortative devotionalism. On the one hand, it was essential to appraise significant positions of scholarship that directly impact an understanding of the biblical material. But having spent time in both the classroom and the pulpit, I am keenly aware of the need to present the material in a manner that has pragmatic applications as well. Perhaps my approach resulted in arguments becoming too "sermonic" in places. Such is the cost of being one who views the classroom and the sanctuary as an inextricably associated pair that support and encourage each other. In the end, I hope there is something of value for both settings, but in good conscience I could not attempt either a purely devotional or a strictly academic work.

One of the lessons reinforced throughout the process of producing this work has been the importance of doing everything to the glory and honor of God alone. In a manner not too dissimilar to the pressure of filling auditoriums on Sunday morning, the academic setting often measures an individual by the output of literature that he or she creates. The academic is tempted to write with the selfish motive of furthering his or her career. Correspondingly, the pastor is enticed to choose songs or sermon topics that feed the ego of success rather than seeking to glorify of God. As I have reflected on this conundrum, the words of the inspired Teacher of Ecclesiastes have come to have new and significant meaning in my life: "There is no end to the making of many books, and much study wearies the body. When all has been heard, the conclusion of the matter is: fear God and keep His commands, because this is for all humanity" (Eccl 12:12b–13; see Col 3:17).

I have constantly prayed as I have completed this task that God alone receives honor from it and that those who visit its pages will be transported into His presence—not because this work itself is capable of such a dramatic effect, but because it draws the reader to the biblical text that reveals Yahweh in a way that nothing else can. Where do we go from here? I hope that we enter into more meaningful worship as both a lifestyle and an event.

# SELECTED BIBLIOGRAPHY

## Theologies and Special Studies

Abba, Raymond. "The Divine Name YAHWEH." *JBL* 80 (1961): 320–28.

Abou-Assaf, A., P. Bordreuil, and A.R. Millard, *La statue de Tell Fekheriye et son inscription bilingue assyro-araméenne.* Editions Recherche sur les civilizations. Paris: Etudes Assyriologiques, 1982.

Ackerman, James. "Who Can Stand before YHWH, This Holy God? A Reading of 1 Samuel 1–15." *Proof* 11 (1991): 1–25.

Ackroyd, Peter. "Isaiah I–XII: Presentation of a Prophet." In *Congress Volume: Göttingen 1977.* Supplements to VT 29, 16–48. Leiden: Brill, 1978.

_____. "Chronicles-Ezra-Nehemiah: the Concept of Unity." *ZAW* 100 Supp (1988): 189–201.

Ahlström, Gosta. *Joel and the Temple Cult of Jerusalem.* Supplements to VT 21. Leiden: Brill, 1971.

Albertz, Rainer. *A History of Israelite Religion in the Old Testament Period.* Vol. 1, *From the Beginnings to the End of the Monarchy.* Translated by John Bowden. OTL, ed. James Mays, Carol Newsom, and David Petersen. Louisville: Westminster John Knox, 1994.

_____. *A History of Israelite Religion in the Old Testament Period.* Vol. 2, *From the Exile to the Maccabees.* Translated by John Bowden. OTL. Edited by James Mays, Carol Newsom, and David Petersen. Louisville: Westminster John Knox, 1994.

Albright, William F. "Contributions to Biblical Archaeology and Philology." *JBL* 43 (1924): 370–78.

_____. "The Archaeological Background of the Hebrew Prophets of the Eighth Century." *JBR* 8 (1940): 131–36.

_____. *Samuel and the Beginnings of the Prophetic Movement.* Cincinnati: Hebrew Union College, 1961.

Alston, William. "Divine-Human Dialogue and the Nature of God." *FaiPhil* 2 (1985): 5–20.

Alt, Albrecht. "The God of the Fathers." In *Essays on Old Testament History and Religion*. Translated by R. A. Wilson, 3–66. Oxford: Basil Blackwell, 1966.

Auld, A. "Prophets Through the Looking Glass: Between Writings and Moses." *JSOT* 27 (1983): 3–23.

Baab, Otto. "The God of Redeeming Grace: Atonement in the Old Testament." *Int* 10 (1956): 131–43.

Baker, David. *Two Testaments, One Bible*, rev. ed. Downers Grove: InterVarsity, 1991.

Bal, Mieki. *Death and Dissymmetry: The Politics of Coherence in the Book of Judges*. Chicago: University Press, 1988.

Balentine, Samuel. *Prayer in the Hebrew Bible: The Drama of Divine-Human Dialogue*. Minneapolis: Fortress, 1993.

Balentine, Samuel. *The Torah's Vision of Worship*. Minneapolis: Fortress, 1999.

Batto, Bernard. *Slaying the Dragon: Mythmaking in the Biblical Tradition*. Louisville: Westminster John Knox, 1992.

Baumgarten, Joseph. "On the Non-Literal Use of *ma'ăśēr/dekatē*." *JBL* 103 (1984): 245–51.

Barr, James. "The Image of God in the Book of Genesis—A Study of Terminology." *BJRL* 51 (1968): 11–26.

_____. "Some Semantic Notes on Covenant." In *Beiträge zur alt-testamentlichen Theologie: Festschrift für Walther Zimmerli zum 70. Geburtstag*, ed. H. Donner and others, 23–38. Göttingen: Vandenhoeck und Ruprecht, 1977.

_____. *Biblical Faith and Natural Theology*. Oxford: Clarendon, 1993.

Barth, Christoph. *God with Us*. Grand Rapids: Eerdmans, 1991.

Barton, George. *Yahweh Before Moses*. New York: MacMillan, 1912.

Baumgarten, Joseph. "Sacrifice and Worship Among the Jewish Sectarians of the Dead Sea." *HTR* 46 (1953): 141–59.

Beckwith, Roger, and Martin Selman, ed. *Sacrifice in the Bible*. Grand Rapids: Baker, 1995.

Beebe, H. Keith. "Ancient Palestinian Dwellings." *BA* 31 (1968): 37–58.

Berman, Saul. "Extended Notion of the Sabbath." *Judaism* 22 (1973): 342–52.

Blenkinsopp, Joseph. *A History of Prophecy in Israel,* rev. ed. Louisville: Westminster John Knox, 1996.

Blocher, Henri. *In the Beginning: The Opening Chapter of Genesis.* Downers Grove: InterVarsity, 1984.

Boadt, Lawrence. "Divine Wonders Never Cease: The Birth of Moses in God's Plan of Exodus." In *Preaching Biblical Texts,* ed. F. Holmgrem and Herman Schaalman, 46–61. Grand Rapids: Eerdmans, 1995.

Boice, James. *Ordinary Men Called By God: Abraham, Moses, and David.* Wheaton: Victor, 1982.

Bonhoeffer, Dietrich. *Creation and Fall.* London: Collins, 1950.

Brichto, Herbert. "On Slaughter and Sacrifice, Blood and Atonement." *HUCA* 47 (1976): 19–56.

Bright, John. *Covenant and Promises.* Philadelphia: Westminster, 1976.

Brown, William and Dean McBride, ed. *God Who Creates: Essays in Honor of W. Sibley Towner.* Grand Rapids: Eerdmans, 2000.

Brownlee, W. H. "The Ineffable Name of God." *BASOR* 226 (1977): 39–45.

Brueggemann, Walter. "Bounded by Obedience and Praise: The Psalms as Canon." *JSOT* 50 (1991): 63–92.

_____. *Theology of the Old Testament: Testimony, Dispute, Advocacy.* Minneapolis: Fortress, 1997.

_____. *Ichabod Toward Home: The Journey of God's Glory.* Grand Rapids: Eerdmans, 2002.

_____. *An Introduction to the Old Testament: The Canon and Christian Imagination.* Louisville: Westminster John Knox, 2003.

Buber, Martin. *Moses: The Revelation and the Covenant.* New York: Harper & Row, 1958.

Burton, Ernest, John Smith and Gerald Smith. *Biblical Ideas of Atonement: Their History and Significance.* Chicago: University of Chicago Press, 1909.

Carney, Sheila. "God Damn God: A Reflection on Expressing Anger in Prayer." *BTB* 13 (1983): 90–99.

Childs, Brevard S. *Memory and Tradition in Israel*. London: SCM, 1962.

_____. *Introduction to the Old Testament as Scripture*. Philadelphia: Fortress, 1979.

Clements, Ronald. *Prophecy and Covenant*. Studies in Biblical Theology 43. London: SCM, 1965.

_____. *Prophecy and Tradition*. Atlanta: John Knox, 1975.

_____. *Old Testament Theology: A Fresh Approach*. Atlanta: John Knox, 1978.

Clines, David J. A. "The Image of God in Man." *TB* 19 (1968): 53–103.

_____. "Theme in Genesis 1–11." *CBQ* 38 (1976): 483–507.

Coats, George. *Moses: Heroic Man, Man of God*. Sheffield: Sheffield Academic, 1988.

Cohen, Gary. "The Doctrine of the Sabbath in the Old and New Testaments." *GJ* 6 (1965): 7–15.

Cohon, Samuel. "The Name of God, A Study in Rabbinic Theology." *HUCA* 23 (1951): 579–604.

Collins, John J. "The Zeal of Phinehas and the Legitimization of Violence." *JBL* 122 (2003): 3–21.

Conner, W. T. *The Gospel and Redemption*. Nashville: Broadman, 1945.

Conrad, Joachim *Die junge Generation in alten Testament*. Stuttgart: Calwer, 1970.

Crenshaw, James. "Wisdom Psalms?" *CurBS* 8 (2000): 9–17.

_____. *The Psalms: An Introduction*. Grand Rapids: Eerdmans, 2001.

Cross, Frank Moore. *Canaanite Myth and Hebrew Epic: Essays in the History of the Religion of Israel*. Cambridge, MA: Harvard University Press, 1973; reprint, Harvard University Press, 1997.

Culpepper, Robert. *Interpreting the Atonement*. Grand Rapids: Eerdmans, 1966; reprint, Wake Forest: Stevens, 1988.

Curtis, Edward M. "The Theological Basis for the Prohibition of Images in the Old Testament." *JETS* 28 (1985): 277–87.

Curtis, John Briggs. "On Job's Response to Yahweh." *JBL* 98 (1979): 497–511.

Daiches, David. *Moses: The Man and His Vision.* New York: Praeger, 1975.

Dalman, Gustav. *Petra und seine Felsheiligtümer.* Leipzig: Hinrichs, 1908.

Davies, Philip R. "Eschatology in the Book of Daniel." *JSOT* 17 (1980): 33–53.

Davis, Ellen. "Swallowing Hard. Reflections on Ezekiel's Dumbness." In *Signs and Wonders: Biblical Texts in Literary Focus,* ed. J. Cheryl Exum, 217–37. SemeiaSt 18. Atlanta: Scholars, 1989.

Denio, Francis. "On the Use of the Word Jehovah in Translating the Old Testament." *JBL* 46 (1927): 146–49.

De Moor, J.C. "The Peace Offering in Ugarit and Israel." In *Schrift en Uitleg: Festschrift W. H. Gispen,* 112–17. Kampen: Kok, 1970.

De Vaux, Roland. *Ancient Israel: Its Life and Institutions.* Translated by John McHugh. London: Darton, Longman, and Todd, 1961; reprint Grand Rapids: Eerdmans, 1997.

_____. *Studies in Old Testament Sacrifice.* Cardiff: University of Wales Press, 1964.

Dodd, Clement H. *The Bible and the Greeks.* London: Hodder & Stoughton, 1954.

_____. *The Bible Today.* Cambridge: Cambridge University Press, 1956.

_____. *More New Testament Studies.* Grand Rapids: Eerdmans, 1968.

Douglas, Mary. *Purity in Danger: An Analysis of the Concepts of Polution and Taboo.* New York: Praeger, 1966.

Driver, G. R. "Studies in the Vocabulary of the Old Testament." *JTS* 34 (1933): 33–44.

Duhm, Bernhard. *Die Theologie der Propheten als Grundlage für die innere Entwicklungsgeschichte der israelitischen Religion.* Bonn: Adolph Marcus, 1875.

Duvall, J. Scott, and J. Daniel Hays. *Grasping God's Word.* Grand Rapids: Zondervan, 2001.

Dyrness, William. "The Imago Dei and Christian Aesthetics." *JETS* 15 (1972): 161–72.

Edersheim, Alfred, *The Life and Times of Jesus the Messiah II.* Grand Rapids: Eerdmans Publishing Co., 1956.

Edwards, David L. and John R. W. Stott, *Evangelical Essentials: A Liberal-Evangelical Dialogue.* Downers Grove: InterVarsity, 1988.

Elliott, Ralph. "Atonement in the Old Testament." *RevExp* 59 (1962): 9–26.

Ellis, E. Earle. *Prophecy and Hermeneutic in Early Christianity.* Grand Rapids: Baker, 1993.

Eichrodt, Walther. *Theology of the Old Testament.* Translated by J. A. Baker. OTL, ed. Peter Ackroyd, James Barr, John Bright, and G. Ernest Wright. 2 vols. Philadelphia: Westminster, 1961, 1967.

Eissfeldt, Otto. *Die Quellen des Richterbuches.* Leipzig: Buchhandlung, 1925.

Erman, Adolf. *Life in Ancient Egypt.* Translated by H. M. Tirad. New York: Dover, 1971.

Farley, Edward. *Good and Evil: Interpreting a Human Condition.* Minneapolis: Fortress, 1991.

Feinberg, E. L. "The Scapegoat of Leviticus 16." *BSac* 115 (1958): 320–33.

Flynn, Eileen. "Beware the Tithing Team." *ThTo* 40 (1983): 195–96.

Freedman, David. "The Name of the God of Moses." *JBL* 79 (1960): 151–56.

Freeman, Hobart E. *An Introduction to the Old Testament Prophets.* Chicago: Moody, 1968.

Frei, Hans. *The Eclipse of Biblical Narrative: A Study in Eighteenth and Nineteenth Century Hermeneutics.* New Haven: Yale University Press, 1974.

Fretheim, Terence. *The Pentateuch.* Nashville: Abingdon, 1996.

_____. *God and World in the Old Testament: A Relational Theology of Creation.* Nashville: Abingdon, 2005.

Friedman, Richard E. "The Tabernacle in the Temple." *BA* 43 (1980): 241–48.

Galling, Kurt. *Biblisches Realliexicon.* Handbuch zum Alten Testament, ed. Otto Eissfeldt. Tübingen: J.C.B. Mohr, 1937.

Garnet, Paul. "Atonement Constructions in the Old Testament and the Qumran Scrolls." *EvQ* 46 (1974): 131–63.

_____. *Salvation and Atonement in the Qumran Scrolls.* Wissenschaftliche Untersuchungen zum Neuen Testament. Tübingen: J. C. B. Mohr, 1977.

Geisler, Norman. *Chosen but Free: A Balanced View of Divine Election,* 2d ed. Minneapolis: Bethany, 2001.

Gese, Hartmut. *Essays on Biblical Theology.* Translated by Keith Crim. Minneapolis: Augsburg, 1981.

Gianotti, Charles. "The Meaning of the Divine Name YHWH." *BSac* 142 (1985): 38–51.

Girard, René. *Violence and the Sacred.* Translated by Patrick Gregory. Baltimore: Johns Hopkins University Press, 1979; reprint London: Continuum, 2005.

_____. *The Scapegoat.* Translated by Y. Frecero. Baltimore: Johns Hopkins University Press, 1984.

_____. *Things Hidden Since the Foundation of the World.* Translated by Stephen Bann and Michael Metteer. Stanford: Stanford University Press, 1987; reprint London: Continuum, 2003.

_____. *I See Satan Fall Like Lightning.* Maryknoll, NY: Orbis, 1999.

_____. *The Girard Reader.* New York: Crossroad, 1996.

Glueck, Nelson. *Hesed in the Bible.* Hoboken. NJ: Ktav, 1968.

Goldingay, John. "Old Testament Sacrifice and the Death of Christ." In *Atonement Today,* ed. John Goldingay, 3–20. London: SPCK, 1995.

_____. *Models for Interpretation of Scripture.* Grand Rapids: Eerdmans, 1995.

_____. *Old Testament Theology.* Vol. 1, *Israel's Gospel.* Downers Grove: InterVarsity, 2003.

Good, Robert. "The Just War in Ancient Israel." *JBL* 104 (1985): 385–400.

Grant, Jamie. *The King as Exemplar: The Function of Deuteronomy's Kingship Law in the Shaping of the Book of Psalms.* SBLAB 17. Atlanta: Society of Biblical Literature, 2004.

Gray, George Buchanan. *Sacrifice in the Old Testament: Its Theory and Practice.* Oxford: Clarendon, 1925.

Green, Joel. *How to Read Prophecy.* Downers Grove: InterVarsity, 1984.

Greenberg, Moshe. "The Design and Themes of Ezekiel's Program of Restoration." In *Interpreting the Prophets*, ed. James Mays and Paul Achtemeier, 215–36. Philadelphia: Fortress, 1987.

Guelich, Robert. "The Matthean Beatitudes: 'Entrance-Requirements' or Eschatological Blessings?" *JBL* 95 (1976): 415–34.

Gunkel, Hermann. *Psalms: A Form-Critical Introduction.* Translated by Thomas Horner. Philadelphia: Fortress, 1967.

Hamilton, James. *God's Indwelling Presence: The Holy Spirit in Old and New Testaments*, NACSBT, ed. E. R. Clendenen. Nashville: B&H, 2006.

Hanby, Michael. "Reclaiming Creation in a Darwinian World." *ThTo* 62 (2006): 476–83.

Haran, M. *Temples and Temple-Service in Ancient Israel.* Oxford: Clarendon, 1978.

Harrelson, Walter. *From Fertility Cult to Worship.* New York: Doubleday, 1969.

Hasel, Gerhard. "The Polemical Nature of the Genesis Cosmology." *EvQ* 46 (1974): 81–102.

Heinisch, Paul. *Theology of the Old Testament.* Translated by William Heidt. Collegeville, MN: Liturgical, 1955.

Helm, Robert. "Azazel in Early Jewish Tradition." *AUSS* 32 (1994): 217–26.

Heschel, Abraham. *The Prophets.* New York: Harper & Row, 1962.

Hess, Richard and David Tsumura, eds. *I Studied Inscriptions from Before the Flood*. Winona Lake: Eisenbrauns, 1994.

Hirth, Volkmar. *Gottes Boten im Alten Testament*. Theologische Arbeiten 32. Berlin: Evangelische Verlagsanstalt, 1975.

Hoenig, Sydney. "The New Qumran Pesher on Azazel." *JQR* 56 (1966): 248–53.

Holladay, William. "The Background of Jeremiah's Self-Understanding: Moses, Samuel, and Psalm 22." *JBL* 83 (1964): 153–64.

_____. "Jeremiah and Moses." *JBL* 85 (1966): 17–27.

Homan, Michael. *To Your Tents, O Israel! The Terminology, Function, Form, and Symbolism of Tents in the Hebrew Bible and the Ancient Near East*. Leiden: Brill, 2002.

Horst, F. "Segen und Segenshandlugen in der Bibel." *EvT* 7 (1947–48): 23–37.

Jacob, Edmond. *Theology of the Old Testament*. Translated by Arthur Heathcote and Philip Allcock. New York: Harper & Brothers, 1958.

Janowski, Bernd. *Sühne als Heilsgeschehen*. Wissenschaftliche Monographien zum Alten und Neuen Testament. Neukirchen-Vluyn: Neukirchener Verlag, 1982.

Jellicoe, Sidney. "The Prophets and the Cultus." *ExpTim* 60 (1949): 256–58.

Jepsen, Alfred. "Berith, Ein Beitrag zur Theologie der Exilszeit." In *Verbanung und Heimkehr, Wilhelm Rudolph zum 70. Geburtstag*, ed. A. Kusskhe, 161–79. Tübingen: Mohr, 1961.

Johnson, Aubrey. "The Prophet in Israelite Worship." *ExpTim* 47 (1935–1936): 312–19.

_____. "The Role of the King in the Jerusalem Cultus." In *The Labyrinth*, ed. S. H. Hooke, 71–112. London: SPCK, 1935.

_____. *The Cultic Prophet in Ancient Israel*. Cardiff: University of Wales Press Board, 1944.

Judisch, Douglas. "Propitiation in the Language and Typology of the Old Testament." *CTQ* 48 (1984): 221–43.

Kaplan, Mordecai. "Isaiah 6:1–11." *JBL* 45 (1926): 251–59.

Keil, C. F. *Manual of Biblical Archaeology I*. Translated by P. Christie. Edinburgh: T&T Clark, 1888.

Kelm, George. *Escape to Conflict: A Biblical and Archaeological Approach to the Hebrew Exodus and Settlement*. Fort Worth: IAR Publications, 1991.

Kennedy, James H. *The Commission of Moses and the Christian Calling*. Grand Rapids: Eerdmans, 1964.

Kittel, Rudolph. *The Scientific Study of the Old Testament: Its Principal Results, and Their Bearing Upon Religious Instruction*. Translated by J. Caleb Hughes. New York: G. P. Putnam's Sons, 1910.

Köhler, Ludwig. *Old Testament Theology*. Translated by A. S. Todd. Philadelphia: Westminster, 1957.

Koch, Klaus. *The Prophets*. Vol. 1, *The Assyrian Period*. Translated by Margaret Kohl. Philadelphia: Fortress, 1983.

König, E. "The Hebrew Word for 'Atone'." *ExpTim* 22 (1910–1911): 232–34.

Kraus, Hans-Joachim. *Worship in Israel*. Translated by Geoffrey Buswell. Oxford: Oxford University Press, 1966.

———. *Theology of the Psalms*. Translated by Keith Crim. Minneapolis: Augsburg, 1986.

Kuntz, J. Kenneth. "Reclaiming Biblical Wisdom Psalms: a Response To Crenshaw." *CBR* 1 (2003): 145–54.

Lambert, Wilfried G. "Babylonien und Israel." *TRE* 5 (1980): 67–79.

Laney, Carl. "A Fresh Look at the Imprecatory Psalms." *BSac* 138 (1981): 35–45.

Lansdell, Henry. *The Sacred Tenth: Studies in Tithe Giving Ancient and Modern*. London: SPCK, 1906; reprint Grand Rapids: Baker, 1955.

———. *The Tithe in Scripture*. London: SPCK, 1908.

LaSor, William. "Prophecy, Inspiration and the *Sensus Plenior*." *TB* 29 (1978): 49–60.

Lete, Olmo. "David's Farewell Oracle (2 Samuel XXIII 1–7): A Literary Analysis." *VT* 34 (1984): 414–37.

Levenson, Jon. "Creation and Covenant." In *The Flowering of Old Testament Theology*, ed. Ben C. Ollenburger et al., 431–35. Winona Lake: Eisenbrauns, 1992.

Levine, Baruch. *In the Presence of the Lord: A Study of Cult and Some Cultic Terms in Ancient Israel*. Studies in Judaism in Late Antiquity. Leiden: Brill, 1974.

Lewis, C. S. *Reflections on the Psalms*. New York: Harcourt, Brace & Company, 1958.

Liebreich, L. J. "The Songs of Ascents and the Priestly Blessing." *JBL* 74 (1955): 33–36.

Lincoln, Andrew. "The Household Code and Wisdom Mode of Colossians." *JSNT* 74 (1999): 93–112.

Lindblom, Johannes. *Prophecy in Ancient Israel*. Oxford: Basil Blackwell, 1962.

Longenecker, Richard N. "Some Distinctive Early Christological Motifs." *NovT* 16 (1974): 526–45.

Longman, Tremper. *How to Read the Psalms*. Downers Grove: InterVarsity, 1988.

Loretz, Oswald. "Wortbericht-Vorlage und Tatbericht-Interpretation im Schöpfungsbericht Gen. 1:1–2:4a." *UF* 7 (1975): 279–87.

MacLaurin, E. "YHWH, the Origin of the Tetragrammaton." *VT* 12 (1962): 439–63.

Marcus, David. *Jephthah and His Vow*. Lubbock: Texas Tech University Press, 1986.

Matthews, Victor. *Social World of the Hebrew Prophets*. Peabody: Hendrickson, 2001.

Mays, James Luther. "The Place of the Torah-Psalms in the Psalter." *JBL* 106 (1987): 3–12.

McBride, Dean. "Divine Protocol: Genesis 1:1—2:3 as Prologue to the Pentateuch." In *God Who Creates: Essays in Honor of W. Sibley Towner*, ed. William Brown and Dean McBride, 3–41. Grand Rapids: Eerdmans, 2000.

McCarthy, Dennis. "The Symbolism of Blood and Sacrifice." *JBL* 88 (1966): 166–76.

McComiskey, Thomas. *The Covenants of Promise: A Theology of the Old Testament Covenants.* Grand Rapids: Baker, 1985.

McConville, J. Gordon. *Law and Theology in Deuteronomy.* JSOTSup 33. Sheffield: JSOT, 1984.

_____. "Deuteronomy's Unification of Passover and Massot: A Response to Bernard M. Levinson." *JBL* 119 (2000): 47–58.

Mendenhall, George. *Law and Covenant in Israel.* Pittsburgh: The Biblical Colloquium, 1955.

Merrill, Eugene. "Remembering: A Central Theme in Biblical Worship." *JETS* 43 (2000): 27–36.

Mettinger, Tryggve. "Abbild oder Urbild? 'Imago Dei' in traditionsgeschichtlicher Sicht." *ZAW* 86 (1974): 403–424.

_____. *No Graven Image? Israelite Aniconism in Its Ancient Near Eastern Context,* Coniectanea biblica: Old Testament Series, ed. Tryggve Mettinger and Magnus Ottosson. Stockholm : Almqvist & Wiksell International, 1995.

Meyer, Frederick B. *Moses: The Servant of God.* Grand Rapids: Zondervan, 1953.

Meyers, Carol. *Tabernacle Menorah: A Synthetic Study of a Symbol from the Biblical Cult.* Winona Lake: Eisenbrauns, 1972.

Milgrom, Jacob. "A Prolegomenon to Leviticus 17:11." *JBL* 90 (1971): 149–56.

_____. "Sin-offering or Purification Offering?" *VT* 21 (1971): 237–39.

_____. "Profane Slaughter and a Formulaic Key to the Composition of Deuteronomy." *HUCA* 47 (1976): 1–17.

Miller, J. E. "The Thirtieth Year." *RB* 99 (1992): 499–503.

Miller, Patrick. *Genesis 1–11: Studies in Structure and Theme.* JSOTSup 8. Sheffield: JSOT, 1978.

_____. *Interpreting the Psalms.* Philadelphia: Fortress, 1986.

_____. *They Cried to the Lord: The Form and Theology of Biblical Prayer.* Minneapolis: Fortress, 1994.

_____. "Preaching the First Commandment in a Pluralistic World." *JP* 27 (2004): 4–11.

Morgenstern, Julian. *Amos Studies I.* Cincinnati: Hebrew Union College, 1941.

Morris, Leon. *The Apostolic Preaching of the Cross*. Grand Rapids: Eerdmans, 1956.

Morrow, William. "Consolation, Rejection, and Repentance in Job 42:6." *JBL* 105 (1986): 211–25.

Morton, Russell. "Glory to God and to the Lamb: John's Use of Jewish and Hellenistic/Roman Themes in Formatting His Theology in Revelation 4–5." *JSNT* 83 (2001): 89–109.

Mowinckel, Sigmund. *Psalmenstudien I–VI*. Kristiana: Dybwad, 1921–1924.

_____. *The Psalms in Israel's Worship I–II*. Translated by D. R. Ap-Thomas. Oxford: Blackwell, 1962.

Moyer, James. "Hittite and Israelite Cultic Practices: A Selected Comparison." In *Scripture in Context II: More Essays on the Comparative Method*, ed. William Hallo, James Moyer, and Leo Perdue, 19–38. Winona Lake: Eisenbrauns, 1983.

Muilenburg, James. *The Way of Israel*. New York: Harper, 1961.

Mullins, Terence Y. "Jewish Wisdom Literature in the New Testament." *JBL* 68 (1949): 335–39.

_____. "New Testament Commission Forms. Especially in Luke-Acts." *JBL* 95 (1976): 603–614.

Murphy, R. E. "A Consideration of the Classification, 'Wisdom Psalms'." In *Congress Volume: Bonn 1962*. Supplements to VT 9, 156–67. Leiden: Brill, 1963.

Neusner, Jacob. *The Idea of Purity in Ancient Judaism*. Studies in Judaism in Late Antiquity. Leiden: Brill, 1973.

Newell, B. Lynn. "Job: Repentant or Rebellious." *WTJ* 46 (1984): 298–316.

Nicholson, Ernest. *God and His People: Covenant and Theology in the Old Testament*. Oxford: Clarendon, 1986.

North, Christopher. "Some Outstanding Old Testament Problems: Sacrifice in the Old Testament." *ExpTim* 47 (1935–1936): 250–54.

Obbink, Herman Theodorus. "The Horns of the Altar in the Semitic World, Especially in Jahwism." *JBL* 56 (1937): 43–49.

Och, Bernard. "The Garden of Eden: From Creation to Covenant; pt 1." *Judaism* 37 (1988): 143–56.

Odell, Margaret. "You Are What You Eat: Ezekiel and the Scroll."
    *JBL* 117 (1998): 229–48.
Oehler, Gustav. *Theology of the Old Testament.* Translated by George
    Day. New York: Funk & Wagnalls, 1883.
Otto, Rudolph. *The Idea of Holy.* Oxford: Oxford University Press,
    1924.
Overholt, Thomas. *Channels of Prophecy: The Social Dynamics of
    Prophetic Activity.* Minneapolis: Fortress, 1989.
_____. "Prophecy in History: The Social Reality of
    Intermediation." *JSOT* 48 (1990): 3–29.
Paton, Lewis B. "Did Amos Approve of the Calf-Worship at
    Bethel?" *JBL* 13 (1894): 80–90.
_____. "The Meaning of Exodus xx. 7." *JBL* 22 (1903): 201–10.
Patterson, Richard D. "The Psalm of Habakkuk." *GTJ* 8 (1987):
    163–94.
Perdue, Leo. *Wisdom and Cult: A Critical Analysis of the Views of
    Cult in the Wisdom Literature of Israel and the Ancient Near
    East.* SBLDS 30. Missoula, MT: Scholars, 1977.
Petersen, David. *The Roles of Israel's Prophets,* ed. David Clines and
    others. JSOTSup 17. Sheffield: JSOT, 1981.
Pfeiffer, Charles. *Egypt and the Exodus.* Grand Rapids: Baker, 1964.
Pierce, Timothy. "Micah as a Case Study for Preaching and
    Teaching the Prophets." *SWJT* 46 (2003): 77–94.
Pinnock, Clark H. "The Destruction of the Finally Impenitent."
    *CTR* 4 (1990): 243–59.
Preuss, Horst Dietrich. *Old Testament Theology.* 2 volumes.
    Translated by Leo Perdue, OTL, ed. James Mays, Carol
    Newsom, and David Petersen. Louisville: Westminster John
    Knox, 1992.
Provan, Iain, Philips Long and Tremper Longman. *A Biblical
    History of Israel.* Louisville: Westminster John Knox, 2003.
Ramm, Bernard. *The Christian View of Science and Scripture.* Grand
    Rapids: Eerdmans, 1954.
Ramsey, George. "Is Name Giving an Act of Domination in Genesis
    2:23 and Elsewhere?" *CBQ* 50 (1988): 24–35.

Ringgren, Helmer. *The Prophetical Conception of Holiness.* Uppsala: Almqvist & Wickselis Boktryckeri, 1948.

_____. *The Faith of the Psalmists.* London: SCM, 1963.

_____. *Israelite Religion.* Translated by David Green. Philadelphia: Fortress, 1966.

Robinson, H. Wheeler. *Corporate Personality in Ancient Israel.* Philadelphia: Fortress, 1980.

Roubos, K. *Profetie en Cultus in Israël.* Achtergrond en Betekenis van Enige Profetische Uitspraken Inzake de Cultus. Wageningen: H. Veenman en Zonen, 1956.

Rowley, H. H. *The Unity of the Bible.* Philadelphia: Westminster, 1953.

_____. *Worship in Ancient Israel: Its Forms and Meaning.* Philadelphia: Fortress, 1967.

Sailhamer, John. "Exegetical Notes: Genesis 1:1–2:4a." *TJ* 5 (1984): 73–82.

_____. *The Pentateuch as Narrative: A Biblical-Theological Commentary.* Grand Rapids: Zondervan, 1992.

Sakenfeld, Katharine Doob. *The Meaning of Hesed in the Hebrew Bible: A New Inquiry.* Eugene, OR: Wipf & Stock Publishers, 2002.

Salstrand, George. *The Tithe: The Minimum Standard for Christian Giving.* Grand Rapids: Baker, 1971.

Savran, George. "1 and 2 Kings." In *The Literary Guide to the Bible,* ed. Robert Alter and Frank Kermode, 146–64. Cambridge: Belknap, 1987.

Schmid, R. *Das Bundesopfer in Israel.* Munich: Kösel, 1964.

Schmidt, Werner H. *Die Schöpfungsgeschichte der Priesterschrift,* 2d ed. Wissenschaftliche Monographien zum Alten und Neuen Testament. Neukirchen: Neukirchener Verlag, 1967.

_____. *Altestamentlicher Glaube in seiner Geschichte.* Neukirchen: Neukirchener Verlag, 1982.

_____. *The Faith of the Old Testament.* Translated by J. Sturdy. Oxford: Blackwell, 1983.

Schroeder, Christoph. "'Standing in the Breach': Turning Away the Wrath of God." *Int* 52 (1998): 16–23.

Schüle, Andreas, "Made in the 'Image of God': The Concepts of Divine Images in Genesis 1–3." *ZAW* 117 (2005): 1–20.

Skinner, John. *Prophecy and Religion: Studies in the Life of Jeremiah.* Cambridge: Cambridge University Press, 1922.

Smith, Mark S. *The Ugaritic Ba'al Cycle.* Vol. 1, *Introduction with Text, Translation & Commentary of KTU 1.1–1.2.* Leiden: Brill, 1994.

Smith, W. Robertson. *Lectures on the Religion of the Semites: The Fundamental Institutions.* Edinburgh: A&C Black, 1889.

Snaith, Norman. *Distinctive Ideas of the Old Testament.* Philadelphia: Westminster, 1946.

_____. *Mercy and Sacrifice: A Study of the Book of Hosea.* London: SCM, 1953.

_____. "Sin-offering and the Guilt-offering." *VT* 15 (1965): 73–80.

Sommer, Benjamin. "Conflicting Constructions of Divine Presence in the Priestly Tabernacle." *BibInt* 9 (2001): 41–63.

Staples, W. E. "The Third Commandment." *JBL* 58 (1939): 325–29.

Steck, Odil. "Bemerkungen zu Jesaja 6." *BZ* 16 (1972): 188–206.

Stedman, Ray Charles. "Giving under Grace, Part 1." *BSac* 107 (1950): 321–28.

Stern, Philip. *Biblical Herem: A Window on Israel's Religious Experience.* Atlanta: Scholars, 1991.

Swartley, Willard, ed. *Violence Renounced: Rene Girard, Biblical Studies, and Peacemaking.* Studies in Peace and Scripture 4. Telford, PA: Pandora, 2000.

Tate, Marvin. "Tithing: Legalism or Benchmark?" *RevExp* 70 (1973): 153–61.

Tawil, Hayim. "Azazel The Prince of the Steppe: A Comparative Study." *ZAW* 92 (1980): 43–59.

Terrien, Samuel. *The Elusive Presence: Toward a New Biblical Theology.* San Francisco: Harper & Row, 1978.

Thomas, Marlin E. "Psalms 1 and 112 As a Paradigm for the Comparison of Wisdom Motifs in the Psalms." *JETS* 29 (1986): 15–24.

Thompson, Michael. *I Have Heard your Prayer: The Old Testament and Prayer.* Peterborough, UK: Epworth, 1996.

Thompson, R. J. *Penitence and Sacrifice in Early Israel Outside the Levitical Law.* Leiden: Brill, 1963.

Towner, W. Sibley. "Clones of God: Genesis 1:26–28 and the Image of God in the Hebrew Bible." *Int* 59 (2005): 341–56.

Torrey, C. C. "The Prophecy of 'Malachi.'" *JBL* 17 (1898): 1–15.

Tozer, Aiden W. *The Knowledge of the Holy.* Lincoln, NE: Back to the Bible, 1971.

Travis, Stephen. "Christ as Bearer of Divine Judgement in Paul's Thought about Atonement." In *Atonement Today,* ed. John Goldingay, 21–38. London: SPCK, 1995.

Tsevat, Matitiahu. "The Meaning of the Book of Job." *HUCA* 37 (1966): 73–106.

Tsumura, David. *The Earth and Waters in Genesis 1 and 2: A Linguistic Investigation.* JSOTSup 83. Sheffield: JSOT, 1989.

Unger, Merrill. *Archaeology and the Old Testament.* Grand Rapids: Zondervan, 1954.

VanGemeren, Willem A. *Interpreting the Prophetic Word: An Introduction to the Prophetic Literature of the Old Testament.* Grand Rapids: Zondervan, 1990.

Van Imschoot, P. *Theology of the Old Testament.* Translated by Kathryn Sullivan. New York: Desclee, 1954.

Vermes, Geza. *Scripture and Tradition in Judaism: Haggadic Studies.* Leiden: Brill, 1961.

von Rad, Gerhad. "The Origin of the Day of Yahweh." *JSS* 4 (1959): 97–108.

———. *The Message of the Prophets.* Translated by D.M.G. Stalker. New York: Harper & Row, 1962.

———. *Old Testament Theology.* Translated by D. M. G. Stalker. 2 vols. New York: Harper & Row, 1965.

———. *The Problem of the Hexateuch and Other Essays.* Translated by E.W. Trueman Dicken. New York: McGraw-Hill, 1966.

———. *Wisdom in Israel.* Translated by J. D. Martin. Nashville: Abingdon, 1972.

———. *Holy War in Ancient Israel.* Translated by Marva Dawn. Grand Rapids: Eerdmans, 1991.

Vos, Johannes G. "The Ethical Problem of the Imprecatory Psalms."
      *WTJ* 4 (1942): 123–38.

Vriezen, Th. C. *An Outline of Old Testament Theology.* Oxford: Basil
      Blackwell, 1962.

Weiss, Meir. "Concerning Amos' Repudiation of the Cult." In
      *Pomegranates and Golden Bells: Studies in Biblical, Jewish,
      and Near Eastern Ritual, Law, and Literature in Honor of Jacob
      Milgrom,* ed. David P. Wright and others, 199–214. Winona
      Lake: Eisenbrauns, 1995.

Welch, Adam. *Prophet and Priest in Old Israel.* New York:
      Macmillan, 1953.

Wellhausen, Julius. *Prolegomena to the History of Israel.* Translated
      by J. Sutherland Black. Edinburgh: A&C Black, 1885.

_____. *Die Kleinen Propheten,* 3d ed. Berlin: G. Reimer, 1898.

Wenham, Gordon. *Story as Torah: Reading Old Testament Narratives.*
      Grand Rapids: Baker, 2000.

Wenham, John. "The Case for Conditional Immortality." In
      *Universalism and the Doctrine of Hell.* Edited by Nigel M. de S.
      Cameron, 161–91. Grand Rapids: Baker, 1992.

Westermann, Claus. *Blessing in the Bible and the Life of the Church.*
      Translated by Keith Crim. Philadelphia: Fortress, 1978.

_____. *Praise and Lament in the Psalms.* Translated by Keith Crim
      and R. N. Soulen. Atlanta: Westminister John Knox, 1981.

_____. *Elements of Old Testament Theology.* Atlanta: John Knox,
      1982.

Whybray, R. N. "The Immorality of God: Reflections on Some
      Passages in Genesis, Job, Exodus, and Numbers." *JSOT* 72
      (1996): 89–120.

_____. "The Wisdom Psalms." In *Wisdom in Ancient Israel: Essays
      in Honour of J. A. Emerton,* ed. John Day and others, 152–60.
      Cambridge: Cambridge University Press, 1995.

Wiener, Harold Marcus. *The Altars of the Old Testament.* Leipzig:
      Hinrich 1927.

Wilson, G. H. *The Editing of the Hebrew Psalter.* SBLDS 76. Atlanta:
      Scholars, 1985.

Wilson, Robert. "Prophecy and Ecstasy: A Reexamination." *JBL* 98 (1979): 321–37.

_____. "Prophecy in Crisis: The Call of Ezekiel." In *Interpreting the Prophets,* ed. James Mays and Paul Achtemeier, 157–69. Philadelphia: Fortress, 1987.

Winden, J. C. M. van. "The Early Christian Exegesis of 'Heaven and Earth' in Genesis 1,1." In *Romanitas et Christianitas: studia Iano Henrico Waszink,* ed. W. den Boer and others, 371–82. Amsterdam: North-Holland, 1973.

Wolff, Hans Walter. *Anthropology of the Old Testament.* Translated by Margaret Kohl. Philadelphia: Fortress, 1974.

Wong, Daniel. "The Tree of Life in Revelation 2:7." *BSac* 155 (1998): 211–26.

Wright, David. *The Disposal of Impurity: Elimination Rites in the Bible and in Hittite and Mesopotamian Literature.* SBLDS. Atlanta: Scholars, 1987.

Zeligs, Dorothy. *Moses: A Psychodynamic Study.* New York: Human Sciences, 1986.

Zimmerli, Walther. *Old Testament Theology in Outline.* Atlanta: John Knox, 1978.

Zohar, Noam. "Repentance and Purification: The Significance and Semantics of חטאת in the Pentateuch." *JBL* 107 (1988): 609–18.

## Other Works on Worship

Allen, Ronald, and Gordon Borror. *Worship: Rediscovering the Missing Jewel.* Portland: Multnomah, 1982.

Card, Michael. *A Sacred Sorrow: Reaching Out to God in the Lost Language of Lament.* Colorado Springs: NavPress, 2005.

Carson, D. A., ed. *Worship: Adoration and Action.* Grand Rapids: Baker, 1994.

Dawn, Marva. *A Royal Waste of Time.* Grand Rapids: Eerdmans, 1999.

Frame, John M. *Worship in Spirit and Truth.* Phillipsburg, NJ: P&R, 1996.

Hill, Andrew. *Enter His Courts with Praise! Old Testament Worship for the New Testament Church.* Grand Rapids: Baker, 1993.

Jeremiah, David. *My Heart's Desire: Living Every Moment in the Wonder of Worship.* Nashville: Integrity, 2002.

Leafblad, Bruce. *Music, Worship, and the Ministry of the Church.* Portland: Western Conservative Baptist Seminary, 1978.

Longman, Tremper. *Immanuel in Our Place: Seeing Christ in Israel's Worship.* Phillipsburg, NJ: P&R, 2001.

Martin, Ralph. *Worship in the Early Church,* 2d ed. Grand Rapids: Eerdmans, 1998.

Peterson, David. *Engaging With God: A Biblical Theology of Worship.* Downers Grove: InterVarsity, 1992.

Ruis, David. *The Worship God is Seeking: An Exploration of Worship and the Kingdom of God.* Louisville: Westminster John Knox, 2005.

Saliers, Don. *Worship As Theology.* Nashville: Abingdon, 1994.

Segler, Franklyn, and Randall Bradley. *Understanding, Preparing For, and Practicing Christian Worship,* 2d ed. Nashville: Broadman & Holman, 1996.

Torrance, James. *Worship, Community & The Triune God of Grace.* Downers Grove: InterVarsity, 1996.

Webber, Robert. *Worship is a Verb.* Waco: Word, 1985.

_____. *Celebrating Our Faith: Evangelism Through Worship.* San Francisco: Harper & Row, 1986.

Willimon, William H. *Worship as Pastoral Care.* Nashville: Abingdon, 1979.

_____. *Word, Water, Wine and Bread: How Worship Has Changed Over the Years.* Valley Forge: Judson, 1980.

# Author Index

# Subject Index

# Hebrew Words

# Scripture Index

## Proverbs

## Ecclesiastes

## Isaiah